The People's Liberation Army and China's Nation-Building

The People's Liberation Army and China's Nation-Building

YING-MAO KAU

INTERNATIONAL ARTS AND SCIENCES PRESS, INC. WHITE PLAINS, N.Y.

Library of Congress Catalog Card Number 72-77203

International Standard Book Number 0-87332-006-9

©1973 by International Arts and Sciences Press, Inc.
901 North Broadway, White Plains, New York 10603

Printed in the United States of America

To Lea E. Williams
and the East Asia Language
and Area Center, Brown University

Contents

III. THE ECONOMIC ROLE OF THE MILITARY

IV. THE ARMY AND SOCIO-CULTURAL CHANGE

V. THE FUNCTIONS OF THE MILITIA

VI. THE STRUGGLE BETWEEN "TWO LINES"

Preface

Data collected by the United States Arms Control and Disarmament Agency reveal that a total of approximately 24 million men are under arms today in the world, and more than $210 billion is spent each year in direct support of military forces. On the average, military expenditures consume roughly 20 percent of the national budget of every country. These staggering figures raise an obvious and serious question: How can this enormous military manpower and these resources be used for the constructive purposes of nation-building and modernization? The question is of particular significance to the developing countries of the "Third World," where material and human resources available for development are scarce, while expectations and demands for modernization are high. The probe into the feasibility of harnessing and converting armed forces into a vehicle of modernization and nation-building clearly goes beyond the confines of academic interests.

Historical evidence throughout the world, however, shows that efforts to enlist the military for the performance of nonmilitary tasks carry certain risks and consequences. Such attempts tend to upset the proper balance of civil-military relations, especially the ideal of civilian supremacy and control of the military. Calling on the armed forces to share power or form a partnership in domestic politics for the purpose of sustaining the political system in crisis often leads to a military takeover of the civilian government. Attempts to utilize the organizational and technical skills of the military for economic development and social modernization frequently introduce military men into the arena of power and policy struggles and eventually prompt the generals to intervene militarily.

Without appropriate normative and organizational arrangements, encouraging the military, intentionally or unintentionally, to play an expanded role in civilian affairs can invite unanticipated disasters. The ubiquity of military coups, praetorian rule, and army dictatorships in the developing countries today clearly attests to this phenomenon. In 1965 alone, for instance, as many as fifty-seven cases of large-scale military revolts, armed insurgencies, and military coups d'état were reported, in which the military succeeded in imposing praetorian control in eleven countries. The results are clear: A civilian government attempting to tap the resources of the military without being victimized by the expanded power and role of the military incurs a great challenge and high risks.

The Chinese experience, in which the Communist leadership has actively and effectively used its armed forces, the People's Liberation Army (PLA), for a wide variety of extramilitary purposes, deserves close attention. Organized on the basis of Mao's theory of "people's war," the Communist Red Army has, since the late 1920s, functioned successfully, as Mao put it, both as a "fighting force" and as a "working force." It fought and won one of the greatest revolutionary wars in human history, played an active role in the creation of Communist power in China, and participated extensively and effectively in economic and social transformation. It was not only during the periods of protracted guerrilla movements that the extramilitary role of the PLA was conspicuous; it was equally evident in the years of postliberation construction. Although on a few occasions the Maoist principle that "the Party commands the gun and the gun shall never be allowed to command the Party" was challenged by military leaders, Mao has managed to avert the crises of military domination or takeover. Evidence to date indicates that Mao has succeeded to a great extent in developing a unique formula of ideological and organizational control capable of effectively using the military for nation-building.

The purpose of this volume is to present, in the Chinese

leadership's own words and conceptualization, the Chinese model of army-building and its contributions to the political development and socioeconomic modernization of China. Special emphasis is placed on the historical roots and organizational characteristics of the model, and on the scope of extramilitary activities. The operational dynamics of the model within the broad context of China's changing political and social systems is also examined in light of the growing challenges to Mao's military thinking stemming from the changes and developments within and outside the PLA as a societal institution.

The documents and writings selected for this book are broadly organized into three parts. The first part (section I) traces the origins of Mao's military doctrines and identifies, in Mao's own words, the major characteristics of the model he has constructed. The second part (sections II-V) covers the specific categories of extramilitary roles that the PLA performs. The selections in this part also deal with the organizational principles and leadership techniques devised by Mao to guarantee the effective performance of the functions assigned to the military. The last part (sections VI-VIII) emphasizes the operational dynamics of the model since 1949, highlighting on the one hand, the struggle between "two lines" and the challenges of military professionalism and military power, and on the other hand, the persistence of the Maoist line of military-building. The editor's introductory essay offers a comprehensive analysis of the development and operation of the Maoist model from historical and theoretical perspectives. It also ties the materials together into a coherent whole focusing on the special role in China's mass-mobilization approach to nation-building of the Chinese military. Owing to the limitations of space, materials that fall within the scope of military training, tactics, and strategy are not included. Fortunately, most of these materials written by Mao himself have been made conveniently available in the Selected Military Writings of Mao Tse-tung (Peking: Foreign Languages Press, 1963).

This volume comprises materials chosen from original Chinese Communist sources. Some are from the official public

press, and others are from Red Guard or other restricted
sources. Included is the complete text of the celebrated "Ku-
t'ien Resolution," drafted by Mao personally in 1929, the major
portion of which has never been published in English. The selections encompass the wide historical span of the model's development, ranging from the inception of the Chinese Red Army
in the late 1920s through the spectacular rise of the PLA's
power and role during the Cultural Revolution in the 1960s and
the dramatic attempt at a military coup led by Lin Piao in 1971.
Many of the items included in the volume were first published
by the editor in Chinese Law and Government, Volume IV,
No. 3-4 (Fall-Winter, 1971-72) and Volume V, No. 3-4 (Fall-
Winter 1972-73); some are drawn from The Political Work
System of the Chinese Communist Military, coauthored with
Paul M. Chancellor, Philip E. Ginsburg, and Pierre M. Per-
role (Providence: East Asia Language and Area Center, Brown
University, 1971).

*   *   *

I am indebted to my former collaborators Edward C. Chan,
Pao-ming Chang, Philip E. Ginsburg, and Pierre M. Perrolle
for their contributions to the larger research project on the
military and modernization in China, which was initiated earlier under the auspices of the East Asia Language and Area Center at Brown University. I owe a special debt of gratitude to
the inspiring leadership and enthusiastic support of Professor
Lea E. Williams, Director of the Center. Without his sustained
stimulation, encouragement and friendship, this volume would
never have been possible.

At various stages of my study of the Chinese military, I have
benefited from constructive suggestions and gracious assistance generously extended to me by many scholars and librari-
ans. I am particularly grateful to A. Doak Barnett (The Brook-
ings Institution), Davis B. Bobrow (University of Minnesota),
Parris H. Chang (Pennsylvania State University), King C. Chen
(Rutgers University), I-min Chiang (Gardner Collection, Brown

University), S. M. Chiu (Temple University), William Hsu
(Union Research Institute, Hong Kong), John Gittings (Far
Eastern Economic Review, Hong Kong), Jerome B. Grieder
(Brown University), Chalmers Johnson (University of Califor-
nia), John W. Lewis (Stanford University), John T. Ma (Hoover
Institution), Thomas W. Robinson (Rand Corporation), Tang
Tsou (University of Chicago), Ezra F. Vogel (Harvard Univer-
sity), Eugene Wu (Harvard-Yenching Institute), and P. K. Yu
(Center for Chinese Research Materials).

I wish to express my appreciation to Fred Ablin, Editorial
Director of International Arts and Sciences Press, and especially to Douglas Merwin, China Publications Editor of the
Press, for their unfailing support and encouragement. My
thanks also go to Philip E. Ginsburg, Alison Huey, Jay Mathews,
Suzanne Ogden, and Douglas Spelman for their superb job of
translation.

Finally, my wife Anna and our three children, Andrew, David,
and Kathy, share and cooperate in my efforts in many ways;
and they are all happy to see that this volume has been completed.

Y. M. K.

Providence, Rhode Island
April 1973

Introduction

Owing to its command of major instruments of coercion and destruction, the military is generally looked upon by civilian authorities with distrust and apprehension. The conventional concept of the military's place in society as evolved from the Western experience emphasizes organizational separation of the military from the rest of society and the functional primacy of the military in national defense and security. In this model the formal institutional arrangements are based on the principle of civilian supremacy and the political neutrality of the military establishment, in order to minimize the risk of military intervention. (1) Functionally, the specialization and professionalization of the armed forces in the military tasks of defense and security are established as the institutional norm. Direct involvement of the military in nonmilitary activities, such as economic development and social reform in society at large, is considered the exception rather than the rule. The contributions of the military to modernization or nation-building, if any, are at most accidental or peripheral. (2)

In China, with the founding of the Red Army in 1927, Mao Tse-tung began developing a different conception of the army's role. (3) He not only emphasized organizational penetration of the Red Army by the Party to guarantee political control over the military but also stressed the importance of a systematic use of the guerrilla forces for a wide range of extramilitary activities. The Red Army was mobilized to organize and indoctrinate the masses, to take part in agricultural and industrial production, and to support social and political reforms. Mao not only argued for the desirability of this approach but also

successfully demonstrated its feasibility both during and after
the revolutionary war. Thus, in contrast with the Western model of military institutions, which stresses a high degree of professional specialization, organizational differentiation, and
political neutrality, the Chinese model, as developed by Mao,
is marked by the multifunctionality, structural diffuseness, and
politicization of the military. An understanding of Mao's military thinking and of the effectiveness of the Chinese model requires a careful analysis of the historical context in which the
Chinese Communist movement and the revolutionary war took
place.

I. The Roots of the Maoist Model

Chalmers Johnson argues that strategies of violent political
revolution tend to be of two basic types: the swift coup d'état
or the protracted guerrilla insurrection. (4) The former generally involves a sudden, strategic attack on the regime in
power and a quick seizure of governmental power through a
military coup or uprising. The latter normally involves prolonged guerrilla warfare and an organized mass movement,
which systematically seek to challenge the legitimate authority
of the existing regime and the effectiveness of its military and
police forces. This guerrilla-type insurrection requires the
revolutionaries to organize a mobile, multifunctional army, to
establish defensible revolutionary bases, to mobilize the population in support of the revolutionary effort, and to maintain
self-sufficiency in necessary supplies. Hence, the political
and the military quality of the guerrillas as a multifunctional
insurgent force becomes the key determinant of the outcome
of any revolutionary struggle.

The development of the Communist revolution in China after
its strategic shift of 1927 typifies the guerrilla model of revolutionary insurrection. From the very beginning Mao tried to
organize the Chinese Red Army of Workers and Peasants into
a new type of politicized and multifunctional army strikingly
different from the traditional Chinese military forces (see

selections 1-3). (5) The Red soldiers were trained to be not
only good guerrilla fighters but also committed revolutionaries
and political workers dedicated to the Communist revolution.
They were inculcated with a progressive political ideology, in-
doctrinated with a new class consciousness, and taught a working style of egalitarianism and friendship toward the masses.
In contrast with the poorly disciplined and exploitative warlord
troops, bandits, or rebel groups, the Red Army was built on
strict organizational discipline and political indoctrination
(see selections 4-9). As Wilson C. McWilliams points out in
his analysis of guerrilla forces, "fighting under great hardship, such forces are normally sustained only by revolutionary
zeal and by individual commitment." (6)

Moreover, in the course of the revolution the Red Army did
not confine itself to battles but participated in a wide range of
nonmilitary tasks as well. From the early stages the Red
Army, partly owing to necessity, undertook the political and
social mobilization of the masses, took part in land reform,
built roads, and labored in agricultural and industrial production in the guerrilla bases (see selections 10-13). (7) As Mao
put it succinctly at the historic Ku-t'ien Conference in 1929,

> The Red Army is an armed group whose responsibility
> is executing class-oriented political tasks. In addition
> to fighting battles, it must also carry out the tasks of
> conducting propaganda among the masses, organizing
> the arming of the masses, and creating organs of polit-
> ical power. Otherwise fighting would lose its signifi-
> cance and the existence of the Red Army would lose all
> meaning. (8)

The Development of the Political Work System

The creation of the so-called "political work system,"
through which Party organization was systematically super-
imposed on the Red Army to ensure Party control of the guerrilla forces and to lead the army in nonmilitary work, was

probably the most important element in the effectiveness of
the guerrilla army (see selection 4). (9) The political work
system, which was introduced by Mao in 1927-28, was modeled
at first after the Soviet system of political commissars. The
early system of Front committees quickly gave way the next
year to a slightly more complex structure of Party representatives and Party committees. (10) From 1929 onward, the
system developed an elaborate infrastructure consisting of a
political commissar, a political department, a Party committee,
a Party secretariat, and Party cells within the larger units of
the Red Army. Under the overall leadership of the political
commissar, it operated as an integrated system for political
work, which in turn formed an integral part of the command
system of the Red Army.

Functionally, the political work structure quickly outgrew
its initial concerns with the political security and loyalty of
the guerrilla army and assumed a broad range of political, social, and economic responsibilities. The political work organs
were given responsibility for ideological indoctrination, morale, mass mobilization, economic production, counterinsur-
gency work, and a host of other noncombat tasks. Indeed, the
political work system became a mechanism through which the
Party leadership was systematically integrated into the army,
and the army became a politicized and multifunctional force. (11)
As early as 1932 the Political Work Regulations issued by the
Red Army categorically stated:

> The combat strength of the Red Army is determined not
> merely by the levels of military techniques, but principally
> by its class-oriented political consciousness, its political
> influence, and its capacity to mobilize the vast masses of
> workers and peasants, to disintegrate the enemy forces,
> and to rally the broad masses of workers and peasants
> around the Red Army. (12)

The extensive extramilitary activities performed by the Red
Army during the 1930s and 1940s under the general label of

"political work" can be grouped analytically into three broad
categories: (1) political work within the army, (2) political
work outside the army among the masses, and (3) political
work against enemy forces. (13)

Internal Political Work

In principle, a division of labor between military and political work within the Red Army was emphasized. While the
commanding officer was in charge of "military matters" related to combat training and military operations, the political
commissar was responsible for "political matters," including
control of personnel, ideological training, political loyalty, the
economic and cultural well-being of the military units, and all
other matters of political significance. In practice, all matters not of a strictly military nature were handled by the political work system. The political commissar, as "co-leader"
of the military unit, was required to ensure that the military
commander's combat plans and training program were in line
with Party policies. The political commissar assumed the
primary responsibility for the recruitment, assignment, transfer, and promotion of cadres. He was also responsible for
rectifying "feudal" attitudes, "backward" value orientations,
and "evil habits," and for inculcating a new political outlook,
eliciting activism and voluntarism among the soldiers, and
developing a new style of "hard work and plain living." (14)
The political work system was also entrusted with coordinating cultural and economic activities, operating schools, the-
aters, and libraries, organizing literacy classes and sports
activities, and directing participation in manual labor, construction projects, and farm work, in order to enrich the cultural and material well-being of the rank and file of the Red
Army. The leadership explicitly stressed the principle that
correct ideological orientation and proper work style were the
very foundation of the solidarity, comradeship, morale, and
effectiveness of the Red Army. (15)
Intensive training in political ideology and practical skills

was a sheer necessity in the early period for the simple reason that many of the army recruits were illiterate and un-
skilled peasants or "vagabond elements" hastily gathered in
the remote areas. Insubordination, desertion, and the "habits
of roving rebels" were matters of routine occurrence. (16)
There is no question that effective measures were urgently
needed to organize and discipline the peasant recruits and convert them into politically motivated and technically skilled soldiers (see selection 1).

From the outset, the leadership under Mao was convinced
that an egalitarian spirit and a democratic style of work were
essential if the leadership was to elicit genuine cooperation
from the rank and file and inspire sincere dedication to revolution. Within the army, solidarity and mutual trust between
officers and men, and among the troops themselves, were always the focal point of educational campaigns. Mass movements for "mutual assistance and cooperation" were launched
repeatedly to encourage the educated, the experienced, and the
"advanced" to help the ordinary soldiers, the new recruits, and
the "backward," respectively. "Revolutionary contests and
comparisons" and "emulation of models" were developed on a
large scale to enhance the military effectiveness among the
troops by developing their self-confidence, activism, and willingness to take the initiative in battle and political work.
Cadres were sent into the ranks to take part in the "company
democratic conferences," "officers-men relationship review
meetings," and "criticism, self-criticism" sessions on an
equal basis with the rank and file, and even to discuss military
tactics with the troops in the so-called "Chu-ko Liang meetings," in order to enlist the support and learn the views of the
troops. (17)

It was during this period of guerrilla operations that the Red
Army eliminated military rank, insignia, and differential pay.
Officers were asked to cast off their traditional status consciousness and to practice the "four togethers," by living, working, studying, and eating together with their men and the peasant masses. While cautioning against the excesses of "absolute

egalitarianism," the Red Army instituted the system of "supply in kind" — providing the daily necessities equally to all — to replace the graduated pay scale, and used the red star to replace the differential insignia of rank. (18) These measures were more than symbolic, having a significant impact on the solidarity of the revolutionary forces (see selection 6).

External Political Work

Although the political work system was an integral administrative component of the Red Army, it was always active outside the army barracks. As the security and effectiveness of guerrilla activities required the cooperation of the masses, the army was instructed to mobilize and organize the masses. Extensive propaganda and educational campaigns were carried out among the masses to convince them of the legitimacy of the revolution and to dissipate the traditional fear and distrust of the military. The masses were mobilized to join the militia and other auxiliary forces and to give direct support to guerrilla activities. In return, the soldiers were organized to work side by side with the peasants on the farms and to teach them how to read and write. (19)

During the period of guerrilla operations, military personnel were also used in organizing Soviets and Party organizations in newly occupied territories and behind enemy lines, wherever the regular Party and Soviet organizations were weak. In those instances, the distinction between the Red Army's political work system and the regular Party organizations virtually disappeared. (20)

Throughout the thirties and the forties, a series of political campaigns was launched by the army aimed at creating a new relationship of "mutual respect and cooperation" between the army and the people. The goal was to build a new image of the army as a respectable, well-disciplined political force, different from the warlord troops, the forces of the KMT, and the armies of the Imperial government. The leadership was convinced that unless the Red Army could win the genuine respect

and voluntary cooperation of the people, it would be impossible
to gain mass support in demolishing the traditional local power
structure, carrying out land reform, and establishing local
Soviets. (21) As early as 1928, for example, the Party representatives started conducting intensive educational and disciplinary campaigns to propagate the "three main rules" and
the "eight points for attention" laid down by Mao, in order to
train the soldiers to treat the people with courtesy, honesty,
and respect. (22) The "three-unity" movement launched after
the Japanese invasion of China in 1937 was meant to create
unity between officers and men, between the army and the people, and among various regional troops. (23)

The period was also marked by an intensification of campaigns to mobilize the masses to support the army, as guerrilla activities extended deep into the vast regions controlled
by the troops of Wang Ching-wei's "puppet government" and
the Japanese occupation army. The campaigns to "support the
government and cherish the people" within the army were always coupled with efforts to educate the masses to "respect the
cadres and cherish the soldiers." (24) Organizations were set
up on a hsien-by-hsien basis in which local people were taught
to respect and support the Red Army, to identify with the cause
of resistance, and to help with intelligence and other tasks.
Villagers were organized by guerrilla cadres into "Self-
Defense Corps" to gather intelligence, post sentries to observe
road traffic, and help relay the wounded to field hospitals. In
return, soldiers helped local peasants with farm work, provided armed cover for planting and harvesting, offered free
medical aid, operated schools and literacy classes, and even
organized village celebrations. (25) Soldiers were instructed
to respect local customs and religious practices and, where
possible, cadres were assigned to work in their native places.
By the late 1930s, army personnel in newly liberated areas
were increasingly involved in setting up local Party organizations as well as "anti-Japanese democratic regimes" based on
the "three-thirds principle" of coalition among the CCP, the
KMT, and neutral elements. (26)

Enemy Political Work

The third category of political work during this period involved extensive activities directed toward enemy forces and
the general populace behind enemy lines. The strategy of guerrilla warfare emphasized the active engagement of army cadres
in counterespionage work, psychological warfare, political propaganda, and sabotage. It was the responsibility of the army's
political personnel to develop and execute plans weakening the
enemy forces from within by nonmilitary means, on the one
hand, and to win their sympathy and support, on the other. They
were also responsible for establishing communication, propaganda, and supply networks, and for replenishing manpower and
supplies from enemy territories. (27)
    In dealing with the "White Army" of the KMT and the "pup-
pet army" of the Wang Ching-wei regime in the forties, the
Red Army emphasized the appeal of nationalism and patriotism
and intensified political propaganda aimed at sharpening class
tensions, undermining solidarity and morale, and encouraging
defection and rebellion among enemy forces. Meanwhile, de-
fectors and prisoners were treated sympathetically. The traditional practices of torture, public humiliation, and indiscrim-
inate execution of prisoners were prohibited; instead, political
education and thought reform were emphasized. Even prisoners who chose to leave the Red Army and return home were
treated with respect; often they were given farewell parties
and travel money in the expectation that they could some day
be won over to the cause of the revolution and be incorporated
into the Red Army. (28)

The Army as a "Working Force"

The most critical test of the capacity of the Red Army as a
multifunctional force came between 1947 and 1949, when the
tide of the civil war turned in favor of the Communists with
unexpected speed. This development confronted the People's
Liberation Army (PLA, formed from the Eighth Route Army

and the New Fourth Army in 1946) with a number of urgent
problems: (1) how to handle the hundreds of thousands of enemy
troops deserting the Nationalist regime; (2) how to organize
and discipline the rapidly expanding Communist forces; (3) how
to convert military manpower to civilian uses in the newly occupied areas; and (4) how to manage the enormous job of taking
over administrative control from the KMT at all levels. Each
of these vast problems became in part the responsibility of the
PLA. Under Mao's call to turn the Army into a "working
force," crash programs were set up to further enlarge the role
of the army. (29) In the meantime, army cadres were transferred in great numbers to civilian areas to perform nonmilitary tasks. (30) Indeed, the activities of the PLA in this transitional period were so extensive and diffuse on all fronts that
it was virtually impossible to draw any meaningful distinction
between the military and the nonmilitary. By the end of 1949,
by relying on strengths developed in its earlier political and
organizational work, the PLA had clearly demonstrated its
capability as a "working force" under the severe test of the
transition. (31)

   In sum, it seems clear that during the long period of more
than twenty years of the revolutionary war, the tradition of
systematic use of the guerrilla forces for a broad range of
noncombat activities was firmly established. The Red Army
served not only as the mainstay of the Party's armed struggle
for power but also as an instrument for social and political reform and economic production in the base areas. Organizationally, the Party penetrated deeply into the military to ensure
control of the army by the political apparatus. Intensive ideological training was conducted to inculcate political loyalty and
commitment, to boost morale and solidarity, and to spread effective methods of leadership and work. On the social and economic front, the Red Army met the critical need for skilled
and well-disciplined manpower to carry on social reform and
economic production in the liberated areas (see selections 1-3).

II. The Army and Nation-Building

In 1949 the Communist movement in China passed from the period of armed insurrection to a new stage of national construction and reform. The ending of the civil war drastically changed the operational environment of the PLA, but the army's assignment continued to involve the employment of its manpower and skills to meet the acute need for loyal cadres and effective organization to assist in the formidable tasks of postwar political control and construction. Thus, despite the new emphasis on "institution-building" and "organizational regularization" in the government bureaucracy and economic enterprises, the PLA did not turn away either organizationally or functionally from its "glorious tradition" of the guerrilla period. (32) The political importance and the multifunctional character of the army continued as before.

During the transitional period, it was of course the PLA that played a key role in managing the takeover of most Nationalist government organizations and public enterprises and in organizing the military control commissions, which governed in the cities. Below the national government, the regional military and administrative committees, dominated by the military, functioned as the highest local authority in the country. To reduce the army's burden on the nation's shaky postwar economy and to strengthen local leadership, large numbers of soldiers were demobilized and transferred to civilian organizations, industry, and administrative organs. Military units were also detailed on a large scale to help with agrarian reform and new industrial projects. (33) The official emphasis on the nonmilitary roles of the PLA was clearly reflected in the formal recognition of the "political work" apparatus of the PLA in both the 1949 Common Program and the 1956 Party Constitution. (34)

After 1949, to be sure, the PLA did play the conventional military role, defending China's national security in the military confrontations in Korea and the Taiwan Strait and in the border conflicts with India and the Soviet Union. These military roles have been duly noted and analyzed by specialists in

military affairs. (35) Yet most of the extramilitary activities
outside the conventional scope of the military have not received
attention commensurate with their importance.

The unconventional nonmilitary role of the PLA can be analyzed conceptually at two levels. At the institutional level, the
army as a whole has been used systematically to promote political development, social mobilization, and economic development. At the individual level, the PLA has played an important
role in the reshaping of the values, behavioral norms, and career patterns of the large number of Chinese who at some point
in their lives have served in or had contact with the military. (36)

In contrast with the Western model, in which the army is
kept structurally and functionally distinct from civilian institutions, the Maoist Chinese model demonstrates a pervasive inter-
systemic diffuseness. (37) The PLA's extramilitary activities since 1949 have been particularly significant in the areas
of political transformation, economic development, socio-
cultural change, and the organization of the militia. The significance of these activities for China's modernization and
nation-building deserves close examination (see sections II-V).

The Political Role of the PLA

The role of the PLA as the mainstay of Communist power
and defender of Party leadership was most dramatically demonstrated under the leadership of Lin Piao in the 1960s. (38)
After the overhauling and restrengthening of the political work
system within the military was completed in 1961-62, the PLA
launched a wavelike series of mass campaigns aimed at developing "correct" ideological orientation. (These included campaigns for the "four firsts," the "three-eight work style," the
"four-good company," and the "five-good fighter.") (39) The
campaigns were first carried out within the army, then in society at large. Beginning in 1963, the entire nation was encouraged to espouse the political loyalty, ideological commitment, and behavioral norms of PLA heroes like Lei Feng,
Wang Chieh, and Mai Hsien-te through the mass movement to

The PLA and the Socio-Cultural Transformation

The policy statement that "the PLA is the defender as well as the builder of the cause of socialism" reflects accurately the leadership's emphasis on using the army to promote socio-cultural change under the leadership of the Party. (51) As in the pre-1949 years, the army has continued to be instrumental in most social and political reform movements. In the 1950s the army played a role in the campaigns for land reform, the new marriage law, the suppression of counterrevolutionaries, the collectivization and communization of the countryside, and the socialist transformation of private enterprises in the cities. (52) During these campaigns, armymen and officers not only undertook propaganda and educational activities but also helped Party and state cadres in the actual organization and administration of the campaigns. In the 1960s, as discussed above, members of the PLA under the vigorous leadership of Lin Piao were held up as models of the Maoist revolutionary for emulation by the people of China. During the Cultural Revolution, it was of course the PLA's "Mao Tse-tung thought propaganda teams" and "support-the-left forces" that led the vigorous campaigns of "struggle-criticism-transformation" against "revisionism" in China (see selections 18-19). (53)

Periodic literacy and educational campaigns carried out by the PLA among the masses are another feature of the military's nonmilitary role. The significance of such campaigns, it should be noted, goes beyond the obvious immediate objectives of the transmission of basic literacy and technical knowledge. The army propagandists are also simultaneously engaged in promoting ideological and cultural change by attacking traditional values and norms and replacing them with new attitudes supportive of the goals and priorities set by the Communist regime (see selections 14-15). (54) The key role the PLA played in effecting significant change in the themes and style of contemporary literature, art, and theater — from the traditional to the revolutionary — testifies to the subtle yet

crucial cultural role of the military in China (see selection
16). (55) In the area of social change, recruitment and conscription techniques favoring poor and lower-middle peasants
serve the function of restructuring patterns of social mobility
and class stratification (see selections 14-19) (56)

The Role of the Militia

The impact of the extramilitary functions of the PLA is
greatly augmented by its control over the vast forces of the
People's Militia at the local level. Operating as an auxiliary
to the regular army, the militia serves as an organizational
link between the PLA and the masses of Chinese peasants. (57)
In times of war or emergency the militia can be mobilized for
national defense and internal security; in times of peace it becomes a mechanism for the training and management of the
enormous reservoir of manpower available in the countryside.

Although the strength and effectiveness of the People's Militia waned at times, the revival of the Maoist line in military
affairs in 1958 brought about a rapid and massive expansion
through the "everyone-a-soldier" movement. By June 1960
the PLA claimed that over 250 million men and women had
been recruited and organized into militia units (see selections
20-21). (58)

The PLA and Human Development

From the perspective of the PLA as a whole, the impact of
the military's "civic action" is indeed clearly visible and statistically conspicuous. From the perspective of the individual
citizen, however, the measurement of such impact is much
more difficult. Nonetheless, its significance should not be
overlooked. To begin with, there are probably nearly three
million men currently under arms in China. Each year about
700,000 young people are drafted to serve from two to three
years in the armed services, and an equal number of veterans
return to civilian life. (59) During their military service, these

men, mostly from rural backgrounds, acquire not only basic literacy but also organizational and vocational skills.

In addition, the education and training provided by the military constitutes an intensive socialization effort aimed at instilling the new citizenship and value orientations emphasized by China's new leaders. As Lucian W. Pye argues, the relatively successful socialization of military personnel into modern values and norms in many underdeveloped countries is due to the highly disciplined and controlled nature of the military environment. (60) If this is the case, we may infer that the PLA can work as an effective vehicle for transmitting "modern" values, impersonal and achievement orientations, and the Chinese Communist ethic of hard work and selfless dedication to a large part of the nation's youth.

The organizational setting in which this political socialization takes place is also highly conducive to the homogenization of parochial identities and the promotion of nationalism and national integration. The military forces, more than any other organization, represent a cross-section of class, ethnic, and regional backgrounds. The use of the national language in the political and military training of conscripts and cadets, for example, can provide the basis of an effective nationwide communication network, which the leadership can in turn use to facilitate the cultural and social integration of all citizens. (61)

The impact of the military is not limited to those who have actually served in the PLA. Skills and values are also transmitted through the vast militia system to the broad masses. The PLA's extensive extramilitary activities bring large segments of the population under the indirect influence of the army. Moreover, the demobilization process makes available roughly 700,000 men each year to be placed in relatively important leadership positions at local levels, because of the special training and skills they received during service. For instance, scattered data on cadre recruitment for Agricultural Producers' Cooperatives in selected areas in 1956 revealed that from 46 to 60 percent of Party and administrative leaders at that level were deliberately recruited from among former servicemen. (62) During the period from 1949 through 1956, over five million veterans were infused into the civilian work force. (63) Thus, the military as a channel of social and political mobility for a wide cross-section of rural youth and as an instrument for controlled social change is clearly a crucial factor in China's nation-building.

III. The Challenges to the Maoist Model

The Maoist model of army-building has consistently emphasized two fundamental principles since the late 1920s: the multifunctionality of the army and control of the military by the Party. As Mao put it, the PLA should forever serve not only as a "fighting force" but also as a "working force." (64) At the same time, according to Mao, "the Party commands the gun and the gun shall never be allowed to command the Party." (65) Derived from these two guiding principles are specific emphases on such priorities as the political work system, the dual command structure within the PLA, the politicization of the army, participation in civic action, the supportive role of the militia, and the "mass line" leadership technique.

These two guiding principles deal with the two most intricate problems of the military as a social institution. The former is concerned with the division of labor within the military and the differentiation of functions between the military and the nonmilitary, while the latter deals with the delicate power relationship between the civilian and the military authorities.

Over the past two and a half decades, the Chinese leadership has by and large sustained the continuity of the Maoist approach to the military's place in society. This was not accomplished, however, without serious challenges and struggles. It is true that the PLA has played a significant extramilitary role in the nation's economic development and socialist reform and that the Party has generally retained its political supremacy over the army. Yet it is also evident that the extent to which the ideal was approximated fluctuated over time. Two major sources of challenge to implementation of the ideal deserve special attention: One source was the military's tendency toward institutionalization and professionalization, which led to an increased demand for the professional autonomy of the military priority for the development of military technology, and exclusive emphasis on the regular army. This was the course advocated by P'eng Te-huai and Lo Jui-ch'ing in the 1950s and early 1960s (see selections 22-24). The other source of difficulty was a continual expansion of the nonmilitary role of the military, leading to military domination and intervention in virtually all areas of society. This was clearly evident in the pervasive influence the Army exercised under Lin Piao's vigorous leadership throughout the Cultural Revolution (see selections 25-29).

These two deviations from the Maoist model, it should be noted, resulted in different types of institutional behavior on the part of the military. Emphasis on institutionalization and professionalization promoted the separation of the PLA from the Party and enhanced the military's desire to withdraw from political and other extramilitary involvements. The expansion of the role of the military, in contrast, furthered the infusion of the military into society and the ascendence of military power, culminating in an attempt by the military to intervene in politics. A careful examination of these two challenges is helpful for an understanding of the operational dynamics as well as the dangers inherent in the Maoist model of army-building.

The Challenge of Military Professionalism

In his penetrating study of the military as a profession, Samuel P. Huntington argues that "the distinguishing characteristics of a profession as a special type of vocation are its expertise, responsibility, and corporateness." (66) According to this formulation, the professional is marked by his specialized knowledge and skills in a vocation, which are acquired only through prolonged training and experience. As a result of this process, he internalizes a code of professional ethics and a sense of social responsibility through the process of

socialization into the profession. He also develops a normative
orientation supportive of the effective performance of the professional functions. The members of the profession tend to
share a collective sense of organic unity, consciousness, and
identity. Once the military becomes highly professionalized,
therefore, the military man is likely to be proud of his special
training and competence in military affairs and to guard jeal-
ously his professional autonomy, prerogatives, and authority
against outside interference. Any external attempt to impose
control over what professionals, in this case the military, define as their legitimate activities is bound to be resented and
resisted.

The history of the development of the PLA as a professional
military establishment suggests the validity of Huntington's
theoretical argument. (67) Even in the late 1920s, when the Red
Army had just been organized from a group of independent
guerrilla armies, the introduction by Mao of Party control and
political work immediately met with considerable opposition
from the military commanders, who resented the dilution of
their prestige and power. It became necessary for Mao, at the
historic Ku-t'ien Conference in December 1929, to reaffirm
the strategic necessity of political work. At the Conference,
Mao and his followers severely criticized the "purely military
viewpoint" of the professional officers, and laid down the basic
principles on which Mao felt the army should be built (see
selections 1-2). (68) Throughout the long period of revolutionary war, although tension always existed between military professionalism and the insistence on political control, and between military needs and the extramilitary services the Red
Army was required to perform, the conflict never rose to crisis proportions. This was due partly to the fact that the guerrilla forces at that period never became a highly "specialized"
and "professionalized" military force, and due partly to the
fact that military commanders had to compromise with the harsh
reality of material poverty and the struggle for political sur-
vival in guerrilla warfare. (69) Under these circumstances,
extramilitary work was essential for developing the ideological

commitment and economic self-sufficiency of the Red Army in
order to compensate for its deficiencies in technology and organization.

The challenge of military professionalism began to emerge
as a major factor following the end of the civil war in 1949, as
the new regime shifted to an emphasis on institutional regularization and modernization. As the government and the Party
assumed more and more of the administrative and economic
functions that had been temporarily assigned to the military
control commissions, the PLA withdrew from its nonmilitary
activities and moved toward specialization and professionalization in military affairs. The military confrontation with the
United States in the Korean War further heightened the military's sense of the need to modernize as rapidly as possible
so as to be able to cope effectively with modern warfare. Moreover, the introduction into China of modern Russian military
equipment and related organizational forms helped establish
the "advanced experience" of the Soviet Union as a model for
the Chinese. (70) Technological modernization gradually affected all aspects of the PLA's command, organization, and
training from the early 1950s on. Military commanders took
on a more professional orientation, favoring the development
of a well-trained officer corps and a pool of skilled military
manpower to conduct new training programs and maintain the
new weapons systems. (71)

By 1954 the PLA had developed an elaborate and highly centralized command and logistics system supported by a large
number of military academies offering specialized, professional training. A conscription system was formalized in 1955 to
emphasize the development of a regular professional army,
downgrading the role of the militia. (72) The adoption of the
Regulations on the Service of Officers in February 1955 formally introduced into the PLA, as part of its movement toward
regularization and professionalization, a highly stratified system of ranks with differential pay and privileges, modeled after
the Soviet pattern. (73)

The professional military leaders and the newly emerged

officer corps now attacked the informality, flexibility, spontaneity, and egalitarianism that had been such central aspects
of the guerrilla tradition as "organizational anarchy" and "in-
discipline." Condemning the old "guerrilla mentality and habits" as obsolete and dysfunctional, they argued that "technical
work" should replace political work as the "lifeline" of the
new military order. The military leaders also began to per-
ceive the strength of the PLA primarily in terms of its professional and technological quality rather than its ideological
commitment and extramilitary capability. (74) Thus, in the
military barracks, the balance of priorities in training tipped
in favor of the professional and technical matters. This was
particularly evident in those units most oriented toward advanced technology, such as the air force, the artillery, and
the armored divisions. Under these circumstances, professional officers came to resent the political work system, which
protected the priority of political considerations in military
training and emphasized political indoctrination and extramilitary activities. (75) It was complained that "When the army
is carrying out the work of modernization, training tasks are
heavy. Participation in national construction will affect training, and will do more harm than good." (76)

The increased emphasis on professionalism and modernization was also frequently articulated in the policy statements of
military leaders. For instance, in a speech on military affairs
at a rally of the National Committee of the Chinese People's
Political Consultative Conference in July 1952, Hsiao Hua,
then deputy director of the General Political Department, declared that the central tasks of the PLA should be the development of "military science, skillful use of modern weapons and
equipment, strict observance of military discipline, and the
art of conducting coordinated action of all branches of the
army." (77) Reporting to the Eighth National Party Congress
held in September 1956, P'eng Te-huai, then defense minister,
declared:

We must intensify our study of modern military science

and technique, the art of commanding a modernized army
in battle, and new military systems. Unless we put greater effort into study of these things, we shall not be able to
master and make use of the most up-to-date weapons, or
command a modernized army in battle, and consequently
we shall not be able to build our army into an excellent
modern revolutionary army. (78)

The Struggle Between "Two Lines"

The growing challenge of professionalism within the military
eventually set the stage for the open struggle between "two
lines" in the late 1950s and early 1960s: the struggle between
the Maoist line and the "revisionist" line on the role of the
military. The supporters of the Maoist model apparently
sensed the challenges of professionalism as early as 1953,
when a nationwide conference of the PLA's senior political
work cadres was called to examine what they considered "deviations" from the "glorious tradition" of the Red Army. (79)
The defenders of the Maoist model argued that the one-sided
stress on military work and technological modernization would
inevitably weaken the Party's control over the army, reduce
the PLA's contribution to socialist construction, erode the
army's commitment to revolution, and undermine the tradition
of solidarity between officers and men and between the army
and the people. Moreover, neglect of political work would lead
to the evils of "commandism," "bureaucratism," and the
"purely military viewpoint" (see selections 4-6).

A new set of Draft Regulations on Political Work was reported to have been adopted in April 1954 in an attempt to re-
assert the primacy of the Maoist line of army construction.
However, judging from the limited press coverage and the absence of a large-scale propaganda campaign in support of the
Draft Regulations, the efforts to check the rise of professionalism were apparently not very successful. (80)

The attempt to control the challenge of professionalism was
renewed in 1957 and 1958 through a series of major mass

movements, such as the rectification campaigns, the movement
to send "officers to the ranks," and the intensification of ideological training. But these efforts came to fruition only when
the whole nation was radicalized by Mao's strenuous push for
the Great Leap Forward and the communization movement in
1958. In the military, the nationwide rectification campaigns
of 1957-58 against bureaucratism, dogmatism, subjectivism,
and conservatism were conducted in conjunction with a stepped-
up movement to send officers, including generals, to the ranks
as privates to practice productive labor and the "four togethers"
with the masses. (81) These campaigns had the threefold purpose of undercutting the organizational power accumulated by
the professional military bureaucrats, educating out-of-touch
officers about conditions among the men under their command,
and rekindling the revolutionary fervor of the professional officers.

As the Great Leap Forward gained momentum, the army was
mobilized on a massive scale to take part in capital construction, perform relief work in flood and drought, and help organize and streamline the management of rural communes. (82)
Beginning in 1958, the militia was once again reinvigorated
through the mass movement to make "everyone a soldier." (83)
The troops and military academies were caught up in an intensive campaign to study Mao's thought and military writings. (84)
As the individual campaigns coalesced into the nationwide push
to put "politics in command of everything" in 1958 and 1959, the
Maoist model seems to have regained the level of strength it
had achieved in the 1940s.

It should be noted, however, that the triumph of the Maoist
military doctrine over the "revisionist" line in the late 1950s
was by no means simple. In addition to the stormy mass campaigns, it required the purge of the top military leaders such
as P'eng Te-huai, minister of defense, and Huang K'e-ch'eng,
chief of staff, to check the influence of professionalism within
the military establishment. (85)

The Continued Challenge of Professionalism

The appointment of Lin Piao as P'eng's successor in September 1959 marked a return to the Maoist line. Under Lin's leadership, as indicated earlier, the political work system and the Party organizations in the army underwent a major overhaul. (86) Political education for the rank and file, stressing the study of Mao's thought, was restored as the central task in the day-to-day activity of the army. In 1961 five sets of important regulations — four on political work and one on management and education at the company level — were issued as guidelines for the systematic revamping of political work. (87) In March 1963 the Party reissued, with great fanfare, a comprehensive set of Political Work Regulations for the PLA in every service and at every level (see selection 4). (88) The Regulations reaffirmed the Maoist line on military matters as the "guidepost of both the political and the military work of the army." By the mid-1960s the PLA had reemerged as a vigorous multifunctional "working force," taking a leading role in every mass movement and actively participating in every aspect of national life.

Even in the midst of this impressive success in putting the Maoist line back in command, however, the "sins" of professionalism continued to be a problem. As revealed during the Cultural Revolution, Lo Jui-ch'ing, the chief of staff from 1959 until 1966, was found to have pursued the same "revisionist" line on the development of the military advocated by his predecessor, the purged Huang K'e-ch'eng. He was accused of sponsoring the mass campaigns for "great competitions in military skills" to enhance the priority of military professionalism, technological superiority, and technical training. It was said that he covertly undermined the political control over the PLA, encouraged the withdrawal of the army from nonmilitary work, and sabotaged the dual-control system in the PLA (see selections 22-24). And once again, in 1966, it required a major purge to rid the military establishment of the tendency toward a "purely military viewpoint." (89) The series of major purges and struggles between "two lines" clearly points to a serious contradiction in the Maoist model: As long as the PLA exists as an autonomous institution responsible for military affairs, the challenge of professionalism can at best only be contained, and not eliminated. Hence, the status of the PLA as a multifunctional force is bound to be subject to periodic challenge.

The Challenge of the Army's Multifunctionality

Aside from the challenge of professionalism, the other source of challenge to the stability of the Maoist model stems from the multifunctionality of the PLA. Expansion of extramilitary functions enables the military to play a major role in political affairs and encourages the military to seek political power. In contrast with the danger from military professionalism, which involves a contravention of Maoist principles, the risk of military domination or intervention results from an overly enthusiastic application of Mao's doctrine with regard to the use of the military as a "working force."

The prominent role played by the PLA during the Cultural Revolution and Lin Piao's attempt at a military coup in 1971 are clear illustrations of the latter type of problem. (90) Western analysts who have considered the theoretical problems and institutional patterns in civil-military relations have only rarely taken the Chinese case explicitly into account. In the West, civilian supremacy over the military has been safeguarded by the segregation of the military establishment from civilian sectors organizationally and functionally, and by an emphasis on the military's political neutrality and professional autonomy. In other words, civil-military conflicts are inhibited by maximizing military professionalism and the norms of institutional specialization and autonomy. (91) Samuel P. Huntington characterizes this pattern as the "objective civilian control" of the military. (92) In the "totalitarian" model, represented by the Soviet Union, the military is also functionally specific and distinct from other sectors. Yet the military is heavily penetrated

by the party organizationally and is turned into a political arm
in complete subordination to political control. Under such a
system, civil-military tensions are also kept at a minimum. (93)
    The Chinese model, while differing completely from the
Western model, is similar to the Soviet model in one respect,
that is, the organizational penetration of the military by the
Party. Functionally, however, the Chinese military, unlike the
Soviet and Western counterparts, maintains a diffuse relationship with the civilian sector. The PLA participates actively
and extensively in extramilitary activities. By virtue of its
organizational strength and nonmilitary activities, the military
acquires influence over a wide variety of policy matters. At
times of political crisis, the military further expands its extramilitary role, often by request of the civilian authorities, by
taking responsibility for the maintenance of social order. A
concomitant of such development is the military's assumption,
first, of a dominant role in policy-making, and then, of control
over all political power.

The Danger of Military Domination

    The pattern of military development in China since 1958 has
vividly illustrated the dangers inherent in the Maoist concept
of the army's extra-military role. The multifunctional character of the PLA was greatly expanded as a result of the chaos
of the Great Leap Forward and the communization movement.
It was further expanded during the Cultural Revolution, culminating in the dramatic coup attempt by military leaders
in 1971.
    Beginning in the late 1950s, particularly during the "three
hard years" between 1959 and 1961, the PLA under the newly
established leadership of Lin Piao started to assume a more
active role in support of the massive campaigns for production,
construction, socialist transformation, and emergency relief.
By 1962, when the process of internal overhaul and reinvigora-
tion had been completed, the army began turning outward even
more, exerting conspicuous influence in society at large. As

mentioned above, army heroes were hailed as revolutionary
models for the whole nation to emulate from 1964 on, as part
of the movement to "Learn from the PLA." Between 1964 and
1966, an organizational structure modeled on the army's political work system was introduced into schools, trade organizations, factories, and even Party organs throughout the nation;
and army cadres were transferred to man the newly organized
political work departments in all sectors of civilian life. (94)

The power and influence of the military grew still further
during the Cultural Revolution. As the regular Party apparatus
and state bureaucracy were paralyzed by the Red Guards' violent attempts to seize power from the "power-holders" and
"capitalist-roaders," the military emerged from early 1967
on as the "mainstay of the dictatorship of the proletariat." (95)
The army was finally asked by the Party to intervene to maintain order when armed conflict seriously threatened the state
(see selections 25-29). Since then, the army's formidable influence and presence have been maintained in every walk of
life through the nationwide "three-support" and "two-military"
campaign (i.e., to mobilize the army to support the broad
masses of the left, support industry, and support agriculture;
and to carry out military control and military training). (96)

The strong military representation in the new "provisional
organs of power" (revolutionary committees) and later in the
reorganized Party committees at all levels is clear evidence
of the dominance of the PLA on the political scene (see the
table on the next page). The large-scale military intervention
in the most chaotic years of 1967 and 1968 was apparently
viewed by Mao and the Party as a matter of necessity for political order and social discipline. But even after the holding of
the Ninth Party Congress and the reestablishment of local
Party committees, which took place at the provincial level between November 24, 1970, and August 19, 1971, the dominance
of the army persisted. (97) As shown in the table, the representation of the PLA in the provincial Party committee leadership was even greater than it had been in the provincial revolutionary committees, which had been organized earlier in the

Military Representation in
the New Power Structure, 1969-71

Organization	Total Membership (number)	Military Representation (number)	%
Politburo [1]	25	13	52
Central Committee [2]			
Full members	170	64	38
Alternate members	109	41	38
Provincial Revolutionary Committee [3]			
Chairmen	29	21	72
Vice chairmen	250	90	36
Provincial Party Committee [4]			
First secretaries	29	22	74
All secretaries	158	95	60

Sources:

1) Issues & Studies VIII: 1 (October 1971), 23-27.
2) Tsu-kuo No. 89 (August 1971), 9-11.
3) Chung-kung yen-chiu VI: 7 (July 1972), p. 2.
4) Tsu-kuo No. 100 (July 1972), 7-8.

Also, Derek J. Waller, "Elite Composition and Revolutionary Change in Communist China, 1965-1969," paper presented at the Association for Asian Studies Meeting, 1972; Donald W. Klein and Lois B. Hager, "The Ninth Central Committee," The China Quarterly, No. 45 (January-March 1971), 37-56. These data are also reported in Ying-mao Kau "The Case Against Lin Piao," Chinese Law and Government, V:3-4 (Fall-Winter 1972-73), p. 8.

period of the greatest disorder between January 31, 1967, and
September 5, 1968. (98) According to statements attributed to
Mao, the tradition of unified leadership by the Party — "the
Party commands the gun — was seriously crippled by the ar-
my's enhanced position of power. (99)

The Crisis of "Reactive Militarism"

Hindsight of the abortive coup attempt suggests that the growing influence of the army may in fact have forced Mao and the
Ninth Party Congress to acquiesce in the unprecedented proclamation of Lin Piao as the official successor in the new Party
Constitution adopted in April 1969. (100) In this light, it is not
surprising to see that in August 1970, when the Second Plenum
of the Ninth Congress was convened at Lushan, the top military
leadership put forth the demand that a state chairmanship for
its chief, Lin Piao, be established under the revised draft state
Constitution, in defiance of Mao's explicit instruction to the
contrary. (101) Its aim was clearly to further consolidate the
army's power over the entire government bureaucracy. But
this time Mao and the Party stood firm and rejected the army's
further advance. This rebuff apparently inspired in the military leadership fear for its own political security and suspicion
of the capability and legitimacy of the civilian authorities.
Finally, in early 1971, Lin Piao and his close military associ-
ates resorted to an attempt at a coup d'état to seize power from
Mao and the Party. (102) Although the plot was uncovered in
September of 1971 in time to prevent its success, the contradiction in the Maoist model between the use of the army as a
"working force" and the Party's command over the "gun" had
been made abundantly clear.

The progress of the PLA from political dominance to military intervention shows clearly the characteristics of "reactive
militarism" as portrayed by Morris Janowitz. (103) Military
intervention and military takeover tend to result from the
"pressures of civilians to expand the military role" because

of a need for the military to participate in national construction and development and/or because of crisis in the civilian sector which requires the military to step in to maintain order. (104)

The Politics of Military Intervention

In this respect, the Chinese case shows considerable similarity with patterns of military intervention in other developing countries. As Lucian W. Pye has pointed out, the army in a modernizing nation represents a relatively well-organized and well-trained modern force in society. (105) Because of its leading role in most revolutionary or other movements for independence, the military tends to be popular and respected. Moreover, the armed forces, as one of the socially and ethnically best-integrated organizations in society, become a symbol of national interest and unity. However, as Henry Bienen observes, the impact of the "Western" model influences the military in the new states to emphasize organizational autonomy and professional specialization, while the heritage of the colonial army generally encourages the army to compete for political power with the civilian authorities. (106) The tendency for the military to intervene is particularly acute in the Third World because many civilian regimes are incapable of developing effective policies and maintaining domestic political order. The lack of a firmly institutionalized norm of political neutrality of the military in the newly independent states tends to induce the military to maximize its political power. Hence, as Moshe Lissak's studies show, the pattern of military intervention in the new nations often progresses from the stage of the exercise of political influence to that of direct military takeover of political and administrative leadership and functions. (107) Such a pattern is clearly revealed in part in Indonesia under Suharto, South Korea under Park Chung Hee, Burma under Ne Win, and Nigeria under Yakubu Gowon, just to cite a few. (108)

It is worth noting, however, that the Chinese situation di-

verges in a number of respects from the general patterns ex-
hibited in the new nations. From the very beginnings of its
guerrilla phase, the Chinese Communist leadership has deliberately emphasized a high degree of diffuseness in the relationship between the military and the nonmilitary. It is virtually
impossible in terms of the historical tradition to regard the
military as a distinct sector, organizationally or functionally
separate from other societal sectors. Moreover, for over four
decades the leadership has consistently insisted that the Party
penetrate the army and control it. (109) A broad consensus
appears to have emerged among the elite in various sectors,
including a substantial segment of the military leadership, that
excessive involvement of the PLA in the power struggle would
inevitably destroy both the military's own basic organizational
unity and the nation's military security. The successful aversion of an armed confrontation at the Wuhan Incident of July
1967 attests to the development of such a consensus. (110)
   In the final analysis, the reasons why Mao was able to avert
a complete military takeover in China may be found in part in
the unique revolutionary heritage and institutional arrangements
developed over the past four decades. In the same vein, the
fact that the military failed to achieve a takeover also revealed
some inherent weaknesses of the PLA as a military institution.
Morris Janowitz argues that the military is in general most
effective in using its organization and coercive power to enforce
policies and carry out concrete programs set by the political
leadership. It lacks the innovative political imagination and
flexible leadership skills needed to take part effectively in the
more complex process of competing for power and making
public policies in the arena of political conflicts. (111)

The Reassertion of the Maoist Model

Although the successful aversion by Mao of the military's
attempt to seize power enabled the Party to restore the primacy of the Maoist model, it also exposed problems in the re-

lationship between army and society. In his theory of contradiction, Mao has consistently emphasized the principle of the
"unity of opposites" in the formulation of his military and
political strategy. (112) His doctrines and techniques of mass-
line leadership and democratic centralism, for example, are constructed by combining and integrating such opposing elements as
democracy and centralism, the elite and the masses, discipline
and spontaneity, centralization and decentralization. (113)

Such emphasis on the unity of opposites, as John W. Lewis
has demonstrated, has indeed become a unique characteristic
of Mao's leadership theory, one that provides an essential basis for the effectiveness and adaptability of China's revolutionary organization. (114) It is emphasized that all institutions
must constantly pay attention to the synthesizing and balancing
of contradictory principles and conflicting demands. According to this model, one-sided emphasis on one principle at the
expense of its counterpart will only undermine the unity of the
two opposites and lead to institutional deviation and dysfunction.

The general theory of the "unity of opposites," of course,
also applies to Mao's model of the military. According to Mao,
the PLA should be a combination of "fighting force" and "working force," engaging in both military work and political activities and emphasizing both military and ideological training.
The function of the "gun" and the power of the Party must also
be correctly integrated. Deviation to either extreme will inevitably upset the "correct balance" of opposites and disrupt
the healthy operation of the PLA in society (see selections
30-32). (115)

From the perspective of this Maoist model, therefore,
P'eng Te-huai and Lo Jui-ch'ing were guilty of the "rightist"
deviation of espousing a "purely military viewpoint," overemphasizing military professionalism and technology at the
expense of their counterparts of nonmilitary work and political
commitment. Lin Piao, in contrast, went to the opposite extreme, espousing a "leftist" deviation by overstressing political work and political power. This one-sided emphasis of

lii THE PLA AND CHINA'S NATION-BUILDING

Lin's eventually turned the PLA, according to Mao, into a
"cultural army," and induced the army to seize political
power. (116)

Apparently by 1970, Mao was alarmed that the military
under Lin Piao's ambitious leadership had overstepped the
limits on political power and extramilitary involvement set by
his dialectic model. Thus, at the Lushan Plenum of August
1970, and particularly following the foiling of the abortive military coup in September 1971, the Maoist leadership pushed a
campaign to restore the proper mix in civil-military relations
(see selections 30-32). The movement to "Learn from the
PLA" in the 1960s was matched by a new campaign based on
the slogan, "The Army Must Learn from the People." (117)
The Three Main Rules of Discipline and the Eight Points for
Attention were reissued in early 1972 in conjunction with the
PLA's campaigns to study and eliminate its arrogance and dis-
obedience. (118) The PLA is now instructed to place equal
emphasis on military and political training. In contrast with
the frenzied movement to "put politics to the fore" during the
Cultural Revolution, the PLA is now told that "politics must
be in command of and lead military affairs, but it cannot replace military affairs." (119) The earlier campaign for "two
militaries" and "three supports" has now been replaced by an
emphasis on "the Party's unified leadership." (120) Although
the general concept of the multifunctionality of the army as
expressed in the effort to make the PLA a "Great School of
Mao's Thought" remains in force, the principle of Party control and the theory of the "unity of opposites" are being restored.

The process of reform progresses slowly, yet the trend is
unmistakable. The increasing numbers of military leaders
removed from positions of power since 1972 and the continued
rehabilitation of Party veterans purged during the ascendance
of military power during the Cultural Revolution, for example,
are indicative of the trend. From the foiling of the coup attempt in September 1971 through the early spring of 1973, a

total of 48 top provincial-level Party leaders (5 first secretaries, 3 second secretaries, and 40 secretaries or deputy
secretaries) appear to have been dismissed. Among them
were 35 professional military commanders and political commissars (representing 73 percent of those dismissed). The
removal of these military leaders reduces the proportion of
the PLA representation in the provincial Party committees
from the 60 percent registered in August 1971 to about 46 percent (61 out of 132 provincial secretaries). In contrast, the
proportion of Party representation increased from 35 to 48
percent in the same period. (121) The balance of civil-military
relations at this particular level of leadership has undoubtedly
begun to shift, statistically at least, in the Party's favor. The
dramatic reappearance after seven years in obscurity of a
Party figure like Teng Hsiao-p'ing, the former general secretary of the Central Committee who was second only to Liu
Shao-ch'i as a target of violent attack during the Cultural Revolution, clearly demonstrates that the Party is regaining strength
vis-à-vis the military. (122) As of the spring of 1973, all evidence points to the continued restoration of the Maoist line of
army-building in China.

IV. Leadership, Mobilization, and Army-Building

The creation and development of the Maoist model of army-
building during the years of the revolutionary war can be explained as an outgrowth of the strategy of protracted guerrilla
warfare, which Mao formulated in response to the unique historical circumstances and harsh operational environment of
that period. The same factors, however, are not adequate to
explain the persistence of the model in the postliberation
period, when the revolution shifted from armed insurrection
to national construction. Three broad causal hypotheses seem
plausible and merit close examination.

First, the general theory of political socialization suggests
that people acquire more or less stable political orientations

and perceptions through their socialization experience. Memories of past experience tend to form a frame of reference in which a political actor perceives political realities and formulates policies. (123) It is therefore likely that the continued emphasis on the Maoist model after 1949 by the top elite is a function of the leadership's preliberation political socialization experience. In the personal experience of these men, the principles laid down by Mao sustained the Red Army through the severe test of protracted revolutionary war, giving rise in them a strong sense of confidence in the continued validity of the model. (124) Indeed, as Tang Tsou has argued, recurrent patterns in the political behavior and leadership style of the old revolutionary elite can be considered in part a manifestation of a "guerrilla mentality" or the so-called "Yenan syndrome." (125) This hypothesis would, then, imply that as long as the old generation of revolutionaries who shared Mao's political and military experience remains in power, the reliance on the PLA for extramilitary work and nation-building is likely to continue. (126)

The second hypothesis maintains that the nonmilitary role of the army in Chinese society is an element of rational, conscious decision in support of China's choice to take a "mobilization" approach to national development and social transformation. The policy of mass mobilization, as David Apter points out, is based on the belief that rapid social transformation and development can only be achieved through the synchronized mobilization of the nation's human and material resources. (127) In China, the PLA has been identified by the leadership as an organization capable of mobilizing both its own resources and those of the masses for general developmental purposes. (128) Indeed, there is no doubt that the PLA as a well-trained and highly organized block of nearly three million men can, if used skillfully, carry out a wide variety of "civic action" tasks. To confine this enormous manpower to military drills in peacetime would constitute a great waste of scarce resources. By coordinating its activities closely with those of the millions of demobilized veterans and the extensive militia network, the

PLA can undoubtedly play an extremely significant role in mass mobilization, policy implementation, and task performance. Thus, the model of the "fighting force," as Mao formulated it, is clearly a product of rational policy choice aimed at maximizing the effect of the military's skills, manpower, and organizational resources for peaceful and constructive purposes in China. (129)

The third hypothesis concerns the link between the persistence of the Maoist model and the continued presence of acute social tensions and political struggle. As long as the revolutionary regime keeps pressing for radical change in political values, social structure, and policy priorities, "class enemies" and political opposition are bound to emerge. (130) This would naturally entail the need for the military to shoulder the extra-military burdens of social reform and political control in support of the Party in "continued revolution." During times of extensive revolutionary change, the coercive power of the military is always needed to ensure internal security and to buttress political authority. The loyalty and subordination of the military to the revolutionary leadership under such circumstances becomes a prerequisite for political stability and the implementation of reform. Thus, as long as the leadership insists on carrying out Mao's policy of "continued revolution," the PLA is likely to remain highly political and active in extra-military work. (131)

If these three broad hypotheses are all valid, the future role of the PLA clearly depends on (1) the persistence of the old revolutionary elite who share Mao's revolutionary experience and outlook, (2) the continued endorsement by the political leadership of a mass mobilization strategy for national development, and (3) the degree of political instability and social conflict present in China's political system. Significant change in any of these three areas would affect the role of the PLA.

When the old elite, still highly influential, passes from the political scene and a new generation with different training, career background, and political outlook arises, it is likely

that a new strategy of development based on different socialization experience will emerge. (132) If the tendency Max
Weber noted for charismatic revolutionary leaders to be succeeded by pragmatic technocrats should operate in China (133),
then the new generation of "revolutionary successors" will
most likely view the link between the extramilitary activities
of the PLA and the task of nation-building differently from
their predecessors, and they may abandon the effort to preserve
it on the ground that it is neither effective nor necessary.

Another powerful force at work which will certainly strongly
challenge the persistence of the Maoist line is the general trend
toward institutionalization and professionalization that China
has been experiencing since 1949 in every sector of society. (134)
Institutionalization and professionalization are bound to enhance
the influence and authority of professionals and bureaucrats. (135)
Within the PLA the conflict between "red" and "expert," between political control and military autonomy, and between political work and military work has been evident for many years.
There is no question that the continued advancement in military
technology, especially after the development of nuclear weapons and the related delivery capability, is going to push the
PLA further in the direction of specialization and centralization. In this modernized stage, the responsible military professionals cannot but view the diversion of the PLA to nonmilitary activities as dysfunctional and counterproductive for national security. (136) In the long run, as Ellis Joffe argues,
the debate over the relative importance of men and weapons,
of political and military work, is likely to be decided by the
formidable force of professionalization and modernization. (137)

The hypothesis that the scope of the military's extramilitary
activity is a function of the nation's instability and internal conflict seems to be well supported by the process of political development in China since 1949. In the early 1950s the absence
of serious power conflicts and political struggles within the
Party leadership and the high prestige of the regime among
the populace were accompanied by a low level of external in-

volvement on the part of the PLA. But in the late 1950s and throughout the 1960s, as the struggle between the "two lines" grew and the intensive reform movements were pressed forward, the extramilitary role of the PLA increased greatly. If this hypothesis is correct, then when socialist transformation of the economy and society is completed and the goals of the Communist system become institutionalized, we would expect that the political role of the PLA and the need for the Party's control of the army would probably decline in proportion. (138) In these circumstances, the danger of military intervention in the form of "reactive militarism" would also be reduced. (139)

While all three of these hypotheses may well be proved valid in the long run, it is premature to argue at this time that the Maoist model of the military's function has outlived its usefulness in China and will be discarded in the near future. The developments of recent years have shown the truth to be otherwise. First, the old revolutionary elite under Mao and his close followers is still very much in charge of the formulation of the general ideological orientation and policies. Second, the leadership continues to rely on the rationality and effectiveness of the mass mobilization strategy of revolutionary change and the model of "people's war." Third, despite the economic progress of the past two and a half decades, China's level of development is still very low in comparison with the West. Fourth, the series of violent struggles between "two lines" since the late 1950s demonstrates clearly that the process of institution-building and the consolidation of the "proletarian dictatorship" are still far from complete. (140) Therefore, it would seem reasonable to conclude that in the near future the Maoist model of army-building will continue to be supported by substantial segments of the leadership and play a positive role in China's mass mobilization approach to nation-building.

Notes*

Abbreviations

CB	Current Background
ECMM	Extracts from China Mainland Magazines
JPRS	Joint Publications Research Service
NCNA	New China News Agency
PWR	Political Work Regulations
SCMM	Selections from China Mainland Magazines
SCMP	Survey of China Mainland Press

1) See, for example, David B. Ralston, ed., Soldiers and States (Boston: Heath, 1966); Samuel P. Huntington, The Soldier and the State (Cambridge: Harvard University Press, 1957).

2) For further analysis of the theme, see Wilson C. McWilliams, ed., Garrisons and Government (San Francisco: Chandler, 1967); Henry Bienen, ed., The Military and Modernization (Princeton: Princeton University Press, 1971).

3) Important works on the PLA's nonmilitary activities include Davis B. Bobrow, "The Political and Economic Role of the Military in the Chinese Communist Movement, 1927-1959"; S. M. Chiu, "A History of the Chinese Communist Army"; John Gittings, The Role of the Chinese Army; Wang Chiahsiang et al., Cheng-chih kung-tso lun-ts'ung [Discussion on Political Work]; Ellis Joffe, Party and Army; Chiang I-shan, "Chung-kung chün-tui ti cheng-chih kung-tso" [Political Work in the Chinese Communist Army], 2-15; and Yingmao Kau, Paul M. Chancellor, Philip E. Ginsburg, and Pierre M. Perrolle, The Political Work System of the Chinese Communist Military.

4) For an excellent discussion of the typology of revolution, see Chalmers Johnson, Revolutionary Change (Boston: Little,

*The bibliographical information for articles and books has not been included in the Notes when the publications have been listed in full in the Bibliography.

Brown, 1966), pp. 150-165.

5) This portion of discussion is based primarily on sources cited in note 3 above. Also, Lo Jui-ch'ing, K'ang-Jih chün-tui-chung ti cheng-chih kung-tso [Political Work in the Anti-Japanese Military Forces], and Ching Ch'in, Chan-shih cheng-chih kung-tso [Wartime Political Work]. For an excellent collection of documents and articles for the post-1949 period, see Chiang I-shan, comp., Chung-kung chün-shih wen-chien hui-pien [Source Book on Military Affairs in Communist China].

6) McWilliams, ed., Garrisons and Government (see note 2), p. 40.

7) For a wide variety of economic activities, see Pa-lu-chün lien-fang-chün cheng-chih-pu, comp., Fa-chan sheng-ch'an yung-cheng ai-min wen-hsien-chi [A Collection of Documents on Advancing Production, Supporting Government, and Loving the People]. See also sources cited in note 5 above.

8) Mao Tse-tung, Chung-kuo kung-ch'an-tang hung-chün ti-ssu-chün ti-chiu-tz'u tai-piao ta-hui chüeh-i-an [Resolution of the Ninth Congress of the Chinese Communist Party of the Fourth Army of the Red Army], p. 4. This Resolution is also known as the Ku-t'ien Resolution of 1929. Part of the texts in English may be found in Mao Tse-tung, Selected Works of Mao Tse-tung, Vol. I, pp. 105-116. The entire text is translated by Philip E. Ginsburg and included as selection 1 of this volume.

9) For a detailed analysis of the political work system and the complete text of the three most important sets of Political Work Regulations issued in 1932, 1939, and 1963 respectively, see Ying-mao Kau et al., Political Work System of the Chinese Communist Military. These three sets of the Political Work Regulations are hereafter cited respectively as PWR, 1932; PWR, 1939; and PWR, 1963.

10) Mao, Selected Works, I, pp. 63-116.

11) See note 8 above.

12) PWR, 1932, Article 1.

13) Lo Jui-ch'ing's work used the same categorization. See Lo, K'ang-Jih chün-tui-chung ti cheng-chih kung-tso, pp. 41-189. As the PWR, 1963, I, puts it, the central tasks of political

work are to "strengthen the internal and external unity of the
Army, that is, internally, between officers and soldiers, between higher and lower levels, between military and political
work, between various types of other work, and between various army units; and externally between the Army and the people, between the Army and local organizations, between our
Army and friendly armies; and to conduct work designed to
disintegrate enemy forces."

14) All these activities are clearly spelled out in great detail in
the political work regulations; see especially PWR, 1932, A; PWR,
1939, A; and PWR, 1963, I. One of the best analyses may be found in
Lo Jui-ch'ing, K'ang-Jih chün-tui-chung ti cheng-chih kung-tso.

15) Ibid.

16) PWR, 1932, A and B X.; Mao, Selected Works, I, pp. 63-
116. Some frank descriptions of the situation by Mao are quite
revealing: "How to deal with the enemy, how to fight, has become the central problem in our daily life," p. 80. "The political ideology of roving rebel bands has emerged in the Red Army
because the proportion of vagabond elements is large and because there are great masses of vagabonds in China," p. 114.

17) All these leadership techniques are detailed in the three
manuals issued by the General Political Department of the
Eighteenth Army Group, entitled Kuan-ping kuan-hsi [Officer-
Men Relations], Ling-tao tso-feng [Leadership Style], and Chün-
min kuan-hsi [Army-People Relations]. See Ti-shih-pa chi-
t'uan-chün tsung-cheng-chih-pu, comp., Ling-tao tso-feng
[Leadership Style]; by the same comp., Kuan-ping kuan-
hsi [Officer-Men Relations]. Also, Koain, "Kyōsangun-
nai ni okeru seiji kunren" [Political Training Within the Communist Army]. Chu-ko Liang was a well-known tactician of the
Three Kingdoms period. The Chu-ko Liang meeting was designed
to have officers and men get together to discuss tactical issues as
a means for improving military operation and morale.

18) Lo Jui-ch'ing, K'ang-Jih chün-tui-chung ti cheng-chih
kung-tso; Mao, Selected Works, I, pp. 73-104; Ho Lung, "Chung-
kuo-jen-min chieh-fang-chün ti min-chu ch'uan-t'ung" [The
Democratic Tradition of the Chinese PLA]; Li Kuang, Hung-chün

shih tsen-yang tuan-lien ti [How the Red Army Is Trained];
and Hihon gaiji kyōkai, comp., Shina ni okeru kyōsan undō [The
Communist Movement in China].

19) See note 14 above.

20) PWR, 1939, B I, for example, declared succinctly: "Political work must rely upon the Party and is in itself Party work.
The major proportion of political work personnel should be
members of the Party. The political organs are the organs of
the Party." See also Pa-lu-chün lien-fang-chün cheng-chih-pu,
comp., Fa-chan sheng-ch'an yung-cheng ai-min wen-hsien-
chi [A Collection of Documents on Advancing Production and
on Supporting the Government and Loving the People].

21) For an excellent analysis of the mass mobilization in the
Kiangsi period, see Ilpyong J. Kim, "Mass Mobilization Pol-
icies and Techniques Developed in the Period of the Chinese
Soviet Republic."

22) Mao Tse-tung, Selected Works, IV, p. 156: "In the spring
of 1928, ...Mao Tse-tung set down Three Rules of Discipline:
(1) Obey orders in your actions; (2) Don't take anything from
the workers and peasants; and (3) Turn in all things taken from
local bullies. In the summer of 1928 he set forth Six Points
for Attention: (1) Put back the doors you have taken down for
bed-boards; (2) Put back the straw you have used for bedding;
(3) Speak politely; (4) Pay fairly for what you buy; (5) Return
everything you borrow; and (6) Pay for anything you damage.
After 1929 Comrade Mao Tse-tung made the following changes:
Rule 2 became 'Don't take a single needle or piece of thread
from the masses,' and Rule 3 was changed first to 'Turn in all
money raised' and then to 'Turn in everything captured.' To
the Six Points for Attention he added two more: 'Don't bathe
within sight of women' and 'Don't search the pockets of captives.' This was the origin of the Three Main Rules of Discipline and the Eight Points for Attention."

23) PWR, 1939, A; see also Tōa keizai chōsakyoku, "Kyōsantō
Shin-Satsu-Ki henku seifu to guntai oyobi minshu dantai to no
kankei" [The Communist Party's Chin-Ch'a-Chi Border Region
Government and Army and Their Relation to the Mass Organiza-

tions], 35-36. The details of proper relationships between the officers and men were spelled out in the well-known "Cadre Compact" and "Soldier Compact." For the texts, see Chiang I-shan, "Chung-kung chün-tui ti cheng-chih kung-tso" [Political Work in the Chinese Communist Army], 2-15.

24) Pa-lu-chün liu-shou ping-t'uan cheng-chih-pu, comp., I-nien-lai ti yung-cheng ai-min kung-tso [The "Support the Government and Love the People" Work of the Past Year]; Lo Jui-ch'ing, K'ang-Jih chün-tui-chung ti cheng-chih kung-tso, pp. 146-150; and note 74.

25) The details of such activities were spelled out in the 10 articles of the "Support the Government and Love the People Compact." For the texts, see Chiang I-shan, "Chung-Kung chün-tui ti cheng-chih kung-tso" [Political Work in the Chinese Communist Army], p. 14, note 11.

26) Pa-lu-chün cheng-chih-pu, Chung-kuo ti-hou k'ang-Jih min-chu keng-chü-ti kai-k'uang [The Conditions of the Anti-Japanese Democratic Bases Behind Enemy Lines in China]; Conrad Brandt et al., A Documentary History of Chinese Communism (New York: Atheneum, 1967), pp. 279-315; Mao Tse-tung, Selected Works, II, pp. 418-419; III, pp. 131-134.

27) Lo Jui-ch'ing, K'ang-Jih chün-tui-chung ti cheng-chih kung-tso, pp. 164-176.

28) Hou Mi, Chung-kung tsen-yang tui-tai fu-lu [How the Chinese Communists Treat Prisoners]; and Lo Jui-ch'ing, K'ang-Jih chün-tui-chung ti cheng-chih kung-tso, pp. 164-189.

29) For the concept of turning the "fighting force" into a "working force," see Mao, Selected Works, IV, pp. 337-340. The crash programs launched in the transitional period include the "four immediates" (immediate capture, resupply, training, and return of Nationalist soldiers to combat on the Communist side), the "three checkups" (check the class origin, performance, and fighting will of each man and officer), and the "three improvements" (improve ideological training, organizational discipline, and correct living and working style). See Mao, Selected Works, IV, pp. 191-193, 271-274, 337-340; Shih Ch'eng-chih, Lun Chung-kung ti chün-shih fa-chan [On the Develop-

ment of the Chinese Communist Military], pp. 87-106. The
"policy of leniency" toward the KMT armies proclaimed in
1947 offered five guarantees: (1) not to confiscate private properties, (2) not to beat up and humiliate, (3) to protect the safety
of life, (4) not to settle old accounts, and (5) to allow free
choice of one's own future.

30) For a fuller treatment of the cadre transfer, see Ying-
mao Kau, "Patterns of Recruitment and Mobility of Urban
Cadres."

31) For an excellent report on the transition, see A. Doak
Barnett, China on the Eve of Communist Takeover (New York:
Praeger, 1961), pp. 315-364.

32) For the trend toward institutionalization, see Ying-mao
Kau, Bureaucracy and Political Development in Communist
China (Stanford: Stanford University Press, forthcoming).

33) Ibid.

34) Article 21 of the Common Program provides: "The People's Liberation Army and the people's public security forces
shall, in accordance with the principle of unity between the
officers and the rank and file and between the army and the
people, set up a system of political work...." Article 35 of the
1956 Party Constitution reads: "The General Political Department in the People's Liberation Army, under the direction of
the Central Committee, takes charge of the ideological and organizational work of the Party in the army."

35) See, for example, Allen S. Whiting, China Crosses the
Yalu (New York: Macmillan, 1960); Samuel B. Griffith, The
Chinese People's Liberation Army.

36) For theoretical speculations on these aspects, see Davis
B. Bobrow, "The Civic Role of the Military: Some Critical
Hypotheses"; Moshe Lissak, "Modernization and Role-Expansion of the Military in Developing Countries: A Comparative
Analysis," Comparative Studies in Society and History, IX:3
(April 1967), 233-255; Marion J. Levy, Jr., Modernization
and the Structure of Societies (Princeton: Princeton University Press, 1966), pp. 517-605; Lucian W. Pye, "Armies in
the Process of Political Modernization," Archives Européennes

de Sociologie, No. 2 (1961), 82-92.

37) For the Western model of military development, see
Morris Janowitz, The Professional Soldier (New York: The Free
Press, 1960); David B. Ralston, Soldiers and States (see note
1); Huntington, The Soldier and the State (see note 1).

38) The growing role of the PLA in the 1960s was the central
theme treated in Chinese Law and Government, V: 3-4 (Fall-
Winter 1972-73); VI: 1 (Spring 1973).

39) PWR, 1963, I. The concept of "four firsts" seems to have
been formulated for the first time at an important enlarged session
of the Military Affairs Committee held between September 14 and
October 20, 1960. For the texts of the Resolution on Strengthening
Political and Ideological Work in the Army, see Kung-tso t'ung-
hsün [Bulletin of Activities], No. 3 (January 7, 1961). For Lin's
own elaboration of the concept, see "Shen-ju lien-tui chia-ch'iang
ssu-hsiang kung-tso" [Go Deep into the Company-level Units to
Strengthen Ideological Work]. The "four firsts" stress to place
"the human factor first in handling the relationship between men
and weapons, political work first in handling the relationship between various kinds of work and political work, ideological work
first within political work, and living ideology first within ideological work." The "three-eight work style" refers to three
phrases and eight characters enunciated by Mao: "a firm and correct political direction, a persevering and simple style of work,
and flexible strategy and tactics;" and "unity, intensity, solemnity,
and liveliness." The "four goods" stress "good in political and ideological work, good in the three-eight work style, good in military
training, and good in management of army livelihood." The "five-
good fighters" refers to the soldiers "good in political ideology,
good in military techniques, good in the three-eight work style,
good in carrying out assigned tasks, and good in physical training."
For the official instructions of the General Political Department
on political work for the entire PLA for 1961, see Kung-tso t'ung-
hsün, No. 1 (January 1, 1961); San-pa tso-feng [Three-Eight
Style]; and Hsiao Hua, "Ssu-hao lien-tui ti chi-pen ching-yen"
[The Basic Experience of the Four-Good Company].

40) John Gittings, "The 'Learn from the Army' Campaign."
In the meantime, political training within the military was further

intensified in 1965 under Lin's new slogan "to read Chairman
Mao's books, listen to Chairman Mao's words, act according to
Chairman Mao's directives, and be Chairman Mao's good fighters,"
see Jen-min jih-pao [People's Daily] (January 19, 1965). An unmistakable sign of the primacy of political work and the efforts to
restore the "guerrilla tradition" of egalitarianism, comradeship,
and democracy in the army was the decision of May 1965 to abolish
all military ranks and honors, and to eliminate distinctive uniforms
and insignia. The decision was formally adopted at the Ninth Session of the Standing Committee of the Third National People's
Congress on May 22, 1965. See Fei-ch'ing nien-pao [Year-
book on Chinese Communism], 1967, pp. 703-704; NCNA, May 24,
1965; also Ho Lung, "Democratic Tradition of the Chinese PLA."

41) Chalmers Johnson, "Lin Piao's Army and Its Role in
Chinese Society," and Ralph L. Powell, "Commissars in the
Economy." For the press coverage on the establishment of
political departments in the areas of finance and trade and
industry and communications, see Jen-min jih-pao [People's
Daily] (June 7, September 30, 1964); Ta-kung pao (February 28,
March 22, 27, June 19, 1965); Jen-min shou-ts'e [People's
Handbook] (1965), pp. 504-518, 537-539. It is interesting to
note that no single article on the civilian political departments
had ever appeared in Hung-ch'i [Red Flag] during the 1964-65
period. This may indicate a strong opposition to the movements
from the "revisionists" at the top level.

42) "Yung-yüan t'u-ch'u cheng-chih" [Forever Give Politics
Prominence].

43) See further discussion and the table below.

44) Ellis Joffe, "The Chinese Army in the Cultural Revolution," and Jurgen Domes, "The Role of the Military in the Formation of Revolutionary Committees, 1967-68." For the broad
power exercised by the so-called "support-the-left" forces
dispatched by the PLA, see an official directive issued jointly
by the Central Committee and other key organs on June 10,
1968, which may be found in Chung-kung nien-pao [Yearbook
on Chinese Communism] (1969), Section VII, pp. 39-41.

45) Fu Chung, "Achievements Made by the Armed Forces in
Support of Socialist Construction"; Hsiao Hua, "Participation

in National Construction Is a Glorious Task of the PLA"; and
Henry Schwartz, "The Chinese Communist Army in Sinkiang."
For activities in the recent period see, for example, "Greater
Successes by the PLA in 1968 Farming and Sideline Occupa-
tions"; "PLA Unit Builds Dyke to Turn Lake into Farmland in
South China Province"; "PLA Scores New Gains in Farm and
Sideline Production Last Year."

46) "A Brief Account of the Achievements of the Sinkiang
Production and Construction Corps of the Army in the Last
Ten Years," China Land Reclamation, No. 2 (February 5, 1960);
translated in ECMM, No. 204 (1960); Chang Chun-han, "Production and Reconstruction Army Corps in Sinking," Jen-min
jih-pao [People's Daily] (July 31, 1966); translated in SCMP,
No. 2318 (1966).

47) See Hsin-Hua pan-yüeh-k'an [New China Semi-Monthly],
No. 1 (January 10, 1957), 98-99; No. 3 (February 10, 1957),
7-8; and Jen-min jih-pao [People's Daily] (February 19, 1958).
See also "PLA Helps in China's Industrial Production" and
"Northwest China Veteran Communists Active in Industry."

48) See, for example, "PLA Active in Production and Political Life in Countryside" and "PLA Medical Workers Go to
Countryside to Temper Themselves."

49)   For example, Fu Chung, "Achievements Made by the Armed
Forces in Support of Socialist Construction"; and NCNA-English,
Peking, February 22, 1958; in SCMP, No. 1724 (March 1958). It
reports that the navy and the air force were used to create artificial
rainfall and combat locust pests.

50)   Jen-min jih-pao [People's Daily] (February 26 and
March 14, 1959).

51)   Second Session of the Eighth National Congress of the Communist Party of China (Peking: Foreign Languages Press, 1958),
p. 54.

52) See, for example, Ezra Vogel, Canton Under Communism
(Cambridge: Harvard University Press, 1970), pp. 88, 142-156;
Hsiao Hua, "Participation in National Construction"; and "PLA
Farm Leads People's Communes in Learning from Tachai."

53) "Lin Piao and the Cultural Revolution"; see also sources

cited in notes 39, 40, 41, 44.

54) Chalmers Johnson, "Lin Piao's Army and Its Role in Chinese Society"; John Gittings, "The 'Learn from the Army Campaign"; Ho Lung, "Democratic Tradition of the Chinese PLA"; "Class Struggle on Literature and Art Front," Chieh-fang-chün pao [Liberation Army Daily], editorial, NCNA-English, Peking, May 23, 1967; in SCMP, No. 3946 (May 25, 1967), 19-20.

55) "Hail Victory of Mao Tse-tung Line on Literature and Art"; "Fine Models of Revolutionary Literature and Art"; "Chinese Armymen on Revolutionary Literature and Art"; "PLA Men on Revolutionary Mass Repudiation in Literature and Art."

56) See further discussion below of the recruitment of veterans in the countryside. Jen-min jih-pao [People's Daily] (January 30, 1957); "Troops Stationed in Fukien Active in Strengthening Ties Between the Military and the Administration."

57) George P. Jan, "Red China's Militia," in George P. Jan, ed., Government of Communist China (San Francisco: Chandler, 1966), pp. 535-542; Ralph L. Powell, "Communist China's Mass Militia."

58) Ralph L. Powell, "Everyone a Soldier: The Communist Chinese Militia"; "PLA Men Help Militia Study Chairman Mao's Ideas on People's War."

59) The Communist Bloc and the Western Alliances (London: Institute for Strategic Studies, 1964), p. 8.

60) Lucian W. Pye argues the point strongly in his "Armies in the Process of Political Modernization" (see note 36).

61) See, for example, Chalmers Johnson, Peasant Nationalism and Communist Power; Ch'en I, Pa jen-min chieh-fang-chün ti wen-i kung-tso t'i-kao i-pu [Raise Higher the Cultural and Art Work of the People's Liberation Army].

62) Jen-min jih-pao [People's Daily] (January 30, 1957). Data collected by Michel Oksenberg indicate a similar proportion. See his "Local Leaders in Rural China, 1962-65," in A. Doak Barnett, ed., Chinese Communist Politics in Action, p. 197.

63) See P'eng Te-hui's report to the Eighth National Party Congress in September 1956, in Chiang I-shan, Chung-kung chün-shih wen-chien hui-pien [Source Book on Military Affairs in Communist China], p. 47.

64) Mao, Selected Works, IV, pp. 337-340.

65) Ibid., II, p. 224.

66) This portion of theoretical discussion is based on Samuel P. Huntington, The Soldier and the State (see note 1), pp. 7-18.

67) A detailed treatment of the professionalization of the military may be found in Ellis Joffe, Party and Army.

68) See also Chun-tu Hsüeh and Robert C. North, trans., "The Founding of the Chinese Red Army"; Chiang I-shan, "Chung-kung chün-tui ti cheng-chih kung-tso" [Political Work of the Chinese Communist Military]; Edgar Snow, Red Star Over China; and Tōa Keizai Chōsakyoku, Shina Sovieto undō no kenkyū [A Study of the Soviet Movement in China].

69) PWR, 1932; and Wu Yün-kuang, "Chung-kung-chün cheng-chih kung-tso ti san-ko shih-ch'i" [The Three Periods of the Chinese Communist Army's Political Work]. As late as October 1933, the urban-based central leadership of the Party under Wang Ming and Po Ku was reported to have ordered the abolition of the Party committee system within the Red Army to prevent political intervention in military operations. However, the order appears to have been ignored by Mao's forces. Chiang I-shan, "Chung-kung chün-tui ti cheng-chih kung-tso" [Political Work in the Chinese Communist Army], p. 40.

70) Ellis Joffe, Party and Army, pp. 1-45.

71) See, for example, Peng Te-huai, "Build Our Army into an Excellent Modernized Revolutionary Force."

72) For a comprehensive collection of original documents on various aspects of the PLA's development, 1949-64, see Chiang I-shan, Chung-kung chün-shih wen-chien hui-pien [Source Book on Military Affairs in Communist China].

73) For the text of the Regulations, see Jen-min jih-pao [People's Daily] (February 9, 1955).

74) Chieh-fang-chün pao [Liberation Army Daily], editorials, (February 13, 1957, January 4 and July 1, 1958).

75) For example, see "Against One-sided Emphasis on Modernization"; and Izaki Kiyota, "Chūkyōgun ni okeru seijibu seido ni tsuite" [On the Political System in the Chinese Communist Army].

76) The complaint was cited by Hsio Hua, "Participation in National Construction Is a Glorious Task of the PLA."

77) NCNA (July 31, 1952), in CB, No. 208 (1952), 37-39, cited in Ellis Joffe, Party and Army, pp. 2-3. For the Chinese text, see Hsiao Hua, "Hsiang-cho hsien-tai-hua mai-chin ti Chung-kuo jen-min chieh-fang-chün" [The PLA Marches Toward Modernization].

78) Eighth National Congress of the Communist Party of China (Peking: Foreign Languages Press, 1956), II, pp. 40-41. I am grateful to Pao-min Chang for calling my attention to this note.

79) This was mentioned in Liu Ya-lou, "Seriously Study Mao Tse-tung's Military Thinking."

80) Ibid.

81) The details of these campaigns may be found in Ellis Joffe, Party and Army, pp. 114-116.

82) See, for example, Li Hsü-ku, "The People's Liberation Army on the Industrial Front."

83) George P. Jan, "Red China's Militia" (see note 57); also sources cited in notes 57-58 above.

84) S. M. Chiu, "The PLA and the Party: Recent Developments," Military Review, XLIII: 6 (June 1963) 58-66; also, Ellis Joffe, Party and Army.

85) David A. Charles, "The Dismissal of Marshal P'eng Teh-huai"; and "From the Defeat of P'eng Teh-huai to the Bankruptcy of China's Khrushchov."

86) It was reported that between July 1960 and February 1961, 82 percent of all Party branches in the army were reorganized. In the same period, over 78,000 cadres were sent down to companies to conduct the rectification campaigns, over 2,200 regular and provisional Party members were expelled from the Party, and about 230,000 new Party members were re-

cruited into the army. Kung-tso t'ung-hsün [Bulletin of Activities], No. 23 (June 1961), 1-6.

87) The Regulations Concerning the Management and Education Work of the Company of the PLA were issued by the General Political Department on June 19, 1961. The texts may be found in Chung-kung nien-pao [Yearbook on Communist China] (1967), pp. 798-804. The political work regulations for the political instructor, Party branch, YCL branch, and the Revolutionary Servicemen's Committee were issued in late 1961. See Jenmin jih-pao [People's Daily] (November 22, 1961). For the texts, see PWR, 1963, IX-XII.

88) PWR, 1963, I. Jen-min jih-pao [People's Daily] (April 29 and May 10, 1963); Chieh-fang-chün pao [Liberation Army Daily], editorial (May 9, 1963). For the text, see Ying-mao Kau et al., Political Work System of the Chinese Communist Military, pp. 217-324.

89) Ralph L. Powell, "The Party, the Government and the Gun."

90) For the details of Lin's coup attempt, see Ying-mao Kau, "The Case Against Lin Piao."

91) Samuel P. Huntington, The Soldier and the State (see note 1), pp. 7-97; Gino Germani and Kalman Silvert, "Politics, Social Structure and Military Intervention in Latin America," Archives Européennes de Sociologie, No. 2 (1961), 62-81.

92) Samuel P. Huntington, The Soldier and the State (see note 1), pp. 83-85.

93) For the Russian model, see D. Fedotov White, The Growth of the Red Army (Princeton: Princeton University Press, 1944); Zbigniew Brzezinski, ed., Political Control in the Soviet Army (New York: Research Program on the USSR, 1954); Pierre Krebs, "The Political Institution of the Soviet Army with Special References to the Role of the Political Commissar" (unpublished Ph.D. thesis, Oxford University, 1958).

94) Sources for this portion of the discussion may be found in notes 38-41 above.

95) "The Great Chinese PLA: Reliable Pillar of Our Proletarian Dictatorship and Great Proletarian Cultural Revolu-

tion." Also, Chinese Law and Government, V: 3-4 (Fall-Winter
1972-73), special issue on the rise of Lin Piao and his coup attempt; Ralph L. Powell, "The Increasing Power of Lin Piao
and the Party Soldier."

96) The "two-military" campaign refers to the movement of
"military control" and "military training." For details, see
Chung-kung nien-pao [Yearbook on Chinese Communism]
(1969), Section II, pp. 33-38; Ellis Joffe, "The Chinese Army in the
Cultural Revolution"; Chiang I-shan, "Tang-ch'ien kung-chün
ti 'san-chih' 'liang-chün' kung-tso" [Current "Three Supports"
and "Two Militaries" Work in the Communist Army], Tsu-kuo
[China Monthly], No. 79 (October 1970), 4-12. The movement
was also well covered by various Red Guards publications. See,
for example, Chu-ying tung-fang-hung [East Is Red, Chu River
Studio] (Canton) (October 1, 1967). For an interview report on
the military control in Canton, see "Kuang-chou-shih ti chün-
shih kuan-chih" [The Military Control in Canton City], Tsu-
kuo [China Monthly], No. 42 (September 1967), 26-27.

97) For a complete listing, see China News Summary
(English ed.), No. 434 (September 7, 1972).

98) A complete listing may be found in China News Summary
(Chinese ed.), No. 239 (October 3, 1968). "The Revolutionary
Committee and the Party in the Aftermath of the Cultural Revolution," Current Scene, VIII: 8 (April 15, 1970). For data on
military domination in the revolutionary committees, see
Chung-kung nien-pao [Yearbook on Chinese Communism]
(1969), Section IX, pp. 27-156.

99) "Summary of Chairman Mao's Talks to Responsible
Local Comrades During His Tour of Inspection"; translated in
Chinese Law and Government, V: 3-4 (Fall-Winter 1972-73),
31-42.

100) The text reads: "Comrade Lin Piao has consistently held
high the great red banner of Mao tse-tung Thought and has
most loyally and resolutely carried out and defended Comrade
Mao Tse-tung's proletarian revolutionary line. Comrade Lin
Piao is Comrade Mao Tse-tung's close comrade-in-arms and
successor." Peking Review, No. 18 (April 30, 1969), 36-39.

101) See note 99. Also, other "top secret" documents included in the issue.

102) For a detailed analysis of Lin's coup attempt, see Ying-mao Kau, "The Case Against Lin Piao."

103) Morris Janowitz, The Military in the Political Development of New Nations (Chicago: University of Chicago Press, 1964), pp. 83-88.

104) The pattern of "designed militarism," in which the army actively undertakes a premeditated campaign for power and a policy of military expansionism, does not apply here. Ibid.

105) Lucian Pye, "Armies in the Process of Political Modernization (see note 36).

106) Henry Bienen, ed., The Military and Modernization (see note 2), pp. 1-34.

107) Moshe Lissak, "Modernization and Role-Expansion of the Military in Developing Countries" (see note 36).

108) See, for example, John J. Johnson, ed., The Role of the Military in Underdeveloped Countries (Princeton: Princeton University Press, 1962); Wilson C. McWilliams, ed., Garrisons and Government (see note 2); Henry Bienen, ed., The Military and Modernization (see note 2); Morris Janowitz, The Military in the Political Development of New Nations (see note 103); S. E. Finer, The Man on Horseback (New York: Praeger, 1962).

109) See Mao's concept of Party control of the gun, Selected Works, II, p. 224.

110) The successful aversion of a major violent confrontation among different military factions in Wuhan in July 1967 is a case in point. See Thomas W. Robinson, "The Wuhan Incident."

111) Morris Janowitz, The Military in the Political Development of New Nations (see note 103), pp. 15-19.

112) Mao, "On Practice," and "On Contradiction," in Selected Works, I., pp. 295-347.

113) For a brief analysis, see Ying-mao Kau, "The Organizational Line in Dispute."

114) John W. Lewis, Leadership in Communist China, especially Chapters II-III.

115) Mao, Selected Military Writings; "Sixty Articles on Work Methods," translated in Chinese Law and Government, V: 1 (Spring 1972), 93-117; "On the Ten Great Relationships," translated in Jerome Ch'en, Mao (Englewood Cliffs: Prentice-Hall, 1969), pp. 65-85.

116) See note 99.

117) See, for example, "Learn Humbly from the Masses"; "PLA Men Develop Revolutionary Tradition in Learning From the Masses"; Chang Yün-t'ien, "Tui Chung-kung-chün chan-k'ai 'Hsiang-jen-min hsüeh-hsi' yün-tung ti fen-hsi" [An Analysis of the 'Learn from the People' Movement of the Chinese Communist Army].

118) "Important Teaching Materials for Education in Ideology and Political Line," Hung-ch'i [Red Flag], No. 12 (November 1, 1971), 7-11; translated in Chinese Law and Government, V: 3-4 (Fall-Winter 1972-73), 82-86.

119) See selection 32 of this volume.

120) See selection 31 of this volume. Also, "Perfect the Party Committee System and Guarantee the Party's Collective Leadership"; "Strengthen Regard for the Party and Uphold the Party's Centralized Leadership."

121) Data taken from Parris H. Chang, "Mao Tse-tung and His Generals," a paper given at the Annual Meeting of the Association for Asian Studies, Chicago, April 1973, p. 5; Chiang I-shan, "Lin Piao tao-t'ai ch'ien-hou ti jen-min chieh-fang-chün" [The PLA Before and After the Downfall of Lin Piao].

122) The New York Times, April 14, 1973.

123) For the theory of political socialization, see Richard E. Dawson and Kenneth Prewitt, Political Socialization (Boston: Little, Brown, 1969); Kenneth P. Langton, Political Socialization (London: Oxford, 1969).

124) See the argument presented in "Cheng-chih t'ung-shuai chün-shih, cheng-chih t'ung-shuai i-ch'ieh" [Politics Commands Military Affairs, Politics Commands Everything].

125) Tang Tsou, "The Cultural Revolution and the Chinese Political System." Benjamin Schwartz, "Modernization and the Maoist Vision," The China Quarterly, No. 21 (January-March

1965), 3-19. The on-going campaigns of "two remembrances" and "three investigations" in the PLA, launched since February 1970, for example, clearly have their roots in the pre-1949 experience. The campaigns emphasize the necessity to "recollect the bitterness of class suffering and the hatred of national humiliation," and to "investigate the three concepts of class struggle and political power, war preparation, and uninterrupted revolution." Chiang I-shan, "I-chiu-ch'i-ling-nien ti Chung-kung chün-shih" [Chinese Communist Military Affairs in 1970], Tsu-kuo [China Monthly], No. 82 (January 1971), 5-14. See also Selection 9 of this volume.

126) John W. Lewis, "Leader, Commissar, and Bureaucrat," in Ping-ti Ho and Tang Tsou, eds., China in Crisis, I, pp. 449-481.

127) David E. Apter, The Politics of Modernization (Chicago: University of Chicago Press, 1965), pp. 357-390.

128) The argument is well presented in Hsiao Hua, "Participation in National Construction Is a Glorious Task of the PLA."

129) Mao, Selected Works, IV, pp. 337-340.

130) For general theoretical discussions, see Morris Janowitz, The Military in the Political Development of New Nations (see note 102); Wilson C. McWilliams, ed., Garrisons and Government (see note 2); Henry Bienen, ed., The Military and Modernization (see note 2). The need for political work in order to manage tensions within the military were best revealed in Kung-tso t'ung-hsün [Bulletin of Activities].

131) See the arguments presented in Selections 25-29; also "The Great Chinese PLA — Reliable Pillar of Our Proletarian Dictatorship and Great Proletarian Cultural Revolution."

132) John W. Lewis, "Revolutionary Struggle and the Second Generation in Communist China," The China Quarterly, No. 21, (January-March 1965), 126-147; Donald W. Klein, "The 'Next Generation' of Chinese Communist Leaders," The China Quarterly, No. 12 (October-December 1962), 57-74; Klein, "The State Council and the Cultural Revolution," The China Quarterly, No. 35 (July-September 1968), 78-95. Ellis Joffe, "The Conflict Between Old and New in the Chinese

Army"; John Gittings, "Military Control and Leadership."

133) Talcott Parsons, ed., Max Weber: The Theory of Social and Economic Organization (New York: The Free Press, 1964), pp. 324-385. See also Suzanne Keller, Beyond the Ruling Class (New York: Random House, 1963); and David Apter, The Politics of Modernization (see note 127), pp. 357-421.

134) For a fuller treatment of the trend, see Ying-mao Kau, Bureaucracy and Political Development in Communist China (see note 32).

135) The hypothesis has been well explored by A. Doak Barnett, Cadres, Bureaucracy, and Political Power in Communist China (New York: Columbia University Press, 1967), and China After Mao; Tang Tsou, "Revolution, Reintegration, and Crisis in Communist China," and John W. Lewis, "Leader, Commissar, and Bureaucrat" both in Ping-ti Ho and Tang Tsou, eds., China in Crisis, I, pp. 277-347, 441-481.

136) The following passage from an editorial of Chieh-fang-chün pao [Liberation Army Daily] (August 18, 1958) is most revealing: "In training work, not a few persons generally stress superficially the training enterprise and stress skill, while slighting the political and ideological factors and even restricting the role of the political command, because they spread the erroneous theory that modern combat techniques determine everything. They speak presumptuously of 'military skills' and of 'military functions,' praising excessively the role of the individual military officer while considering the Party committee as something alien and slighting the collective power of the broad masses. They see only things, not men, and say that military techniques are something very mysterious." Quoted in Ellis Joffe, Party and Army, p. 62.

137) Ellis Joffe, Party and Army, pp. 1-45.

138) For the concept of "political institutionalization," see Samuel P. Huntington, "Political Development and Political Decay," World Politics, XVII: 3 (1965), 385-430.

139) For a theoretical discussion, see Morris Janowitz, The Military in the Political Development of New Nations (see note 103), pp. 79-90; Samuel P. Huntington, The Soldier and the State (see note 1), pp. 59-97.

140) This generalization of current development in China is clearly supported by "Hsin-nien hsien-tz'u" [New Year's Message], a joint editorial by Jen-min jih-pao [People's Daily], Hung-ch'i [Red Flag], and Chieh-fang-chün pao [Liberation Army Daily], see Hung-ch'i, No. 1 (January 1, 1973), 5-8; translated in Peking Review, No. 1 (January 5, 1973), 9-11.

The People's Liberation Army
and China's Nation-Building

I

The Maoist Model
of Army-Building

1

RESOLUTION OF THE NINTH CONGRESS
OF THE CHINESE COMMUNIST PARTY OF
THE FOURTH ARMY OF THE RED ARMY*

Ku-t'ien (Western Fukien) Conference,
December 1929

Mao Tse-tung

I. The Question of Correcting Mistaken Tendencies Toward Nonproletarian Ideas in the Party

Various types of nonproletarian ideas are extremely common in the Fourth Army, and they greatly hinder the application of the Party's correct line. Unless these ideas are thoroughly corrected, the Fourth Army cannot possibly shoulder the tasks assigned to it in China's great revolutionary struggle. The

---

*Mao Tse-tung, Chung-kuo kung-ch'an-tang hung-chün ti-ssu-chün ti-chiu-tz'u tai-piao ta-hui chüeh-i-an (Hong Kong: Hsin-min-chu, 1949); published as part of the early series of Mao Tse-tung hsüan-chi [Selected Works of Mao Tse-tung]. Recently, the complete text has been reproduced in the Japanese edition of Mō Takutō shū [Collected Works of Mao Tse-tung] (Tokyo: Hokubō-sha, 1972), Vol. II (1927-1931), pp. 77-125. Chapter I of this document, "The Question of Correcting Mistaken Tendencies Toward Nonproletarian Ideas in the Party," in its revised form is the only part included in the official Mao Tse-tung hsüan-chi (Peking: Jen-min, 1951-1965), Vols.

general source of such incorrect tendencies in the Party organization lies, of course, in the fact that its basic units are composed largely of peasants and other elements of petty-bourgeois
origin; yet the failure of the Party's leading bodies to wage a
concerted and determined struggle against these incorrect tendencies and to educate the members in the Party's correct line
is also an important cause of their existence and growth. In
accordance with the spirit of the September letter of the Central
Committee, this Congress points out the sources of the mistaken tendencies toward nonproletarian ideas, their manifestations, and the methods of correcting them, and calls upon all
comrades to thoroughly eliminate them.

A. The Purely Military Viewpoint

1) The sources of the purely military viewpoint.*
a) The political level is low. Because of this, some comrades
do not recognize the leading role of politics and do not recog-

---

I-IV; published in English as Selected Works of Mao Tse-tung
(Peking: Foreign Languages Press, 1961-1965), Vols. I-IV.
The chapter appears under the title "On Correcting Mistaken
Ideas in the Party," in the official English edition, Vol. I, pp.
105-116. The present translation is based on the 1929 text.
However, for Chapter I, where the original text is identical
with its revised version, the official English translation in Selected Works of Mao Tse-tung is used. Apart from changes in
style and terminology, the revised version drops some significant passages and tones down some of Mao's unorthodox analysis of organizational and strategical problems of the rural
revolution in China. In our translation of Chapter I, passages
that are eliminated in the revised official version are underlined for the reader's attention.

*In Selected Works, the underlined passages in this section
are edited out of this place and inserted seven paragraphs
later, preceding the section on "Methods of Correction" —
Ying-mao Kau.

nize the fundamental points of difference between the Red Army's mission and the White Army's mission.

b) Remnants of the mercenary viewpoint. Especially because we often take large numbers of prisoners in battle; when this type of element joins the Red Army, it introduces a strong mercenary outlook. This gives the purely military viewpoint a foothold at the lower levels.

c) These two reasons give rise to a third, which is an excessive belief in military power and a lack of belief in the power of the masses.

d) The Party has not energetically attended to and discussed military matters, which also constitutes a reason for the purely military viewpoint among some comrades.

2) The purely military viewpoint is very highly developed among a number of comrades in the Red Army. It manifests itself as follows:

a) These comrades regard military affairs and politics as opposed to each other and refuse to recognize that military affairs are only one means of accomplishing political tasks. Some even say: "If you are good militarily, naturally you are good politically; if you are not good militarily, you cannot be any good politically." This is to go a step further and give military affairs a leading position over politics.

b) They think that the task of the Red Army, like that of the White Army, is merely to fight. They do not understand that the Red Army is an armed body for carrying out the political tasks of a class. Especially in the China of the present, the Red Army should certainly not confine itself to fighting; besides fighting, it should also shoulder such important tasks as carrying out propaganda among the masses, organizing the masses, arming the masses, helping the masses, establishing political power, as well as other important tasks. The Red Army fights not merely for the sake of fighting; rather it fights entirely in order to conduct propaganda among the masses, organize the masses, arm them, help them, and establish political power. Without these objectives, fighting loses its meaning and the Red Army loses the reason for its existence.

c) Hence, organizationally, these comrades subordinate the departments doing political work to those doing military work, and put forward the slogan, "Let Army Headquarters handle outside matters." If allowed to develop, this idea would involve the danger of estrangement from the masses, a monopoly of the government by the army, and a departure from our class stand. It would be to take the path of the Kuomintang Army.

d) At the same time, they overlook the important tasks of the propaganda teams in propaganda work. On the question of mass organization, they neglect the organizing of soldiers' committees in the army and the organizing of local workers and peasants. As a result, both propaganda and organizational work are abandoned.

e) They become conceited when a battle is won and dispirited when a battle is lost.

f) Fourth Army departmentalism. They think only of the basic units of the Fourth Army and do not realize that it is an important task of the Red Army to arm the local masses. This is cliquism in magnified form.

g) Unable to see beyond their limited environment in the Fourth Army, a few comrades believe that no other revolutionary forces exist, hence their extreme addiction to the idea of conserving strength and avoiding action. This is a remnant of opportunism.

h) Some comrades, disregarding the subjective and objective conditions, suffer from the malady of revolutionary impetuosity; they will not take pains to do minute and detailed work among the masses but, riddled with idealistic illusions, want only to do big things. This is a remnant of putschism.

3) Methods of correction.

a) Raise the political level in the Party by means of education; destroy the theoretical roots of the military viewpoint. At the same time, eliminate the remnants of opportunism and putschism and break down the departmentalism of the Fourth Army.

b) Intensify the political training of officers and men and especially the education of ex-prisoners when they join our ranks. At the same time, as far as possible let the local government select workers and peasants who are experienced in struggle to join the Red Army, thus organizationally weakening or even eradicating the source of the purely military viewpoint.

c) Arouse the local Party organizations to criticize the Party organizations in the Red Army and the organs of mass political power (soviets) to criticize the Red Army itself, in order to influence the Party organizations and the officers and men of the Red Army.

d) The Party must actively attend to and discuss military work. All the work must be discussed and decided upon by the Party before being carried out via the mass line.

e) Draw up Red Army rules and regulations that clearly define its tasks, the relationship between its military and its political apparatus, the relationship between the Red Army and the masses of the people, and the powers and functions of the soldiers' committees and their relationship with the military and political organizations.

B. Ultra-Democracy

1) Since the Fourth Army of the Red Army accepted the directives of the Central Committee, there has been a great decrease in the manifestations of ultra-democracy. For example, Party decisions are now carried out fairly well, and no longer does anyone bring up such erroneous demands as the Red Army should apply "democratic centralism from the bottom to the top," or should "let the lower levels discuss all problems first and then let the higher levels decide." Actually, however, this decrease is only superficial and does not mean that ultra-democratic ideas have already been thoroughly eliminated from the outlook of Party members in general. In other words, the poisonous shoots of ultra-democracy are still deeply rooted in the minds of many comrades. Witness as proof the various expressions of reluctance to carry out Party decisions.

2) Methods of correction.

First, in the sphere of theory, destroy the roots of ultra-

democracy. First, it should be pointed out that the danger of
ultra-democracy is that it damages or even completely wrecks
the Party organization and weakens or even completely un-
dermines the Party's fighting capacity, rendering the Party
incapable of fulfilling its fighting tasks and inevitably leading
to the defeat of the revolution, while at the same time pro-
longing the life of the ruling class's counterrevolution. Next,
it should be pointed out that the source of ultra-democracy is
the individualistic aversion to discipline of the petty bourgeoisie
([because of its] small peasant production and small urban
capital). When this characteristic is brought into the Party, it
develops into ultra-democratic political and organizational
ideas. These ideas are utterly incompatible with the fighting
tasks of the proletariat and, objectively speaking, constitute a
type of counterrevolutionary thinking. A person with this kind
of thinking, if he does not diligently correct it but rather allows
it to continue to develop, will inevitably take the counterrevolutionary path.

Second, in the sphere of organization, ensure democracy
under centralized guidance. This should be done along the following lines:

a) The leading bodies of the Party must give a correct line
of guidance and find solutions when problems arise, in order to
establish themselves as centers of leadership.

b) The higher bodies must be familiar with the situation in
the lower bodies so as to have a basis in society for correct
guidance.

c) No Party organization at any level should make casual
decisions in dealing with matters. Once a decision is reached,
it must be firmly carried out.

d) All decisions of any importance made by the Party's higher
bodies must be promptly transmitted to the lower bodies and
the Party rank and file. The method is to call meetings of activists, or general membership meetings of the Party branches
or even of the columns (when circumstances permit), and to assign people to attend and make reports at such meetings.

e) The lower bodies of the Party and the Party rank and file must discuss the higher bodies' directives in detail in order to understand their meaning thoroughly and decide on the methods of carrying them out.

C. Disregard of Organizational Discipline

Disregard of organizational discipline in the Party organization in the Fourth Army manifests itself as follows:

1) Failure of the minority to submit to the majority. For example, when a motion is voted down, they are ill-tempered and do not sincerely carry out the decision.

Methods of correction:

a) At meetings, all participants should be encouraged to voice their opinions as fully as possible. The rights and wrongs in any controversy should be clarified without compromise or glossing over. What cannot be settled at one meeting should be discussed at a subsequent meeting (providing there is no interference with work).

b) One requirement of Party discipline is that the minority should submit to the majority. If the view of the minority has been rejected at a Party meeting, during the period before the next meeting it must support the decision passed by the majority. If necessary, it can bring up the matter for reconsideration at the next meeting, but apart from that it must not act against the decision in any way.

2) Criticism made without regard to organizational discipline.

a) Inner-Party criticism is a weapon for strengthening the Party organization and increasing its fighting capacity. In the Party organization of the Red Army, however, many do not understand this purpose of criticism, but instead mistakenly use it for personal attacks. Damage to the Party organization as well as to individuals is the result. This is entirely a manifestation of petty-bourgeois individualism. The method of correction is to help Party members understand that the purpose of criticism is to increase the Party's fighting capacity in order to achieve victory in the class struggle, and that it absolutely cannot be used as a means of personal attack.

b) Many Party members make their criticisms not inside, but outside, the Party. The reason is that we have not built an understanding of the political significance of the Party organization in the minds of the Party members in general, and therefore they do not understand the importance of the Party's organization (meetings and so forth) and erroneously believe that there is no difference at all between criticism within and outside the organization. This kind of belief is sufficient to lead the Party along a destructive path. The method of correction is to build up an understanding of the political significance of the Party organization in the minds of Party members in general, and in this way fundamentally eradicate all irresponsible disregard of organizational discipline and its damaging effect on the masses.

3) The development of a special group among Party members.

Using as a pretext the fact that they are very busy, but actually because they are unwilling to draw close to the masses, and also because they fear the criticism of the masses, some Party members do not attend branch membership meetings and group meetings, or they attend the meetings but do not make work reports. They differ with the ordinary Party members on all sorts of matters, and as a result they become isolated from the masses and from the Party. Not only do the responsible persons in the branch fail to correct this kind of phenomenon but, on the contrary, they fear these privileged Party members.

The reasons for the occurrence of this phenomenon: One, the Red Army has up to now made a great mistake in that the Party organs have given very little attention to the discussion of military matters. Because of this they have also failed to oversee the responsible comrades in military affairs to regularly bring forth plans (for example, training plans, administrative plans, combat plans, etc.) and reports at Party meetings. As a result, the Party's discussions have neglected military matters, and responsible comrades in military affairs have forgotten that they should be under the direction of the

Party and report to the Party. This has caused the Red Army's military affairs to become a sort of special area which the Party organs and the average Party member do not understand. Not only does this present a great obstacle to the militarization of the Party members, but it also separates the Party from military matters and creates the danger that the Party will be unable to lead in military affairs. Two, because of the above-mentioned great mistakes in regard to the Party's tasks, some of the comrades responsible for military affairs have become a special group within the Party. At the same time, among comrades with responsibility in other areas there also are a good many who set themselves apart as a special group who do not like to go to branch meetings, or who go to meetings and do not speak. This is one reason why the Party's branch life has become as distorted and unsound as it is now.

Methods of correction: One, Party meetings at every level (from the branch to the front committee) must list plans and reports concerning military matters on their agendas and should discuss and decide on them. Two, Party members, no matter in what area they have responsibility, must attend branch membership meetings and group meetings and make work reports, and they must not fail to attend unless there is a reason.

D. Absolute Equalitarianism

1) Absolute equalitarianism was once quite serious in the Red Army. After many struggles we have actually reduced it a great deal, but there still exist a good many remnants. Here are some examples. On the matter of allowances to wounded soldiers, there were objections to differentiating between light and serious cases, and the demand was raised for equal allowances for all. When officers rode on horseback, it was regarded not as something necessary for performing their duties but as a sign of inequality. Absolutely equal distribution of supplies was demanded, and there was objection to somewhat larger allotments in special cases. In the hauling of rice, the

demand was made that all should carry the same load on their backs, irrespective of age or physical condition. Equality was demanded in the allotment of billets, and the Headquarters would be abused for occupying larger rooms. Equality was demanded in the assignment of fatigue details, and there was unwillingness to do a little more than the next man. It even went so far that when there were two wounded men but only one stretcher, neither could be carried away because each refused to yield priority to the other. Absolute equalitarianism, as shown in these examples, has certainly not been totally eliminated from the minds of the masses of officers and men in the Red Army; when we say some of it has been eliminated, we mean only partially and superficially.

2) Absolute equalitarianism, like ultra-democracy in political matters, is the product of a handicraft and small peasant economy — the only difference being that one manifests itself in material affairs, while the other manifests itself in political affairs.

3) The method of correction: In the realm of theory, we should point out that before the abolition of capitalism, absolute equalitarianism is a mere illusion of peasants and small proprietors, and that even under socialism there can be no absolute equality, for material things will then be distributed according to the needs of the individual and of the work. The distribution of material things in the Red Army must reach the greatest degree of equality, as in the case of equal pay for officers and men, and so forth, because this is required by the present circumstances of the struggle. But absolute equality beyond reason must be opposed because it is not required by the struggle; on the contrary, it hinders the struggle.

E. Idealism

1) Idealism exists to a serious degree among Party members in the Red Army, causing great harm to analysis of the political situation, guidance of work, and Party organization. This is because idealist analysis of a political situation and idealist

guidance of work inevitably result either in opportunism or in putschism. As for idealist criticism, loose and groundless talk, or suspicion, such practices inside the Party often breed unprincipled and meaningless disputes and undermine the Party organization.

Another point that should be mentioned in connection with inner-Party criticism, apart from idealist criticism, is nonpolitical criticism. It is not understood that the main task of criticism is to point out political mistakes, and then to point out organizational mistakes. As for shortcomings in personal life or small technical matters, unless they are closely related to political and organizational mistakes, there is no need to be overcritical and to embarrass the comrades concerned. Moreover, once such technical criticism develops, there is the great danger that the Party members will concentrate on minor technical faults and everyone will become timid and overcautious and forget the Party's political tasks. Technical, nonpolitical criticism within the Party in the Red Army is the same as idealist, nonscientific criticism, and will inevitably have (and moreover has already had) extremely damaging results.

2) The sole method of correction is to educate Party members so that a political and scientific spirit pervades their thinking and their Party life. To this end we must (a) teach Party members to apply the Marxist method in analyzing a political situation and appraising the class forces, instead of making an idealist analysis and appraisal; (b) direct the attention of Party members to social and economic investigation and study, so as to determine the tactics of struggle and methods of work and help comrades to understand that without investigation of actual conditions they will fall into the pit of fantasy and putschism; (c) in inner-Party criticism, eradicate the idealist and technical spirit; statements should be based on facts, and discussion should concentrate on the political significance of a matter.

F. Individualism

1) Individualism in the Red Army Party organization manifests itself as follows:
a) Retaliation. Some comrades, after being criticized inside the Party by a soldier comrade, look for opportunities to
retaliate outside the Party, and one way is to beat or abuse the
comrade in question. There are a great many examples of
this. They also seek to retaliate within the Party: "You have
criticized me at this meeting, so I'll find some way to pay you
back at the next." There are also quite a few examples of that.
This kind of retaliation arises from purely personal considerations, to the neglect of the interests of the class and of the
Party as a whole. Its target is not the enemy class, but individuals in our own ranks. It is a corrosive that weakens the
organization and its fighting capacity.
b) Cliquism. On the surface this seems to be an extension
of individualism; in reality it exemplifies the narrowest individualism and has the same strong corrosive and centrifugal
effect. Cliquism used to be rife in the Red Army, and although
as a result of our efforts we have eliminated quite a bit of it,
there are still remnants, and further effort is needed.
c) The employee mentality. Some comrades do not understand that the Party and the Red Army, of which they are members, are both instruments for carrying out the tasks of a class.
They do not realize that they themselves are makers of the
struggle, but think the struggle has no relation to themselves
and that their responsibility is only to their superiors in the
Red Army or the Party organization, and not to the revolution.
This mentality of an "employee" of the revolution is highly developed in the Red Army. This is why there are not many activists who work unconditionally for the revolution. Unless it
is eliminated, the number of activists will not grow, and the
heavy burden of the revolution will remain on the shoulders of
a small number of people, much to the detriment of the struggle.
d) Pleasure-seeking. In the Red Army there are also quite
a few people whose individualism finds expression in pleasure-

seeking. They always hope that their unit will march into the big cities. They want to go there not to work but to enjoy themselves. The last thing they want is to work in the Red areas where life is hard. The result of pleasure-seeking is that they only think of individual benefit, and do not think of the whole revolution or the actions of their unit.

e) Passivity. Some comrades become passive and stop working whenever anything goes against their wishes. This of course is mainly due to individualism, because they do not really recognize their own class mission; but it is also due to objective factors such as improper conduct of affairs, assignment of work, or enforcement of discipline in the Party and army.

f) The desire to leave the army. The number of people who ask for transfers from the Red Army to local work is increasing. The reason for this does not lie entirely with individualism but also with (1) the material hardships of life in the Red Army, (2) exhaustion after long struggle, and (3) improper conduct of affairs, assignment of work or enforcement of discipline, and other objective factors in the environment.

2) The source of individualism lies in the influence in the Party of outlooks ranging from the small-peasant mentality to bourgeois ideology. The method of correction is primarily to use educational means to rectify individualism ideologically. Next, it is to conduct affairs, make work assignments, and enforce discipline in a proper way. In addition, ways must be found to improve the material life of the Red Army, and every available opportunity must be utilized for rest and rehabilitation in order to improve objective conditions.

G. Roving-Rebel Ideology

1) The sources of roving-rebel ideology in the Red Army are: (a) the lumpen-proletariat makes up a majority in the Red Army — this is an immediate reason; (b) throughout all of China, and especially in all the provinces of South China, there exist great masses of rootless persons — this is a remote rea-

son. Because of these two factors, there have developed within
the Red Army calls for roving-rebel political thinking and action. But large-scale roving-rebel actions of the Huang Ch'ao
or Li Chuang or Hung Hsiu-ch'üan type, in a China ruled by imperialism, especially in present-day China when there are im-
ported advanced weapons (hand grenades, artillery, machine
guns, etc.), advanced methods of communication (military tele-
phones and radios), and advanced means of transportation (au-
tomobiles, steamships, and railroads), are not permissible.
Naturally, therefore, roving-rebel thinking will not become
something that ultimately is strongly advocated for the Red
Army in the realm of action. But its influence is still manifest
on a large scale in every area. For example, (a) some people
want to increase our political influence only by means of roving
guerrilla actions, but are unwilling to do it by working hard and
patiently helping the masses build up political power. (b) In
expanding the Red Army, some people follow the line of "hiring
men and buying horses" and "recruiting deserters and accept-
ing mutineers," rather than the line of expanding local Red
Guards and the local Red Army units and thereby strengthen the
nonlocal Red Army. (c) Some people lack the patience to carry
on arduous struggles together with the masses and only want to
go to the big cities to eat and drink to their hearts' content. All
these manifestations of the roving-rebel ideology seriously obstruct the carrying on of the revolution and the Red Army's great
tasks; consequently, their eradication is an important objective
of ideological struggle within the Red Army Party organization.

2) Methods of correction.

a) Through education, reform incorrect thinking within the
Party that has its basis in the rootless elements, in order to
eradicate the roving-rebel ideology.

b) Intensify education among the basic sections of the Red
Army and among future newly recruited captives to counter the
vagabond outlook.

c) Draw active workers and peasants who are experienced
in struggle into the ranks of the Red Army so as to change its
composition.

d) Create new units of the army from among the masses of militant workers and peasants.

H. The Remnants of Putschism

1) The Party organization in the Red Army has already put tremendous effort into struggles against putschism, but still not to a sufficient degree. Therefore, although we have already overcome a great deal of the thinking and actions of putschism in the Red Army, remnants still exist. Putschism is a by-product of the combination of lumpen-proletariat outlook and the petty-bourgeois outlook. Its manifestations are (a) blind action regardless of objective conditions; (b) inadequate and irresolute application of the Party's policies for the cities; (c) slack military discipline, especially in moments of defeat; (d) acts of house-burning without regard for our mass base, which still occur among some members of all units; and (e) the practices of shooting deserters and of inflicting corporal punishment, both of which have certain elements that smack of putschism.
2) Methods of correction.
a) Eradicate putschism ideologically.
b) Correct putschist behavior through rules, regulations, and policies.

II. The Party's Organizational Problems

Organizational matters of the Party in the Red Army have now reached an especially critical period, particularly with the poor quality of Party members and organizational slackening. The effect on the Red Army's leadership and execution of policy is especially great. The Congress has formulated a detailed analysis and decision on this problem. Comrades should take their stand in the spirit of the Congress, and work hard to reform the Party's organization. They must make the Party's organization truly able to bear the burden of its political tasks. Only then will they be regarded as having achieved success.

A. The Party's Organizational Line

1) The line on the recruitment of Party members takes the fighting soldier as its main target. At the same time, non-fighting personnel, like porters, service workers, etc., must not be neglected.

2) Each company establishes a [Party] branch; each squad establishes a [Party] group: this is one of the important organizational principles of the Party in the army. In the case of a unit where the number of Party members is too small, and in practice it is not possible for each squad to establish a group, then the platoon may be taken temporarily as the unit in which a group is established; and there may be a planned distribution of group members among all the squads. But it must be understood that this is a transitional method.

3) The original methods of organizing Party groups in the Red Army, in which cadres were mixed with ordinary personnel, and intellectuals were mixed with laborers, were quite correct. But we still have not worked out a very good systematic method of blending the different abilities of the various elements. From now on we must pay greater attention to this. As for taking the cadres alone and organizing them into groups, that is not acceptable.

B. The Problem of Slackening of the Party Organization

1) The present state of the Party organization in the Fourth Army.

a) The methods of joining the Party are too haphazard, and many people with insufficient qualifications as Party members are taken in. Officers in particular are taken in without exception and with no requirements. Because of this, the quality of the Party has become very poor.

b) The work of the Party organizations at various levels has achieved the solving of problems, but it has completely neglected the mission of educating the comrades. As far as conferences of a training nature are concerned, like general meetings of activists, combined meetings of the Secretariat and the Propaganda Department, combined meetings of Party committee and work departments, branch general meetings, brigade or detachment general Party membership meetings and so forth, very few have been held.

c) General discipline has slackened. Especially in circumstances where there is nobody else to replace the individual responsible for important work, often his mistakes are overlooked and he is not disciplined. If one person is treated in this way, it is not possible to do anything but treat others in this way as well. Because of this, discipline in general is relaxed.

d) Since the officers have all become Party members, very few of the persons working in military and political organizations pay attention to their occupational work. They assume that occupational work is the Party's work, and the two cannot be separated. For example, there are almost no military work conferences and political work conferences at the various levels. Everybody assumes that once the Party reaches a decision, a matter is closed. The fact that Party members are to function as the nucleus of professional work is simply never mentioned.

e) Relations between higher and lower levels are not close. The reports of the lower levels rarely receive an official answer or guidance from the higher level. When the lower levels have conferences, the higher levels rarely send anyone to attend. This is so because the organization of the higher-level organs is not sound. But the unenthusiastic attitude of the higher-level organs toward their work is another reason that guidance of the lower levels is nonexistent, or is not detailed and complete. Particularly the guidance of practical work — for example, directing a unit that sets out on a guerrilla attack, or the like — in general lacks detail and thoroughness. There are still certain units that have hardly even the sketchiest guidance.

f) Many branch general meetings and group meetings are not held as scheduled.

2) The correct line.

a) Take strong measures to eliminate the old practices, like erroneous political viewpoint, smoking opium, fortune-seeking, gambling, and so forth. Repeated offenders who do not reform, no matter whether they are cadres or non-cadres, shall be purged from the Party.

b) Requirements for new members entering the Party in the future.

The prospective member must:

(1) have no erroneous political views (including class consciousness);

(2) be loyal;

(3) have a sacrificing spirit and the ability to work actively;

(4) have no fortune-seeking notions;

(5) not smoke opium, nor gamble.

Only when an individual satisfies the above five conditions can he be sponsored for Party membership. The sponsoring individual should investigate in advance whether or not the candidate truly meets the above conditions. After he has passed through the necessary introduction procedures and been proposed for entry into the Party, the new member should be informed in detail about life in the branch (including secret work) and the essential points a Party member should comply with. The sponsor should undertake a certain degree of responsibility in regard to the candidate. The branch committee should send someone to interview an individual who is about to join the Party, to investigate whether or not he has met the conditions for joining the Party.

c) The Party unit at each level not only solves problems and guides practical work but also has the important mission of educating comrades. All types of conferences for training comrades, and other methods of training — training classes, discussion meetings, and so forth — should be systematically carried out.

d) Put discipline strictly into effect and eliminate the phenomenon of perfunctory discipline.

e) Distinguish the nature of the Party member's social occupation from that of his Party work. Each Party member

(except individuals who have undertaken important or specialized assignments within the Party, whose profession is that of a
revolutionary) must assume an occupation in society and at the
same time, while carrying on his occupation, must undertake
work given him by the Party.

f) The work attitude of the Party organization at each level
should become even more enthusiastic than before. The lower
levels should report in detail to the higher levels; the higher
levels should discuss and answer these reports in detail and,
moreover, should make every effort to send someone to attend
conferences at the lower levels. They must not make the excuse that workers are few, that their work ability is poor, and
that work time is insufficient, in order to cover up their own
lack of enthusiasm and to neglect these tasks.

g) Party organs at the branch committee level or higher
should systematically provide materials for discussion at the
regular monthly branch meeting and group meeting, regulate
the schedule of meetings, and be thorough in supervising
meetings.

C. How to Make Party Members Attend Meetings and
   Take an Interest

1) Reasons for Party members having little interest at a
meeting.

a) The purpose of the meeting is not understood. The first
purpose of the branch meeting is to solve problems. The meeting should concentrate on discussing and solving questions of
struggle and internal problems of the unit. If someone does
not attend meetings, or attends meetings but does not actively
express his views, he does not comprehend the political significance of the meeting, and he will not have any interest in
struggle. All those who are enthusiastic about struggle will of
course be eager to attend meetings and eagerly speak out. The
second purpose is to educate comrades. The meeting not only
solves problems but also, in the process of solving problems,
should explore the surrounding circumstances of the problem

and consult instructions received from higher levels. In this way the thoughts and abilities of the comrades will be mobilized; by politicizing and giving practical substance to the meeting, we will also politicize and give practical effect to the mind of every comrade. When every comrade is politicized and "practicalized" in this way, the Party's fighting capacity will have become great. This is the educational purpose of the meetings. Party members in the Red Army do not understand these purposes, and this has become the primary reason for their not liking to attend meetings, or attending meetings and having little interest.

b) When resolutions are passed but not put into effect, or an item is requested from the higher level and a long time passes without an answer being received, this diminishes interest in discussions.

c) Responsible persons do not properly prepare in advance. They do not prepare an agenda; they do not understand the substance and the circumstances of the problems; they do not prepare even the smallest idea about how the problems should be solved.

d) The chairman thoughtlessly stops Party members from speaking out. When someone speaks on a matter that accidentally arises outside the topic, he immediately forbids that person to speak. The person feels he has been rebuffed and will not express himself. If a speaker makes a mistake, in addition to stopping him, the chairman also ridicules him.

e) The meeting is carried on in feudal style, stiff and lifeless, and going to a meeting is like sitting in jail.

2) Methods of correction.

First, the meeting should be politicized and practicalized. Second, the comrades, especially new Party members and Party members who work without enthusiasm, should be reminded often of the important purposes of meetings. Third, resolutions should not be taken lightly; as soon as one is passed, it should be firmly put into effect. Fourth, higher-level organs should diligently answer questions from the lower levels and should not delay excessively long to let the matter cool off. Fifth, the responsible leaders should prepare an agenda in advance, and

the agenda should make things concrete: they should investigate
and clarify the substance and circumstances of the problem in
advance and also consider how to solve it. Sixth, the chairman
should adopt good techniques for directing the meeting and
should guide the flow of the masses' discussion toward a certain
question; but if there should be an important or significant development that is outside the topic, the chairman not only should
not hurt someone's feelings by cutting him off too abruptly, but
he should value highly and take up the essential point of this development, introduce it to the masses, and establish a new subject of discussion. In this way the meeting will be utilized and,
at the same time, the meeting will achieve genuine educational
significance. Seventh, eliminate the feudal procedure of the
meeting; a communist meeting place should reflect the enthusiastic, lively, and straightforward spirit of the proletariat,
and this must be put into the proceeding.

D. The Party's Youth Organization in the Red Army
    and Its Work

   1) What is of benefit to young people and what is of benefit
to adults in a unit cannot be separated. The [Communist Youth]
League does not have separate work targets. Moreover, the
basic unit of the Party group should be the squad in order to
facilitate struggle; because of this, there is no need to set up
League groups in Party branches.
   2) The young among the Party members, because their feelings are not the same as the adults', need to receive, apart
from ordinary Party training, a special type of youth education.
Also, since winning over the young worker and peasant masses
is one of the Party's important tasks, we must have a specialized organization to undertake this kind of work. Therefore,
Party members in the branch who are less than twenty years
of age should be separated out (except for special situations
such as those where they are responsible for important Party
work), and the youth-work conference should be set up. This
kind of meeting, except where meetings are systematically and

regularly held with the brigade as the basic unit, should also be convened by each detachment and column at suitable intervals.

3) For the purpose of planning the education of young Party members and the winning over of the young worker and peasant masses, as well as for the leadership of youth-work confer- ences, there should be established within each front Party com- mittee and brigade Party committee a five-member youth- work committee; the detachment Party committee and the branch Party committee should each then establish a youth of- ficer [a member of the committee] to work under the guidance of the Party organ at each level.

E. The Relationship Between the Political Commissar and Internal Party Work

The secretary of the Party organ at the two levels of brigade and detachment in principle should not simultaneously be the political commissar. But in units where work personnel are lacking, he may continue to serve as both temporarily. A po- litical commissar who does not assume the responsibility as the Party secretary may be appointed by the higher-level Party organ, after investigating the situation and in circumstances where the conditions are appropriate, as the Party's spe- cial emissary with the task of guiding the Party's work at that level.

F. The Question of the Highest Party Organs in Direct- Command Units

The direct-command units of the army and each column should all organize direct-command committees as the highest Party organ. There should be between five and seven com- mittee members.

G. The Question of the Party and League in the Soldiers' Committee

The brigade soldiers' committee does not set up Party and

League units; its work is directed by the Party branch committee. The column soldiers' committee should set up Party
and League units; these Party and League units will receive
the guidance of the column Party committee.

III. The Question of Education in the Party

A. Significance

Education should be regarded as the most urgent problem
within the Party in the Red Army. For the Red Army to
be completely sound and to expand, for it to be able to bear the
burden of the struggle, education within the Party must be the
basis. If we do not raise the political level within the Party, if
we do not eliminate deviations of all kinds within the Party,
then we definitely will not be able to perfect and expand the
Red Army; still less will we be able to bear the burden of the
struggle. Because of this, one of the Party's essential tasks
is the systematic implementation of intra-Party education, correcting the unplanned state of affairs of the past in which things
were allowed to take their natural course. General meetings
shall stipulate and use the following materials and methods in
order to educate the Party members; and the Party's leading
organs shall have still more detailed discussions in order to
carry out this task.

B. Materials

1) Political analysis.
2) Publicity for discussion by higher-level leading organs.
3) Organizational general knowledge.
4) Correction of eight kinds of erroneous thinking within the
Party in the Red Army.
5) Discussion of the question of the opposition of the opportunist and Trotskyite cliques.
6) Strategy and tactics of mass work.
7) Social and economic investigation and study of guerrilla
regions.

8) Study of Marxism-Leninism.

9) Social, economic, and scientific research.

10) The question of the revolution's current phase, and its future.

These ten items, except for those parts (like social, economic, and scientific research) which in practice are limited to cadres in their application, are all applicable to Party members in general.

C. Methods

1) Party newspapers.

2) Political newsletters.

3) Editing all kinds of pamphlets for the education of the comrades.

4) Training classes.

5) Systematic distribution and reading of books.

6) Reading of books and newspapers to illiterate Party members.

7) Individual discussions.

8) Criticism.

9) Group meetings.

10) Branch general membership meetings.

11) Joint meetings of branch committees and groups.

12) Meetings of activists above the level of group leader, with the column as the unit.

13) Meetings of activists above the level of branch secretary, with the entire army as the unit.

14) Party general membership meetings, with the column as the unit.

15) Combined conferences of secretariats and propaganda departments of all levels, with the column as the unit.

16) Combined conferences of secretariats and propaganda departments above the level of detachment, with the entire army as the unit.

17) Political discussion meetings.

18) Suitable allocation of Party members to participation in practical work.

IV. The Question of the Red Army's Propaganda Work

A. The Significance of the Red Army's Propaganda Work

The mission of the Red Army's propaganda work is to expand our political influence and win over the broad masses. Only when this propaganda mission has been carried out will we be able to achieve the Red Army's general tasks, such as organizing the masses, arming the masses, building political power, destroying the power of the reactionaries, promoting the revolutionary high tide, and so on. Therefore, the Red Army's propaganda work is work of the first importance for the Red Army. If we neglect this work, then we will abandon the essential mission of the Red Army, and it will be equivalent to helping the ruling class strip the Red Army of its strength.

B. The Present Status of the Red Army's Propaganda Work

1) Shortcomings in the content of propaganda.
a) A concrete political platform has not been promulgated (political platforms promulgated in the past, like the "Four-Word Proclamation" and so on, were not concrete).
b) [Red Army propaganda] neglects propaganda and agitation on behalf of the day-to-day struggle of the masses.
c) [It has] neglected to win over the urban poor.
d) [It has] neglected to propagandize the masses of women.
e) Propaganda directed at the masses of young people is inadequate.
f) Propaganda directed at the lumpen-proletariat is inadequate.
g) [It has included] extremely little propaganda [aimed at] destroying the armed organizations of the landlord class (people's regiments, pacification guards, etc.).
h) The propaganda is not timely or adapted to a given locality.
2) Shortcomings of propaganda techniques.
a) Propaganda teams have not been perfected.
(1) Propaganda personnel have shrunk from five in each bri-

gade to three; there are some that have only one or two; there
are some that have only one; and there are a minority of units
that do not even have one.

(2) Propaganda personnel are from very inferior elements:
there are captured soldiers; there are bearers and grooms;
there are opium-smokers; there are those who, on suspicion
of desertion, are disarmed and put in the propaganda teams;
there are those who, not suited to be clerks, are sent to the
propaganda units; and there are those who are crippled and un-
wanted by any other organizations and they are sent to the propaganda teams. The present propaganda teams have simply
become shelters, completely incapable of carrying out their
mission.

(3) Almost all officers and soldiers reject propaganda teams
(partly because propaganda personnel are from very inferior
elements and their work achievements are few, which leads to
a general dissatisfaction), so the people call them "layabouts,"
and "quack medicine men."

(4) Propaganda teams do not have enough money for propaganda.

(5) The training of propaganda personnel is unsystematic
and, at the same time, supervision of their work is also bad.
Because of this, propaganda units simply take it easy in their
work, and nobody pays attention to whether they do anything or not.

b) Handbills, bulletins, and proclamations are old-fashioned,
not up-to-date, and we have not found correct methods of distributing and mailing.

c) Very few wall newspapers are issued; the contents of political broadsides are too abbreviated and very few are issued;
and the characters are too small and cannot be read clearly.

d) As for revolutionary songs, there simply are none.

e) Only a few pictorial papers have been issued.

f) As for propaganda with costume and makeup, there is
absolutely none.

g) Clubs, with the dual purpose of providing recreation for
the soldiers and approaching the worker and peasant masses,
have not been set up.

h) Verbal propaganda is both meager and ineffective.

i) The Red Army's discipline at the present time has slackened compared with the past. Because of this it has had a negative influence on the masses.

j) [If you enter a peasant's home], knock before entering, help clean up weeds and sweep the floor, speak politely, buy and sell fairly, return what you borrow and pay for any damages; all these are a type of Red Army propaganda work. At present these practices are too seldom carried out.

k) Very few mass meetings are held, and they are conducted badly.

l) The methods of propaganda aimed at White Army soldiers are bad.

C. The Correct Line

1) The content of propaganda.

a) Promulgate a concrete political platform, called "The Red Army Political Platform."

b) Propaganda must conform to the mood of the masses. Aside from the generally promulgated insurrection slogans, we also should have slogans appropriate to the fighting mood of the masses and suitable to day-to-day local life in order to promote the day-to-day struggle and link up with the insurrection slogans.

c) The urban poor (middle-sized and small businessmen and students) are a considerable force in the process of the revolution of the people's rights [min-ch'üan ke-ming]. To neglect to win over this force is no different from taking it and handing it over to the gentry and the bourgeoisie. In the future we should do intensive propaganda work directed at the urban masses of middle-sized and small businessmen and students in order to win them over.

d) Women make up half the population. The position of working women in the economy — their especially oppressed situation — not only proves the pressing need of women for revolution but also that they are a decisive factor in the victory or defeat of

the revolution. In the future we should have effective slogans
for women and make widespread propaganda.

e) The masses of young toilers make up more than 30 percent of the population, and in the struggle they are also the
bravest and most resolute. Because of this, propaganda to win
over the masses of youth is an important mission within the
overall mission of propaganda.

f) China's broad masses of rootless people, if they stand on
the side of the revolutionary classes, become tools of the revolution; if they stand on the side of the reactionary classes,
they become tools of counterrevolution. Therefore, seizing the
rootless masses and taking them out from under the influence
of the reactionary classes is one of the tasks of Party propaganda. In carrying out propaganda work, we must pay attention
to differences in the life and character of the various elements
of the rootless masses, and direct separate propaganda at
them.

g) The destruction of the armed organizations of the landlord class and the winning over of their members constitutes
one of the conditions for the victory of the agrarian revolution
in the countryside. In the future we should pay special attention
to propaganda work aimed at the people's regiments and pacification guards and their members.

h) Upon arriving in a locality, we should have propaganda
slogans and insurrection slogans appropriate to that locality.
We should also produce different propaganda and insurrection
slogans for different times (like the autumn harvest and the
end of the year, the Chiang-kuei [Chiang Kai-shek-Kwangsi
Warlord] war period, and the Wang [Ching-wei]-Chiang [Kai-
shek] war period.

2) Techniques of propaganda.

a) The problems of propaganda teams.

(1) Significance.

The propaganda teams of the Red Army are the essential
tool of the Red Army's propaganda work. If the propaganda
teams do not do a good job, then they will have neglected a
great part of the Red Army's propaganda task. Therefore, the

question of putting the training of propaganda teams in order is one toward which the Party must intensify its efforts at the present time. As the first step in this work, we must correct the theoretical viewpoint generally held among officers and men of underestimating propaganda work and the propaganda units. In this way we will prevent their being called "loafers," "quack medicine men," and other strange names.

(2) Organization.

(a) Based on the detachment as the unit, or the army and column or direct-command force as the unit, each unit shall organize a [propaganda] platoon, with a commander, a vice commander, sixteen propaganda personnel, a bearer (to carry propaganda materials), and two messengers. The propaganda personnel of each platoon shall be divided into a number of subunits [teams]. (The number of subunits shall be determined according to the number of personnel in the brigade and other units or organs.) Each team shall have a leader and three propaganda personnel.

(b) Each detachment's propaganda teams are under the command of the detachment's political commissar. When brigades split off for guerrilla operations, each brigade should have a propaganda team to work with it under the command of the brigade's political commissar. The propaganda team of a direct-command unit is under the command of the chief of the propaganda section of the political department; the propaganda teams of a column are under the command of the propaganda section of the column political department; and all the propaganda platoons of the army are under the command of the propaganda section of the army political department.

(c) Funds for the propaganda teams shall be supplied by the political department, which ensures that they are sufficient.

(d) [Adopt] methods to reform the makeup of propaganda personnel. Aside from inviting local governments to select progressive elements to participate in the Red Army's propaganda units, select outstanding elements from among the soldiers of each unit to be propaganda personnel (not squad leaders, if possible). The political department should regularly

promulgate plans for training propaganda personnel, regulate
training materials, methods, times, teachers, etc., and actively
improve the quality of the propaganda personnel.

b) In regard to propaganda handbills, bulletins, proclamations, and other propaganda materials, the old ones should be
checked over and new ones should quickly be drafted. The
suitable and effective distribution of propaganda materials
should be considered one of the important technical problems
for the propaganda unit. The political work organs should attend to the mailing of propaganda materials, the smuggling of
propaganda materials in with the mail, or the stamping of propaganda and agitation slogans on the mail; and, moreover, they
should do it well.

c) Wall-newspapers are an important method of propaganda
directed at the masses. The army and the column each man-
ages a wall-newspaper, responsibility for which is taken
by the propaganda section of the political department. It is
called "Current Events Bulletin." The contents are (1) international and domestic political news; (2) the situation in the
mass struggle in the guerrilla areas; (3) the status of the Red
Army's work. Each week they should put out at least one page,
always using a large paper and characters, not using mimeo-
graph, and each time making an effort to write a few pages. In
editing and printing the political bulletin, attention should be
paid to the following items: (1) it should be put out quickly;
(2) the contents should be rich; (3) the characters should be
quite large and quite clear.

d) Each political department shall take the responsibility for
compiling and producing revolutionary songs and ballads that
express the various moods of the masses. The army political
department publications committee is responsible for supervising and inspecting [this work].

e) The art subsection of the propaganda section of the army
political department should be strengthened, and it should publish printed or mimeographed pictorial papers. In order to
strengthen the army art subsection, the work of the artistically
talented from the entire army should be centralized.

f) Propaganda with costume and makeup is a most practical and effective kind of propaganda method. The propaganda unit of each detachment and each direct-command unit should set up a section for propaganda with costume and make-up to organize and direct propaganda with costume and makeup to the masses.

g) Set up clubs, with the brigade as the unit, within the soldiers' committee.

h) Within the propaganda unit, a verbal propaganda section and a written propaganda section shall be set up to research and direct verbal and written propaganda techniques.

i) Rigorously implement the "Three Main Rules."

j) The political department and propaganda team should, in a planned and organized way, convene various kinds of mass meetings, and they should determine beforehand the procedure of the meeting, speakers, the speakers' topics, and the time.

k) Propaganda directed at the soldiers and lower-level officers of the White Army is particularly important. In the future we should pay attention to the following methods:

(1) Propaganda should be written in a simple and brief manner; it should be such that it can be read through quickly. It should be refined and lively, so that it makes an impression as soon as it is seen.

(2) In addition to the organized writing of slogans related to certain actual units along the sides of the road where the enemy passes, we should also store handbills in the Party headquarters and mass organizations along the route. Later, when the enemy army passes, they can be surreptitiously passed out among them.

(3) From captured officers and men and from inspection of mail, find out the names of enemy officers and men and the numerical designations of the units they are attached to, and mail them propaganda material, or write letters to them.

(4) Treating captured enemy soldiers well is an extremely effective method of propaganda toward the enemy armies. Methods of treating captured enemy soldiers well: First, do not search their bodies for money and other articles; past con-

duct of Red Army soldiers in searching captured soldiers for valuables should be resolutely abolished. Second, we should, with an extremely warm welcome to captured soldiers, make them feel happy in spirit and oppose any insulting comment or act toward them. Third, give captured soldiers the same treatment as veteran soldiers in regard to supplies. Fourth, for those who do not want to stay, after they have undergone propaganda, give them traveling money and send them back; let them spread the influence of the Red Army within the White Army. Oppose those who are only greedy for more soldiers, who coerce [enemy soldiers] to stay against their will.

Each of the above items, except in special circumstances, is entirely applicable to captured officers.

(5) Treating wounded enemy soldiers is also an extremely effective method of propaganda toward the enemy army. Treatment and allowances for wounded enemy soldiers should be exactly the same as for wounded Red Army soldiers. Moreover, we should take advantage of all possible conditions to send recovered enemy soldiers, who have been treated well with medicine and given travel allowances, back to the enemy army. The same applies to the treatment of wounded enemy officers.

V. The Question of Political Training for Soldiers

A. The Question of Materials

Concerning each of the following items, textbooks should be artistically edited and produced to serve as educational material for the soldiers:

1) Current political analysis and the Red Army's tasks and plans.

2) All aspects of the agrarian revolution.

3) Armed organization and related military tactics.

4) The reasons for the establishment of the "Three Main Rules."

5) Slogans, before and after roll call.

6) The literacy movement.

7) How to do mass work.

8) Explanation of individual Red Army slogans.

9) Correction of all types of deviations.

10) The Soviet Russian Red Army.

11) The current phase of the revolution and its future.

12) Comparisons of the Red Army and the White Army.

13) Comparisons of the Communist Party and the Kuomintang.

14) Stories of the revolution.

15) Stories of the evolution of society.

16) Hygiene.

17) General knowledge of the geography and political economies of the guerrilla regions.

18) Revolutionary songs.

19) Illustrated papers.

B. Methods

1) Attending political classes.

a) Divide into three classes: ordinary, special, and cadre. The ordinary class should be further divided into two forms: when one detachment is together, take the detachment as the unit to hold class. The faculty consists of the detachment political commissar as director and the brigade political commissars as responsible for various classes. In addition to combat troops, who must attend class, messengers, service workers, head bearers, grooms, and bearers also must attend class. The purpose of the ordinary class is to enable the average soldier to gain the basics of political knowledge.

b) The special class is based on the detachment as the unit. From among the soldiers of each brigade, fifty of those who are slightly literate and have a little political knowledge should be selected by examination for enrollment. The detachment political commissar is the instructor in charge; the brigade political commissar shares the responsibility for each class. The purpose of the special class is to create trained individuals with a higher level of political knowledge than that taught in the ordinary class, and to prepare them to become lower-level cadres in the future.

c) The cadre class is based on the column as the unit; the army direct-command units may also constitute the unit. The class shall be made up of brigade commanders and deputy commanders, regimental commanders and deputy commanders, officers at the various levels, as well as other assigned personnel. The purpose is to raise the political level of present lower-level cadres and enable them to lead the masses, and ensure that in the future they will be able to serve as middle-level cadres. The political commissar, the director of the political department, and the column commander and other individuals of suitable ability shall serve as instructors.

d) A political training committee shall be organized, with the detachment as the basic unit. It shall be composed of those among the detachment's political commissars and military commanders who have ability in political training, with the detachment political commissar as director. Its task is to discuss various questions concerning implementation of the soldiers' political training within a detachment.

e) Political training in the army and each column and direct-command unit shall be carried out by a political training committee to be organized by the political propaganda section of the army and each column.

f) Teaching methods.

(1) A stimulating style (abolish the "pouring-in style").

(2) From the near to the distant.

(3) From the shallow to the deep.

(4) Speak in a colloquial style (new terms should be explained simply).

(5) Speech should be understandable.

(6) Speaking should be interesting.

(7) Use gestures to aid speaking.

(8) Later sessions should repeat concepts from earlier sessions.

(9) Prepare outlines.

(10) The cadre classes should use the discussion method.

2) Speaking before and after roll call.

a) Speaking time should not be more than half an hour each time.

b) Materials.

(1) Report political news.

(2) Criticize everyday living.

(3) Explain each week's political slogans.

3) Lecture meetings.

a) Once a week for the detachment, once every half month for the column, and at no set interval for the army.

b) For each meeting there must be systematic consultation by the political work organ (in the detachment, by the political commissar) with the military work organs to set the contents of speeches, to assign speakers, and to apportion speaking time.

c) Except for those responsible for fatigue duties, no one is permitted to miss any lecture session.

d) The lower-level political organs must report to the higher-level political organs on the contents, and effect on the masses, of each lecture session.

4) Conversations with individuals.

a) [We must have] separate conversations with the following types of person:

(1) Those who have deviations.

(2) Those who have been punished.

(3) Wounded soldiers.

(4) Ill soldiers.

(5) New soldiers.

(6) Captured soldiers.

(7) Those who do not work steadily.

(8) Those whose thinking wavers.

b) Before such a conversation, one must investigate the psychology and circumstances of the person with whom he is to speak.

c) When conversing, one must put himself in his comrade's position, and adopt a sincere attitude in speaking with him.

d) After talking, one must record the main points and the effects of the conversation.

5) Recreation.

a) Based on the brigade as the unit, improve the work of the recreation department of the soldiers' committee, carrying on the following types of recreation:

(1) Hide and seek, etc.

(2) Soccer.

(3) Music.

(4) Military techniques.

(5) Traditional folk opera.

(6) Old plays.

b) Under each propaganda team, set up a corps for propaganda with costume and makeup.

c) Funds for recreation equipment shall be supplied by the government (for the brigade, by approval of the column political department).

6) Improve treatment.

a) Resolutely abolish physical punishment.

b) Abolish insults and cursing.

c) Give special treatment to wounded and ill soldiers.

d) Reinstitute the system of paying out forty cents for straw-shoe money each month.

7) How to carry out special education for new and captured soldiers.

a) Lecture to new and captured soldiers on the Red Army's living style — for example: first, the equality of living of officers and men (between officers and men there is only a difference of duties, there is no class difference; officers are not an exploiting class, soldiers are not an exploited class); second, the "Three Main Rules" and the reason for them; third, the significance and function of the soldiers' committee; fourth, the economic system within the Red Army (economic resources, organization for the management of the economy, the openness of economic matters, and the system of inspection by the soldiers); fifth, the economic committee's management of the brigade provisions and division of the balance of provisions; sixth, the abolition of physical punishment and insulting curses; seven, preferential treatment of prisoners; and other items.

b) Relate the history of the Red Army's struggle in brief.

c) The Red Army's goals: (1) the ways in which the Red Army and the White Army are different; this point should be explained in detail to captured soldiers; (2) the ways in which the Red Army and bandits are different; (3) the three great tasks of the Red Army.

d) Describe the organizational system of the Red Army.

e) Ordinary political knowledge. For example: (1) the Kuomintang and the Communist Party; (2) the aggression against China of the three great imperialists, England, Japan, and the United States; (3) the various warlord cliques, under the command of the imperialists, that are fighting chaotically everywhere; (4) dividing the land; (5) the Soviet; (6) the Red Guards; and so forth.

VI. Special Education for Young Soldiers

A. Each column political department is responsible for producing a young people's character-learning textbook (consulting elementary school teaching materials from the Commercial Publications Press [Shang-wu kuan], the thousand-character courses of the civilians, the Dragon Cliff Culture Society [Lung-yen wen-hua she] textbook, and so forth).

B. Within each column shall be established a young soldiers' school divided into three or four classes, with each detachment having one class, and one class to a direct-command unit. There should not be more than twenty-five men in a class. The director of the political department shall be the principal, and the chief of the propaganda section shall be head of education. Each class shall establish a head teacher; a class shall have ninety hours of instruction in one semester.

C. Issue to the students, paper, pens, ink, and other supplies purchased with government funds.

VII. The Question of Abolishing Corporal Punishment

A. The Effects of the Use of Corporal Punishment in the Red Army

Among the various units, in all those where the men are

beaten most severely, the hatred of the men and the number who run away are the greatest. The most prominent examples: In the Eighth Detachment of the Third Column, a certain officer liked to beat the men, with the result that not only almost all the messengers and bearers ran away, but the supply sergeant and deputy commander ran away as well. The Twenty-fifth Brigade of the Ninth Detachment, during one period in the past had a commander who liked to beat the men so much that the masses gave him the nickname "Blacksmith." As a result, the soldiers felt there was no way out and were filled with feelings of hatred. Only when this commander was transferred were the men liberated. The beating of men in the Third Brigade of the Special Tasks Detachment resulted in the desertion of four bearers, a special task officer, and two veteran squad leaders. Among these, one named Hsiao Wen-ch'eng left a letter just before departing, explaining clearly that he was not a counter-revolutionary, but ran away only after the oppression became unendurable. When the Fourth Column was first established, the First, Second, and Third Columns transferred over brigade commanders, and they were constantly beating the men bar-barically. As a result, many soldiers ran away, and finally, unable to stand by themselves, the squad leaders had no choice but to leave the Fourth Column. The Second Column had more deserters than any other column; although there was no single reason, one of the most important was the vicious habit of the great majority of the lower-level officers in the Second Column of beating the men. There have occurred in the Second Column three instances of suicide (one platoon commander and two soldiers). This is the Red Army's greatest shame; its signifi-cance is particularly critical. It is impossible not to say that this is a result of the especially widespread practice of beating the men in the Second Column. Now the cry of the soldiers in the Red Army is, "Officers, do not beat the soldiers; those who beat them shall die!" Uncovering this kind of complaint and hatred among the masses truly merits our serious attention.

B. The Origins of Corporal Punishment and the Reason for Its Abolishment

The feudal class, in order to maintain its feudal exploitation, had no choice but to use the most brutal punishment as a tool to suppress the resistance and rebellion of those who were exploited. This is why physical punishment is an outgrowth of the feudal era. With economic development, there was an advance to the capitalist system; it was then necessary to set forth a doctrine of freedom for the development of the individuality of the worker, peasant and soldiers masses, increasing their labor capacity and their war-making capacity in order to create the conditions for development of the capitalist system. Because of this, the capitalist nations in general abolished physical punishment, and for a long time men have not been beaten in their armies. Then, economic development reached the stage of the birth of socialism and the development of class struggle, and the worker and peasant classes overthrew the power of the ruling class and the exploitation that depends on that power. Only when they wanted to mobilize the force of the broad masses of their own class were they able to obtain victory in the struggle. The Soviet government is the government of the most advanced class; it must not have any remnants of the feudal system. Therefore, not only has physical punishment long since disappeared from the Red Army of the Soviet Union but also, in general, the use of physical punishment has been completely prohibited by law. The Red Army's Fourth Army was created in a China where the feudal system has still not been exterminated, and its main force has been recruited from within the feudal warlord armies. The thinking and habits of the feudal system are still very common among the officers and men in general. Thus, the custom of beating the men and the belief that there is no respect without beating are still the same as the customs within the feudal warlord armies. Although we long ago advanced the slogan "Officers, do not beat soldiers," and provided the soldiers' committee with the right to appeal their grievances, it was simply ineffectual. The result was the creation of a gulf between the officers and men, and a lowering of the morale of the soldiers as well as of the officers; more and more ran away daily, and the army was pervaded by an atmosphere of hatred, even to the point that cases of suicide occurred. This is a phenomenon completely contrary to the Red Army's fighting mission; if it is not corrected quickly, it will be dangerous beyond words.

C. The Methods of Correction

1) Resolutely abolish corporal punishment.

2) Conduct an "Abolish Corporal Punishment Movement." This movement should work on both sides, officers and men, to create [an understanding of] the significance of "abolish corporal punishment to facilitate the struggle right now," and spread it throughout the masses of officers and men. In this way we will then be able not only to make the officers feel that the abolition of corporal punishment will not result in an inability to lead the soldiers, but also to understand that after we eliminate corporal punishment it will be advantageous for leadership and training. As for the soldiers, not only will they not be more obstructive because of the elimination of corporal punishment, but also, owing to the elimination of corporal punishment, their fighting morale will be increased. As the separation of officers and men is removed, they will voluntarily accept leadership, training, and general discipline.

3) After the abolition of corporal punishment, because of the origins of the historical custom, it is possible that some temporary bad phenomena may occur. This should intensify our responsibility to diligently advocate the spirit of persuasion and the spirit of voluntary adherence to discipline, in order to overcome this most evil feudal system, which is opposed to the aims of our struggle. We definitely must not take these bad phenomena as a pretext to serve as a protective cover for the feudal custom of beating the men. All those who use temporary bad phenomena as a pretext to oppose the abolition of corporal punishment or to sabotage the movement to abolish corporal

punishment are then, in objective terms, an obstacle to the development of the revolutionary struggle, and an ally of the ruling
class.

4) Legal procedure for the Red Army's abolition of corporal
punishment: (a) revise the Red Army's punishment regulations;
(b) under the authority of the highest military and political organs, promulgate a general order on the abolition of corporal
punishment, and also promulgate new Red Army punishment
regulations; (c) after the general order has been promulgated,
on the one hand, the military and political organs shall convene
meetings of officers and explain in detail the reasons for the
abolition of corporal punishment, to make the entire body of
officers support the major reform embodied in this general
order and implement it fully and energetically in the units;
(d) on the other hand, the soldiers' committee shall convene a conference of soldiers' representatives which, besides supporting
this reform and then later voluntarily observing discipline,
shall also rigorously tighten the disciplinary control of the
masses in order to achieve the greatest gains from the abolition
of corporal punishment.

VIII. The Question of Preferential Treatment
for Wounded Soldiers

A. The Phenomena and the Effects of the Suffering of the
Wounded and Sick

1) The health organs of the various units in the army are
not sound, doctors are few, medicine is in short supply, stretch-
ers and equipment are inadequate, and administrators are few
and unsound, so that many wounded and ill soldiers are not only
unable to get adequate treatment but also are sometimes unable to get even general, rudimentary treatment.

2) The attention paid by the army's military and political
organs to the wounded and ill is inadequate. For example, (a) Regarding the soundness of the health organs, not only are they
not exerting the greatest effort, they have simply paid no at-

tention at all; in the various types of conferences, discussions of the health problem are very few. (b) Officers do not take the time to comfort wounded and ill soldiers; for example, customs such as officers getting tea for the wounded and ill soldiers, covering them with blankets, inquiring solicitously about them, and so on, simply do not exist in the Red Army. The officers adopt an unheeding attitude toward the wounded and ill soldiers, even to the point of expressing disgust toward them. (c) When on the march, officers and even soldiers express not one bit of sympathy for wounded soldiers who fall behind along the way, and not only fail to try to do something for them but, on the contrary, constantly curse them or heartlessly drive them away.

3) Supplies and allowances for seriously wounded and seriously ill soldiers are insufficient; seven or eight days after being wounded, a soldier still does not have a change of clothes. A wounded officer may get some allowance, but a wounded soldier gets none.

4) The shortcomings of the Chiao-yang [Rear Area] Hospital: (a) it is in a state of organizational chaos; (b) doctors and medicine are insufficient; (c) doctors sell medicine privately; (d) it is dirty; (e) there are not enough winter clothes and quilts; (f) there are too few soldier-nurses; (g) food and drink are poor; (h) the building is cramped; (i) relations with the local masses are bad. Therefore, wounded and ill soldiers see the hospital as a jail, and they do not want to stay in the rear area.

The various types of evils in the treatment of wounded and ill soldiers listed above create the following effects: (a) They make the soldiers dissatisfied with the Red Army. ("The Red Army is all right, but only as long as you aren't wounded or sick.") This kind of opinion is actually widespread among the entire body of soldiers, as well as among the lower-level officers. (b) Soldiers and officers are not contented, which adds still more to the gulf between officers and men. (c) Soldiers and lower-level officers are all afraid of being wounded, and because of this, the Red Army's fighting capacity is reduced. (d) There are many deserters. (e) It affects the worker and peasant masses, reducing their courage for joining the Red Army.

B. Means of Solution

1) Military and political organs cannot continue to ignore health questions as they have done. In the future all meetings should adequately discuss health problems.

2) The organization of health organs should be made especially sound. Able administrators should be sought out; we should not take a person because he cannot be used at some other place and put him into a health unit. Moreover, we should increase the size of the staff and reach the goal of complete care. We should exert every effort to find solutions to the problem of the shortage of doctors and medicine. As for the doctors, we should be sure to urge them to examine the sick thoroughly, not carelessly.

3) Officers, especially officers who have close contact with the soldiers, should visit wounded and ill soldiers from time to time, take tea for them to drink, and in the night cover them with quilts. If they feel cold, [the officers] should think of ways to help them, like borrowing additional clothing from other men. The above methods of caring for wounded and ill soldiers should be formalized as a system and put into effect by everybody, because this is the method most effective for winning over the masses.

4) With regard to wounded soldiers who fall behind along the way when the army is on the march: (a) Forbid anyone's cursing or ridiculing them. (b) When wounded and ill soldiers make way for others, the latter should speak kindly to them, and not push them aside. (c) No matter what unit or organization, all those that have a man who falls behind because of illness or wounds, no matter whether he is a combat soldier or a non-combatant, should immediately assign someone to take care of him; if he is seriously wounded or ill, wherever possible hire a bearer to carry him. (d) On the march the rear guard should patiently help wounded and ill soldiers who have fallen behind

and, when necessary, also carry their rifles and ammunition.

5) Distribute pocket money to wounded and ill soldiers; the seriousness of the wound or illness should be considered, and the seriously wounded or ill should be given a bit more than the slightly wounded or ill. In the matter of allowances, in regard to the especially seriously wounded and ill, without distinguishing among officers, soldiers, and bearers, give them an appropriate amount.

6) On the problem of clothing and quilts for wounded and ill soldiers, apart from the government doing its best to procure them, donations should be solicited from the officers and soldiers of each unit. This will not only serve to increase the pocket money for wounded and ill soldiers, but it is also a good method of arousing in the whole army a spirit of mutual aid and support.

7) The many shortcomings of the Chiao-yang Rear Area Hospital should be corrected in a systematic way. Apart from this, we should also initiate a collection of donations among the worker and peasant masses of Western Fukien (clothes, bedding, cash, and food) in order to unite the worker and peasant masses closely with the Red Army.

IX. The Question of the Relations Between the Military and Political Systems of the Red Army

A. Before high-level local organs of political power have been established, the military organs and political organs of the Red Army carry out their work side by side under the direction of the Front Committee.

B. Relations between the Red Army and the masses.

1) In all matters with significance for the entire army, like the promulgation of the political platforms, the two organs, military and political, should promulgate them jointly.

2) Mass work, like propagandizing the masses, organizing the masses, establishing government organs, as well as the

direction and supervision of confiscation, trials, punishment, taking up donations, raising money, helping the needy, and other matters, before organs of local government have been established, shall all come under the authority of the political department.

3) In all localities where government organs have not been established, the political department of the Red Army shall serve as the government organ of that locality until local government organs have been established. In all localities where local government organs have already been established, it should as a matter of principle make the local government organs independent in dealing with all matters, and strengthen confidence in them among the masses. Only where local government organs are still not completely sound and the Red Army has affairs related to the locality, may the method of joint control by local government organs and the Red Army political department be used.

4) Helping in the establishment and development of local armed forces is the responsibility of the political department; helping in the peacetime military training of the local armed forces and in the wartime combat command is the responsibility of the military commander. But both must make every effort to go through the local government organs of political authority and do their utmost to avoid dealing with these matters directly.

C. As for the internal personnel administration of the Red Army, the two systems, military and political, have independent channels. When the two have relations with each other — for example, when transferring personnel between them or transmitting information between them — they should communicate with official letters on an equal basis.

D. In putting into effect courtesy and military discipline, the two systems, military and political, shall mutually observe the principle of class obedience; they must not take the difference of systems as a pretext to ignore or fail to obey commands.

E. In all matters of provisions, health, the march, combat, pitching camp, etc., the political system should accept the direction of the military system. In all matters of political training and mass work, the military system should accept the direction of the political system. But the form of the direction can only be by a direct line through the subordinate organs within the opposite system (the general affairs section, the adjutant department, etc.).

F. Command of all Red Army fund-raising and decisions and outlays on expenditures for political work is within the competence of the political department, and the military organs must not interfere. (In regard to the procedures for obtaining cash, the political department [deals] directly with the military supplies office.) Funds for the Party shall be supplied by the political department.

G. All the orders of military organs, except for those which the political commissar must countersign, need not be signed by the director of the political department. All the orders of political organs shall be executed by the political department alone, and the political commissar does not need to countersign them.

2

CHAIRMAN MAO TSE-TUNG
ON PEOPLE'S WAR*

Mao Tse-tung

Joint Editorial Note by Red Flag, People's Daily,
and Liberation Army Daily

   To commemorate the fortieth anniversary of the founding
of the Chinese People's Liberation Army, we are publishing
quotations from Chairman Mao on people's war.
   Chairman Mao's theory of people's war constitutes an im-

---

   *"Mao chu-hsi lun jen-min chan-cheng," jointly published in
Hung-ch'i [Red Flag], No. 12 (August 1, 1967), 2-16; Jen-min
jih-pao [People's Daily], August 1, 1967; and Chieh-fang-chün
pao [Liberation Army Daily], August 1, 1967. The English
translation of this selection is taken, in slightly revised form,
from Peking Review, No. 32 (August 4, 1967), 5-13. The ed-
itors of Peking Review note: "The page number given for the
source of a quotation refers to the latest English edition of the
book or pamphlet cited as published by the Foreign Languages
Press, Peking. In cases where a word or phrase linked to the
preceding text has been omitted in the opening sentence of the
quotation, (*) is placed after the source. This is also done in
a number of places where the English rendering has been re-
worded to make up for omission of context or to improve the
translation."

portant part of Mao Tse-tung's thought — Marxism-Leninism
of the present era.

In this era, Mao Tse-tung's thought is the guide for all oppressed peoples and oppressed nations in their struggles for
liberation. The most important thing is to arm oneself with
Comrade Mao Tse-tung's theory of people's war and, with the
barrel of a gun, smash the old state apparatus, topple imperialism and its running dogs, and transform the whole world.

After the proletariat attains political power and throughout
the entire historical period of socialism, there exists the
struggle between the proletariat, which is endeavoring to consolidate its dictatorship, and the bourgeoisie, which is trying to
overthrow it. In attempting to overthrow the dictatorship of the
proletariat, the bourgeoisie always tries desperately to get a
grip on the gun through its representatives within the Communist Party. In the Soviet Union, the Khrushchev revisionist
clique usurped military power and staged a counterrevolutionary
coup d'etat. This is a serious lesson for us. In China, the top
Party person in authority, taking the capitalist road, colluded
with the big conspirators, careerists, and warlords Peng Te-
huai and Lo Jui-ch'ing for seventeen years in order to bring
about the restoration of capitalism. They engaged in frenzied
underhand activities to usurp army leadership in a vain attempt
to turn our people's army into their tool for a counterrevolutionary restoration. The imperialists, headed by the United
States, are vainly attempting to invade and subvert the socialist
countries. Therefore, revolutionary people in the socialist
countries must also conscientiously study Chairman Mao's
theory of people's war and skillfully grasp this sharpest of
ideological weapons in order to smash the schemes for capitalist restoration and to consolidate the dictatorship of the proletariat. They must be vigilant at all times against armed aggression by imperialism and its accomplices, ensure that the
gun is firmly and safely in the hands of the proletariat, and
prevent the revisionists from usurping military power or
changing the nature of the proletarian army. This is the vital
factor for preventing the restoration of capitalism.

Armed with Mao Tse-tung's thought, the Chinese People's Liberation Army has fulfilled its great role as the pillar of the dictatorship of the proletariat in the unprecedented Great Proletarian Cultural Revolution, and gained new merits; at the same time it has been educated, tempered, and tested anew in the storms of this great revolution. The Chinese People's Liberation Army has participated in the Great Proletarian Cultural Revolution in the localities. This is the latest development of our great supreme commander Chairman Mao's theory of building a proletarian revolutionary army.

Today, it is of vital significance for the whole Party, the entire army, and the Chinese people to restudy Chairman Mao's theory of people's war.

Revolutions and Revolutionary Wars Are Inevitable in Class Society

War is the highest form of struggle for resolving contradictions, when they have developed to a certain stage, between classes, nations, states, or political groups, and it has existed ever since the emergence of private property and of classes.

> "Problems of Strategy in China's Revolutionary War" (December 1936), Selected Works, Vol. I, p. 180.

Revolutions and revolutionary wars are inevitable in class society, and without them it is impossible to accomplish any leap in social development and to overthrow the reactionary ruling classes, and therefore impossible for the people to win political power.

> "On Contradiction" (August 1937), Selected Works, Vol. I, p. 344.*

History shows that wars are divided into two kinds, just and unjust. All wars that are progressive are just, and all wars

that impede progress are unjust. We communists oppose all
unjust wars that impede progress, but we do not oppose progressive, just wars. Not only do we communists not oppose
just wars, we actively participate in them.

> "On Protracted War" (May 1938),
> Selected Works, Vol. II, p. 150.

War, this monster of mutual slaughter among men, will be
finally eliminated by the progress of human society, and in the
not too distant future. But there is only one way to eliminate
it, and that is to oppose war with war, to oppose counterrevolutionary war with revolutionary war, to oppose national counterrevolutionary war with national revolutionary war, and to oppose
counterrevolutionary class war with revolutionary class war.

> "Problems of Strategy in China's Rev-
> olutionary War" (December 1936),
> Selected Works, Vol. I, pp. 182-183.

Political Power Grows Out of the Barrel of a Gun

The seizure of power by armed force, the settlement of the
issue by war, is the central task and the highest form of revolution. This Marxist-Leninist principle of revolution holds
good universally, for China and for all other countries.

> "Problems of War and Strategy"
> (November 6, 1938), Selected
> Works, Vol. II, p. 219.

Every communist must grasp the truth, "Political power
grows out of the barrel of a gun."

> Ibid., p. 224.

According to the Marxist theory of the state, the army is the
chief component of state power. Whoever wants to seize and

retain state power must have a strong army. Some people ridicule us as advocates of the "omnipotence of war." Yes, we are advocates of the omnipotence of revolutionary war; that is good, not bad — it is Marxist. The guns of the Russian Communist Party created socialism. We shall create a democratic republic. Experience in the class struggle in the era of imperialism teaches us that it is only by the power of the gun that the working class and the laboring masses can defeat the armed bourgeoisie and landlords; in this sense we may say that only with guns can the whole world be transformed.

Ibid., p. 225.

Without armed struggle neither the proletariat, nor the people, nor the Communist Party would have any standing at all in China, and it would be impossible for the revolution to triumph. In these years [the eighteen years since the founding of the Party] , the development, consolidation, and bolshevization of our Party have proceeded in the midst of revolutionary wars; without armed struggle the Communist Party would assuredly not be what it is today. Comrades throughout the Party must never forget this experience for which we have paid in blood.

"Introducing The Communist"
(October 4, 1939), Selected
Works, Vol. II, p. 292.*

Imperialism and All Reactionaries Are Paper Tigers

All reactionaries are paper tigers. In appearance, the reactionaries are terrifying, but in reality they are not so powerful. From a long-term point of view, it is not the reactionaries but the people who are really powerful.

"Talk with the American Correspondent
Anna Louise Strong" (August 1946),
Selected Works, Vol. IV, p. 100.

Just as there is not a single thing in the world without a dual nature (this is the law of the unity of opposites), so imperialism and all reactionaries have a dual nature — they are real tigers and paper tigers at the same time. In past history, before they won state power and for some time afterwards, the slave-owning class, the feudal landlord class, and the bourgeoisie were vigorous, revolutionary, and progressive; they were real tigers. But with the lapse of time, because their opposites — the slave class, the peasant class, and the proletariat — grew in strength step by step, struggled against them more and more fiercely, these ruling classes changed step by step into the reverse, changed into reactionaries, changed into backward people, changed into paper tigers. And eventually they were overthrown, or will be overthrown, by the people. The reactionary, backward, decaying classes retained this dual nature even in their last life-and-death struggles against the people. On the one hand, they were real tigers; they devoured people, devoured people by the millions and tens of millions. The cause of the people's struggle went through a period of difficulties and hardships, and along the path there were many twists and turns. To destroy the rule of imperialism, feudalism, and bureaucratic-capitalism in China took the Chinese people more than a hundred years and cost them tens of millions of lives before the victory in 1949. Look! Were these not living tigers, iron tigers? But in the end they changed into paper tigers, dead tigers, bean-curd tigers. These are historical facts. Have people not seen or heard about these facts? There have indeed been thousands and tens of thousands of them! Thousands and tens of thousands! Hence, imperialism and all reactionaries, looked at in essence, from a long-term point of view, from a strategic point of view, must be seen for what they are — paper tigers. On this we should build strategic thinking On the other hand, they are also living tigers, iron tigers, real tigers which can devour people. On this we should build our tactical thinking.

Speech at the Wuchang Meeting of the
Political Bureau of the Central Com-

mittee of the Communist Party of
China (December 1, 1958), quoted in
the explanatory note to "Talk with the
American Correspondent Anna Louise
Strong," Selected Works, Vol. IV,
pp. 98-99.*

Make trouble, fail, make trouble again, fail again ... till
their doom; that is the logic of the imperialists and all reactionaries the world over in dealing with the people's cause,
and they will never go against this logic.   This is a Marxist
law.   When we say "imperialism is ferocious," we mean
that its nature will never change, that the imperialists will
never lay down their butcher knives, that they will never become Buddhas, till their doom.

Fight, fail, fight again, fail again, fight again ... till their
victory; that is the logic of the people, and they, too, will never
go against this logic. This is another Marxist law. The Russian people's revolution followed this law, and so has the Chinese people's revolution.

"Cast Away Illusions, Prepare for Struggle"
(August 14, 1949), Selected Works, Vol. IV,
p. 428.

People of the world, unite and defeat the U.S. aggressors and
all their running dogs! People of the world, be courageous,
dare to fight, defy difficulties, and advance wave upon wave.
Then the whole world will belong to the people. Monsters of
all kinds shall be destroyed.

"Statement Supporting the People of the Congo
(L) Against U.S. Aggression" (November 28,
1964), People of the World, Unite and Defeat
the U.S. Aggressors and All Their Lackeys,
2nd ed., p. 14.

The Decisive Factor of Victory and Defeat in War Is People, Not Things

The people, and the people alone, are the motive force in the making of world history.

> "On Coalition Government" (April 24, 1945), Selected Works, Vol. III, p. 257.*

Weapons are an important factor in war, but not the decisive factor; it is people, not things, that are decisive. The contest of strength is not only a contest of military and economic power, but also a contest of human power and morale. Military and economic power is necessarily wielded by people.

> "On Protracted War" (May 1938), Selected Works, Vol. II, pp. 143-144.

The richest source of power to wage war lies in the masses of the people. It is mainly because of the unorganized state of the Chinese masses that Japan dares to bully us. When this defect is remedied, then the Japanese aggressor, like a mad bull crashing into a ring of flames, will be surrounded by hundreds of millions of our people standing upright; the mere sound of their voices will strike terror into him, and he will be burned to death.

> Ibid., p. 186.

Take the case of China. We have only millet plus rifles to rely on, but history will finally prove that our millet plus rifles is more powerful than Chiang Kai-shek's airplanes plus tanks. Although the Chinese people still face many difficulties and will long suffer hardships from the joint attacks of U.S. imperialism and the Chinese reactionaries, the day will come when these reactionaries are defeated and we are victorious.

The reason is simply this: the reactionaries represent reaction, we represent progress.

"Talk with the American Correspondent Anna Louise Strong" (August 1946), Selected Works, Vol. IV, p. 101.

The Revolutionary War Is a War of the Masses

The revolutionary war is a war of the masses; it can be waged only by mobilizing the masses and relying on them.

"Be Concerned with the Well-being of the Masses, Pay Attention to Methods of Work" (January 27, 1934), Selected Works, Vol. I, p. 147.*

What is a true bastion of iron? It is the masses, the millions upon millions of people who genuinely and sincerely support the revolution. That is the real iron bastion which it is impossible, absolutely impossible, for any force on earth to smash. The counterrevolution cannot smash us; on the contrary, we shall smash it. Rallying millions upon millions of people round the revolutionary government and expanding our revolutionary war, we shall wipe out all counterrevolution and take over the whole of China.

Ibid., p. 150.*

Considering the revolutionary war as a whole, the operations of the people's guerrillas and those of the main forces of the Red Army complement each other like a man's right arm and left arm, and if we had only the main forces of the Red Army without the people's guerrillas, we would be like a warrior with only one arm.

"Problems of Strategy in China's Revolutionary War" (December 1936), Selected Works, Vol. I, p. 238.

This army is powerful because it has the people's self-
defense corps and the militia — the vast armed organizations
of the masses — fighting in coordination with it. In the Liberated Areas of China, all men and women, from youth to middle
age, are organized in the people's anti-Japanese self-defense
corps on a voluntary and democratic basis and without giving
up their work in production. The cream of the self-defense
corps, except for those who join the army or the guerrilla units,
is brought into the militia. Without the cooperation of these armed
forces of the masses it would be impossible to defeat the enemy.

"On Coalition Government" (April 24,
1945), Selected Works, Vol. III, p. 265.*

This army is powerful because of its division into two parts,
the main forces and the regional forces, with the former available for operations in any region whenever necessary and the
latter concentrating on defending their own localities and attacking the enemy there in cooperation with the local militia
and the self-defense corps. This division of labor has won the
wholehearted support of the people. Without this correct division of labor — if, for example, attention were paid only to
the role of the main forces, while that of the regional forces
were neglected — it would likewise be impossible to defeat the
enemy in the conditions obtaining in China's Liberated Areas.
Under the regional forces, numerous armed working teams have
been organized, which are well trained and hence better qualified for military, political, and mass work; they penetrate into
the rearmost areas behind the enemy lines, strike at the enemy, and arouse the masses to anti-Japanese struggle, thus
giving support to the frontal military operations of the various
Liberated Areas. In all this they have achieved great success.

Ibid., pp. 265-66.*

The imperialists are bullying us in such a way that we will

have to deal with them seriously. Not only must we have a powerful regular army, we must also organize contingents of the people's militia on a big scale. This will make it difficult for the imperialists to move a single inch in our country in the event of invasion.

> Interview with a Hsinhua News Agency
> correspondent (September 29, 1958).

The Establishment of Rural Bases and Using the Villages to Surround the Cities

Armed struggle by the Chinese Communist Party takes the form of peasant war under proletarian leadership.

> "Introducing The Communist"
> (October 4, 1939), Selected Works,
> Vol. II, p. 291.

The anti-Japanese war is essentially a peasant war.

> "On New Democracy" (January 1940),
> Selected Works, Vol. II, p. 366.

Since China's key cities have long been occupied by the powerful imperialists and their reactionary Chinese allies, it is imperative for the revolutionary ranks to turn the backward villages into advanced, consolidated base areas, into great military, political, economic, and cultural bastions of the revolution from which to fight their vicious enemies who are using the cities for attacks on the rural districts, and in this way gradually to achieve the complete victory of the revolution through protracted fighting; it is imperative for them to do so if they do not wish to compromise with imperialism and its lackeys but are determined to fight on, and if they intend to build up and temper their forces, and avoid decisive battles with a powerful enemy while their own strength is inadequate.

> "The Chinese Revolution and the Chinese
> Communist Party" (December 1939),
> Selected Works, Vol. II, pp. 316-17.

What, then, are these base areas? They are the strategic bases on which the guerrilla forces rely in performing their strategic tasks and achieving the object of preserving and expanding themselves and destroying and driving out the enemy. Without such strategic bases, there will be nothing to depend on in carrying out any of our strategic tasks or achieving the aim of the war.

> "Problems of Strategy in Guerrilla War
> Against Japan" (May 1938), Selected
> Works, Vol. II, p. 93.

... the protracted revolutionary struggle in the revolutionary base areas consists mainly in peasant guerrilla warfare led by the Chinese Communist Party. Therefore, it is wrong to ignore the necessity of using rural districts as revolutionary base areas, to neglect painstaking work among the peasants, and to neglect guerrilla warfare.

> "The Chinese Revolution and the Chinese
> Communist Party" (December 1939),
> Selected Works, Vol. II, p. 317.

And stressing the work in the rural base areas does not mean abandoning our work in the cities and in the other vast rural areas which are still under the enemy's rule; on the contrary, without the work in the cities and in these other rural areas, our own rural base areas would be isolated and the revolution would suffer defeat. Moreover, the final objective of the revolution is the capture of the cities, the enemy's main bases, and this objective cannot be achieved without adequate work in the cities.

> Ibid., p. 317.

From 1927 to the present, the center of gravity of our work has been in the villages — gathering strength in the villages, using the villages in order to surround the cities, and then taking the cities.

> "Report to the Second Plenary Session of the Seventh Central Committee of the Communist Party of China" (March 5, 1949), Selected Works, Vol. IV, p. 363.

The People's Liberation Army Is an Armed Body for Carrying Out the Political Tasks of Revolution

Without a people's army the people have nothing.

> "On Coalition Government" (April 24, 1945), Selected Works, Vol. III, pp. 296-97.

Our principle is that the Party commands the gun, and the gun must never be allowed to command the Party.

> "Problems of War and Strategy" (November 6, 1938), Selected Works, Vol. II, p. 224.

This army is powerful because all its members have a conscious discipline; they have come together and they fight not for the private interests of a few individuals or a narrow clique, but for the interests of the broad masses and of the whole nation. The sole purpose of this army is to stand firmly with the Chinese people and to serve them wholeheartedly.

> "On Coalition Government" (April 24, 1945), Selected Works, Vol. III, p. 264.*

The Chinese Red Army is an armed body for carrying out the political tasks of the revolution. Especially at present, the Red Army should certainly not confine itself to fighting; besides fighting to destroy the enemy's military strength, it should shoulder such important tasks as doing propaganda among the masses, organizing the masses, arming them, helping them to establish revolutionary political power, and setting up Party organizations. The Red Army fights not merely for the sake of fighting but in order to conduct propaganda among the masses, organize them, arm them, and help them to establish revolutionary political power. Without these objectives, fighting loses its meaning and the Red Army loses the reason for its existence.

> "On Correcting Mistaken Ideas in the Party" (December 1929), Selected Works, Vol. I, p. 106.*

Another highly significant and distinctive feature of the Eighth Route Army is its political work, which is guided by three basic principles. First, the principle of unity between officers and men, which means eradicating feudal practices in the army, prohibiting beating and abuse, building up a conscious discipline, and sharing weal and woe — as a result of which the entire army is closely united. Second, the principle of unity between the army and the people, which means maintaining a discipline that forbids the slightest violation of the people's interests, conducting propaganda among the masses, organizing and arming them, lightening their economic burdens, and suppressing the traitors and collaborators who do harm to the army and the people — as a result of which the army is closely united with the people and welcomed everywhere. Third, the principle of disintegrating the enemy troops and giving lenient treatment to prisoners of war. Our victory depends not only on our military operations but also on the disintegration of the enemy troops.

> "Interview with the British Journalist James Bertram" (October 25, 1937), Selected Works, Vol. II, p. 53.*

The People's Liberation Army is always a fighting force. Even after country-wide victory, our army will remain a fighting force during the historical period in which classes have not been abolished in our country and the imperialist system still exists in the world. On this point there should be no misunderstanding or wavering.

> "Report to the Second Plenary Session of the Seventh Central Committee of the Communist Party of China" (March 5, 1949), Selected Works, Vol. IV, p. 362.

The People's Liberation Army should be a great school. In this great school, our armymen should learn politics, military affairs, and culture. They can also engage in agricultural production and side occupations, run some medium-sized or small factories, and manufacture a number of products to meet their own needs or for exchange with the state at equal values. They can also do mass work and take part in the socialist education movement in factories and villages. After the socialist education movement is over, they can always find mass work to do, so that the army will forever be at one with the masses. They should also take part in the struggles of the cultural revolution, whenever they occur, to criticize the bourgeoisie. In this way the army can concurrently study, engage in agriculture, run factories, and do mass work. Of course, these tasks should be properly coordinated, and a distinction should be made between the primary and secondary tasks. Each army unit should engage in one or two of the three fields of activity — agriculture, industry, and mass work, but not in all three at the same time. In this way our army of several million will be able to play a very great role indeed.

> "Letter to Comrade Lin Piao," quoted from Jen-min jih-pao editorial, August 1, 1966, The Whole Country Should Become a Great School of Mao Tse-tung's Thought, Foreign Languages Press, pp. 5-6.

The Strategy and Tactics of People's War

You fight in your way and we fight in ours; we fight when we can win and move away when we can't.

> Quoted from Comrade Lin Piao's article
> Long Live the Victory of People's War
> (September 1965), Foreign Languages
> Press, p. 36.

Note:

Comrade Mao Tse-tung has provided a masterly summary of the strategy and tactics of people's war: You fight in your way and we fight in ours; we fight when we can win and move away when we can't.

In other words, you rely on modern weapons and we rely on highly conscious revolutionary people; you give full play to your superiority and we give full play to ours; you have your way of fighting and we have ours. When you want to fight us, we don't let you and you can't even find us. But when we want to fight you, we make sure that you can't get away and we hit you squarely on the chin and wipe you out. When we are able to wipe you out, we do so with a vengeance; when we can't, we see to it that you don't wipe us out. It is opportunism if one won't fight when one can win. It is adventurism if one insists on fighting when one can't win. Fighting is the pivot of all our strategy and tactics. It is because of the necessity of fighting that we admit the necessity of moving away. The sole purpose of moving away is to fight and bring about the final and complete destruction of the enemy. This strategy and these tactics can be applied only when one relies on the broad masses of the people, and such application brings the superiority of people's war into full play. However superior he may be in technical equipment and whatever tricks he may resort to, the enemy will find himself in the passive position of having to receive blows, and the initiative will always be in our hands.

> Lin Piao: Long Live the Victory of
> People's War (September 1965), For-
> eign Languages Press, pp. 36-37.

Our strategy is "pit one against ten" and our tactics are "pit ten against one" — this is one of our fundamental principles for gaining mastery over the enemy.

> "Problems of Strategy in China's
> Revolutionary War" (December 1936),
> Selected Works, Vol. I, p. 237.

Ours are guerrilla tactics. They consist mainly of the following points:

"Divide our forces to arouse the masses, concentrate our forces to deal with the enemy."

"The enemy advances, we retreat; the enemy camps, we harass; the enemy tires, we attack; the enemy retreats, we pursue."

"To extend stable base areas, employ the policy of advancing in waves; when pursued by a powerful enemy, employ the policy of circling around."

"Arouse the largest numbers of the masses in the shortest possible time and by the best possible methods."

These tactics are just like casting a net; at any moment we should be able to cast it or draw it in. We cast it wide to win over the masses and draw it in to deal with the enemy.

> "A Single Spark Can Start a Prairie Fire"
> (January 5, 1930), Selected Works, Vol. I, p. 124.

Our principles of operation are:

1) Attack dispersed, isolated enemy forces first; attack concentrated, strong enemy forces later.

2) Take small and medium cities and extensive rural areas first; take big cities later.

3) Make wiping out the enemy's effective strength our main objective; do not make holding or seizing a city or place our main objective. Holding or seizing a city or place is the outcome of wiping out the enemy's effective strength, and often a city or place can be held or seized for good only after it has changed hands a number of times.

4) In every battle, concentrate an absolutely superior force (two, three, four, and sometimes even five or six times the enemy's strength), encircle the enemy forces completely, strive to wipe them out thoroughly, and do not let any escape from the net. In special circumstances, use the method of dealing the enemy crushing blows, that is, concentrate all our strength to make a frontal attack and an attack on one or both of his flanks, with the aim of wiping out one part and routing another so that our army can swiftly move its troops to smash other enemy forces. Strive to avoid battles of attrition in which we lose more than we gain or only break even. In this way, although inferior as a whole (in terms of numbers), we shall be absolutely superior in every part and every specific campaign, and this ensures victory in the campaign. As time goes on, we shall become superior as a whole and eventually wipe out all the enemy.

5) Fight no battle unprepared, fight no battle you are not sure of winning; make every effort to be well prepared for each battle, make every effort to ensure victory in the given set of conditions as between the enemy and ourselves.

6) Give full play to our style of fighting — courage in battle, no fear of sacrifice, no fear of fatigue, and continuous fighting (that is, fighting successive battles in a short time without rest).

7) Strive to wipe out the enemy when he is on the move. At the same time, pay attention to the tactics of positional attack and capture enemy fortified points and cities.

8) With regard to attacking cities, resolutely seize all enemy fortified points and cities which are weakly defended. At op-

portune moments, seize all enemy fortified points and cities
defended with moderate strength, provided circumstances permit. As for all strongly defended enemy fortified points and
cities, wait till conditions are ripe and then take them.

9) Replenish our strength with all the arms and most of the
personnel captured from the enemy. Our army's main sources
of manpower and matériel are at the front

10) Make good use of the intervals between campaigns to
rest, train, and consolidate our troops. Periods of rest, training, and consolidation should not in general be very long, and
the enemy should so far as possible be permitted no breathing
space.

These are the main methods the People's Liberation Army
has employed in defeating Chiang Kai-shek. They are the result of the tempering of the People's Liberation Army in long
years of fighting against domestic and foreign enemies and are
completely suited to our present situation. . . . Our strategy and
tactics are based on a people's war; no army opposed to the
people can use our strategy and tactics.

> "The Present Situation and Our Tasks"
> (December 25, 1947), Selected Military
> Writings, 2nd ed., pp. 349-50.*

Our Chief Method Is to Learn Warfare Through Warfare

The laws of war are a problem which anyone directing a war
must study and solve.

The laws of revolutionary war are a problem which anyone
directing a revolutionary war must study and solve.

The laws of China's revolutionary war are a problem which
anyone directing China's revolutionary war must study and
solve.

We are now engaged in a war; our war is a revolutionary
war; and our revolutionary war is being waged in this semi-
colonial and semifeudal country of China. Therefore, we must
study not only the laws of war in general, but the specific laws

of revolutionary war, and the even more specific laws of revolutionary war in China.

It is well known that when you do anything, unless you understand its actual circumstances, its nature, and its relations to
other things, you will not know the laws governing it, or know
how to do it, or be able to do it well.

> "Problems of Strategy in China's
> Revolutionary War" (December 1936),
> Selected Works, Vol. I, p. 179.

A commander's correct dispositions stem from his correct
decisions, his correct decisions stem from his correct judgments, and his correct judgments stem from a thorough and
necessary reconnaissance and from pondering on and piecing
together the data of various kinds gathered through reconnaissance. He applies all possible and necessary methods of reconnaissance and ponders on the information gathered about the enemy's
situation, discarding the dross and selecting the essential, eliminating the false and retaining the true, proceeding from the one to
the other and from the outside to the inside; then, he takes the conditions on his own side into account, and makes a study of both sides
and their interrelations, thereby forming his judgments, making up
his mind, and working out his plans. Such is the complete process
of knowing a situation which a military man goes through before he
formulates a strategic plan, a campaign plan, or a battle plan.

> Ibid., p. 188.

Unquestionably, victory or defeat in war is determined mainly
by the military, political, economic, and natural conditions on
both sides. But not by these alone. It is also determined by
each side's subjective ability in directing the war. In his endeavor to win a war, a military strategist cannot overstep the
limitations imposed by the material conditions; within these
limitations, however, he can and must strive for victory. The
stage of action for a military strategist is built on objective

material conditions, but on that stage he can direct the performance of many a drama, full of sound and color, power and grandeur.

Ibid., pp. 190-91.*

Reading is learning, but applying is also learning, and the more important kind of learning at that. Our chief method is to learn warfare through warfare. A person who has had no opportunity to go to school can also learn warfare — he can learn through fighting in war. A revolutionary war is a mass undertaking; it is often not a matter of first learning and then doing, but of doing and then learning, for doing is itself learning.

Ibid. pp. 189-90.

3

TURN OUR ARMY INTO A GREAT
SCHOOL OF MAO TSE-TUNG THOUGHT*

Liberation Army Daily

Our great leader Chairman Mao recently gave us extremely important directions regarding army-building.

Chairman Mao said: "The People's Liberation Army should be a great school. In this school, armymen should study politics, military affairs, and culture. They can also engage in actual agricultural production and side occupations, run some medium-sized and small factories, and manufacture a few products to meet their own needs or to exchange with the state at equal value. In this school, they can also do practical work among the masses and take part in the socialist education movement in the factories and rural villages. When the socialist education movement is concluded, they can always find work to do among the masses. They should also take every opportunity to participate in criticizing the bourgeoisie in the struggles of the Cultural Revolution. In this way, the army can study, engage in agriculture, run factories, and work among the masses, all at the same time. Of course these tasks should be properly coordinated, and there should be a distinction between primary

---

*"Pa wo-chün pan-ch'eng Mao Tse-tung ssu-hsiang ti ta-hsüeh-hsiao," Chieh-fang-chün pao, August 1, 1966; reprinted in Jen-min jih-pao [People's Daily], August 2, 1966. This was an editorial of the Liberation Army Daily commemorating the thirty-ninth anniversary of the founding of the PLA.

and secondary tasks. Each army unit can engage in only one
or two of the three tasks of agriculture, industry and work
among the masses, not in all three at the same time.

Chairman Mao said: "In this way, our army of several million will be able to play a very great role"

These directions from Chairman Mao are a great call to our army
at a time when our country's Great Proletarian Cultural Revolution
is developing with vigor and vitality, and the class struggle at home
and abroad is becoming more acute and complex. This clarion call
comes at a time when our army is carrying out the instructions of the
Military Affairs Commission of the Central Committee of the Chinese
Communist Party and of Comrade Lin Piao, a time when our army is
making a living study and living application of Chairman Mao's works,
energetically putting politics to the fore and making great progress
in all fields of work. It is a great call that requires our army to go
forward along the road toward becoming an extremely proletarian,
extremely militant army and reach an even higher stage.

Chairman Mao wants us to turn our army into a great school. The
army's main responsibility is that of a fighting force, but at the same
time it studies, engages in agriculture, runs factories, and does work
among the masses. It maintains and carries forward the fine traditions of our Party and our army, and it cultivates and trains millions
of successors to the proletarian revolutionary cause; thus our people's army can play an even greater role in the cause of socialist revolution and socialist construction. The army is a great school for
the study of Mao Tse-tung thought, for the implementation of Mao
Tse-tung thought, for the propagation of Mao Tse-tung thought,
and for the safeguarding of Mao Tse-tung thought.

It is already thirty-nine years since Chairman Mao himself
founded this army of ours. This army is a workers' and peasants' army under the absolute leadership of the Chinese Communist Party, built up according to the principles of Marxism-
Leninism. It is a completely new type of people's army, radically different from feudal-warlord and bourgeois armies.

At an early stage in the creation of our army, Chairman Mao
clearly pointed out that our army was certainly not exclusively
a fighting army, that it should also serve as an armed body for

carrying out the political tasks of the revolution. In the famous Decision of the Ku-t'ien Conference, Chairman Mao wrote: "The Red Army fights not merely in order to fight but also in order to conduct propaganda among the masses, organize them, arm them, and help them to establish revolutionary political power. Without these objectives, fighting loses its meaning, and the Red Army loses the reason for its existence."

Chairman Mao set for our army the three great tasks of fighting, work among the masses, and production. He pointed out that our army was always a fighting force, but at the same time it was a work force and a production force.

On the eve of nationwide victory, Chairman Mao said: "The army is a school," and "we must consider the field armies, with their 2.1 million men, as a gigantic school for cadres."

In the last few decades our army has worked precisely according to Chairman Mao's teachings.

The directions recently issued by Chairman Mao are the most recent summation of our army's experience in previous decades. In Chairman Mao's consistent concern with army-building, these directions represent new developments in his thought under new historical conditions. These directions are of great historic and strategic importance in that they enable our army to maintain forever its true colors as a people's army. They are of importance in that they enable our army to consolidate the dictatorship of the proletariat, to promote China's socialist revolution and socialist construction, strengthen national defense, bring into full play the mighty force of the people's war, and counter possible attacks by U.S. imperialism and its accomplices.

Chairman Mao's thought on army-building is the most thorough, correct, and comprehensive proletarian body of thought on the subject.

Chairman Mao's thought on army-building is diametrically opposed to the purely military viewpoint, which considers only military matters and entirely disregards politics, and which considers the army's task to be limited entirely to combat duties. Chairman Mao's thought on army-building is diametrically opposed to all bourgeois military ideas.

Throughout our army's thirty-nine year history, the struggle between Chairman Mao's thinking and line on army-building and bourgeois military ideas of various kinds has never ceased. This was true during the entire period of the democratic revolution, and it is equally true in the period of the socialist revolution.

In the sixteen years since the founding of the People's Republic of China, we have had three big struggles with representatives of the bourgeois military line who wormed their way into the Party and the army.

The first big struggle started when the War to Resist the U.S. and Aid Korea ended. Under the label of "regularization" and "modernization," a handful of representatives of the bourgeois military line [refers to P'eng Te-huai, Hsiao K'o, etc.], directly copying foreign practices, vainly attempted to deny our army's historical experience and fine tradition, and to lead our army onto the road followed by bourgeois armies. The bourgeois military dogmatism that they tried to implement was strongly resisted and opposed by the broad masses of cadres and soldiers in our army. Responding to Chairman Mao's call of "down with the slave mentality; let's bury dogmatism," the 1958 Enlarged Session of the Military Affairs Commission of the Central Committee of the Chinese Communist Party crushed their frantic attack and defended Chairman Mao's thinking and line on army-building.

The second big struggle took place at the same time as our Party's struggle against the right opportunist anti-Party clique in 1959. Taking advantage of the important posts they held in the army, the principal members of the clique [refers to P'eng Te-huai, Huang K'o-ch'eng, Hung Hsüeh-chih, etc.], later exposed at the Party's Lushan Conference, exerted great efforts in their attempt to do away with the Party's absolute leadership over the army, to abolish political work, to abolish the responsibility that the army has for taking part in socialist construction and doing mass work, and to abolish the local armed forces and the militia. In this way, the clique attemped to negate completely Chairman Mao's thought on the people's army and people's war. They vainly hoped to refashion our army in accordance with the bourgeois revisionist military line so that it would be an instrument to help them usurp leadership of the Party and the government, and to help them realize their personal ambitions. The Enlarged Session of the Military Affairs Commission held after the Party's Lushan Conference thoroughly settled accounts with them according to their crimes and dismissed them from office. This was a great victory for Mao Tse-tung thought.

Since he took charge of the work of the Military Affairs Commission of the Party Central Committee, Comrade Lin Piao has been most resolute and thorough in carrying out Chairman Mao's thinking and line regarding army-building. In 1960, under the concerned guidance of the Party's Central Committee and Chairman Mao, the Enlarged Session of the Military Affairs Commission, presided over by Comrade Lin Piao, further eradicated the influence of the bourgeois military line, corrected the political-work orientation, adopted a "decision on strengthening the army's political-ideological work," and continued and further developed the spirit of the Ku-t'ien Conference, thus becoming a new milestone on the road of our army's progress. In the last few years, under the leadership of the Military Affairs Commission of the Party Central Committee and Comrade Lin Piao, the whole army has raised high the great red banner of Mao Tse-tung thought, studied and applied Chairman Mao's works with full vigor, put politics to the fore, adhered firmly to the "four firsts," cultivated vigorously the "three-eight work style," given full scope to democracy in the three main fields of work,* launched the "four-good" companies movement, participated in the socialist education movement and the Great Proletarian Cultural Revolution, and shared and helped in socialist construction, so that a fine, flourishing situation has developed in building our army into a thoroughly

---

* Democracy in the three main fields of work refers to democracy in the political, economic, and military fields — Ying-mao Kau.

revolutionized army in all its fields of work.

The third big struggle took place not very long ago. In this struggle, we exposed representatives of the bourgeoisie who held important posts in the army and were important members of the counterrevolutionary anti-Party, antisocialist clique recently uncovered by our Party [refers to Lo Jui-ch'ing, etc.]. They had opposed the Party Central Committee and Mao Tsetung thought, had outwardly agreed with but inwardly opposed Comrade Lin Piao's directives on putting politics to the fore, had talked about putting politics in command but in practice had given first priority to military affairs, technique, and specialized work. They had waved the "red flag" to oppose the red flag, and vigorously spread eclecticism, i.e., opportunism, in a vain attempt to substitute a bourgeois military line for Chairman Mao's proletarian military line. Our Party's thorough exposure and denunciation of this handful of anti-Party careerists is a great new victory for Mao Tse-tung thought!

Since the founding of our country, these big struggles in the army have exposed the representatives of the bourgeoisie who opposed Chairman Mao's principle of building a powerful, revolutionary army of the proletariat, opposed the absolute leadership of the Party over the army, opposed political work, and opposed the mass line. They wanted only bourgeois regularization, not proletarian revolutionization. They threw away our army's glorious traditions, reduced its three great responsibilities to the single responsibility of combat training in peacetime and actual combat in war. In sum, everything they did was diametrically opposed to Chairman Mao's ideas on armybuilding and on turning the army into a great school. Their sinister aim was to turn our army into a bourgeois army serving a few careerists, one divorced from Mao Tse-Tung thought, from proletarian politics, from the masses, and from productive labor.

The struggle between two sets of ideas on army-building and between two different lines is a reflection within the army of the struggle between the proletariat and the bourgeoisie, between the socialist road and the capitalist road. As long as

there are still classes and class struggle, this struggle will
never end. Any class enemy, at home or abroad, who is vainly
hoping for our country to change its color must first try to
make our army change its color. The tiny handful of bourgeois
representatives who wormed their way into our army always
stepped forward and tried to stir up trouble whenever the class
struggle grew very intense. However, under the radiant light
of great Mao Tse-tung thought, the broad masses of cadres
and soldiers in our army, including some who were temporarily
misled, have invariably been able to detect their ugly faces,
expose them to the light of day, and frustrate their plots.

The few decades of our army's history have amply proved
that Chairman Mao's thinking and line on army-building are
indisputably true and are the vital roots of our army. At no
time and under no circumstances is it permissible to depart
in the slightest from the realm of Chairman Mao's thinking
and line on army-building.

We must enthusiastically answer the great call of Chairman
Mao, adopt and carry forward the fine traditions of our army,
and turn our army into a great school.

We will resolve to study politics, military affairs, and culture according to Chairman Mao's directions. We will participate actively in the socialist education movement and the Great
Proletarian Cultural Revolution. Everyone should take up Mao
Tse-tung thought, the sharpest of weapons, and use it to criticize the bourgeoisie. We should at all times hold ourselves in
readiness to crush any possible attack by U.S. imperialism
and its accomplices.

We will adhere resolutely to Chairman Mao's directions that
the army should simultaneously study, engage in agriculture,
run factories, and work among the masses. Everyone should
take part in productive labor and always maintain the essential
qualities of the working people. Everyone should work among
the masses, abiding by the three main rules of discipline and
the eight points for attention,* so that the army will always be

---

* The three main rules of discipline are (1) obey orders
in everything you do, (2) don't take a single needle or piece of
thread from the masses, (3) turn in everything captured. The

as one with the masses. Militia work should be done well, and the idea of the people's war should be carried to the masses of the people. We must enthusiastically share and help in socialist construction, actively help with local work, be modest in learning from the local areas, and strengthen the unity between the army and the local areas.

In order to manage this great school of the army successfully, the most important and fundamental thing is to study and apply Chairman Mao's works with full vigor. We must study them and put them into practice in the course of struggle. This great school must always raise high the great red banner of Mao Tse-tung thought and always put proletarian politics to the fore, using Mao Tse-tung thought as the guideline for all work and arming everyone with Mao Tse-tung thought!

This great school of ours is a great school of Mao Tse-tung thought!

We absolutely must manage this great school of Mao Tse-tung thought well!

Let us march valiantly forward under the great banner of Mao Tse-tung thought!

---

eight points for attention are (1) speak politely, (2) pay fairly for what you buy, (3) return everything you borrow, (4) pay for anything you damage, (5) don't hit or swear at people, (6) don't damage crops, (7) don't take liberties with women, (8) don't ill-treat captives — Ying-mao Kau.

II

The Political Work
of the PLA

4

HOLD HIGH THE GREAT RED FLAG OF MAO TSE-TUNG THOUGHT AND RESOLUTELY AND THOROUGHLY IMPLEMENT THE POLITICAL WORK REGULATIONS*

Liberation Army Daily

The Central Committee of the Chinese Communist Party promulgated the "Regulations Governing the Political Work of the Chinese People's Liberation Army" on March 27. This event was important in the history of our army-building. The promulgation of the political work regulations was of great and far-reaching significance in strengthening our army's political work, guaranteeing the Party's absolute leadership over the troops, preserving and developing the fine traditions of our Party and army, and turning our army into a revolutionary force of a markedly proletarian and militant nature, so as to perform successfully the great tasks of defending our motherland, the East, and world peace.

The political work regulations consist of nineteen regulations, which include the general principles and regulations concerning the General Political Department, Party committees, and political commissars. The regulations promulgated at this time were drawn up on the basis of the "Draft Regulations Gov-

---

*"Kao-chü Mao Tse-tung ssu-hsiang ti wei-ta hung-ch'i chien-chüeh kuan-ts'e chih-hsing cheng-chih kung-tso t'iao-li," Chieh-fang-chün pao editorial, May 8, 1963; reprinted in Jen-min jih-pao [People's Daily], May 10, 1963.

erning Political Work in the Chinese People's Liberation Army,"
issued by the Central Committee of the Chinese Communist
Party and its Military Affairs Commission in 1954. Since the
founding of the Chinese People's Liberation Army, the Party
and Chairman Mao have established revolutionary political
work in the military units. The Decision of the Ku-t'ien Conference,
drafted by Chairman Mao himself, laid the foundation for our
army's political work. During the various periods in the development of our army, regulations governing political work were
issued. During the past ten years, since the promulgation of
the draft political work regulations in 1954, there have been
great changes in the international and domestic situation and
new developments in our army-building and political work.
The political work regulations promulgated at this time are
based on relevant directives from the Party Central Committee
and Chairman Mao issued during that period, on the Party Constitution adopted by the Eighth National Party Congress, on the
resolution on the strengthening of political and ideological work
in the armed forces adopted by an enlarged meeting of the Military Affairs Commission, and on new experiences gained in
our army-building and political work. The regulations were
endorsed by the All-Army Political Work Conference in February 1963, after having been extensively discussed in the armed
forces, and were then submitted to the Central Committee of
the Chinese Communist Party for approval and official promulgation. The regulations explicitly embody Mao Tse-tung thought,
sum up the rich experience gained from the political work in
the armed forces over the past several decades, explain the
important principles of political work in the armed forces, and
preserve and develop the fine traditions of the People's Liberation Army. They therefore constitute our army's basic rules
for political work and the guidepost for action.

What, then, are the basic spirit and the main content of the
regulations governing political work?

First, the political work regulations, from beginning to end,
implement Mao Tse-tung thought and clearly point out that his
thought is the guide to the Chinese people's revolution and so-

cialist construction and also the guide to our army-building
and political work.

Comrade Mao Tse-tung is a great contemporary Marxist-
Leninist. In an era when imperialism is heading toward collapse and socialism is moving toward victory, Mao Tse-tung
thought is Marxism-Leninism creatively developed through the
application of its universal truth to the concrete practice of
the Chinese revolution and the collective struggle waged by the
Party and the people. His thought is a strong ideological weapon against imperialism, modern revisionism, and dogmatism.
The Marxist-Leninist political and military lines which were
instituted by the Party and Chairman Mao are the fundamental
guarantee for the building of our army and for achieving all
victories. Under the leadership of the Party and Chairman Mao,
and together with the people of the whole country, our army
went through a protracted and arduous struggle, completely
overthrew the reactionary rule of imperialism, feudalism, and
bureaucratic capitalism in China, and fulfilled its historic role
in the people's democratic revolution. As a result of the wisdom and correct strategic guidance of the Party and Chairman
Mao, the Chinese people's volunteers won a great victory in
the struggle to "resist America and aid Korea." In the more
than ten years since the founding of the People's Republic, just
as in the postwar years [pre-1949], whenever we confronted
crucial problems in the building of national defense and in military struggles, we always received the correct direction from
the Party and Chairman Mao and arrived at successful solutions. More than thirty years of our army's history prove that
as long as we carry out our work in line with Mao Tse-tung
thought, at all times and in all circumstances, we will be correctly guided and will be able to win victory. However, if we
commit even a slight deviation from his thought, we will lose
our bearings and meet with defeat. Today we face a situation
in which the class struggle in the international sphere is raging,
while domestically the class struggle is protracted and complicated. It rises and ebbs and sometimes becomes very acute at
home. Under these circumstances, our army must hold even

higher the great red flag of Mao Tse-tung thought so that we can successfully carry out the great historic tasks of safeguarding our country's sovereignty, territorial integrity, and security, of liberating Taiwan, and of defending peace in the East and the rest of the world. As pointed out in the political work regulations, Mao Tse-tung thought "has not only provided the basic guarantee for our army's victories attained in the past but also serves as a guideline that must be followed in all its future activities."

As early as the army's inception, Chairman Mao clearly set forth the nature of the army and its tasks, and the fundamental principles for army-building and for the army's political work. In the various subsequent stages of building and developing the army, he also gave many extremely important instructions. Chairman Mao pointed out that our army was an army of workers and peasants led by the Chinese Communist Party. It was a new type of people's army. He said: "Our army is not and cannot be an army of any other kind; it must be an instrument subordinate to the ideological leadership of the proletariat and in the service of the struggle of the people and the building of revolutionary base areas"; "It is an armed group for carrying out revolutionary political tasks." He also pointed out: "Our principle is that the Party commands the gun, and the gun must never be allowed to command the Party"; "The sole purpose of this army is to stand firmly with the Chinese people and to serve them wholeheartedly." Chairman Mao stipulated that our army must shoulder the three-in-one task of fighting, doing mass work, and raising funds (which later evolved into production work). He personally built up the system of revolutionary political work for our army and always taught us that political work is the lifeline of a revolutionary army which must be strengthened in every possible way. He established the three principles for the political work of our army: the principle of unity between officers and soldiers, the principle of unity between the army and the people, and the principle of disintegrating enemy forces. He also formulated a series of systems, the content, and the methods for political work. The People's Lib-

eration Army, which was established under the guiding light of
Mao Tse-tung thought, has become the first people's army — a
completely new form — to emerge in the history of our country.
The political work of this revolutionary army as developed under the guidance of Mao Tse-tung thought has clearly marked
the distinction between our army and all the old-style armies.
The political work regulations relating to our army's nature
and tasks, to the Party's leadership over the army, to the tasks,
content, and style of political work, and to the establishment
and functioning of Party committees, political commissars, political organs, and political workers at various levels were all
formulated on the basis of the great Mao Tse-tung thought, [par-
ticularly] his thought on people's war and the people's army.

No matter how many sets of regulations and articles there
are in the political work regulations, their soul and kernel are
Mao Tse-tung thought. Mao Tse-tung thought runs through them
like a red thread. Once we hold this red thread firmly in our
hands, we will be able to grasp the spirit and true nature of
these regulations. Therefore we must learn well Mao Tse-tung
thought: his theories pertaining to class, class struggle, proletarian revolution, and proletarian dictatorship; his works
"On Practice," "On Contradictions," and "On the Correct Handling of Contradictions Among the People"; his comments on
"the East wind prevailing over the West wind" and on the
general line of foreign policy; his theory pertaining to "all imperialists and reactionaries being paper tigers"; his theory of
"despising the enemy strategically and taking full account of
him tactically"; his theory pertaining to war, peace, and "the
decisive factor for a victory in war being not material but men";
his theory and policy concerning the General Line for socialist
construction, the Great Leap Forward, and the people's communes; his comments on the relationship between economic
construction and the building of national defense; his works on
the concept of people's war and the principle of the strategy
and tactics of revolutionary war; his comments on "politics
being the commander and the soul," and on the relationship between "red and expert"; his works on the building of the Party

and the principle of democratic centralism; his works elaborating on the mass line and work style of the Party; on the goal and principle of building the people's army; on the absolute leadership of the Party over the army; on the system of Party committees, political commissars, and political work; on the fundamental principle of unity between officers and soldiers, unity between the army and the people, and the disintegration of enemy forces; on the democratic system and fighting style of the army; on the militia and the concept of "everyone a soldier."

After having learned all this well, we will be able to let Mao Tse-tung thought take command of all our undertakings and to carry out our assignments in conformity with Chairman Mao's instructions. Only by so doing can we correctly implement the regulations governing political work.

Second, the political work regulations expound the principle of the Party's absolute leadership over the army, and they stipulate that the army must implement the systems of Party committees, political commissars, and political work.

Chairman Mao pointed out long ago that in order to realize the Party's absolute leadership over the army, to ensure the thorough implementation of Party lines, principles, and policies in the army, and to preserve and develop the tradition of the people's army, it was essential to set up Party committees in the army at all levels, to organize Party branches in the companies, to establish a system of political commissars in all military units, and to create a system of political work in the army. As Chairman Mao stated, "These systems have never been instituted in the history of China. The introduction of these systems will give our army a new outlook." These systems were established and consolidated in the course of the protracted armed revolutionary struggle of the people and the struggle against various forms of bourgeois military ideology. This has laid the foundation organizationally for realizing the Party's absolute leadership over the army.

Party committees established by the Party at all levels of the army are the nucleus of the unified leadership and maintain the unity of the armed forces. The system of division of work and responsibility among the leading officers under the unified and collective leadership of the Party committees is the fundamental system ensuring the Party's leadership over the army. This system is built according to the principle of democratic centralism. It is a concrete application to army units of the provision of the Party Constitution that "all Party organizations operate on the principle of combining collective leadership with individual responsibility." The system has correctly solved the relationship between Party committees and military commanders and has at the same time organically linked them together. Except under emergency conditions that require prompt action by leading officers, all important problems in army units must be fully discussed at Party committee meetings, and all decisions must be made in accordance with the principle of democratic centralism. The military commander is responsible for the implementation of military decisions, and the political commissar is responsible for carrying out decisions related to political work. Only in this manner can we ensure a high degree of centralization and unification of the army under the unified collective leadership of the Party, bring collective wisdom into full play, prevent subjectivism and one-sidedness — which may arise from an individual's making decisions on important questions — and achieve the creation of a correct leadership. On the other hand, the army is a highly centralized organization with combat duties. The responsibility for carrying out decisions made by Party committee meetings on important questions in the army must be delegated to the commanders and political commissars. Other cadres must work under their guidance. Therefore the military commanders must, with a sense of responsibility to the Party, report in good time to the Party committees important situations and problems within their jurisdiction and request instructions. They must set personal examples for carrying out decisions made by the Party committees and actively take the initiative in discharging their duties.

The regulations stipulate that both political commissars and military commanders are leading officers of army units and are jointly responsible for the work of their army units. Generally, the political commissars are in charge of the daily work of the Party committees, and their primary duty is to lead Party work and political work in the armed forces. They must devote their efforts chiefly to matters of principle and policy and to political and ideological work in order to guarantee that the Party's line and policies, and the state's laws and decrees, will be thoroughly carried out in the army, and that the army units resolutely implement orders and directives from higher levels and that they fulfill the tasks of fighting, training, and other responsibilities. After adopting the system of making both the political commissars and military commanders leading officers, we can effectively ensure the Party's leadership over the army, strengthen the army's political and ideological work, and guard against the tendencies toward a purely military viewpoint and warlordism.

Following the establishment of the system of Party committees and political commissars, an effective system of political work must also be built. Political work is Party work, and political work organs are the Party's work organs. The regulations stipulate that political work organs should be set up in army units from the general headquarters down to the regimental level. The political work organs are responsible for the Party's ideological and organizational work and for organizing and implementing political work in the army. [They carry out their work] under the leadership of the political work organs at higher levels and the Party committees and political commissars at the same level. All this has made it even more clear that the function of political organs is to organize and carry out Party work and political work, and not to deal with general administrative work. In addition to the assignment of political commissars at the regimental level and above, political instructors and political supervisors are assigned at the battalion and company levels. They are political work personnel assigned by political work organs to battalions and companies to carry out Party and political work under the leadership

of political work organs and leaders at higher levels, and under
Party committees at the same level. This organization thus
forms a complete network for directing and implementing political work from the highest to the lowest level [of army units].
By instituting the system of Party committees, political commissars, and political work, the whole army will be placed under the absolute leadership of the Party. Politically, ideologically, and organizationally, it guarantees that our army will
advance victoriously according to the directives of the Party
and Chairman Mao.

Third, the regulations elaborate the direction of the army's
political work and set forth its fundamental tasks and main
content.

Proceeding from the concept of people's war and a people's
army, Chairman Mao has always given top priority to work related to men and to that of a political and ideological nature.
He said: "Weapons are an important factor in war, but not the
decisive factor. It is men, not materials, that are decisive."
He also said that political work is an important factor in our
army's effort to defeat the enemy because "soldiers are the
foundation of an army; unless they are imbued with a progressive political spirit, and unless such a spirit is cultivated
through progressive political work, it will be impossible to
achieve genuine unity between officers and men, impossible to
fully arouse their enthusiasm for the War of Resistance [Against
Japan], and impossible to provide a sound basis for the most
effective use of all our technical equipment and tactics." Chairman Mao instructed us: "To master ideological education is
the major link in uniting the whole Party to carry out great political struggle. If we fail to come to grips with this task, it
will be impossible to fulfill any of the political tasks of the Party." He also stressed that ideological education "must not be
limited solely to words and phrases in books." Creatively applying Mao Tse-tung thought, Marshal Lin Piao pointed out that
the factor of political ideology was the foremost factor determining the fighting strength of our army. He elaborated, on the
basis of instructions of the Party and Chairman Mao, the four

relationships in the sphere of political work. In line with this concept, the political work regulations explicitly point out that first place must be given to the human factor in handling the relationship between weapons and men, to political work in handling the relationship between political and other work, to ideological work in relation to other aspects of political work, and to living ideas in ideological work. This "four-first" principle is the direction for both the political work and the building of our army. We should firmly head in this direction now and in the future, as we did in the past.

The regulations have stipulated the fundamental tasks of our army's political work according to the correct direction and principles of political work established by Chairman Mao. These are to educate the armed forces in Marxism-Leninism-Mao Tse-tung thought; to raise the proletarian consciousness of all armymen and to thoroughly carry out the Party's program, lines, and policies and the state's laws and decrees; to consolidate the Party's absolute leadership over the army; to cultivate the "three-eight work style"; to preserve a high degree of centralization, unification, and strict discipline in the army; to strengthen internal and external unity — internally strengthening the unity between the officers and men, between the higher and lower levels, between military, political, and other work, and between various army units, and externally strengthening the unity between the army and the people, between the army and local organizations, and between our army and the friendly troops — to carry out the work of destroying enemy forces; so as to consolidate and raise the fighting strength of our army, maintain its unity, and defeat the enemy.

The regulations also lay down the major contents of political work on the basis of the above-mentioned fundamental tasks. Our army's political work must be effectively carried out in accordance with the regulations. In dealing with the work of political ideology, the most important and frequent job is to get a firm grip on living ideas, to arm the cadres and soldiers ideologically with Mao Tse-tung thought, to cultivate proletarian ideology and liquidate bourgeois ideology, and to constantly consolidate and extend the ideological position of the proletariat. The regulations also stipulate that it is necessary to creatively study and apply the works of Chairman Mao; to transmit resolutions and directives of the Party; to have a firm grip on the ideological trends among army units; to strengthen education in living ideas; to commend good people and good deeds; to overcome unhealthy trends; to prevent the corrosive influence of modern revisionist and bourgeois ideology; to make all armymen loyal to the motherland, the people, and the cause of the Party; to pay attention to the major events of the state, the international communist movement, the liberation movement of the oppressed nations, and the revolutionary struggle of the people of the world; to hate and despise imperialism and all reactionaries; to develop patriotism, internationalism, and revolutionary heroism; to strengthen fighting spirit and maintain combat readiness at all times. In taking a firm grip on living ideas, efforts should be made to discover in time and to fully understand all existing ideological problems among army units so that they can be solved correctly. When the work of political ideology is properly carried out, the result will be the emergence of thousands of "four-good" companies like the "Good Eighth Company" [on Nanking Road in Shanghai] and an even larger number of "five-good" combatants like Lei Feng, capable of standing up to the test of any difficult circumstance and any political storm, overcoming and fully developing the immense power of a "spiritual atom bomb."

Fourth, the regulations stipulate that our army's political work should develop the work style of the Party and thoroughly carry out the mass line.

The work style of the Party is a style that links theory with practice, a style that keeps close ties with the masses, and a style that practices self-criticism. This is the work style of our Party, formed in the course of protracted revolutionary struggle under the leadership of Chairman Mao, and it is an important component of Mao Tse-tung thought. This style of work, as Chairman Mao put it, is a conspicuous characteristic of the Marxist-Leninist party that distinguishes it from all other political parties. Since the army's political work is the Party work in the army, we should naturally take this work style of the Party as our own work style. And, of course, we must not permit ourselves to deviate for a single moment from the work style of the Party in carrying out our work.

Chairman Mao has taught us that in all our work it is necessary to carry out the principles of "from the masses, to the masses," and "summing up the ideas, and carrying them out with perseverence." We should also employ the methods of linking the leading group with the broad masses, adopt the attitude of seeking truth from facts, and develop the habit of investigation and research. The reason our army has made tremendous achievements in its political work is because we have followed the instructions of Chairman Mao. In the work of recent years we have gained remarkable results in further insisting on dealing with facts, on keeping close ties with the masses and the company-level units, and on adopting concrete measures. The regulations point out that in strengthening the political work of our army it is extremely important to follow persistently the work style and work method outlined by Chairman Mao.

Marshal Lin Piao once said: "Our political work is the mass work of the Communist Party in the army. In the same manner that local governments mobilize the masses, we organize the masses who carry weapons and are clad in uniforms." Mass work naturally depends on the broad masses to carry it out. For this, the regulations emphatically point out, political work must develop democracy under centralized leadership and must thoroughly enforce the mass line. Political work must rely on Party organizations at all levels and on cadres and Party members to carry out the mobilization of the masses so that everyone may supervise and give his views and encourage and help the other. In other words, political work is to be carried out not only by political cadres but also by military cadres, administrative cadres, and technical cadres; not only by cadres but also by soldiers; not only by a few progressive elements but also by the broad masses. All of us should confront problems, think about problems, discuss problems, and solve problems.

Only in this way can political work be carried out universally, in good time, and effectively.

The regulations also stipulate that, while handling the internal relationships and solving ideological problems among the masses, it is necessary to follow persistently Chairman Mao's teachings, such as the method of "unity-criticism-unity" and the principle of combining strict demands with patient persuasion. Only in this way can there be developed correctly in our army the practice of criticism and self-criticism aimed at raising the level of consciousness, distinguishing right from wrong, strengthening unity, and consolidating discipline.

In order to carry out thoroughly the work style of the Party, execute the mass line, and do well in political work, all political cadres must set an example with their own conduct. The regulations provide that they must endeavor to study Marxism-Leninism and Chairman Mao's writings, resolutely enforce Party lines and policies, solidify their stand, uphold principles, fight valiantly, work energetically, cope with hardship, lead a simple life, maintain ties with the masses, and play an exemplary role in the implementation of various tasks. In education personal example is more important than words. The exemplary role of cadres is like silent command. This is an important guarantee in the implementation of political work and all other work.

The promulgation of the political work regulations will undoubtedly promote a further development and advancement of our political work and army-building. At present, the great task confronting all Party committees, political organizations, political workers, and the entire body of cadres is to make an all-out effort to put the provisions of the regulations into practice. Consequently, this requires that we first study the regulations in earnest. The study of the regulations is the study of Mao Tse-tung thought, as well as the study of the fine traditions of the army's political work. Not only leading cadres but also basic-level cadres must study; and not only cadres but also the broad masses of Party members, Youth League members, and combatants must study. [We must] study not only now but continue to do so for generations to come. We should realize that each provision of the regulations must be thoroughly carried out, and that no violation will be tolerated. However, our regulations are flexible, and not rigid. In the course of carrying out the regulations, it is necessary to take actual conditions into consideration, to apply creatively the principle embodied in the regulations according to varied conditions, and to enrich the regulations with new experience, so as to improve and develop them constantly. Let us hold still higher the great red flag of Mao Tse-tung thought. We must carry out the political work regulations thoroughly through the movement of the "four-good" company and the implementation of various military tasks. We must endeavor to build our army into an excellent, modernized revolutionary army by persisting in the principle of "four firsts" and by strengthening its political and ideological work.

5

THE REVOLUTIONARY SIGNIFICANCE
OF CADRES WORKING AS SOLDIERS
IN THE ARMED FORCES*

August 1 Magazine

Equality Between Officers and Men
Is a Persistent Tradition of Our Army

The relationship between officers and men in the Chinese
People's Liberation Army is a relationship of equality among
ordinary workers. This sort of equality is the embodiment of
the communist spirit. It is a glorious tradition long held by
the Chinese People's Liberation Army. Early in the founding
of the Chinese People's Liberation Army, Chairman Mao established the unity of officers and men as one of the principles
of PLA military development. For several decades the Chinese
People's Liberation Army has consistently followed Chairman
Mao's instructions, taking the principle of unity of officers and
men and the idea of equality between officers and men, and
making them the basic principles in managing relationships
within the army. Under the guidance of these principles, army
officers are leaders, but they also live among the masses of
soldiers. Their appearance is that of an ordinary soldier, and
they are under the surveillance of the masses. Soldiers are

---

*"Pu-tui kan-pu tang-ping ti ke-ming i-i," Pa-i tsa-chih,
No. 3 [n.d.]; reprinted in Jen-min jih-pao [People's Daily],
November 8, 1959.

followers, but they also have the right to take part in the management of their companies. Soldiers and officers are politically equal. This kind of equality is an extremely important
factor in guaranteeing that our army will defeat even those enemies that are much more powerful than we are.

Regularization Has Influenced the Equality
of Officers and Men

Throughout its history, the People's Liberation Army has
certainly not been without conflict regarding whether to support
the principle of unity of officers and men. In the last few years,
under the slogan of "regularization," the idea of a set of special
bourgeois privileges appeared as an adverse current in the army. Some people called our fine tradition of unity of officers
and men and equality of officers and men a "country hick work
style," a "guerrilla warfare style," "inappropriate to the requirements of regularization," etc., while opposing our fine
tradition. As a result, the original cohesion of officers and
men and the fine tradition of living together as equals were
weakened. Many officers began to put on superior airs and cut
down on their contact with the soldiers. The relations between
officers and men had become "regularized." Emotionally they
kept their distance. What did all this prove? It proved and demonstrated that the so-called "regularization" of relations between officers and men was precisely the "bureaucratization"
that we so resolutely opposed. The so-called "country-hick work
style" and "guerrilla warfare style" are precise manifestations
of the Marxist work style. They are in fact the communist
spirit that we want to bring into full play.

The Key to Equality Between Officers and Men
Is to Have Cadres Work as Soldiers

In establishing the relationship of equality between officers
and men, the most important point was to destroy the idea of
bourgeois privileges in the cadres' ideology and to set up the

idea of communist equality in its stead, thoroughly getting rid of all bureaucratic airs. There were some cadres who, having been influenced by the idea of special privileges for the exploiting class, saw the relationship between officers and men as one in which "I command you and you obey me." They took the specific power to implement work given by the people and made it into a power for personal privileges, etc. These points of view have nothing in common with the Marxist outlook. We believe that officers and men alike are members of a revolutionary army. Both officers and men are ordinary workers, and their jobs and responsibilities are differentiated only insofar as there is a division of labor necessary for the overall work of the revolution. Since officers are charged with the task of leadership, the functions and powers of the work of leadership often can easily conceal an officer's original status as an ordinary worker. If we do not see the substance underneath this sort of superficial appearance, there is the danger that the officer will make himself stand out from the masses as someone special, setting himself apart from the masses. We advocate that cadres go down to the companies and work as soldiers — that cadres go down to the companies, live the life of a soldier, and be subordinate to squad and platoon leaders. This will enable them to understand keenly the thoughts and feelings of the soldiers, and make them learn from experience about life in the companies. This is indispensable in getting rid of bureaucratic airs among the cadres, building a really equal relationship between officers and men, and fostering communist virtues among the cadres.

Promote the Growth of the Idea of Equality Among the Soldiers

The phenomenon of cadres going down to the companies to work as soldiers is not only changing the spiritual appearance of the cadres themselves but is also promoting the growth of the idea of communist equality among the soldiers. Ideas of inequality exist not only among some cadres but also in the

minds of some soldiers. There are some soldiers who are generally of the opinion that officers still should be somewhat special in comparison with soldiers, and that officers cannot be
the same as soldiers. The reason that this idea has arisen
stems from three important factors: (1) the influence of the
old concept of bourgeois legal rights, (2) the "bureaucratic
airs" of a group of cadres, and (3) the fact that the soldiers
have comparatively little contact with cadres and therefore
do not know enough about them. The [eradication of the] influence of this sort of old concept of legal rights in the soldiers'
minds depends, on the one hand, on education to transform all
their views of inequality. Even more importantly, it depends
on the cadres dropping their airs, working among them as soldiers, at every point merging with them, and using facts to influence them so that they will learn that there are no differences between cadres and soldiers. In that way all their views
of inequality regarding officers will be transformed. The experience of Commander Yang Te-chih's going down to the
companies to work as a soldier proves this point. Before the
soldiers had seen Commander Yang they still had the idea in
their heads that a high-level commander was certainly different from a soldier. However, when Commander Yang had gone
down to the company to work as a soldier, he was just like an
ordinary soldier in every way, eating with the soldiers, living
with them, taking part in drills with them, and laboring with
them. He rushed to do fatigue duty and was a model soldier in
adhering to all rules and regimes of daily life. In this way, in
their contact with Commander Yang, the soldiers did not feel
at all that there was any distance between them. It was entirely
an equal relationship among comrades-at-arms. After this
sort of spirit of equality was established in the minds of the
soldiers, they could return with this spirit and demand that
cadres live together with them as equals. This situation has
already appeared in the army. The soldiers say to some cadres
who have bureaucratic airs: "The chief commanders can all
live with us as equals, why can't you?" This then puts pressure on those cadres. This sort of pressure will be of great

help in overcoming the "bureaucratic airs" of cadres.

Prepare Conditions for the Transition to Communism

Cadres going down to the companies to work as soldiers has an even more profound meaning. It serves to prepare conditions for the transition to communism. At present our whole country is in the midst of a great era in which a single day is equal to twenty years. Following the tremendous pace of the Great Leap Forward in agriculture and industry, and following the powerful development of the people's commune movement throughout the country, we are faced with an extremely urgent problem — to speed up the building of socialism and to prepare conditions for communism. As for conditions within our army itself, it has become a crucial matter to lessen, in a preliminary way, the extent to which the difference between brain work and manual work is a reflection of a difference between officers and soldiers. In this way we can raise communist consciousness to a great height and bring forth a communist equal relationship between officers and men, built on an even higher foundation. Cadres going down to the companies to work as soldiers is one of the steps to take in order to lessen this sort of difference between manual work and brain work.

The movement of cadres going down to the companies to work as soldiers has now turned into a flaming tide sweeping through the entire army. We fully believe that if we continue to carry through this revolutionary measure our glorious tradition of equality between officers and men will undoubtedly flourish greatly on a new foundation, making our army-building develop with extraordinary brilliance.

(When the article was reprinted by this paper, there were some alterations, and the title was revised.)

6

IMPORTANT MEASURE TO PROMOTE
THE REVOLUTIONIZATION OF OUR ARMY*

Liberation Army Daily

The Standing Committee of the National People's Congress
has decided to abolish the system of military ranks in our army. Chairman Liu Shao-ch'i has issued an order promulgating
this decision. The State Council has, in accordance with the decision of the Standing Committee of the National People's Congress and the order of Chairman Liu Shao-ch'i, decided that
after the abolition of the system of military ranks all members
of the army, the navy, the air force, and the public security
forces under the Chinese People's Liberation Army shall uniformly wear a red-star hat insignia and a red collar badge.
This is an important measure for the promotion of the revolutionization of our army. It fully conforms to our army's revolutionary spirit and glorious tradition and is an expression of
the desires and demands of the broad masses of cadres and
fighters. All the commanders and fighters of the Chinese People's Liberation Army give this decision their enthusiastic support.

Our army is a people's army founded and led by the Chinese
Communist Party and Chairman Mao. The unity between officers

---

*"Ch'u-chin wo-chün keng-chia ke-ming-hua ti chung-ta
ts'o-shih," Chieh-fang-chün pao editorial, May 25, 1965; reprinted in Jen-min jih-pao [People's Daily], May 26, 1965.

and soldiers, between higher and lower levels, and between the army and the people is a fine tradition inherent in our army. Our cadres and fighters are intimate comrades-in-arms and class brothers. Our army and the people are bonded by flesh and blood and are as closely related as fish and water. Our army had no military ranks during the protracted revolutionary wars of the past. The rank system came into effect from 1955 onwards, after victory throughout the country. Ten years of practice has proved that this system of military ranks is not compatible with our army's glorious tradition; nor is it in line with the close relations between officers and soldiers, between higher and lower levels, and between the army and the people. The primary tasks in the building of our army are to take Mao Tse-tung thought as the guide, to strengthen political and ideological work, to raise class consciousness among the commanders and fighters, to develop a good style of work, to enhance the military quality of the armed forces, and to make our army still more proletarian and militant. Therefore the abolition of the military-rank system is completely correct and necessary. It enhances the unity between officers and soldiers, between higher and lower levels, and between the army and the people, and it encourages the further development of the glorious tradition of our army.

The abolition of the system of military ranks will further revolutionize the ideology of commanders and fighters. Chairman Mao said: "These troops of ours are wholly dedicated to work for the liberation of the people and the interests of the people." Our cadres and fighters are all servants of the people. Their devotion to revolution is neither for fame nor for personal interest, but for rendering wholehearted service to the people. The abolition of the explicit differentials of rank serves to remove the conditions that foster the ideas of rank, fame, and personal interest; helps the people to regard themselves more consciously as ordinary soldiers and ordinary workers and to reform themselves ideologically; further strengthens the ideology of serving the people wholeheartedly.

Our army is a highly centralized and unified fighting collectivity which maintains a strict organizational discipline. The centralized unity and organizational discipline are based on the high level of political consciousness among cadres and fighters. Chairman Mao said: "This army is powerful because all its members . . . have joined together to fight for the interests of the broad masses and the whole nation." The lower levels obey the higher levels, and the fighters respect the cadres. This phenomenon originates from the conscientious conduct of every army man as required by revolution, and does not depend on the function of military ranks or grades. Only the people's fighters with a high level of political consciousness can obey commands and follow instructions in all their actions. In peacetime these fighters do their jobs well and perform their tasks voluntarily and conscientiously. In wartime they throw themselves against the enemy lines, attacking the enemy enthusiastically.

In decades past we had no military ranks, yet we defeated strong enemies both at home and abroad just the same. In the War to Resist America and Aid Korea, the Chinese people's volunteers had no military ranks either, yet, displaying a spirit of patriotism and internationalism and fighting shoulder to shoulder in excellent consort with the Korean People's Army, they defeated the United States imperialists and achieved a great victory. This outcome demonstrates that the absence of military ranks adversely affects neither leadership in war nor joint operation and unified command with the armies of fraternal countries.

After the abolition of military ranks, every member of the army, the navy, the air force, and the public security forces, under the Chinese People's Liberation Army, will wear on his hat a red star insignia and on his collar a red badge. The new hat insignia and collar badge are dignified and simple, and show the brilliant redness of revolution. The red star on the hat symbolizes the leadership of the Party and Chairman Mao, and the red revolutionary flag on the collar symbolizes the proletarian and very militant nature of our army. They thus provide a very striking and vivid expression of the revolutionary character and glorious tradition of our army.

The abolition of military ranks is a measure that will develop further our army's glorious tradition and promote the revolutionization of the army. We ought to have a profound understanding of the far-reaching significance of this measure, and resolutely strengthen our army in accordance with Chairman Mao's principles on the building of a people's army. The cadres should cherish the fighters more, and the fighters should respect the cadres more; superiors should be more concerned for their inferiors, and inferiors should be more obedient to their superiors. Both unity and discipline should be further strengthened to create a vigorous and lively political climate in which both centralism and democracy, discipline and freedom, unity of will and personal ease of mind can prevail. Let us hold still higher the great red flag of Mao Tse-tung thought and, under the wise leadership of our great Party and our great leader, Chairman Mao, develop further the revolutionary spirit and glorious tradition of our great people's army, and march forward bravely on the road of proletarianization and "combativization."

7

LEARN BETTER FROM THE LOCAL GOVERNMENT
AND THE MASSES AND PROMOTE STILL CLOSER
RELATIONS BETWEEN THE MILITARY AND THE
GOVERNMENT AND THE ARMY AND THE PEOPLE*

People's Daily

On December 23, the General Political Department of the
Chinese People's Liberation Army issued a bulletin requesting
the whole army, during the period from the New Year to the
Spring Festival, 1964, to carry out extensive "support-the-
government and cherish-the-people" activities, to learn more
successfully from local government and the masses, and to
promote still closer relations between the military and the
government and between the army and the people.

The bulletin says: Regular activities of "supporting the government and cherishing the people," of actively participating
in socialist construction, of seriously learning from the local
governments and from the masses, and of promoting still closer
relations between the military and the government and between
the army and the people are all excellent traditions of our army, as well as an important aspect of the army's political and
ideological work. In the past year, through studying Chairman
Mao's writings, through conducting education in socialism and

---

*"Keng-hao ti hsiang ti-fang ho ch'ün-chung hsüeh-hsi chin-
i-pu mi-ch'ieh chün-cheng chün-min kuan-hsi," Jen-min jih-
pao, December 25, 1963. This report was a news release of
the New China News Agency, December 24, 1963.

learning from Lei Feng and the Good Eighth Company, and through the practice of participating in socialist construction, struggle against drought and flood, and fighting against enemies in the coastal and border defense areas, the broad masses of commanders throughout the army have universally heightened their class consciousness and their awareness of policy and discipline. There has been continual evidence of good people and of good deeds showing respect for the government, love for the people, and willingness to sacrifice oneself for others and to help others. The tradition of supporting the government and cherishing the people has developed greatly. We should realize that the accomplishments of our army in its various tasks are inseparable from the concern, support, and help given by the local Party and government leadership organs and the masses throughout the country. In order to unite with the people of the whole country in attaining new victories in socialist construction and new achievements in building the army, we must further develop the tradition of supporting the government and cherishing the people, and learn more successfully from the local governments and the masses. We must try to do a better job of supporting the government and cherishing the people, and promote still closer relations between the military and the government and between the army and the people.

The bulletin requests the whole army to achieve the following tasks during the period from the New Year to the Spring Festival, 1964: (1) By paying visits to communes and factories and by inviting local comrades to make reports, the army should be modest in learning from local Party and government leadership organs, from local cadres, and from the masses. (2) The army should propagate the Party's various policies extensively among the local masses. (3) The army should carry out extensive activities involving good deeds for the people. It should actively support the people's communes with manpower and technical forces, and help in the construction of water conservancy projects, in spring plowing, winter irrigation, and manure accumulation, in overhauling agricultural machines and farm tools, and in making other preparations for agricultural production so that they can lay the foundation for reaping a bumper harvest in agriculture next year. (4) The army should celebrate the New Year and the Spring Festival together with the local Party and government organs and the masses, sending their festival congratulations and greetings. (5) The army must conduct intensive education in "supporting the government and cherishing the people" throughout its ranks, as well as education in the "three main rules of discipline" and "eight points for attention." There should be a general investigation of the army's execution of the Party's policies and decrees and the observance of discipline toward the masses.

8

ARMYMEN HELP CIVILIANS STUDY
MAO TSE-TUNG'S WRITINGS*

New China News Agency

The commanders and fighters of the Chinese People's Liberation Army, themselves fine students of Mao Tse-tung's writings, are helping civilians in their studies so as to give maximum publicity to Mao Tse-tung's thought.

In this way they are maintaining the fine tradition of the army, which has always been both a fighting force and a working force at one and the same time.

The armymen have deep, infinite love for and confidence in the Communist Party and Chairman Mao Tse-tung. They regard the spreading of Mao Tse-tung's ideas as their binding duty and the most fundamental task in carrying out work among the masses of the people. They say that the more the people are in command of Mao Tse-tung's thought, which is the supreme instruction for all work, the stronger will the revolutionary forces become.

In the course of a long-distance march, a company under the Peking Military Command passed through 32 hsien towns and more than 300 villages and hamlets. During the march, the commanders and fighters of the company gave priority to spreading Mao Tse-tung's ideas among the people. In any village where they stopped, they told the peasants about their own

---

*This text is based on the English-language release of the New China News Agency, Peking, August 1, 1966; minor editorial revisions have been made.

experience in studying and applying Mao Tse-tung's writings. The company's medical corpsmen carried out their propaganda work as they treated the villagers. They discussed with their patients the question of how to act in accordance with the ideas expressed by Chairman Mao, and with the medicine they prescribed they gave away leaflets on which some of Mao Tse-tung's sayings were written.

A company under the Canton Military Command has been stationed in five different places during the last four years. The commanders and fighters of the company have, during that time, helped factories, communes, and schools set up twenty-five groups, cultural rooms, and evening classes for the study of Mao Tse-tung's writings. They have, in addition, trained ninety-five men and women from among the local people to play a leading part in these organizations. Thanks to their efforts, eleven of these factories, people's communes and schools have been singled out as advanced units in the study of Mao Tse-tung's writings by their respective localities.

The Chinese People's Liberation Armymen pay special attention to arming the people with Mao Tse-tung's teachings on classes and class struggle. On Hainan Island, the nationally known "Red Outpost" Company has repeatedly studied these teachings of Chairman Mao together with the local people. As a result, all have heightened their revolutionary vigilance. Over the years, this company, supported by the local militia and people, has smashed all enemy sabotage and harassing activities.

When the current Proletarian Cultural Revolution first got under way, commanders and fighters of an air force unit organized the local people in a series of discussions on the significance of the movement in the light of Mao Tse-tung's teachings on classes and class struggle. Thanks to their efforts, the people acquired a correct understanding of the present phase of the class struggle in China and of its special features. They held meetings to express their great indignation and published wall newspapers to condemn the sinister gangs which are opposed to the Party, socialism, and Mao Tse-tung's thought.

As they help the people to study Mao Tse-tung's writings, the armymen try their best to help them, at the same time, to make a fundamental change in their world outlook. They consider this as one of the most important aspects of the study and application of Mao Tse-tung's thought.

The commanders and fighters of another air force unit worked in collaboration with the Party Committee of a local commune and taught the commune members to study Mao Tse-tung's "Serve the People" and "In Memory of Norman Bethune." Their express purpose was to help the peasants develop a collective spirit and eradicate their own individualism. They initiated a discussion among the commune members centering on the question "For whom do we farm?" In the course of the discussion, those taking part came to realize how their work was an integral part of the revolution in China and throughout the world.

The armymen also pay attention to educating the people in the spirit of daring to struggle and daring to win, as formulated by Chairman Mao. Their efforts in this field have borne fruit in the peasants' dogged fight for better harvests in the teeth of harsh natural conditions.

When a regiment in Fukien Province learned that the commune members and cadres in one or two local production brigades were somewhat discouraged in the face of a big drought, it sent its best political workers and soldiers to help the commune members study not only Mao Tse-tung's writings but also the experience of the Tachai Production Brigade, which is the national pacesetter in the revolutionary spirit of self-reliance and hard work. Inspired by Mao Tse-tung's saying, "Resolute and unafraid of any sacrifice, surmount every difficulty to win victory," the peasants set to work to dig wells and irrigation ditches. When, in the following year, they reaped a good harvest, the grateful peasants attributed their success to Mao Tse-tung's thought, brought to them by the People's Liberation Armymen.

9

DIRECTIVE OF THE POLITICAL DEPARTMENT
OF THE PEKING MILITARY REGION ON THE
LAUNCHING OF THE "TWO REMEMBRANCES AND
THREE INVESTIGATIONS" EDUCATIONAL CAMPAIGN*

Bulletin of Activities

    In accordance with the directives of Chief Lin** and the
General Political Department, and on the basis of education in
domestic conditions and policies, the Party Committee of the
Military Region has decided to launch a "Two Remembrances
and Three Investigations" educational campaign among the

---

    *"Pei-ching chün-ch'ü cheng-chih-pu kuan-yü k'ai-chan
'liang-i san-ch'a' chiao-yü yün-tung ti chih-shih," Kung-tso
t'ung-hsün, No. 4 (January 11, 1961), 11-20. The Bulletin is
the so-called secret military papers published by the General
Political Department of the PLA for restricted circulation
above the regimental level. The first thirty issues of the Bulletin, published between January 1 and August 26, 1961, became
available in the West in 1962. The document is a rare and rich
source of information on the broad activity of the PLA.
    **Chief Lin refers to Lin Piao, then minister of national de-
fense. The title "chief" was used to address Lin Piao, instead
of the more formal titles such as "minister" or "commander,"

troops of the entire Region during the first quarter of 1961.

In "On the Great Victory in the Northwest and on the New Type of Ideological Education Movement in the Liberation Army,"* Chairman Mao pointed out: "This victory has proven that by using the methods of speaking bitterness and three investigations to carry on a new type of rectification campaign, the People's Liberation Army will make itself invincible in the world." The present "Two Remembrances and Three Investigations" educational campaign is another political rectification campaign within our army under new historical conditions, and it has tremendous significance. The two remembrances (remember class hardship, remember national hardship) and the three investigations (of standpoint, of the determination to fight, and of work) are class education, traditional education, and a living education. They are an extremely effective method for heightening the troops' class consciousness and determination to fight, and are the keys for educational cadres and soldiers in applying the methods of class viewpoint and class analysis to assess problems and distinguish right from wrong. They are a very good path for our army to follow in heightening our troops' class awareness and stimulating their determination to fight in the period of socialist construction, and are a very good way for us to study Marxism-Leninism-Mao Tse-tung thought. This Marxist-Leninist, mass-line educational method is a fine tradition in our army's political education. During the last few years, however, we have not emphasized it enough. As a result of Chief Lin's pointing this out, we must now speedily revive this glorious tradition and develop it further under these new conditions.

At present, the ideological situation among our cadres and

---

throughout the Bulletin of Activities. Although it suggests certain informality, the title also signifies the respect, affection, and prestige that Lin had commanded in the PLA — Ying-mao Kau.

*For the text in English translation, see Mao Tse-tung, Selected Works of Mao Tse-tung (Peking: Foreign Languages Press, 1961), IV, pp. 211-218 — Ying-mao Kau.

soldiers is, in general, stable. Especially after having gone through a period of education about current conditions and policies, the majority of comrades vigorously support the Three Red Flags. They have a clear-cut standpoint, are full of energy and the determination to fight, have a correct attitude towards service, and are resolved to establish and staunchly protect socialism. However, among some personnel there exist many confused views and much incorrect thinking, mainly the following: First, on the question of food and markets there exist a considerable number of confused ideas and much incorrect knowledge. Some people have violated Party policy, and a few have even begun to doubt and falter [in their support of] the Three Red Flags. Second, on the question of war and peace, some people have begun to fear war and dream of peace. Third, among a minority of cadres there exists the more serious problem of bourgeois individualism. The chief manifestations of this are a flagging of revolutionary determination, a desire for ease and comfort, an infatuation with family life, and a concern with rank, grade, and pay; tiring of army life, fearing stress, and thinking of leaving the army are particularly serious. Fourth, some soldiers joined the army for incorrect reasons, and their attitude toward service is improper.

Objectively speaking, the reason for these kinds of ideological problems is the reflection within our troops of domestic and international class struggle. From the point of view of leadership, they show our lack of living ideology and our insufficient linking up of theory and practice in political education. From the point of view of the situation with regard to the political thinking of our cadres and soldiers, they stem from the fact that a considerable number of people do not understand class exploitation and class oppression and do not deeply comprehend class struggle. Many young basic-level cadres and soldiers lack sympathetic understanding of the class struggle during the democratic revolution period, are not clear about the meaning of class struggle during the socialist revolution period, and lack correct understanding of the Party's general and specific policies during the socialist revolution period. They do not

understand very well the hardships of the old society; nor do
they understand very well how this present well-being and happy
life were achieved — their thinking is that of one who is living
well but cannot see it because he has forgotten where it came
from. They do not know enough about the circumstances of
current international class struggle, do not realize that imperialism is inherently aggressive, and do not understand the
criminal history of imperialist aggression, especially American imperialism, in China. Their hatred of American imperialism is not deep, so they do not take great precautions.
As a result, they do not have that implacable class hatred for
domestic and international class enemies, and when they encounter problems, they cannot apply the method of class viewpoint and class analysis to distinguish right from wrong.

To solve effectively the above-mentioned problems of cadres
and soldiers, and to anticipate the effect that current economic
difficulties of a temporary nature may have on the thinking of
every cadre and soldier, we must, in the first quarter of 1961,
show the power of political and ideological work to teach everyone that while the present situation is a difficult one, the future
is bright, and by uniting and being of one mind these difficulties
can be overcome. [We must] make each cadre and soldier
able, in the most difficult times, to assess correctly the situation, maintain his standpoint, withstand this ordeal, and develop the glorious tradition of our army; moreover, [we] must
lay down a firm ideological foundation for the training, operations, and all other tasks of 1961. And so we must, on the
basis of education about current conditions and policies, launch
this "Two Remembrances and Three Investigations" educational
campaign. Facts prove that in those test units where "Two
Remembrances and Three Investigations" education was conscientiously carried out, and in those units where the methods
of remembering hardships and thinking of sweetness were conscientiously adopted to carry out education to increase production and practice economy, the class awareness of cadres
and soldiers rose universally, the ideological picture took on
a whole new cast, increasing production and practicing economy

became the thing, all were full of energy and the determination to fight, and internal unity was greatly strengthened.

The "Two Remembrances and Three Investigations" educational campaign must take Mao Tse-tung's thought as its guide, the works of Chairman Mao as its weapon, the domestic situation as its main content, and the mass line as its method. The purpose of this campaign is to heighten the class awareness and strengthen the class viewpoint of our troops so that all officers and men will fervently love socialism, the Party and Chairman Mao, firmly uphold the Three Red Flags, correctly assess the situation, maintain their standpoint, sustain their determination to fight, correctly deal with problems, continue to go all out, further our army's glorious tradition, strive for strength, rely on their own efforts, lower their heads and push ahead, struggle against hardship, work hand in hand with local cadres, share happiness and hardship with the masses, and — under the correct leadership of the Party and Chairman Mao — unite, full of confidence, to conquer difficulties and march courageously forward.

In order to carry through the above guiding principles and achieve our educational goals, leadership at all levels must conscientiously take charge of and carry through the following points:

First, the entire campaign must keep to the policy of taking Mao Tse-tung's thought as the guide and the works of Chairman Mao as a weapon. In essence the campaign is a concrete application under new historical conditions of Chairman Mao's thoughts on a new type of army rectification. For this reason, those backbone cadres at all levels leading the campaign must study and grasp Chairman Mao's thoughts on this new type of army rectification and use this to lead the campaign. The minds of cadres and soldiers must be armed with Mao Tse-tung's thought. During the course of the campaign, according to the needs of cadres and soldiers, study sessions of works of Chairman Mao that are relevant to their concerns should be organized. When the need arises, study; when study is over, use the knowledge. Use Mao Tse-tung's thought to answer the questions raised by cadres and soldiers.

Second, the "Two Remembrances and Three Investigations" educational campaign is living education, education about current domestic and international class struggle, education about general and specific Party policies. For this reason, this education must be integrated with the domestic socialist revolution and socialist construction, the Party's line and general and specific policies, and the Three Red Flags. It must also be combined with the international revolutionary struggle to oppose imperialism and aid the peoples of all countries. It must use all possible means to strengthen the class viewpoint of cadres and soldiers; their class awareness must be heightened, for when it is, problems are easy to solve. It must link up theory and practice, use the numerous vital examples that come forth in recalling hardships and thinking of sweetness to elucidate the universal Marxist-Leninist principles of class struggle and, moreover, use these universal principles to solve the immediate ideological problems of the troops. It should oppose the tendency towards empty dogmatism, as well as the tendency towards matter-of-fact empiricism.

Third, another important aspect of Chairman Mao's ideas on this new type of army rectification is the mass-line educational method. This idea of Chairman Mao's must be carried through the whole campaign. To adopt the method of uniting the leadership and the masses to carry out education means to trust the masses, to mobilize fully the masses. As long as the masses are mobilized and undergo self-education, all problems can be solved. The collective wisdom of the masses must be relied upon to solve problems. To arouse the masses fully, every stage, every step of ideological mobilization work must be carefully done. Experience in the key-point test shows that the responsibility of ideological mobilization work is very great. The campaign is very rigorous — each step leads to the next, each link is tied to the next. Each step and each link requires much careful ideological work. As the campaign proceeds step by step, the thought of cadres and soldiers changes very quickly; ideological work must follow closely the progress of the campaign, must correspond to this progress, and must become progressively more detailed. All types of educational methods must be used together in the campaign. Each should be used when appropriate, and they should all complement each other.

On the basis of experience in the key-point test, the following five operational procedures have been decided upon for the "Two Remembrances and Three Investigations" educational campaign.

I. Thorough Investigation and Preparation

Prior to carrying out "Two Remembrances and Three Investigations" education, leadership at each level must conscientiously do the following preparatory work.

1. Thorough investigation. Thorough investigation is the key to preparatory work, the precondition for handling well this education, and the starting point for carrying out this education. Investigation consists of determining the following four things about the troops: their level of class awareness, their hardships, their attitude toward the campaign to recall hardships, and their ideological condition (their attitude toward and reaction to the Three Red Flags and their present economic life, especially the questions of food and supply and demand in the markets). If this investigative work is well done, it not only allows leadership [cadres] to take charge of the education but also gives them facts to use in explaining the necessity and possibility of carrying out this education; then, with the leadership's thought unified, they can vigorously criticize the kind of incorrect thinking which assumes that "young soldiers have no hardships to recall" or those who say "I can't recall anything."

2. Mobilization. At the beginning of the campaign, mobilization work must be done well. Cadres and soldiers must be organized to study Chairman Mao's "On the Great Victory of the Northwest and on the New Type of Ideological Education Movement in the Liberation Army" and Chief Lin's directive on "Two Remembrances and Three Investigations" education. Make clear the great significance of "Two Remembrances and

Three Investigations" education, unify the understanding, explain the policies, and rectify the attitudes. The campaign's
policies, goals, stages, and methods must be clearly explained
to cadres and company-level backbone elements who will take
charge of it.
  3. Cultivate models of recalling hardships. In the process
of investigative work, attention must be paid to discovering
models of recalling hardships. The main criteria for selecting
these models are: the hardship must have been deeply felt, the
model must have a good work record, his consciousness must
be high, and he must have the ability to express himself well.
After models have been selected, they must be cultivated. The
quality of this cultivation will directly affect the success of
recall-hardship meetings. In cultivating typical cases, stick to
the facts; cases cannot be manufactured, and they should not be
falsified.

II. Recalling Hardships

  The purpose of this stage is, through the several methods of
recalling hardships, settling accounts, digging out the roots,
etc., to arouse the class hatred of cadres and soldiers, awaken
their class awareness, overcome their tendency to forget the
roots [of their life], arouse hatred of imperialism, eradicate
thoughts of peace, and strengthen the determination to fight.
  Recalling hardships. In units which have not previously recalled hardships, recall class hardships and national hardships
together, but with emphasis on class hardships. Begin with recalling class hardships, and when hardships caused by class
exploitation and oppression have all come out, carefully lead
into recalling national hardships. Encourage everyone — cadres
and soldiers — to participate in recalling hardships together.
Having leading cadres begin is an effective method for creating
a high tide of recalling hardships. Generally, a combination of
large meetings for recalling typical cases of hardships with
small meetings in which everyone speaks should be the method
used. Good preparation must be done for large meetings; good

typical cases must be cultivated (have two kinds of cases: class hardships and national hardships). Do not hold a big meeting until it is assured that it will go well. Recalling hardships is a serious occasion, a moment in which cadre and soldiers may be deeply grieved. Therefore, pay attention to maintaining the discipline of the meeting, to the physical arrangements of the meeting place, and to the general atmosphere. In addition, food should be provided.

Settling accounts. Recalling hardships should lead naturally to everyone settling accounts, to making clear exactly what are the hardships of the working people. In settling accounts there are three main areas: economic exploitation, political oppression, and imperialist aggression. In general, the method for settling accounts is to begin with one's own squad and platoon, and then extend to one's native place, region, all of China, and the whole world. In this process, make the soldiers understand the truth of the sayings that "the hardships of poor people are unending; the poor people of the world are all of one family; and all of the world's reactionaries are the deadly enemies of the working people." Make them connect their own personal hatred with the hatred of their class, their race, and finally with that of all the working people of the world. Actually, recalling hardships and settling accounts are interconnected; in order to settle accounts, hardships must be brought up and thoroughly discussed. If in recalling hardships, national hardships are lacking, they should be supplemented at this point. To make clear the true face of American imperialist aggression, study articles by Chairman Mao such as "Cast Away Illusion, Prepare for Struggle," "Farewell, Leighton Stuart," "'Friendship,' or Aggression?"* and the history of American imperialist aggression in China published by the Liberation Army Daily.

Digging out the roots of hardships. After settling accounts,

---

*These works may be found in Selected Works of Mao Tsetung (Peking: Foreign Languages Press, 1961), IV, pp. 425-440; 447-450 — Ying-mao Kau.

lead everyone to dig out the roots of hardships and discuss where these hardships come from. Make sure cadres and soldiers are clear about class exploitation and class oppression, know how to use class analysis, and concretely understand that domestically the exploitation and oppression of class enemies and internationally the aggression of imperialism are the roots of hardships. Make everyone understand that the reason the poor are poor is because of the exploitation of landlords and capitalists and the private ownership of the means of production. Then dig deeper by discussing what sustains the system of economic exploitation. Make the soldiers understand that it depends on the reactionary political power of the Kuomintang and Chiang Kai-shek, that the reactionary political power of Chiang Kai-shek and his army is the root of exploitation. At this point dig deeper yet and pose the question of who the reactionary regime of Chiang Kai-shek relies upon. Finally dig down to imperialism, and particularly American imperialism. Make the soldiers understand that American imperialism is the big boss of all the reactionaries in today's world, and connect domestic and international class enemies, domestic class struggle and international class struggle, and thus arouse hatred of imperialism. To show everyone how to use class analysis, study Chairman Mao's articles "Analysis of the Classes in Chinese Society," "Report of an Investigation into the Peasant Movement in Hunan," and "How to Differentiate the Classes in the Rural Areas."*

After the roots of hardships have been uncovered, discuss the state of affairs with regard to domestic and international class struggle, and make everyone see that domestic class enemies have by no means been totally eliminated — that they are still attempting last-ditch resistance. Internationally, imperialism, particularly American imperialism, is still actively preparing for war and is menacing us by forcibly occupying

*The texts of these articles are included in Selected Works of Mao Tse-tung (Peking: Foreign Languages Press, 1964), I, pp. 13-62; 137-140 — Ying-mao Kau

Taiwan, part of our country. The majority of the world's working people are still suffering, and domestically we are still
faced with temporary difficulties. From this arouse the troops'
determination to fight, to heighten their precautions, strive for
greater power, conquer difficulties, and establish the desire to
follow forever the Party and Chairman Mao and carry the revolution through to the end.

In this stage, hardships must be thoroughly discussed and
their roots completely uncovered; American imperialism must
be totally exposed and discussed, and its evils summed up.

III.   Making Comparisons and Thinking of Sweetness

The purpose of this stage is, through the process of making
comparisons, settling accounts, and seeking the roots of sweetness, and on the basis of heightened awareness, to lay out the
differences between the socialist road and the capitalist road,
define our political direction, fervently love the Party, Chairman Mao, and socialism, uphold the Three Red Flags, clearly
assess the situation, maintain our standpoint, conquer difficulties, heighten precautions, strengthen the determination to
fight, establish the idea of continuous revolution, and carry the
socialist revolution through to the end.

Making comparisons and thinking of sweetness. On the basis
of having settled accounts and dug out the roots of hardships,
now organize the troops to compare the hardships of the past
with the sweetness of today. Have them talk contentedly about
their present happy lives, about their personal well-being,
about sweetness they have seen and heard in their native places
and in the whole country. Look at the great changes, in politics,
economics, and culture, in the face of our nation in the eleven
years since liberation. Compare these three aspects of the
old and new societies: political power, economic life, and cultural life. Through making comparisons and thinking of sweetness, inspire everyone more fervently to love the new society,
to despise the old society, and to eliminate the thinking of those
who are living well but cannot see it because they have forgotten

where it came from. Discuss the great changes in our country
in the eleven years since liberation, the Three Red Flags, and
the great significance of socialist revolution and socialist construction. Take stock of the great changes in the eleven years
since liberation, contrast going-it-alone [i.e., individual
farming] with cooperatives, and cooperatives with communes;
take stock of the development in industry and agriculture, as
well as the rise in living standards. Make everyone distinguish
clearly between the two paths, and eliminate the incorrect
thinking which holds that "Although the revolution was done
well, there has not been much progress since liberation" and
that "Each year is worse than the last."

Finding the source of sweetness. After making comparisons
and thinking of sweetness, encourage everyone to find the
source of sweetness. Discuss where sweetness comes from.
Lead everyone to find the sources of sweetness: the Party and
Chairman Mao have led everyone in the country to defeat the
three great enemies and gained victory for the democratic revolution: the Party has directed the victory of the socialist revolution; the Party has led everyone in the country along the
path of socialist revolution — the correct path from going-it-
alone to cooperativization, and from cooperativization to communization; the Party has led everyone in the country to the
great accomplishments of socialist construction and the unparalleled excellences of the Three Red Flags — the General
Line, the Great Leap Forward, and the People's Communes;
and the Party has led all the people of the country to victory
in the struggle against imperialism. Then, discuss the history
of revolutionary struggle and the glorious tradition of bitter
striving, recall the spirit of bloody sacrifice and bitter striving
of the martyrs and the older generation during the period of
revolutionary struggle. Make everyone realize today's well-
being was won by the bloody sacrifice and bitter striving of
revolutionary martyrs and the working people, and from this
inspire cadres and soldiers more fervently to love the Party
and Chairman Mao, cherish the fruits of revolutionary victory, fervently love the socialist system, staunchly main-

tain the socialist road, and uphold the Three Red Flags.

Looking forward to the future. On the basis of heightened class awareness and finding the sources of sweetness, we must look to the future. Erect firmly the idea of continuous revolution and carrying the revolution through to the end. Discuss together the beautiful prospects for socialism and communism, the good situation but temporary difficulties of domestic class struggle, and the Party's policies, especially the current twelve-article policy on the people's commune in rural areas (this should be the central content). Encourage everyone to compare today and tomorrow. Show the connections between today's bitter striving and the good life of the future. Through a comparison between the situation during and after disasters in the past and today, and a comparison between present production and everyday needs, make clear in a down-to-earth fashion today's generally favorable situation and partially unfavorable situation and the true reasons for these temporary difficulties. Strengthen the confidence that these difficulties can be overcome with determination and hard work. Through a discussion of the situation with regard to international and domestic class struggle and the Party's history, make everyone see that everywhere in the world imperialism and the exploitative system which gives rise to war will be eliminated, and the beautiful ideals of communism will be realized; and make them see that at present imperialism is still crazily preparing for war, still slaughtering and oppressing the people. From this [encourage them] to heighten their precautions, strengthen their determination to fight, and firmly erect the idea of carrying the revolution through to the end and continuing forever to be fighting units. In sum, make everyone clearly assess the situation, clearly understand the direction, and resolutely follow the Party and Chairman Mao toward the bright future.

In the education during the stage of making comparisons and thinking of sweetness, the leaders should explain the relevant works of Chairman Mao and the policies of the Party as everyone's needs dictate. Sweetness must be thoroughly discussed, the sources of sweetness accurately located, the [present] conditions and policies thoroughly explained, and the general [level of] knowledge truly raised.

The stages of recalling hardships, making comparisons, and thinking of sweetness are the crucial ones for the success of the "Two Remembrances and Three Investigations" educational movement. Most time should be spent on the recalling-hardships and thinking-of-sweetness stages to ensure that they are done thoroughly, for only then can the class awareness of the broad masses of cadres and soldiers be truly raised, and the three investigations can then be carried out well on this basis. Leadership at all levels must clearly recognize the point that the form of education must be varied, interesting, and lively. "Recalling, settling, comparing, studying, explaining, commenting (discussing)" must all be used together; moreover, the methods of on-the-spot inspection, interview, giving reports, movies, exhibitions, and broadcasts can be used if needed.

IV. Three Investigations

The purpose of this stage is, through the three investigations, to make all the troops hold firm in their class standpoint, resolutely to uphold the Party line and policies, with one mind to overcome difficulties, firmly to erect the idea of continuous revolution and maintaining their fighting units forever, to strengthen the revolutionary will to fight, and to raise the fighting strength of the troops.

The three investigations are a process which, on the basis of the class awareness heightened by recalling hardships and thinking of sweetness, uses the proletarian class viewpoint to reform thought and finally solve problems. Leadership must take careful charge here.

The three investigations involve investigating standpoint, the determination to fight, and work. In concrete terms this means, on the basis of a person's work and behavior record, to investigate his understanding of the country's economic situation and

his attitude toward the Party's line, policies, and the Three
Red Flags; to investigate the question of his revolutionary determination to fight, and whether his political vigilance is high;
to investigate his attitude toward perpetual struggle and toward
service. In a word, it is to investigate class awareness. As
for method, cadres and soldiers must carry it out separately.
Each person's investigation should have a focal point: if someone has a particular problem, that problem should be investigated. Most work should be self-investigation conducted in
small groups and should allow each individual to go as far as
he can; there should be no key-point criticism. Emphasize
self-awareness and not assistance for others.

To carry out the three investigations well, the following tasks
should be attended to: First, ideological mobilization work
should be well done. Explain in detail the goals, significance,
and policies of the three investigations; and through mobilization, preliminary discussions, and preparation, fully arouse
the masses' self-awareness of thought reform, dispel doubts,
and rectify understanding. Second, conscientiously organize
the troops to study articles of Chairman Mao relevant to the
three investigations, such as "On Criticism and Self-Criticism"
(in Documents on Rectification)* and "Combat Liberalism."
These can heighten self-awareness and rectify one's investigative attitude. In the process of investigation, as the need arises,
use articles such as Chairman Mao's "Serving the People,"
"In Memory of Pai Ch'iu-en [Norman Bethune]," "Carry the
Revolution Through to the End," and the introduction to the
Resolution of the Enlarged Meeting of the Military Affairs Commission to arm everyone with Mao Tse-tung's thought.** Third,

---

*See Cheng-feng wen-hsien [Documents on Rectification]
(Hong Kong: Hsin-min-chu, 1949); the documents have been
translated into English in Boyd Compton, trans., Mao's China:
Party Reform Documents, 1942-1944 (Seattle: University of
Washington Press, 1952) — Ying-mao Kau.
**Mao's articles mentioned here may be found in Selected
Works of Mao Tse-tung (Peking: Foreign Languages Press,

since the three investigations are self-education of the masses, they depend chiefly on arousing self-awareness to rectify ideology and solve problems. The direct education and heightened awareness will bring to the [self-] investigator a sense of ease and happiness. For this reason, do not carry out model criticism, struggle against key points, or large struggle meetings; any pressure or coercion and, even more, any beatings or scoldings are not permitted.

V. Concrete Implementation

After the three investigations, we must use the results of the "Two Remembrances and Three Investigations" education, namely, the awareness and enthusiasm of the masses, to carry out the Resolution of the Enlarged Meeting of the Military Affairs Commission to struggle for the creation of four-good companies and five-good soldiers. They should be carried out in our training, work, and study. We must guide the troops to go in the progressive direction, draw up progressive plans, honor model soldiers, raise the Red Flag, strive to excel, publicize good men and good deeds, and hold leap-forward and unity meetings. We must exhort all cadres and soldiers to hold high the great red banner of Mao Tse-tung's thought, resolutely carry out the Party's policies, go all out and aim high, and accomplish the tasks of 1961 with distinction. Mobilize all cadres and soldiers to bring into play their high enthusiasm and creativeness, firmly answer the call of the Military Affairs Commission and Chief Lin, adhere consistently to the Resolution of the Enlarged Meeting of the Military Affairs Commission, and strive valiantly to create four-good companies and five-good soldiers.

1961-1964), II, pp. 31-34; 337-338; III, pp. 227-228. The Resolution of the Military Affairs Commission refers to that adopted on October 20, 1960, "On Strengthening Political and Ideological Work in the Army." The text may be found in J. Chester Cheng, ed., The Politics of the Chinese Red Army (Stanford: The Hoover Institution, 1966), pp. 66-94 — Ying-mao Kau.

Concerning organizational leadership and a few concrete problems:

1. The "Two Remembrances and Three Investigations" educational campaign is a new political rectification campaign in the army and is the focus of political work in the first quarter of 1961. If this campaign is handled well, it will enable the troops to overcome difficulties, weather any storms, and withstand any trials in the future. It will greatly raise the level of our army's fighting strength. As Chairman Mao says, "We will be unrivaled in the world." Therefore, Party committees and leadership organs at all levels must place great emphasis on this campaign; they must be determined, when leading other political campaigns such as the rectification of the Party branches, to proceed vigorously on a grand scale to make this campaign succeed.

2. Party committees at all levels must take direct charge, and leaders on all levels must lead cadres within their organizations to the front line of supervision; political units must use all of their resources to lead and coordinate the efforts of headquarters and the logistics departments. Both the army and division levels must organize work teams or work groups to go down and direct the campaign. Before the work groups go down, they must be trained.

3. To set the time for the "Two Remembrances and Three Investigations" educational movement, the Military Region's 1961 training year will begin around February 15; thus, the campaign should begin during the first ten days of January and be basically completed by about February 10. During the campaign, although attention must be paid to the combination of labor with rest, and therefore no night battles may be held, still, activities must be stepped up. During the period of the campaign, the Military Region must try its best not to call meetings of lower-level comrades nor call them together for training. Every unit must take pains to use its time well. The programs of supporting the government and loving the people, carrying out democratic investigations, and recruitment and return to civilian life must all be carried out in combination

with the "Two Remembrances and Three Investigations" educational campaign.

4. Basic-level cadres and soldiers must all participate in the campaign and be educated. Company cadres especially must take part along with the soldiers to solve their ideological problems. By no means should they be allowed to remain outside this campaign because of work or for other reasons. Administrative organs should organize seventy percent of their cadres to go down and help with this work — as many young intellectuals in administrative offices as possible should go down and take part in the campaign so that they too can be educated.

5. The "Two Remembrances and Three Investigations" educational campaign is carried out on the foundation of education about present domestic conditions and policies. If education about conditions and policies has been done well, then a good foundation will have been laid for this campaign. Therefore, education about present conditions and policies must be handled well. Before the campaign begins, the situation with regard to education about conditions and policies must be looked into a bit. In units where this education has not been handled well, a few days should be given to continuing it. When discussing present ideological problems, take advantage of the actual situation to expedite the "Two Remembrances and Three Investigations" educational campaign.

6. Those units which have already carried out "Two Remembrances and Three Investigations" education should conscientiously carry out an inspection. In general, most of those units which had some recalling-hardships education during the campaign to increase production and practice economy, excluding individual trial units, did not fully reveal their hardships, did not completely dig down to the roots of their hardships, and did not comprehend thoroughly the source of their sweetness; so, in these units this campaign is still quite relevant. Those units which did not carry [these things] out thoroughly, or which only carried out one stage, should continue to develop them. Those which recalled hardships but did not "dig out the roots" nor [carry out] the "Three Investiga-

tions" should continue with the work of "digging out the roots,"
"Three Investigations," and "concrete implementation." Those
which recalled class hardships but not national hardships
should do so, and then proceed to "digging out the roots,"
"Three Investigations," and "concrete implementation." Just
as in the above examples, each unit should do what it has not
done to carry out this education completely and thoroughly.

7. Administrative cadres at the regimental level and above
should, on the basis of education about conditions and policies,
launch the "Three Investigations" ("Two Remembrances" will have
been carried out when they went down and took part in recalling
hardships and education about current conditions and policies
with the troops); if they have no time, they can receive this education at the company level and make up their work when they
return to their jobs. Soldiers and staff and families of administrative organs must all take part in this campaign. Most of
the students in schools of our military region are company and
platoon cadres, so they must also carry on this education (the
administrative cadres of schools should also participate). The
methods used should differ somewhat from those of the company — the time can be a little shorter; more documents
can be read. Those schools which have already carried out
this campaign should hold an inspection to see whether they have
achieved the goals of Chief Lin's directive. If they have not,
they should solve their problems with selective emphasis on
the basis of the previous stage of education.

8. Cadres of the Provincial Military District who took part
in the tidying-up movement of local communes should, along
with the commune tidying-up, handle well education of current
conditions and policies; and when they return, carry out the
"Three Investigations." Whether those cadre who stayed at
home should first carry out the "Two Remembrances and
Three Investigations" is up to the provincial military district
to decide. Garrison divisions and regiments should conscientiously carry out the campaign; standards should be even stricter, and great efforts should be made to handle it well.

9. There can be some differences in the campaign in hos-

pitals and warehouses — without halting medical work and other tasks, time may be allotted according to the concrete situation. Labor teams, work groups, productive and other dispersed units should make proper arrangements according to their own circumstances and conscientiously carry out the campaign. Leadership organs must strengthen their guidance for these groups.

10. All units must pay attention to using relevant material from newspapers and other publications to carry out "Two Remembrances and Three Investigations" education, and they must use them to publicize the experience of "Two Remembrances and Three Investigations."

11. Young intellectuals from the exploiting classes must also without exception take part in this educational campaign. For them, this education is not only profound class education but also a practical test of their class standpoint. But take heed that recalling hardships is recalling class oppression and class exploitation. Therefore, for them it is not a question of recalling hardships or speaking bitterness, but rather a question of how they can correctly deal with their exploiting family, how they can realize the true nature of their exploiting family in order to draw a class line between themselves and the exploiting classes and stand with the proletarian class. In this educational campaign, the following specific work must still be carried out with them: First, organize them to study the sections about thought reform in Chairman Mao's "The Orientation of the Youth Movement" and "Talks at the Yenan Forum on Literature and Art."* Second, talk with them before holding a large meeting to disclose hardships to prevent them from doing or saying anything that would destroy the seriousness of the meeting. Third, allow those whose day-to-day record is good or those who are particularly mature to present the various methods that landlords and capitalists use in exploitation.

---

*For the texts, see Selected Works of Mao Tse-tung (Peking: Foreign Languages Press, 1965), II, pp. 241-250; III, pp. 69-98 — Ying-mao Kau.

12. If during the campaign there appear any counterrevolutionary, bad, or seriously unruly or disruptive elements, after the situation has been investigated and ascertained by leadership organs at the regimental level or higher, transfer them from the company and treat them as a separate case; do not mix this up with the educational campaign itself.

[Issued on] January 3, 1961

III

The Economic Role
of the Military

10

REPORT OF THE PARTY COMMITTEE OF
THE GENERAL LOGISTICS DEPARTMENT
ON CONTINUING TO DEVELOP ENERGETICALLY
THE CAMPAIGN TO INCREASE PRODUCTION
AND PRACTICE ECONOMY*

Bulletin of Activities

I

This year, under the correct leadership of the Military Affairs Commission and the Central Committee, the entire army
has energetically developed the campaign to increase production
and practice economy, and the accomplishments have been
great. Especially since the issuance of the Central Committee's
directives "Concerning the Implementation of the Campaign to
Increase Production and Practice Economy Centering on Preserving Grain and Steel" and "Energetically Restrict the Purchasing Power of Social Groups," Party committees at all levels have conscientiously studied the situation, made specific
arrangements, and put forth concrete requirements. With the
enthusiastic participation of the broad masses of officers and
soldiers, the whole army has set in motion a new high tide of

---

*"Tsung hou ch'in pu tang wei kuan-yü chi-hsü ta-li k'ai-chan
ts'eng-ch'an chieh-yüeh yün-tung ti pao-kao," Kung-tso t'ung-
hsün, No. 1 (January 1, 1961), 21-28. The report was approved by
the Military Affairs Commission on December 22, 1960, and was
transmitted to all units for study and implementation. See also
the source note for the preceding selection.

increasing production and practicing economy. The following
is a report on the main features of the campaign during this
year [1960].

Economizing on grain. By appropriately reducing food rations, universally instituting the planned use of grain, and
adopting various other economy measures, it will be possible
to save 35 million catties of foodstuffs (included are 6.045 million
catties of horse feed) from the beginning of September to the
end of the year. During the past two years the entire army
overdrew more than 27 million catties of grain; this year, with
more careful management, there has in general been no over-
drawing. Since the strengthening of supervision over distribution in September, instances of getting too much grain by
false reporting have been essentially eliminated. In this way,
the amount of grain saved has been greatly increased.

Economizing on cloth and cotton. By adopting various measures such as issuing fewer new articles, increasing the use
of used, mended articles, careful planning, taking careful in-
ventory, using things longer than usual, wearing used in place
of new, and urging economy in the use of cloth ration tickets,
the entire army has saved the equivalent of over 150,000 bolts
of new cloth and 1.13 million catties of new cotton. Besides this,
the collection of used articles in just the past half-year has
amounted to 2.7 million catties of used cloth; 1.32 million catties
of used cotton; over 119,300 used cotton suits; and over 780,000
catties of used rubber shoe soles.

Economizing on fuel. The entire army, through measures
like stricter supervision, stepped-up installation of condensation and injection equipment on vehicles and engines, and improved organization of transportation, has saved over 8,000
tons of various kinds of fuel.

Economizing on construction materials. By adopting a series
of measures such as a changed design for barracks construction, which combines native and Western elements, lowering
the standards for the use of materials, and maintenance, overhaul, and manufacture of parts for armaments and vehicles by
units themselves, it will be possible, according to preliminary

statistics, to save 3,774 tons of steel material, 1,459 tons of cement, and 1,423 cubic meters of lumber. In addition, the Military Equipment Department has saved 117 tons of copper material.

Economizing on expenditures. As a result of adopting such measures as readjusting operational plans, reducing expenditures, and restricting group purchasing power, we have saved over the year more than 18 million yuan, thus fulfilling the state reduction plan figure by 156.76 percent.

In addition, the whole army has saved a great deal in areas like medicine, health, miscellaneous administrative expenses, and necessities of life such as water, electricity, and fuel.

The accomplishments with regard to disaster relief have also been outstanding — the whole army has contributed over 2,113,400 catties of grain and over 500,000 articles of clothing.

There have also been outstanding achievements with regard to production, and this situation is very good.

On the basis of last year's Great Leap Forward, sideline production in the army has experienced a continued leap forward. According to statistics at the end of September, the entire army was raising over 1.353 million pigs, over 50,000 cattle, 300,000 sheep, and 2.9 million domestic fowl. The army's pig production, excluding the over 53,800 supplied for feeding the nation and those which were slaughtered or died within the army, stands at present at 929,000, an average of one for each 2.9 persons, which is an increase over the end of last year of 56 percent. The army operates over 700 large and small farms with over 1.1 million mou under cultivation. This averages out to 0.4 mou per person, an increase of 90 percent over the end of last year. Vegetable production stands at 541 million catties, more than twice as much as during the same period last year. The development of sideline agricultural production has played an important role in guaranteeing the supply of supplementary foodstuffs to the troops, improving life, and reducing the necessity of being supplied through the markets.

Production of steel, iron, and cement has expanded throughout

the entire army. According to statistics through the end of
September, 24 high furnaces with a total capacity of 252
cubic meters, one three-ton electric furnace, and 2 three-
ton revolving furnaces have been built and have already produced 22,400 tons of pig iron. Also, 33 cement factories have
been built or enlarged, and have produced 70,900 tons of cement. By the end of the year it should be possible to complete
59 high furnaces with a total capacity of 640 cubic meters, 5
electric furnaces, and 3 revolving furnaces. This year's plan
calls for the production of 42,000 tons of pig iron, 2,200 tons
of steel, and 119,300 tons of cement.

Working on the principle of repairing and making parts at
the same time, the army's repair shops have manufactured
parts for military equipment, vehicles, planes, and ships — altogether 269 different items and over 440,000 individual pieces —
and have made 2,461 lathes of various types and 9,165 electric
motors. All of this has supplied the army and aided local construction.

Labor productivity, in production for army needs, rose 20.44
percent over last year; production costs fell by 1.62 percent;
the quality of goods produced also improved.

II

Although [the campaign] in the army to increase production
and practice economy achieved the foregoing results, it has still
not penetrated deeply enough; even more stringent economy
can be practiced in many areas. In order to intensify the campaign, the following requirements are set forth for 1961:

1. Economizing on grain. From now on the point of emphasis
for economizing on grain is to strengthen supervision. Mess
halls must be run well, the method of increasing the amount of
cooked food must be put into practice everywhere, and the standard ration must not be exceeded. In order to save on grain
and yet increase nutrition, the whole army must emphasize
substitute food and must grow a lot of vegetables. By June of
next year, everyone must strive to have about five catties of

food to substitute for grain. At present, fall vegetables should be stored and preparation made for spring planting; those troops which are stationed in the south should still plant their winter vegetables well to make sure they will have vegetables for themselves.

2. Economizing on cotton cloth. Next year the supply of cotton cloth for residents in the city and countryside alike will be reduced. Likewise, fewer cotton ration tickets should be issued to officers. Determination of the actual figures will have to wait until after the level of supply for the whole country is set. Unlined clothing and work clothes for officers and soldiers should also be appropriately reduced according to the situation. Cloth for official uses should be strictly controlled; if it is not specially needed, do not use cotton cloth for this purpose.

Special attention must be placed on the efforts to collect and utilize used articles; if used things can be utilized, do not issue new ones; if things can be repaired and used, do not make new ones. Collect used articles according to the regulations for this; strive for a return rate higher than 90 percent.

Take positive steps to carry out uniform reform. In addition to increased study of the problem, fittings should be organized, and production quickly begun. When uniform reform is com-pleted, in one year the army can save over 500,000 bolts of cloth and over 50,000 piculs of cotton.

3. Economizing on construction materials. Make great ef-forts to build the arched type of barracks. It is estimated that we will construct 2.73 million square meters of this type of bar-racks next year. In this way we can use 7,769 tons less steel and 191,345 cubic meters less lumber than needed to build earth and lumber barracks. In addition, we should promote the construction of arched warehouses built with cement and oil drums, and the adoption of new construction techniques to save even more steel and lumber.

In the construction and design of barracks and warehouses, we must stick firmly to the principles of strength, usefulness, and simplicity; and we must resolutely oppose ostentatious stan-dards, extravagance, and waste. The principles for barracks maintenance are to prevent leaking and collapse and to prolong the useful life of the rooms; we must oppose frivolous decoration and additional construction in the name of maintenance.

In order to meet the demands of the new strategic policies, during the next several years barracks construction should center on barracks needed because of troop redeployment, those needed for troops involved in scientific research, and those needed for newly built schools, warehouses, and factories. Buildings used by [administrative] organs should in general not be built; the construction of guest houses and meeting halls should be stopped.

4. Economizing on oil and fuel. Promote the general use of fuel-saving devices, and require all army vehicles and motorized equipment to save 20-30 percent over the original basic fuel-consumption standards.

Use vehicles rationally; require the whole army to save 20 percent over the quotas of vehicle-kilometers. Methods for economizing are experimentation with refitting vehicles with technical devices, increasing the load vehicles can carry, making the most of empty return trips, and utilizing trains, ships, and animals as much as possible for transportation purposes.

The whole army should put coal on a rationed supply basis and should promote the adoption of new techniques such as gas burners, gas stoves, steam cooking, pressure cookers, etc. As regards coal used in production or daily life, we must strive not to use too much, and even attempt to have some surplus.

5. Economizing on expenditures. Organs at all levels of the army should have plans for administrative and miscellaneous expenses; if something is not strictly necessary, do not buy it. Reduce group purchasing power to support the markets. Use special funds correctly and strictly adhere to the regulation of the Central Committee about not sending gifts, not inviting guests, and not "using the back door." Miscellaneous income should be put under the centralized supervision of the various military regions, military arms, or branches of service, and be strictly supervised according to the method of

management for extrabudgetary income and expenditures.

6. Promote sideline agricultural production. The task for subsidiary agricultural production should be, on the present foundation, to consolidate and develop even further the goal of energetically striving to make the lower-level troops totally self-sufficient in meat and vegetables, and partially so in cooking oil. The production target for 1961, excluding those troops on combat duty, on construction tasks, and in special situations, is to strive for each person, on the average, to provide himself with about 25 catties of meat and 500-700 catties of vegetables (due to considerations of soil and manpower, city-based high-level organs and high-level academies and schools can reduce these production targets according to their situations). Cooking oil (mainly animal oil; work hard to produce vegetable oil where conditions permit) should be set according to the concrete situation by the various military regions, military arms, and branches of service. For sideline agricultural production in the army, except for labor power within the army or that of dependents accompanying the units, it is not permissible to hire local labor serving the front line of agriculture.

Sideline agricultural production should implement the twin policies of spare-time production and running small-scale farms well. The main thing in spare-time production is to plant vegetables for use now, and then raise a few hogs. For farms the main thing is to plant many vegetables, much animal feed, and raise a good number of hogs. In raising hogs, however, we must put into practice the policy of controlling quantity, raising quality, and producing fat hogs. On the average, it is enough for three to five persons to raise one hog; do not increase the quantity boundlessly.

7. Manage well army-run industry. Army-run iron, steel, and cement production should adhere firmly to the policy of using native methods to begin, going from small to big, from native methods to foreign methods, and having production spur more production. Estimated production for 1961 is 180,000 tons of pig iron, about 30,000 tons of steel, and about 300,000 tons of cement.

All repair shops should, based on the policy of repairing and making new parts at the same time, realize their present potential and, in addition to fulfilling their repairing responsibility, devise methods for expanding the scope of their manufacturing. The requirements for 1961 are to make ourselves 50-70 percent of all vehicle parts and over 60 percent of weapons parts. Production responsibility for parts for planes, ships, and tanks should be established by military arms and branches of service themselves. In addition we should use our present mechanized production capacity to make some of the facilities that we need.

In the production of military-related products we should continue to raise quality, organize well the dissemination of advanced experience, and rationally organize our labor power. The requirements for 1961 are to make marked improvements in product quality, raise labor productivity by 5 percent, and reduce production costs by one percent. We should strive to build a rubber plant and begin production quickly to provide ourselves with part of the rubber we need.

Army-run industrial and sideline agricultural production must strengthen supervision, improve the organization of production, make great efforts in technical renovation, raise quality, economize on labor power, and reduce production costs.

III

The key to the all-army campaign to increase production and practice economy and attainment of the foregoing important achievements lies in the fact that the whole army enthusiastically responded to the Central Committee's call for diligent striving and self-reliance, and adhered firmly to the Central Committee's directives on increasing production and practicing economy. The Military Affairs Commission and Chief Lin repeatedly instructed the whole army to maintain our army's excellent tradition of bitter striving, to share sweetness and hardship with the masses, and never to allow army life to become privileged, never allow army buildings to exceed local standards. They also clearly laid down the principle that strenuous efforts must be made to ensure that military expenditures focus on key items, and that, in general, financial outlays are reduced. All of these are the principles on which [the campaign] to increase production and practice economy has been run, and they have played a great role in this effort. In the work of organizing and implementing [the campaign] to increase production and practice economy, it should be kept in mind that there are three main problems.

First, Party committees at all levels have shown vigorous leadership, strengthened ideological education, and aroused the masses. The work of the various military regions, military arms, and branches of service in increasing production and practicing economy has been handled by Party committees and personally supervised by their leaders. This includes not only general exhortation but specific measures. For instance, they set the instructions for increasing production and practicing economy and for reducing grain rations, implemented regulations for increasing the portions of cooked food and reducing the purchasing power of social groups, and even suggested how to save on clothing. Moreover, Party committees, with their leaders taking personal command, are responsible for making the decisions which enabled the Army's production of iron, steel, and cement to increase in such a short time. This has only been realized because their determination has been great, they have promoted education to build up the nation and the army through industry and thrift, and they have aroused the masses and relied on them to overcome many difficulties. The development of the campaign to increase production and practice economy during the last year has been uneven — within a general picture of great accomplishment by the whole army, some units have achieved much and others little. The situation is complex, but the key is whether or not the Party committees have taken firm charge, whether or not their leaders have exercised careful supervision, and whether or not they have aroused and relied on the masses.

Second, the whole army's cultivation of a "three-eight work style" has been a huge, invisible force in spurring efforts to increase production and practice economy. In fact, striving to increase production and practice economy and loving public property are important elements in the style of hard work and plain living. Most of the accomplishments in increasing production and practicing economy mentioned above were achieved in over four months during the last half of the year. This is the result of a general upsurge in the "three-eight work style" and the flourishing of the "three-anti campaign."* During this campaign, the good working style of running things industriously and thriftily and loving public property was greatly developed, and the bad working style consisting of corruption, waste, and not loving public property was criticized and stopped. On this basis, there was a great positive turnabout in the supervision of expenditures, materials, and techniques, and in the implementation of regulations and systems. The combination of a great upsurge in the "three-eight work style" with conscious strengthening of supervision, perfecting of the pertinent regulations and systems, and strict handling of extravagance and waste, has even more firmly consolidated and heightened the accomplishments in increasing production and practicing economy.

Third, the fundamental measures for all aspects of increasing production and practicing economy have been vigorous development of technical renovation and technical revolution and effective dissemination of successful advanced techniques and advanced experience. For example, pushing ahead with increased portions of cooked food, emphasizing substitute foodstuffs, extending the installation of condensation and injection equipment on vehicles and engines, and promoting arched barracks, etc., have all played a direct role in practicing economy.

---

*The "three-anti campaign" referred to anticorruption, antiwaste, and anti-not-loving-public-property. However, it was not developed into a large scale movement in that period — Ying-mao Kau.

The current uniform reform is the comprehensive application of the results of [changes] in techniques of designing and making uniforms, and it is also an important measure in economizing on cloth. It will also facilitate fighting, operation, and the logistics of supplies. The leadership task of the campaign to increase production and practice economy is, on the basis of ideological education and working-style cultivation, to bring the enthusiasm and creativity of the broad masses of officers and soldiers to bear on technical renovation and technical revolution in order continuously to extend the results of the campaign.

We feel that the foregoing three points have universal significance for the intensified development of the campaign to increase production and practice economy; hereafter we should step up our study and determination to make the accomplishments of the campaign even greater in 1961.

[Issued on] November 23, 1960

11

THE GENERAL POLITICAL DEPARTMENT
OF THE PLA DRAWS UP THE "IMPLEMENTATION
PLAN FOR THE ARMY'S PARTICIPATION IN
AND SUPPORT OF THE AGRICULTURAL
COOPERATIVIZATION MOVEMENT AND
AGRICULTURAL PRODUCTION"*

People's Daily

In order to mobilize the whole army in all-out, concrete support of the National Program for Agricultural Development
(Draft) for 1956-1967, submitted by the Politburo of the Central
Committee of the Chinese Communist Party, the General Political Department of the Chinese People's Liberation Army
drew up the "Implementation Plan for the Army's Participation
in and Support of the Agricultural Cooperativization Movement
and Agricultural Production." The Plan directs that the whole
army should step up training, accelerate the modernization of
the army, actively deal a heavy blow to the harassing activities
of Chiang Kai-shek's forces, make active preparation for liberating Taiwan, resolutely suppress counterrevolutionaries,
and vigilantly safeguard socialist construction of the motherland. Apart from these tasks, all army units should, as far as pos-
ble, utilize the intervals between fighting and training to join
the people of the whole country in the struggle to perform each

_____

*"Chung-kuo jen-min chieh-fang-chün tsung-cheng-chih-pu
chih-ting 'kuan-yü chün-tui ts'an-chia ho chih-yüan nung-yeh
ho-tso-hua yün-tung chi nung-yeh sheng-ch'an ti shih-shih
fang-an,' " Jen-min jih-pao, February 9, 1956.

146

of the tasks outlined in the National Program for Agricultural Development.

There are twenty points in the "Implementation Plan for the Army's Participation in and Support of the Agricultural Cooperativization Movement and Agricultural Production." The contents of this plan are as follows:

1. All officers and soldiers will continually be urged and organized to write frequently to their dependents, relatives, and friends, prompting and encouraging them to take the road of socialism. Those dependents, relatives, and friends who have already joined the cooperatives should be urged to observe labor discipline, strive to increase production, and become active elements in the cooperatives. Those who have not yet joined the cooperatives should be persuaded to join the cooperatives at an early date. Workers should be encouraged to display greater activism and creativity, participate in socialist labor emulation, raise labor efficiency, and fulfill and overfulfill production tasks. Handicraftsmen and various independent workers should be persuaded to obey state plans and tread the path of cooperativization. Members of the capitalist class should be led to realize the law of social development, give up the practice of exploitation, accept the [socialist] transformation and strive to be the active elements, and become self-supporting workers. Landlords and rich peasants should be directed to obey the laws and decrees of the government, stop practicing exploitation, engage in labor, and accept [thought] reform.

2. In the areas where army cadres are required to take part in the work of building and reorganizing cooperatives (particularly areas liberated late, border regions, coastal islands, and minority nationality areas), the Party committees of the local garrison forces should take the initiative and consult the local Party committees about assigning a number of officers and soldiers to form some work teams. These work teams, under the unified leadership of the local Party committees, after being trained, will help carry out agricultural cooperativization or other socialist transformation work. Apart from

this, the army should systematically supply the local governments each year with a number of officers who are suited to local work in order to support socialist construction and transformation in the country.

3. All armymen will be urged to carry on the drive to practice economy, oppose extravagance and waste, strictly observe financial and supply systems, and take good care of weapons, equipment, and public properties, with a view to saving as much money as possible for socialist construction. Those officers and soldiers who have families in the rural villages should be encouraged to save money so that they can send it back to their homes to be invested in the cooperatives to provide funds for developing production. All officers should also be urged to subscribe to the state economic construction bonds. Banks in the garrison areas should be assisted to launch a "patriotic savings campaign" in the army so that capital funds can be accumulated for socialist construction of the country.

4. In the three-year period from 1956 through 1958, the army will internally raise funds for the establishment of 30 tractor stations, and provide them with various technicians selected from among the demobilized servicemen, to support agricultural production. (These will consist of 5 large, 10 medium and 15 small tractor stations with working capacities for each station of 200,000, 100,000, and 50,000 mou respectively.) These tractor stations, when completed, will be turned over to the Ministry of Agriculture for distribution and employment. The present plans envisage building 2 large, 3 medium, and 5 small tractor stations in 1956; 2 large, 3 medium, and 5 small tractor stations in 1957; and 1 large, 4 medium, and 5 small stations in 1958.

5. A system of compulsory labor in support of socialist construction should be carried out. Various military units, offices, and schools should, according to their respective conditions, get in touch with local Party committees and people's councils so as to arrange in the course of a year a number of labor days for their members' systematic participation in socialist construction in their localities. On the average, each

person is expected to contribute five to seven voluntary workdays annually. In the countryside the members of military units will mainly help the agricultural producers' cooperatives in performing all kinds of farm work, and will participate in constructing water conservancy projects, building dikes and roads, and reclaiming land. In cities they will help primarily in municipal construction.

6. The personnel of the entire army will be mobilized and organized to participate, during spare time and holidays, in the drive to eliminate the "four pests" [rats, sparrows, flies, and mosquitoes]. It is expected that these four pests will be largely eliminated in all barracks by the end of this year. In addition, members of military units should be organized to help local people eliminate the four pests. Whenever local residents start a campaign to destroy other kinds of harmful animals, birds, or insects, troops stationed in the area should take an active part in it. Moreover, the military service bureaus at all levels may organize militia within a set period of time to hunt and kill dangerous wild beasts in the mountains. While engaging in the elimination of harmful insects, birds, or animals, the troops should at the same time be taught to protect those insects, birds, and beasts that are useful.

7. Troops should take an active part in planting trees and building forests. Within a two-year period, from 1956 through 1957, all barracks and military schools are to be landscaped with more trees. When troops build highways or railways they should line both sides with trees. In military defense zones, unless the planting of trees will create obstacles to the operation of weapons, troops should as far as possible "turn the land green." In addition, garrison troops should also provide a certain amount of manpower to help local people plant trees and develop forests in accordance with the local plan. Troops stationed on the coast should actively engage in building and protecting forests to serve national defense. Troops assigned to protect forests or stationed in the vicinity of forests should take good care of the forests and always be on the alert to extinguish forest fires.

8. Troops stationed in urban areas or in the countryside should make arrangements with local people's councils or agricultural cooperatives to collect feces and dung for the cooperatives.

9. Troops should often join with local inhabitants in the disposal of garbage so as to keep the surroundings in a clean and hygienic condition. Military hygiene service personnel should organize propaganda campaigns at least once or twice every month to give the soldiers as well as the civilians the necessary knowledge, according to the conditions of public health, for maintaining health and for the prevention of diseases, and should help the civilians in clinic work and in the prevention of serious diseases. Whenever an epidemic breaks out, the military hygiene service personnel should enforce quarantines, carry out disinfection, and endeavor to bring the epidemic quickly to an end. When there are emergency cases, all hygiene service companies or battalions, medical departments, and hospitals under the military should, without exception, provide clinic service to members of agricultural producers' cooperatives, dependents of servicemen or martyrs, and disabled servicemen in the area, or send out medical personnel on call.

10. Military forces should actively participate in the protection and breeding of livestock, and should strictly prohibit the slaughter of draft animals and calves. Army veterinarians should devote part of their time each month to assisting the local cooperatives in the prevention and cure of animal diseases and help the cooperatives train their own veterinarians. Army horses that are no longer fit for military purposes may be turned over to local people's councils to be distributed to the agricultural producers' cooperatives. Except when stationed in cities, all military units in villages and market towns should raise pigs in the ratio of one pig for every fifty persons, provided this will not cause waste of food grains.

11. Whenever a natural calamity or emergency situation arises, such as the occurrence of floods, droughts, insect pestilence, windstorms, or hailstorms, troops stationed in the affected area should, under the unified leadership of the local

Party committee and the people's council, do their best to help the people fight the disaster and arrange relief. They should do all they can to conquer all kinds of natural calamities and to minimize the resultant damage. When military units receive a forecast of an impending natural disaster, they should immediately pass the information to the residents in the area and help the local people's council organize the residents for early precautionary measures.

12. Military units should systematically assist the cooperatives, factories, and mines in the garrison area to set up primary schools and evening schools, and participate in the drive to eliminate illiteracy. They should help the local government train teachers and help the cooperatives train bookkeeping personnel. Apart from this, they should also help the cooperatives set up libraries and clubs, supply them with teaching materials, books, pictures, and musical instruments, and arrange lectures on scientific subjects and current events and policies. The troops should also carry on internally the program to eliminate illiteracy. It should be guaranteed henceforth that all those servicemen who have been demobilized will possess the educational level of a junior primary school student and will have been taught to speak Mandarin.

13. The existing movie projector teams, cultural work troupes, and spare-time cultural groups of the armed forces should work out plans according to local conditions, and allocate a fixed amount of their time each month or each season to give shows and performances for the local residents. In general it is expected that each movie projector team of military units stationed in villages and suburbs will give ten shows annually, and each cultural work troupe five performances annually, for the agricultural producers' cooperatives. The troops' spare-time cultural work teams should hold a reception party jointly with the cooperatives each season. When movies are shown or performances staged by the troops, as many local people as possible should be invited to attend. In addition, military units should also assign personnel to help local people develop cultural entertainment and sports, to

assist peasants in the villages in organizing spare-time theatrical companies, and to train cultural and entertainment activists among the peasants.

14. Army signal units, without affecting their regular duties, should actively assist in establishing broadcasting and telephone networks in rural areas. In addition to constructing the military communications network and assisting local authorities in drawing up plans for the construction of a rural telephone and relayed broadcasting network, the army shall permit the local authorities to hang, free of charge, additional lines on the poles of military telephone lines already in existence or to be constructed, provided they do not interfere with the military's use of them. Moreover, the army shall be responsible for the maintenance [of the added civilian lines]. Telephone detachments on the army and division level of the PLA should assign signal troops and equipment at the rate of not less than ten workdays per signal soldier every year to help the agricultural producers' cooperatives install telephone wires. Within a three-year period, from 1956 through 1958, the telephone detachments should strive to assist the local postal and telecommunications services to basically complete the construction of a rural telephone and broadcasting network. The repair workshops and technicians of military signal units at various levels should assist the local cooperatives in repairing telephone receivers and switchboards, radio transmitters and receivers, etc. Moreover, they should help the cooperatives train telephone maintenance, repair, and administrative personnel.

15. In addition to fulfilling their regular tasks, the army's repair shops should try their best to help the agricultural producers' cooperatives repair farm implements and agricultural machines if the facilities of the workshops permit.

16. When the army plans to build electrical power stations to meet its own requirements for electricity, it should as far as possible take into consideration the demands for electricity of the local agricultural producers' cooperatives, and consult the people's council of the area to map out a comprehensive plan.

17. When the army has to requisition land to meet the need
for construction and training, it must make accurate calcula-
tions and provide rational controls in order to economize land
and to avoid waste.

18. The central theme of the education of soldiers to be demobilized should be an emphasis on their active participation
in the nation's socialist construction, and particularly their
active participation in the agricultural producers' cooperatives,
so that, when they return home, they can become the backbone
of the cooperatives. As for the technical personnel among the
demobilized servicemen, the army should consult local administrative authorities in advance and make coordinated arrangements for their resettlement. It must be ensured that every
tank crewman, truck driver, mechanic, telephone operator,
or hygiene service crewman demobilized from the army is
sent to a production post where he is most needed.

19. Army officers at various levels should educate their dependents, who are accompanying them and are not engaged in
any work, on the "glory of labor." The officers should encourage them to join the local agricultural producers' cooperatives
or organize them to engage in productive labor in order to create wealth for society.

20. Army units should maintain frequent contact with local
agricultural producers' cooperatives. Every military unit,
office, or school stationed in the countryside or in a suburban
area should be associated with a local agricultural producers'
cooperative, and regularly extend to it all kinds of assistance.
Moreover, military units should frequently send their soldiers
to visit associated cooperatives, invite comrades from the cooperatives to address them, and hold various festival activities
and parties jointly with the cooperatives. Model personnel
from the army and cooperatives may establish personal contacts among themselves for mutual encouragement and mutual
assistance. Following a similar method, military units in cities
should also establish contacts with local factories and mines,
or with local agricultural producers' cooperatives in the out-
skirts.

12

THE GENERAL POLITICAL DEPARTMENT ISSUES AN OUTLINE FOR THE PARTICIPATION OF THE ARMED FORCES IN CONSTRUCTION WORK*

People's Daily

The General Political Department of the Chinese People's Liberation Army recently issued an outline concerning the participation of the Armed Forces in the work of socialist construction. It called for each military unit to make an even greater contribution by participating in socialist construction in an organized and planned way in order to realize gradually the industrialization of the nation and the commune, and the mechanization and electrification of agriculture.

The outline points out that in the past several years the record of the military's participation in socialist construction has been formidable. In doing such work, the army was not only helpful in the socialist construction of our country but, moreover, through its productive labor together with the people, military personnel were intimately linked with the masses and with production, and the army was further united with local units and the people. Participation by the military units in socialist construction enabled the military personnel to gain a certain knowledge of production and much good experience in local work. It also elevated the military personnel's consciousness of labor and communism.

The outline states that the armed forces' participation in socialist construction must proceed in a planned and organized manner. According to the decision of the Military Affairs Commission of the Central Committee on the military's "using one

*"Tsung-cheng fa-ch'u chün-tui ts'an-chia chien-she kung-tso kang-yao," Jen-min-jih-pao, February 26, 1959.

to two months a year to participate in production," each unit should take about fifty percent of the time to participate in various kinds of local construction work, with the rest of the time devoted to the operation of the army's internal industrial and agricultural production. The military units' support of local production work should be carried out primarily in places near or not too far from where they are stationed. Moreover, the army ought to put the emphasis on participating in capital construction projects in the areas of agricultural irrigation, factory building, culture, and education.

The outline demands that all officers and men actively participate in various work projects that are beneficial to the development and consolidation of communes; educate their family members, relatives, and friends to become activists in the communes; and, moreover, use a certain amount of their labor and skills to help the communes in construction and production. Given the premise of absolutely guaranteeing the fulfillment of military production and teaching tasks, factories, repair shops, service detachments of the army, and workshops, laboratories, experimental and research departments of various technical schools will undertake the production of machinery and parts urgently needed by the people's communes or local industries; will dispatch technical personnel to assist the people's communes in constructing factories and technical repair stations; will carry out the tasks of designing and installing the factories to be built, and will train local technical personnel.

Given the premise of not interfering with war preparation and military training, various communications and transportation equipment of the army should be used to actively support local communications and transportation enterprises. The Air Force ought to participate as much as possible in the tasks of surveying, investigating, and drawing up plans for the civil aeronautics network. Communications troops should assist the people's communes near their stations in building either wired or wireless broadcasting and communications systems. In addition, each military unit ought to participate in the seasonal agricultural productive labor, and in planting trees and making forests; help the commune in the tasks of culture, education, and hygiene; manage well various kinds of collective welfare enterprises. In cases of emergency brought on by calamities, it must make every effort to deal with the situation and help the local people eliminate the danger of calamities. In the southeastern coastal areas, the military units, under feasible conditions, ought to protect fishing and navigation in order to ensure the safety of the fishermen and boatmen.

The outline demands that every military unit frequently pay attention to assisting the locale improve and strengthen the people's militia, carry out the Party's policy of "everyone a soldier," and make the people's militia truly become the shock force on the production front and the military's excellent reserve force. Those military units stationed in areas of ethnic minorities, in border regions, and on islands, should pay special attention to carrying out the Party's nationality policies, treating the people with sincerity and modesty, doing well the tasks of consolidating the border and coastal defense, and, moreover, helping the local people develop production and improve their livelihood.

Finally, the outline points out that, while the military units participating in socialist construction must proceed under the unified planning of the local Party committees, the military personnel must also treat and study their local work experience seriously.

13

NEW CONTRIBUTIONS IN RAILROAD CONSTRUCTION
BY THE LIBERATION ARMY RAILWAY CORPS*

Bright Daily

Under the guidance of the line of unity and victory adopted
by the Ninth Party Congress, the Railway Corps of the Chinese
People's Liberation Army has in the past year further implemented Chairman Mao's great policy of "grasp revolution,
promote production and other work, and prepare against war,"
and has gone all out in building railroads and making new contributions to socialist construction of the motherland.

The Railway Corps plays an important role in the motherland's railroad construction. Last year, braving intense heat
and severe cold, the commanders and fighters together with
the broad masses of people stepped up the rate of construction.
Not only was there a great increase in the quantity of major
projects completed over that of 1970, their engineering quality
was also excellent. At the construction sites, one tunnel after
another penetrated rapidly through the mountains, and one bridge
after another went across rivers and streams. Displaying
the spirit of fearing neither hardship nor death, they overcame
all sorts of difficulties and fulfilled their construction task with
"greater, faster, better, and more economical results." Some

---

*"Chieh-fang-chün t'ieh-tao-ping pu-tui tsai t'ieh-lu chien-
she-chung tso-ch'u hsin kung-hsien," Kuang-ming jih-pao,
January 20, 1972.

of the railroad lines have already been completed and successfully opened to traffic.

"The line is the key link; once it is grasped, everything falls
into place." The achievements attained by the Railway Corps
are a result of the thorough implementation of Chairman Mao's
proletarian revolutionary line. In the past year or more, commanders and fighters of various units, in accordance with
Chairman Mao's teaching on "carrying out education in ideology
and political line," have conscientiously read the works of
Marx and Lenin, as well as the writings of Chairman Mao, and
carried out in-depth repudiation of revisionism and rectification. Giving further play to their revolutionary spirit, they
struggled arduously in high spirit and fine mettle to fulfill and
overfulfill the task of construction. During the construction
last year, many units achieved new records and set new standards. While digging a big tunnel through a high and formidable
mountain, a certain unit came upon a subterranean stream in the
course of construction. Jets of high pressure water shot out
from the rock at a rate of 10,000 tons per day. The commanders and fighters had to battle in waist-high water against the
hardship to dig their way through the mountain. Not only was
the schedule of construction unaffected, they even speeded up
the excavation and set a new record. In the early spring of last
year, the company to which the late "mountain-climbing hero"
Yang Lien-ti belonged when he was alive took part in the construction of a big bridge. Braving severe cold, the fighters
leaped into the bone-chilling current to build foundations for
the bridge. Working together with other sister companies,
they constructed a forty-five-meter abutment in the river in a
few short months. Another unit was involved in constructing a
railroad along the hill and by the side of water. The line had
to cross a number of streams. During the dry season when the
water ran low, the commanders and fighters concentrated their
efforts in building abutments and foundations in the water; and
during the rainy season they worked hard digging tunnels.
They set a record of completing more than thirty kilometers
of bridges and tunnels in a year.

Giving play to the glorious tradition of arduous struggle, various units of the Railway Corps have carried out construction work according to [the principle of] building the country by thrift and doing everything by thrift. Many units, under the condition of heavy tasks with insufficient material, transportation facilities, and machinery, used every means to tap potentials, to improve techniques, and to use old and obsolete tools for building the railway by thrift. A certain unit, by utilizing local material, tested and popularized the method of mixing pebbles with cement for the building of bridge piers and railway tunnels and for surfacing walls and other plastering work. This reduced the amount of cement for plastering by about 35 percent, and thereby saved a large amount of cement and labor while ensuring the quality of work. Another unit, doing construction work in an inaccessible mountain region, had its commanders and fighters open up a water transportation route across dangerous shoals and waves to transport a large amount of construction material to meet the needs of the project. Other units in close support of construction operated a number of small plants for producing explosives, cement, light bulbs, and bridge beams, and for repairing machine tools. They performed the function of facilitating construction. In the course of laying tiles for the construction of a new railway, a regiment overcame difficulties by integrating indigenous with foreign methods, and produced more than 300 pieces of reinforced ore-stressed concrete beams and a simple tile-laying machine of their own design and manufacture. They not only satisfied their own needs for tiles and beams, but also supported the railroad and bridge construction of other units. Many units paid attention to investigation and study for improving construction designs. A unit, by adopting the "three-in-one" combination of leading members, technical personnel, and soldiers, and in cooperation with the design department, made improvements in 174 areas in the designing of railroad line and saved a large amount of capital investment for the state.

In the course of the construction of railroads, the masses

of people living along the various lines, under the leadership of the local Party committees, actively participated in the construction by opening transportation links and transporting equipment and materials. The laboring of armymen and civilians shoulder to shoulder in building the railroad together has not only accelerated the rate of construction, but also forged still closer the ties between the army and the government and between the army and the people. They also played an important part in stimulating the revolutionization and construction of the army.

At the present time, the broad masses of commanders and fighters are conscientiously summing up their experience. They are determined to go all out in the new year and aim still higher to make new contributions to the motherland's cause of railroad construction.

IV
The Army and Socio-Cultural Change

14

CONCERNING THE QUESTION OF POLITICAL AND
CULTURAL TRAINING IN MILITARY UNITS*

T'ao Chu

I. Ideological Development and Cultural Improvements
Should Be the Main Substance of Our Tasks
in Training and Consolidation

1. China's war of liberation has basically achieved victory
throughout the country. The entire Central-South area, with
the exception of Hainan Island, has been liberated. Now, aside
from the military task of successfully completing the liberation of Hainan Island, our army should gradually relieve all the
troops of their combat duties in order for them to go into training and production. Those troops that are undertaking bandit
suppression have also basically completed their task in some

---

*T'ao Chu, "Kuan-yü pu-tui cheng-chih wen-hua cheng-hsün
wen-t'i," Ch'ang-chiang jih-pao [Yangtze Daily], April 4, 1950;
reprinted in Hsin-Hua yüeh-pao [New China Monthly], II:1
(May 1950), 166-170. This was a report delivered at a meeting
of high-level cadres of the Fourth Field Army and the Central-
South Military Region. T'ao was then concurrently director of
the Political Department of the Fourth Field Army and the
Central-South Military Region.

parts of the provinces. In the parts of those provinces where the bandit situation is still relatively serious the troops should strive to complete their suppression within the first half of this year. Work teams will then finish up land reform in due course. Our army's responsibility towards training and production should therefore be considered as a long-term and primary responsibility, both now and in the future, with the goal of building an army for national defense and participating in the national economic construction.

2. As regards training and production, since the army should always be essentially a combat army, the troops should therefore also consider training as their most basic responsibility. The aim of training is to make our troops an even stronger force, sufficient to protect our victory and to ensure that our people's new motherland will never again be the victim of aggression by any of the imperialists. The past history of China, particularly the history of the last hundred years, shows that because our country was internally backward and weak it was often beaten and ridiculed. Now we have stood up, we have made progress, we are strong; but standing up, making progress, and becoming strong should first be reflected in a military strength that is adequate to defend the country. Otherwise we will still be beaten. Comrade Stalin aptly said: "Much of Russia's past history shows that because Russia was backward it was trounced. The Mongol Khan beat Russia, the Turkish nobility beat her. The Swedish feudal lords beat her; the feudal lords of Poland and Lithuania beat her. British and French capitalists beat her. Japan's nobles beat her. Everyone beat her, and just because she was backward. Because her armaments, her culture, her national government, her industry and agriculture were all backward and underdeveloped, everyone beat her. They knew that they could win and would not suffer retribution. You remember, in the period before the revolution, a poet's words were as follows: 'Mother Russia! You are prosperous, but also poor; you are strong, but also weak.' All these overlords had memorized these words of the old poet very thoroughly. While beating us, they teased: 'Since you are prosperous'

it is all right to depend on you to become rich. While beating us, they also teased us, saying, 'Since you are weak and poor' it is all right to beat and rob you at our discretion. To strike the backward and the weak — this is the law of exploitation. This is the capitalist way of getting rich, in which 'the weak are the prey of the strong.' You are backward, weak, without strength? Then that means that you have no rights, and that therefore you can be beaten and enslaved. You are great and strong? Then that means that you are always in the right, and that you should be treated carefully. Because this is the way things are, we cannot afford to be backward again." Therefore we too, following our victory, should first, without hesitation, build up and strengthen our present army. Only when we are under the protection of an even stronger national defense army can we start talking about national construction. Otherwise, even supposing we should succeed in construction, it would amount to spilling our heart's blood in vain. This is our meaning when today we indicate that the training of military units is our most basic task.

3. Accordingly, it is certain that by using training to continuously improve and strengthen our army we can build it into a strong and modernized national defense army. Right now the most important work is that of carrying out ideological development and cultural improvement among the troops. Without solving these two problems, which are basic to our present and future construction, it will be impossible to raise the level of the troops' ability and to acquire the most advanced learning of military science and technology. Ideological development, therefore, should first concentrate on thoroughly and systematically resolving the many presently emerging or already existing ideological scruples regarding army training. We should make sure that the idea of the army as a permanent fighting force is consolidated and accepted throughout the army in order to lay the ideological foundations for building a national defense army. On raising the cultural level of the troops, the report of Political Commissar T'an Cheng clearly points out: "In the army's military-political and cultural training, cultural

training is presently the most important. Cultural education should form the main content of army training for the next several years." At the present time, therefore, the stress in army training should be put on politics and culture rather than on military training. In reference to political rectification and cultural training, the report of Political Commissar T'an Cheng pointed out that within the first six months of this year, using the time between bandit suppression or production, all units of the army should carry out ideological education, and patriotism should certainly be taken as the core of this education. Starting with the second half of the year, for at least one year, seventy percent of the time should be taken up with cultural education and thirty percent with military-political education. In other words, by first using political education to resolve the troops' ideological problems we can then carry out cultural and military education even better. What is more, political education, with the help of cultural education, will continuously raise the political consciousness of the officers and men. After having achieved the goal of raising the level of culture we can then exert our efforts on all fronts to carry out military education and training.

II. How to Carry Out Ideological Development in Military Units

1. The Current Ideological Situation and Characteristics in Military Units

A. Generally speaking, the transition from war to peaceful construction constitutes a great turning point in history. Because of our inadequate education, there are many people in the army who, facing this great turning point in history, have either an incomplete or a biased understanding of revolutionary development and outlook, basic conditions, tasks, government policies, and so on. This inadequate understanding easily gives rise to all sorts of individualist attitudes. As a result of the new conditions of victory and peace, the revolutionaries are unquestionably inspired to advance with even more steadfast courage, but it is also easy under these new conditions for the fighting spirit of the revolutionaries to be eroded. Having undergone this process of erosion, individualist attitudes are manifested in several ways. On the one hand there is the feeling of longing for enjoyment and slackening efforts; on the other hand there is the idea of being tired of army life and wanting to change profession. Another attitude is that of considering oneself to be an honored statesman, an attitude of proud conceit. In a word, these people display their irresolute hesitation in the face of victory, and in some serious cases they even want to fall back and leave the army. According to the most recent materials from all army units reflecting the ideological situation, regardless of whether they had been continuously on combat duty on the sea, or on bandit suppression duty, or had been in training in the rear areas, or had originally been organizational units in the rear areas, there was evidence of the ideological situation described above. In the case of units that had been fighting on the sea, when they were given further combat duty after the victorious battle in Kwangsi, their thoughts underwent relatively great fluctuation. Now that they have undergone education and mobilization, the fluctuations in their thoughts have subsided, and their combat spirit has rallied. On the whole they still show an easy acceptance of the idea of the army as a permanent fighting force in which the will to fight cannot be weakened in the least bit. However, there are a number of people who are obedient to their organizations, but with reservations. They will not speak out now, but keep their feelings hidden in their hearts. "Wait until we have finished fighting in Hainan Island, and then we will talk." The same sort of situation has emerged among the troops engaged in bandit suppression. Now that the big fighting is over they are not willing to fight to suppress bandits. They grumble that the hardship and suffering is endless and hope that they will soon be able to settle down. They want to enjoy things a bit by being among men in the national defense army. Some cadres want to change their line of work, and soldiers want to demobilize and go home. After having gone through preliminary education, although most of their emotions have stabilized, the strength of a minority is not enough and the problem has not yet been thoroughly resolved. In the case of military units that were withdrawn from the front for training and organizational units that were originally in the rear areas, since the former were the first to receive training they felt that the upper levels had appointed them to be a national defense army and took it as a great honor. In general, their spirit was very high, but they did not have a correct understanding regarding a national defense army and had considerable ideological problems. As the latter started receiving education earlier — cadres had been undergoing training for six months — so their idea of lifelong service for the national defense army was relatively clear. Nevertheless, there was still some ideological resistance manifested toward training and production, and it still could not be said that problems were solved ideologically. We can see from the situation described above regarding the problem of ideology among the troops after the war that, because we were aware of these problems relatively early, each unit then began, to a greater or lesser extent, to undertake the resolution of this problem. We are still unable, however, to resolve the problems of the postwar ideology of the troops in a relatively penetrating and systematic manner. Therefore, because it is impossible to implant the idea of lifelong service in the construction of a national defense army clearly and throughout the whole army, at this time we should say that the incorrect thoughts and emotions in military units are still in the midst of agitation and growth, and if we do not take this into account it will be very harmful to our work.

B. We should look at another aspect of the situation: our troops are the people's army, and they have grown out of the revolutionary struggle. They have long been tempered and led by the firm leadership of the Party, have laid the foundation of Party organizations (Party members constitute 30-40 percent, of which the great majority are working people), and for a long time have taken education in the ideology of the proletariat as their main guide, so that generally speaking they have a certain degree of political consciousness. What is more, this great turning point in history will be one important aspect in spurring the victorious people and the victorious army to continuously forge ahead, making even greater progress. Therefore the ideological fluctuations emerging among the troops can only be considered as a by-product of conditions brought about by victory. This point is further explained by the fact that most of the military cadres, particularly the young cadres, acquire the determination to establish a national defense army as soon as they have gone through ideological mobilization. This is most clearly evident in the enthusiasm with which they study. What is more, soldiers show a high level of activism regarding the establishment of national defense after the war. According to statistics from an investigation of the Fifth Company, 348th Regiment, XXX Army, 167 of the 193 veteran soldiers in that company were resolved to establish a national defense army. Among these veteran soldiers, more than 60-70 percent bought paper and pencils after the war in preparation for cultural studies.

C. Ideological problems arising among the troops are always seen when soldiers find themselves in new situations and carrying out new responsibilities. Naturally these problems have their class and historical roots. The most important of these roots are to be found in the class character of the peasants and the petty bourgeoisie, which is conservative and clings to private ownership, showing a very narrow and restricted revolutionary outlook. We should admit that our reform of the backward peasant and petty bourgeois ideology existing among the troops up until today has not been sufficient. Our army is an army of peasants in military dress, and it is certainly no easy matter to reform their ideology into a proletarian ideology. If our current efforts are insufficient, then how much more insufficient was our education to reform this ideology during the long period when we were in the midst of war! Moreover, new elements are continually being added. As new conditions and new responsibilities arise, it is naturally very difficult to come suddenly to a correct understanding, and it is very easy to latch onto all sorts of ideas for individual benefit. Therefore, although the development of problems in the troops' ideology manifests all kinds of signs of conscious individualism, it also bears the semiconscious nature of a natural blindness. (Those who in full consciousness commit willful offenses are a very small minority.) This is to say that in general, although always supported by individualist ideology, problems of ideology among the troops are not only due to individualism but also to the added effect of a lack of understanding or a one-sided understanding of the long-term prospects of the revolution, the basic situation, the tasks of the military and politics, and various other phenomena. Right now the greatest number of ideological problems evident among army cadres are most commonly centered around their personal situation and prospects and around family and marital problems. The soldiers all want to go home to see how things are. They hope that after the adoption of the conscription system there will be a changing of the guard and that they will be able to shift their obligations. (The most important questions are home and marital ones.) This arises from a lack of understanding or an inadequate understanding of our meaning when we say that in regard to the great future of China's revolution our victory is only like the first step in a journey of ten thousand li. This arises from a lack of understanding or an inadequate understanding of the great significance of the construction of a national defense army and of the glorious responsibility to be borne in that construction by the veteran cadres of worker and peasant origin. This arises from a lack of understanding or inadequate understanding of the temporary hardships after the war and of the country's need for construction, a lack of understanding of the principle that because the new nation belongs to the people themselves, only after the nation has been rebuilt can individual people prosper. This arises from a lack of understanding or an inadequate understanding of the fact that past achievements of the revolution can only be significant if they [the army cadres] are now even more active in forging ahead on the road of the revolution. Otherwise, being maimed in midcourse is equivalent to making an effort in vain. This arises from an unclear and confused understanding of the things mentioned above. When we add to this lack of understanding all the demands of the individual (such as his working and living conditions, family and marital problems) that cannot obtain immediate solution and satisfaction, then we inevitably come up with ideological problems. Naturally there is presently a serious manifestation of ideological problems among our troops. Some are themselves conscious of their bad ideology, but still, only seeking to enjoy life, become corrupt and decadent. They only want to build up their own individual fortunes, and resolutely demand to be demobilized. But the cadres among whom these various phenomena are manifested constitute a very small minority. Those among the soldiers who resolutely demand demobilization and want to go home are only a very few among the veteran soldiers, and most of them are older soldiers and soldiers in bad physical condition. There are comparatively many [malcontents] among the new soldiers, but this too is important evidence of the problem of inadequate education.

2. We Must Thoroughly Conduct Ideological Education in
   Patriotism

Under the conditions of victory, patriotic education is launched to point out the great future of the revolution, and to educate the people to continue the struggle for its realization with incomparably brave bearing. Patriotic education bears the sacred responsibility of eternally protecting the nation's territories. The conscious and armed workers and peasants should develop education with the idea of building a permanent fighting force. Education in patriotism is the ideological education for the demands of the new nation's construction and for the people to actively participate in national construction with exemplary conduct. Patriotic education in the achievements that led to the victory of the revolution, with an attitude neither proud nor satisfied, should foster further accomplishments and maintain the glories. In sum, education in patriotism should serve mainly to actively arouse people so that they will find happiness and a sense of honor in revolution and develop revolutionary heroism....*

III. How to Raise the Cultural Level in Military Units

1. Basic Situation and Needs

A. The level of culture and science in our army is presently very low. If we do not resolve this problem it will be impossible to succeed in building the modernized national defense army that we want. The situation is this: (1) The level of illiteracy and semiliteracy in most companies (semiliteracy means to know a few hundred Chinese characters but not to have the "four capabilities" [the ability to read, write, speak articulately, and practice what you have learned]) is estimated at more than 80 percent in each company. If we take the level of an upper primary school education as a yardstick, then those who do not measure up to the upper primary school level constitute more than 90 percent in each company. (2) The cultural levels of platoon and above, with about 80,000 or 90,000 of them the entire army ranks, where there are 120,000 cadres at the levels of platoon and above, with about 80,000 or 90,000 of them of worker and peasant origin, shows that their working position as cadres and their cultural level do not correspond at all. Insofar as reading ability is concerned, there are a great many illiterates among the cadres at the battalion level and above, and it is even worse among the cadres at the company and platoon levels. Most nonilliterate cadres at the battalion level and above have only a rough idea of Chinese characters, without the ability to read theoretical books or literary works. In writing, they are only able to write sentences that do not fully convey their meaning. If we consider knowledge of the natural sciences, the majority of these cadres are even more

---

*Three paragraphs are omitted here because they are not very relevant to the subject of education — Ying-mao Kau.

seriously deficient. Some of them have no knowledge of the sciences at all. Therefore we should devise means to raise the cultural level of the entire army. The raising of the cadres' cultural level especially will be of decisive significance in the establishment of a national defense army.

B. Today we should consider the raising of the army's cultural level as the core of military training. This problem is an urgent one, not only for the leadership but also for the whole army — officers and men. Some military units have found that after study begins the esprit de corps of the troops has risen rapidly. The majority of officers and soldiers use their monthly allowance to buy stationery for study. Their achievements in reading are quickly apparent. Moreover, quite a few veteran cadres, having first been forced against their will to study, are now already desperately determined to study culture. In one case, a battalion commander in the 153rd Division, Comrade Liu T'ai, learned more than 800 characters in only two months. Everyone already recognizes that after the victory of the revolution it will not do to be without culture, no matter what the job. With literary training, the prospects for being a member of the national defense army certainly will be better, and even those who later do not remain in the army will still be capable of finding other work and fitting in anywhere. The current fluctuations of ideology among officers and men are particularly strong among veteran cadres without cultural training because they are generally worried about their own future. When we solve this problem on our own initiative it has great significance in the consolidation of the military units as well. At the same time, it is very important in cultivating human talent for national construction. After solving its own cadre needs, the army still has other responsibilities. The army should continue to send cadres into other fields of national construction. Because of the glorious origins of army cadres (the army is a workers' and peasants' organization with the consciousness of having gone through an ordeal), the high tide of cultural development will first rise from the army, and in the future the army will become a vast school for cadres.

C. The actual needs for raising the cultural level of military
units: We plan to start in July of this year (before June, in a
three-month period, we pulled together the current ideological
problems in military units and carried out patriotic education
in order to lay an ideological foundation for training in the construction of a national defense army) and in a three-year period carry out training with cultural studies as the main content.
(First we decided that in the first year we would spend 70 percent of our time on cultural training and the remaining 30 percent on military and political training.) We aim to raise the
cultural level of ordinary soldiers to the level of a graduate of
a senior primary school, and that of company and platoon cadres to the level of a junior middle school graduate. Cadres at
the battalion level and above should reach a level comparable
to that of a senior middle school graduate. In this, the most
important point is to raise their knowledge of the national language so that they will be able to read relatively profound theoretical books and all sorts of written directives necessary in
order for them to exercise leadership. As for mathematics,
metaphysics, etc., it will suffice if we raise their level just a
bit, about to that of a graduate of a junior middle school. Cadres who go so far as to study specialized military science and
technology should emphasize training in natural science. (See
attached plan for three varieties of education for the specific
levels required.)

2. Develop and Implement Plans Concretely

A. The organization of cadres' cultural study and education
is as follows: Raising the cadres' level of culture is a decisive
link in the process of raising the cultural level of the troops,
but it is also a most difficult and formidable task. Therefore
we should adopt methods of on-the-job remedial cultural training and have each person selected by lot to take his turn in
training (to study culture exclusively). By these methods, work
and study will go hand in hand and cultural training can be realized. (1) We decided to take the regiment as the unit in forming

cadres' schools for remedial cultural study. (Military units belonging directly to the division or above or military organs belonging directly to the division or above should ordinarily establish remedial study schools in the same way.) These schools should set up both junior primary school classes and senior primary school classes and admit only those higher-level cadres who do not recognize many characters or have already reached the cultural level of primary school. As for platoon-level cadres who still do not recognize many characters, they can generally be organized into study groups in the companies or in cultural classes affiliated to the above-mentioned schools. (Certain remedial schools, depending on their needs, can set up junior middle school classes now or sometime later in the second year.) (2) In selecting each person by lot to take his turn in training, we should establish schools for intensive cultural training at each division and army. The schools at divisions should first take company-level cadres who do not recognize many characters and cadres at the company and platoon levels who are equivalent to the level of a junior primary school graduate (of "four capabilities" who are able to handle one thousand characters or more) in order to raise these cadres to the level of a senior primary school graduate. The junior middle school classes in the division schools can wait until the second year to be established. Meanwhile, intensive schools at the army level should take cadres at the levels of battalion, regiment, and above who have graduated from junior primary schools or studied at senior primary schools, and raise their level respectively to that of a senior primary school graduate and of a junior middle school graduate. When so doing, the senior middle school classes can be adopted in the following year. It is expected that courses from the junior primary level through the senior primary level will take about one year (students admitted to this program include those of "four capabilities" who can handle one thousand characters or more). Courses from the senior primary level through the junior middle school level, and from the junior middle school level through the senior middle school level, will in general also take one year.

(In the case of those whose original level was comparatively
low and whose progress is also slow, the course can be extended to a year and a half.) Therefore, given this state of affairs, we should start now to raise the cultural level of 80,000
cadres to the junior middle school and senior middle school
level. Apart from the 15,000 cadres being sent to study at the
[Central-South] Military and Political University in the second
half of the year, there are still 60,000 to 70,000 cadres left. If
we set up 80 intensive cultural training schools, and each school
accepts an average of 300 students, it will add up to more than
20,000 people in all. If this is well coordinated with remedial
study schools, then, after the second school year, at the end of
every school year the intensive schools at the army and the
divisional level will graduate students and accept newly entering students. The plan is that within 3 years all 60,000 to 70,000
cadres will go through remedial cultural study schools and intensive cultural training schools, and that in this way we can
solve the problem of their cultural level. If this is not possible,
then the problem can be solved by extending the intensive
schools for an extra 6 months or a year.

　B. The organization of cultural study and education for soldiers will be as follows: To raise the cultural level of the soldiers in general to a senior primary school level, we should
first begin with literacy study. We should have achieved this
in 3 years' time, because the necessary curriculum will take
a total of 2,100 hours. In comparison with a regular primary
school, where all the required courses take a total of 5,100 hours
in a 6-year period, the length of time needed for our literacy
classes will be less than one-half of that total. It is possible
because most of the soldiers today have some foundation in
reading, their faculty for understanding is strong, and their
power of memory has not yet begun to decay. However, cultural studies for the soldiers should be organized on the basis of
the company unit, with the company unit transformed into a
school. We should work to turn every company into a regular
primary school. This can be done by such means as dividing
the classes according to the students' level of achievement;

having specially assigned teachers; setting forth a school system and curriculum; having a classroom and issuing textbooks;
having a commencement ceremony for graduation; having ex-
aminations, rewards, and punishments; exploring teaching methods; establishing all kinds of teaching conventions, systems,
etc. The difference between the company schools and regular
schools is that the company is still a combat organization in
the army; the soldiers still live the exacting life of armymen
and still have to bear the burden of specific military operations
and political training as well as the responsibility for taking
part in production. Because the study undertaken by military
units in the past was very irregular, it only served to make the
soldiers know a few more characters. This could not solve the
bigger problems of education in military units.

C. Concerning the question of teachers: If we want to organize such lasting and large-scale cultural study throughout the
army, we will have to solve the problem of teachers. How many
teachers do we need? We are following the principle of considering the field army units as the main target today in raising
the cultural level of the army. (This will include localized field
armies and all authorized independent divisions in the military
regions.) In these field units there are more than 4,000 companies. Calculating 3 teachers at the junior middle school level
for each company (not counting a soldier at the senior primary
school level to serve as a teaching assistant from each company) we need a total of 12,000 to 13,000 junior middle school
graduates. In order to strengthen cultural education in the companies, each battalion should count on one central teacher (at
a higher educational level than the company teachers) for a
calculated 800 battalion units. Therefore we will need 800 senior middle school graduates. Counting approximately 400
regimental remedial study schools and remedial study schools
for military organizations run directly by the division or above,
with each remedial study school having 3 to 6 teachers, we
should have 1,600 teachers at the senior middle school level
and 800 at the junior middle school level. There will be 80 intensive cultural study schools, of which 20 will be for armies.

Each of these schools should have 10 teachers either at the university level or who have previously been teachers at universities or middle schools. Thus we will need 200 people who are either at the university level or who have previously taught at universities or high schools. There are 60 schools established for divisions, each of which will need 10 teachers, of which 5 should be at the university level or should previously have been teachers at universities or middle schools and the other 5 should be at the level of senior middle school graduates. Altogether the division schools will take 600 teachers. According to the combined estimates above, we will need a total of 16,000 to 17,000 teachers in all. This problem could never have been solved in the past, but today we should be able to solve it. Each unit should select from among its new and old intellectual cadres and thus find core teachers for every battalion and company and key teachers for remedial study schools and intensive schools. (They may be selected from among the propaganda and education cadres, students of the Southbound Work Regiment, members of the army theatrical troupes and propaganda teams, and those army-trained students who are not yet dispersed.) As for the remaining 2 teachers for each company and all the teachers still needed for the remedial study schools and intensive schools, we can fill these positions by transferring on a large scale all the 10,000 intellectuals in the Military and Political University who are above the junior middle school level. If this is still not enough, then each army can work through local governments to mobilize civilian teachers to serve as teachers in the army.

D. Concerning the question of teaching materials: Textbooks for the junior primary and senior primary levels should be compiled and published centrally by the Political Department of the Fourth Field Army. They should include 6 volumes for the national language, covering 2,000 frequently used characters. The first and second volumes will emphasize learning characters. In the third and subsequent volumes both learning characters and simple compositions will be emphasized. The common knowledge of arithmetic and natural science will be published in three volumes suitable for adult readers and will aim at practical use by the enemy. They should also combine with ideology and politics. Elementary history and geography should be published as part of the national language textbooks after the second volume. The junior middle school and senior middle school classes should just use those textbooks that are currently being adopted in regular middle schools rather than publish their own. Inapplicable parts, however, should be expunged from the textbooks and other necessary information should replace them. In order to make it possible for officers and men to study energetically and well, no matter whether cadres go to remedial study schools or to intensive cultural study schools, there should always be one of each textbook per person. For each soldier there should be one text for the national language and one for arithmetic; and for the subject of natural science there should be one textbook for each group. It is also intended that a small dictionary be issued to each cadre, and one to each platoon of soldiers. . . . *

———————

*The last paragraph, dealing with organizational and budgetary matters, is omitted — Ying-mao Kau.

15

MILITARY AND POLITICAL TRAINING IS GOOD*

People's Daily

Today this newspaper publishes a report on the experience
of the 4672nd Unit of the People's Liberation Army, the Peking
garrison forces, in supporting the Left while carrying out military and political training in Peking Normal College. This experience is very good and well worth propagating.

Military and political training in universities and middle
schools is carried out with the wholehearted concern of our
great leader, Chairman Mao.

Chairman Mao directs us: "It is very good to use the method of sending army cadres to train revolutionary teachers and
students. Even a little training is very different from no training at all. In this way, students can learn politics, military affairs, the 'four firsts,' the 'three-eight work style,' and the
'three main rules of discipline and the eight points for attention'
from the Liberation Army. They can learn to strengthen their
sense of organization and discipline."

Chairman Mao also teaches: "The army should carry out
military training of university, middle school, and older primary school students by stages and by groups. It should also
take part in work regarding the reopening of schools, training and consolidation of organizations, setting up 'three-way

---

*"Chün-cheng hsün-lien hao," Jen-min jih-pao editorial,
May 16, 1967.

alliance' leadership organizations,* and carrying out struggle-criticism-transformation. It should first set up a key-point test to gain experience, and then gradually widen the area."

This brilliant observation of Chairman Mao's adds a new and important dimension to the Great Proletarian Cultural Revolution in the universities and middle schools throughout the country. It is one more great creation of the Great Proletarian Cultural Revolution, and it has real strategic significance.

The broad masses of revolutionary teachers and students in the universities and middle schools most enthusiastically support Chairman Mao's directives. The broad masses of cadres and soldiers in the Liberation Army are carrying out Chairman Mao's directives with firm resolution.

In the course of military and political training, the broad masses of cadres and soldiers in the Liberation Army raise high the great red banner of Mao Tse-tung thought. They hold fast to Chairman Mao as the representative of the proletarian revolutionary line, cooperate closely with the broad masses of revolutionary teachers and students, and devote themselves heart and soul to carrying out the Great Proletarian Cultural Revolution successfully in the universities and middle schools. They have had important accomplishments, and their overall orientation is correct. When there were shortcomings and mistakes in the course of their work, they were able to listen with an open mind to the opinions of the masses, sincerely carry out self-criticism, and rectify their mistakes in time. They have received the warmhearted welcome and resolute support of the broad masses of revolutionary teachers and students.

The Liberation Army comrades who carried out the task of military and political training at Peking Normal College have set an example in this respect, and provided rich experience.

In conducting military and political training, the army must definitely support and rely on the Left. The revolutionary Left

---

* An alliance of leading members of the revolutionary mass organizations, leaders of local PLA units, and revolutionary cadres of the Party and government organs — Ying-mao Kau.

is the vanguard of the Great Proletarian Cultural Revolution and the most resolute defender of Chairman Mao's proletarian revolutionary line. The overall direction of the revolution is embodied in the Left. Every cadre and soldier who takes part in military and political training should make sure that he himself has the standpoint, ideology, and feelings of the Left. At the same time, he must carry on study, research, and class analysis, and be good at recognizing and discovering leftists. Only in this way can the standpoint of the Left be firm and its colors vivid in the midst of the struggle between two lines. Only in this way can military and political training be conducted so that it supports the Left, depends on the Left, unites with the majority, and goes forward along the route marked by Chairman Mao.

The basic task of military and political training is to carry out the living study and living application of Chairman Mao's works and promote ideological revolutionization, all within the framework of the struggle between the two lines. In military and political training, the latter should be in the forefront, and politics should take command. To put politics in command is to put Mao Tse-tung thought in command. Only by grasping Mao Tse-tung thought, this weapon of unlimited power, can the broad masses of revolutionary teachers and students be victorious in conducting large-scale criticism and struggle against the biggest handful of Party persons in authority taking the capitalist road. Only by grasping Mao Tse-tung thought can they be victorious in conducting struggle-criticism-transformation within their own units. It is definitely necessary to organize the broad masses of teachers and students very well, and to take on problems that arise in the course of the struggle between the two lines by sitting down to study sincerely the relevant works of Chairman Mao. If there is real and penetrating forward movement embodied in action, then that will show that military and political training really has accomplished something. If we do not grasp the living study and living application of Chairman Mao's works firmly and well, then we will not be able to purge people's minds of all sorts of such erroneous and nonproletarian ideologies as anarchism, mountaintop-ism, factionalism, showing-off-ism, individualism, etc. In that case military and political training will become a mere formality, and will be unable to attain its goal of basically elevating the forces of the Left and elevating the broad masses.

To grasp living ideas fiercely and firmly and to persevere in patiently persuading and educating are important factors in achieving unity among the majority. The Liberation Army should, in conjunction with the actual situation of the Great Proletarian Cultural Revolution in the schools, apply Mao Tse-tung thought to the solution of all sorts of ideological problems in the ranks of the Left and all sorts of ideological problems among cadres who have committed mistakes and members of the masses who have been deluded. It must repeatedly admonish the revolutionary Left to follow Chairman Mao's teachings and to understand the principle that only when the proletariat has liberated all of mankind can it finally liberate itself. It should, moreover, accept this principle as a guide to action. Left organizations that have committed some errors and members of the masses who have participated in conservative organizations must be treated correctly. Rather than driving them away and discriminating against them, the PLA should strengthen political and ideological work among them. It must help the revolutionary Left learn the difficult skills of doing mass work, be good at taking the ideological pulse of the masses, grasp all kinds of ideology at the source and, using the model of frank and intimate discussions, develop ideological mutual help. It must be good at taking Chairman Mao's thought and the Party's policy and turning them into the thought and policy of the broad masses themselves, letting the masses teach themselves and liberate themselves.

The army comrades who participate in military and political training must consider trusting and depending on the masses as the most basic requirements in adhering consistently to Chairman Mao's proletarian revolutionary line. In realizing the great revolutionary alliance in the schools, they must definitely adhere to the principle of "clear-cut stand, resolute struggle, requisite conditions, and careful method." They must have an activist spirit of "seize the hour, seize the day," and not be impatient in their work and anxious for accomplishments.

The broad masses of revolutionary teachers and students should enthusiastically respond to Chairman Mao's great call to support the army and love the people. They should learn from the Liberation Army with an open mind, work closely with the PLA, unite as one, make a success of military and political training in the universities and middle schools, and carry the Great Proletarian Cultural Revolution in the universities and middle schools through to the end!

16

SUMMARY OF THE FORUM ON THE WORK IN
LITERATURE AND ART IN THE ARMED FORCES
WITH WHICH COMRADE LIN PIAO ENTRUSTED
COMRADE CHIANG CH'ING*

Red Flag

I

Entrusted by Comrade Lin Piao with the task, Comrade
Chiang Ch'ing invited some comrades in the armed forces to a
forum held in Shanghai from February 2 to 20, 1966, to discuss
certain questions concerning the work in literature and art in
the armed forces.

Before these comrades left for Shanghai, Comrade Lin Piao
gave them the following instructions: "Comrade Chiang Ch'ing
talked with me yesterday. She is very sharp politically on

---

*"Lin Piao t'ung-chih wei-t'uo Chiang Ch'ing t'ung-chih
chao-k'ai ti pu-tui wen-i kung-tso tso-t'an-hui chi-yao," Hung-
ch'i, No. 9 (May 27, 1967), 11-20. This translation is taken,
with minor editorial revisions, from Peking Review, No. 23 (June
2, 1967), 10-16. The extraordinary significance of this document
is reflected in a cover letter that Lin Piao sent to the Standing Committee of the Military Affairs Commission of the Central Committee. He said in part: "The summary, which has been repeatedly
gone over by the comrades attending the forum and has been personally examined and revised by the Chairman three times, is
an excellent document."

questions of literature and art, and she really knows art. She
has many opinions, and they are very valuable. You should pay
careful attention to them and take measures to ensure that they
are applied ideologically and organizationally. From now on,
the army's documents concerning literature and art should be
sent to her. Get in touch with her when you have any information for her to keep her well posted on the situation in literary
and art work in the armed forces. Ask her for her opinions,
which will help improve this work. We should not rest content
with either the present ideological level or the present artistic
level of such work, both of which need further improvement."
Comrade Hsiao Hua and Comrade Yang Cheng-wu expressed
enthusiastic approval of and support for the forum and instructed
us to act in accordance with Comrade Chiang Ch'ing's opinions.
They also expressed their thanks to Comrade Chiang Ch'ing for
her concern for the work in literature and art in the armed
forces.

At the beginning of the forum and in the course of the exchange of views, Comrade Chiang Ch'ing said time and again
that she had not studied Chairman Mao's works well enough
and that her comprehension of Chairman Mao's thought was
not profound, but that whatever points she had grasped she
would act upon resolutely. She said that during the last four
years she had largely concentrated on reading a number of literary works and had formed certain ideas, not all of which
were necessarily correct. She said that we were all Party
members, and that for the cause of the Party we should discuss things together on an equal footing. This discussion should
have been held last year but had been postponed because she
had not been in good health. As her health had recently improved, she had invited the comrades to join in discussions according to Comrade Lin Piao's instructions.

Comrade Chiang Ch'ing suggested that we read and see a
number of items first and then study relevant documents and
materials before discussing them. She advised us to read
Chairman Mao's relevant writings, had eight private discussions
with a comrade from the army, and attended four group dis-

cussions, thirteen film shows, and three theatrical performances together with us. She also exchanged opinions with us while watching the films and the theatrical performances. And she advised us to see twenty other films. During this period, Comrade Chiang Ch'ing saw a sample copy of the film The Great Wall Along the South China Sea, received the directors, cameramen, and part of the cast, and talked with them three times, which was a great education and inspiration to them. From our contacts with Comrade Chiang Ch'ing we realize that her understanding of Chairman Mao's thought is quite profound, and that she has made a prolonged and fairly full investigation and study of current problems in the field of literature and art and has gained rich practical experience through her personal exertions in cultivating "experimental plots of land." Taking up her work while she was still in poor health, she held discussions and saw films and theatrical performances together with us and was always modest, warm, and sincere. All this has enlightened and helped us a great deal.

II

In the course of about twenty days, we read two of Chairman Mao's writings and other relevant material, listened to Comrade Chiang Ch'ing's many highly important opinions, and saw more than thirty films, including good and bad ones and others with shortcomings and mistakes of varying degrees. We also saw two comparatively successful Peking operas on contemporary revolutionary themes, namely, Raid on the White Tiger Regiment and Taking the Bandits' Stronghold. All this helped to deepen our comprehension of Chairman Mao's thought on literature and art and raise the level of our understanding of the socialist cultural revolution. Here are a number of ideas which we discussed and agreed upon at the forum.

1. The last sixteen years have witnessed sharp class struggles on the cultural front.

Actually, in both stages of our revolution, the new-democratic stage and the socialist stage, there has been a struggle between

the two classes and the two lines on the cultural front, that is,
the struggle between the proletariat and the bourgeoisie for
leadership on this front. In the history of our Party, the struggle against both "Left" and Right opportunism has also included
struggles between the two lines on the cultural front. Wang
Ming's line represented bourgeois thinking which was once
rampant within our Party. In the rectification movement which
started in 1942, Chairman Mao made a thorough theoretical
refutation first of Wang Ming's political, military, and organizational lines and then, immediately afterwards, of the cultural line he represented. Chairman Mao's "On New Democracy," "Talks at the Yenan Forum on Literature and Art," and
"Letter to the Yenan Peking Opera Theatre After Seeing Driven
to Join the Liangshan Mountain Rebels," are the most complete,
the most comprehensive, and the most systematic historical
summaries of this struggle between the two lines on the cultural front. They carry on and develop the Marxist-Leninist
world outlook and theory on literature and art. After our revolution entered the socialist stage, Chairman Mao's two writings,
"On the Correct Handling of Contradictions Among the People"
and "Speech at the Chinese Communist Party's National Conference on Propaganda Work," were published. They are the
most recent summaries of the historical experience of the
movements for a revolutionary ideology and a revolutionary
literature and art in China and other countries. They represent
a new development of the Marxist-Leninist world outlook and
of the Marxist-Leninist theory on literature and art. These
five writings by Chairman Mao meet the needs of the proletariat
adequately and for a long time to come.

    More than twenty years have elapsed since the publication of
the first three of these five works by Chairman Mao, and nearly
ten years since the publication of the last two. However, since
the founding of our People's Republic, the ideas in these works
have basically not been carried out by literary and art circles.
Instead, we have been under the dictatorship of a black anti-
Party and antisocialist line which is diametrically opposed to
Chairman Mao's thought. This black line is a combination of

bourgeois ideas on literature and art, modern revisionist ideas on literature and art, and what is known as the literature and art of the 1930s (in the Kuomintang areas of China). Typical expressions of this line are such theories as those of "truthful writing," "the broad path of realism," "the deepening of realism," opposition to "subject matter as the decisive factor," "middle characters," opposition to "the smell of gunpowder," and "the spirit of the ages as the merging of various trends." Most of these views were refuted long ago by Chairman Mao in his "Talks at the Yenan Forum on Literature and Art." In film circles there are people who advocate "discarding the classics and rebelling against orthodoxy," in other words, discarding the classics of Marxism-Leninism-Mao Tse-tung thought, and rebelling against the orthodoxy of people's revolutionary war. As a result of the influence or domination of this bourgeois and modern revisionist countercurrent in literature and art, there have been few good or basically good works in the last decade or so (although there have been some), which truly praise worker, peasant, and soldier heroes and which serve the workers, peasants, and soldiers; many are mediocre, while some are anti-Party and antisocialist poisonous weeds. In accordance with the instructions of the Central Committee of the Party, we must resolutely carry on a great socialist revolution on the cultural front and completely eliminate this black line. After we are rid of this black line, still others will appear and the struggle must go on. Therefore, this is an arduous, complex, and long-term struggle which will take decades, or even centuries. It is a cardinal issue which has a vital bearing on the future of the Chinese revolution and the future of the world revolution.

A lesson to be drawn from the last decade or so is that we began to tackle the problem a little late. We have taken up only a few specific questions and have not dealt with the whole problem systematically and comprehensively. So long as we do not seize hold of the field of culture, we will inevitably forfeit many positions in this field to the black line, and this is a serious lesson. After the Tenth Plenary Session of the Central Com-

mittee in 1962 adopted a resolution on the unfolding of class
struggle throughout the country, the struggle to foster proletarian ideology and liquidate bourgeois ideology in the cultural field has gradually developed.

2. The last three years have seen a new situation in the great
socialist cultural revolution. The most outstanding example is
the rise of Peking operas on contemporary revolutionary themes.
Led by the Central Committee of the Party, headed by Chairman Mao, and armed with Marxism-Leninism-Mao Tse-tung
thought, literary and art workers engaged in revolutionizing
Peking opera have launched a heroic and tenacious offensive
against the literature and art of the feudal class, the bourgeoisie, and the modern revisionists. Under the irresistible impact of this offensive, Peking opera, formerly the most stubborn of strongholds, has been radically revolutionized, both in
ideology and in form, which has started a revolutionary change
in literary and art circles. Peking operas with contemporary
revolutionary themes like The Red Lantern, Shachiapang, Taking
the Bandits' Stronghold, and Raid on the White Tiger Regiment,
the ballet Red Detachment of Women, the symphony Shachiapang, and the group of clay sculptures, Rent Collection Court-
yard, have been approved by the broad masses of workers,
peasants, and soldiers and acclaimed by Chinese and foreign
audiences. They are pioneer efforts which will exert a profound and far-reaching influence on the socialist cultural revolution. They effectively prove that even that most stubborn of
strongholds, Peking opera, can be taken by storm and revolutionized and that foreign classical art forms such as the ballet
and symphonic music can also be remolded to serve our purposes. This should give us still greater confidence in revolutionizing other art forms. Some people say that Peking operas
with contemporary revolutionary themes have discarded the
traditions and basic skills of Peking opera. On the contrary,
the fact is that Peking operas with contemporary revolutionary
themes have inherited the Peking opera traditions in a critical
way and have really weeded out the old to let the new emerge.
The fact is not that the basic skills of Peking opera have been

discarded but that they are no longer adequate. Those which cannot be used to reflect present-day life should and must be discarded. In order to reflect present-day life, we urgently need to refine, create, and gradually develop and enrich the basic skills of Peking opera through our experience of real life. At the same time, these successes deal a powerful blow at conservatives of various descriptions and such views as the "box-office earnings" theory, the "foreign exchange earnings" theory, and the theory that "revolutionary works cannot travel abroad."

Another outstanding feature of the socialist cultural revolution in the last three years is the widespread mass activity of workers, peasants, and soldiers on the fronts of ideology, literature, and art. Workers, peasants, and soldiers are now producing many fine philosophical articles which splendidly express Mao Tse-tung's thought in terms of their own practice. They are also producing many fine works of literature and art in praise of the triumph of our socialist revolution, the big leap forward on all the fronts of socialist construction, our new heroes, and the brilliant leadership of our great Party and our great leader. In particular, both in content and in form the numerous poems by workers, peasants, and soldiers appearing on wall-newspapers and blackboards represent an entirely new age.

Of course, these are merely the first fruits of our socialist cultural revolution, the first step in our long march of ten thousand li. In order to safeguard and extend these achievements and to carry the socialist cultural revolution through to the end, we must work hard for a long time.

3. The struggle between the two roads on the front of literature and art is bound to be reflected in the armed forces, which do not exist in a vacuum and cannot possibly be an exception to the rule. The Chinese People's Liberation Army is the chief instrument of the dictatorship of the proletariat in China. It represents the mainstay and hope of the Chinese people and the revolutionary people of the world. Without a people's army, neither the victory of our revolution nor the dicta-

torship of the proletariat and socialism would have been possible, and the people would have nothing. Therefore, the enemy will inevitably try to undermine it from all sides and will inevitably use literature and art as weapons in his attempt to corrupt it ideologically. However, after Chairman Mao pointed out that, basically, literary and art circles had not carried out the policies of the Party over the past fifteen years, certain persons still claimed that the problem of the orientation of literature and art in our armed forces had already been solved, and that the problem to be solved was mainly one of raising the artistic level. This point of view is wrong and is not based on concrete analysis. In point of fact, some works of literature and art by our armed forces have a correct orientation and have reached a comparatively high artistic level; some have a correct orientation but their artistic level is low; others have serious defects or mistakes in both political orientation and artistic form; and still others are anti-Party and antisocialist poisonous weeds. The August First Studio has produced as bad a film as the Pressgang. This shows that the work in literature and art in the armed forces has also come under the influence of the black line to a greater or lesser degree. Besides, we have as yet trained relatively few creative workers who are really up to the mark; the ideological problems in creative work are still numerous, and the ranks are still not so pure. We must analyze and solve these problems properly.

4. The Liberation Army must play an important role in the socialist cultural revolution. Comrade Lin Piao has kept a firm hold on the work in literature and art since he has been in charge of the work of the Military Commission of the Central Committee of the Party. The many instructions he has given are correct. "The Resolution on Strengthening Political and Ideological Work in the Armed Forces," adopted at the enlarged session of the Military Commission, clearly specified that the aim of the work in literature and art in the armed forces was "to serve the cause of fostering proletarian ideology and liquidating bourgeois ideology and consolidating and improving fighting capacity in close conjunction with the tasks of

the armed forces and in the context of their ideological situation." There is already a nucleus of literary and art workers in the armed forces whom we have trained and who have been tempered in revolutionary war. A number of good works have been produced in the armed forces. Therefore, the Liberation Army must play its due role in the socialist cultural revolution and must fight bravely and unswervingly to carry out the policy that literature and art should serve the workers, peasants, and soldiers and serve socialism.

5. In the cultural revolution, there must be both destruction and construction. Leaders must take personal charge and see to it that good models are created. The bourgeoisie has its reactionary "monologue on creating the new." We, too, should create what is new and original, new in the sense that it is socialist and original in the sense that it is proletarian. The basic task of socialist literature and art is to work hard and create heroic models of workers, peasants, and soldiers. Only when we have such models and successful experience in creating them will we be able to convince people, to consolidate the positions we hold, and to knock the reactionaries' stick out of their hands.

On this matter we should have a sense of pride and not of inferiority.

We must destroy the blind faith in what is known as the literature and art of the 1930s (in the Kuomintang areas of China). At that time, the leftwing movement in literature and art followed Wang Ming's "Left" opportunist line politically; organizationally it practiced closed-doorism and sectarianism; and its ideas on literature and art were virtually those of Russian bourgeois literary critics such as Belinskii, Chernyshevskii, and Dobroliubov, and of Stanislavsky in the theatrical field, all of whom were bourgeois democrats in tsarist Russia, with bourgeois ideas and not Marxist ones. The bourgeois-democratic revolution is a revolution in which one exploiting class replaces another. It is only the proletarian socialist revolution that finally destroys all exploiting classes. Therefore, we must not take the ideas of any bourgeois revolutionary as guiding

principles for our proletarian movement in ideology or in literature and art. There were, of course, good things in the
1930s too, namely, the militant leftwing movement in literature
and art led by Lu Hsün. Around the middle of the 1930s, some
leftwing leaders under the influence of Wang Ming's right capitulationist line abandoned the Marxist-Leninist class standpoint and put forward the slogan of "a literature of national
defense." This was a bourgeois slogan. It was Lu Hsün who
put forward the proletarian slogan of "a mass literature for
the national revolutionary war." Some leftwing writers and
artists, notably Lu Hsün, also raised the slogans that literature
and art should serve the workers and peasants and that the
workers and peasants should create their own literature and
art. However, no systematic solution was found for the fundamental problem of the integration of literature and art with the
workers, peasants, and soldiers. The great majority of those
leftwing writers and artists were bourgeois nationalist democrats, and a number failed to pass the test of the democratic
revolution, while others have not given a good account of themselves under the test of socialism.

We must destroy blind faith in Chinese and foreign classical
literature. Stalin was a great Marxist-Leninist. His criticism
of the modernist literature and art of the bourgeoisie was very
sharp. But he uncritically accepted what are known as the
classics of Russia and Europe, and the consequences were bad.
The classical literature and art of China and of Europe (including Russia), and even American films, have exercised a
considerable influence on our literary and art circles, and
some people have regarded them as holy writ and accepted them
in their entirety. We should draw a lesson from Stalin's experience. Old and foreign works should also be studied, and
refusal to study them would be wrong; but we must study them
critically, making the past serve the present and foreign works
serve China.

As for the relatively good Soviet revolutionary works of literature and art which appeared after the October Revolution,
they too must be analyzed and not blindly worshiped or, still

less, blindly imitated. Blind imitation can never become art.
Literature and art can only spring from the life of the people,
which is their sole source. This is borne out by the whole history of literature and art, past and present, Chinese and foreign.

The rising forces in the world invariably defeat the forces
of decay. Our People's Liberation Army was weak and small
at the beginning, but it eventually became strong and defeated
the U.S.-Chiang Kai-shek reactionaries. Confronted with the
excellent revolutionary situation at home and abroad and our
glorious tasks, we should be proud to be thoroughgoing revolutionaries. We must have the confidence and courage to do
things never previously attempted, because ours is a revolution to eliminate all exploiting classes and systems of exploitation once and for all and to root out all exploiting-class ideologies, which poison the minds of the people. Under the leadership of the Central Committee of the Party and Chairman
Mao, and under the guidance of Marxism-Leninism-Mao Tse-
tung thought, we must create a new socialist revolutionary
literature and art worthy of our great country, our great
Party, our great people, and our great army. This will be a
most brilliant new literature and art that opens up a new era in
human history.

But it is no easy matter to create good models. Strategically,
we must take the difficulties in creative work lightly, but tactically we must take them seriously. To create a fine work is
an arduous process, and the comrades in charge of creative
work must never adopt a bureaucratic or casual attitude but
must work really hard and share the writers' and artists' joys
and hardships. It is essential to get firsthand material as far
as possible, or when this is impossible, at least to get the material at second hand. There should be no fear of failures or
mistakes. Allowance should be made for them, and people must
be permitted to correct their mistakes. It is necessary to rely
on the masses, follow the line of "from the masses, to the
masses," and repeatedly undergo the test of practice over a
long period, so that a work may become better and better and
achieve the unity of revolutionary political content and the best

possible artistic form. In the course of practice it is necessary to sum up experience in good time and gradually grasp the laws of various forms of art. Otherwise, no good models can be created.

We should give the fullest attention to the themes of socialist revolution and socialist construction, and it would be entirely wrong to ignore them.

A serious effort should now be made to create works of literature and art about the three great military campaigns of Liaohsi-Shenyang, Huai-Hai, and Peiping-Tientsin and other important campaigns while the comrades who led and directed them are still alive. There are many important revolutionary themes, historical and contemporary, on which work urgently needs to be done in a planned and systematic way. A success must be made of the film The Great Wall Along the South China Sea. The film The Long March must be revised successfully. A nucleus of truly proletarian writers and artists should be trained in the process.

6. People engaged in the work of literature and art, whether they are leaders or writers and artists, must all practice the Party's democratic centralism. We favor "rule by the voice of the many" and oppose "rule by the voice of one man alone." We must follow the mass line. In the past, some people pressed the leadership to nod and applaud when they produced something. This is a very bad style of work. As for the cadres in charge of creative work in literature and art, they should always bear two points in mind: First, be good at listening to the opinions of the broad masses; second, be good at analyzing these opinions, accept the right ones, and reject the wrong ones. Completely flawless works of literature and art are nonexistent, and as long as the keynote of a work is good, we should help improve it by pointing out its shortcomings and errors. Bad works should not be hidden away, but should be shown to the masses for their comment. We must not be afraid of the masses but should have firm trust in them, and they can give us much valuable advice. Besides, this will improve their powers of discrimination. It costs several hundred thousand yuan, or as

much as a million, to produce a film. To hide a bad film is wasteful. Why not show it to the public to educate writers and artists and the masses and at the same time make up for its cost to the state, and thus turn it to good account ideologically and economically? The film Beleaguered City has been shown for a long time but it received no criticism. Shouldn't the Chieh-fang-chün pao write an article criticizing it?

7. We must encourage revolutionary and militant literary and art criticism by the masses and break the monopoly over literary and art criticism by a few so-called critics (those wrong in orientation and deficient in militancy). We must place the weapon of literary and art criticism in the hands of the masses of workers, peasants and soldiers, and integrate professional critics with critics from among the masses. We must make this criticism more militant and oppose unprincipled vulgar praise. We must reform our style of writing, encourage the writing of short, popular articles, turn our literary and art criticism into daggers and hand grenades, and learn to handle them effectively in close combat. Of course, we must at the same time write longer, systematic articles of theoretical depth. We oppose the use of terminology and jargon to frighten people. Only in this way can we disarm the self-styled literary and art critics. The Chieh-fang-chün pao and the Chieh-fang-chün wen-i should set up special columns, regular or occasional, for comment on literature and art. Warm support should be given to good or basically good works, and their defects should be pointed out in a helpful way. And principled criticism must be made of bad works. In the theoretical field, we must thoroughly and systematically criticize typical fallacies on literature and art and the many other fallacies spread by certain people who attempt to falsify history and to boost themselves in such books as the History of the Development of the Chinese Film, A Collection of Historical Data on the Chinese Drama Movement in the Last Fifty Years, and A Preliminary Study of the Repertory of Peking Opera. We must not mind being accused of "brandishing the stick." When some people charge us with oversimplification and crudeness, we must analyze these charges.

Some of our criticisms are basically correct but are not sufficiently convincing because our analysis and evidence are inadequate and should be improved. With some people it is a
matter of understanding; they start by accusing us of oversimplification and crudeness but eventually drop the charge. But
when the enemy condemns our correct criticisms as oversim-
plified and crude, we must stand firm. Literary and art criticism should become one of our day-to-day tasks, an important
method both in the struggle in the field of literature and art and
in Party leadership in this field of work. Without correct literary and art criticism it is impossible for creative work to
flourish.

8. In the struggle against foreign revisionism in the field of
literature and art, we must not only catch small figures like
Chukhrai. We should catch the big ones, catch Sholokhov and
dare to tackle him. He is the father of revisionist literature
and art. His And Quiet Flows the Don, Virgin Soil Upturned,
and The Fate of a Man have exercised a big influence on a number of Chinese writers and readers. Shouldn't the army organize people to study his works and write convincing critical
articles containing well-documented analysis? This will have
a profound influence in China and the rest of the world. The
same thing should be done with similar works by Chinese writers.

9. As for method, we must combine revolutionary realism
with revolutionary romanticism in our creative work, and must
not adopt bourgeois critical realism or bourgeois romanticism.

The fine qualities of the worker, peasant, and soldier heroes
who have emerged under the guidance of the correct line of the
Party are the concentrated expression of the class character
of the proletariat. We must work with enthusiasm and do everything possible to create heroic models of workers, peasants,
and soldiers. We should create typical characters. Chairman
Mao has said that "life as reflected in works of literature and
art can and ought to be on a higher plane, more intense, more
concentrated, more typical, nearer the ideal, and therefore
more universal than actual everyday life." We should not con-

fine ourselves to actual persons and events. Nor should we
portray a hero only after he is dead. In fact, there are many
more living heroes than dead ones. This means that our writers
must concentrate and generalize experience from real life accumulated over a long period of time to create a variety of
typical characters.

When we write about revolutionary wars, we must first be
clear about their nature — ours is the side of justice and the
enemy's is the side of injustice. Our works must show our
arduous struggles and heroic sacrifices, but must also express
revolutionary heroism and revolutionary optimism. While depicting the cruelty of war, we must not exaggerate or glorify
its horrors. While depicting the arduousness of the revolutionary struggle, we must not exaggerate or glorify the sufferings involved. The cruelty of a revolutionary war and revolutionary heroism, the arduousness of the revolutionary struggle,
and revolutionary optimism constitute a unity of opposites, but
we must be clear about which is the principal aspect of the
contradiction; otherwise, if we make the wrong emphasis, a
bourgeois pacifist trend will emerge. Moreover, while depicting our people's revolutionary war, whether in the stage in which
guerrilla warfare was primary and mobile warfare supplementary, or in the stage in which mobile warfare was primary, we
must correctly show the relationship between the regular forces,
the guerrillas, and the people's militia and between the armed
masses and the unarmed masses under the leadership of the
Party.

Regarding the selection of subject matter, only when we
plunge into the thick of life and do a good job of investigation
and study can we make the selection properly and correctly.
Playwrights should unreservedly plunge into the heat of the
struggle for a long period. Directors, actors and actresses,
cameramen, painters, and composers should also go into the
thick of life and make serious investigations and studies. In the
past, some works distorted the historical facts, concentrating
on the portrayal of erroneous lines instead of the correct line;
some described heroic characters who nevertheless invariably

violate discipline, or created heroes only to have them die in
a contrived tragic ending; other works do not present heroic
characters but only "middle" characters who are actually backward people, or caricatures of workers, peasants, or soldiers;
in depicting the enemy, they fail to expose his class nature as
an exploiter and oppressor of the people, and even glamorize
him; still others are concerned only with love and romance,
pandering to philistine tastes and claiming that love and death
are the eternal themes. All such bourgeois and revisionist
trash must be resolutely opposed.

10. Reeducate the cadres in charge of the work of literature
and art and reorganize the ranks of writers and artists. For
historical reasons, before the whole country was liberated it
was rather difficult for us proletarians to train our own workers
in literature and art in the areas under enemy rule. Our cultural level was relatively low and our experience limited. Many
of our workers in literature and art had received a bourgeois
education. In the course of their revolutionary activities in
literature and art, some failed to pass the test of enemy persecution and turned traitor, while others failed to resist the
corrosive influence of bourgeois ideas and became rotten. In
the base areas, we trained a considerable number of revolutionary workers in literature and art. Especially after the publication of the "Talks at the Yenan Forum on Literature and
Art," they had the correct orientation, embarked on the path
of integration with the workers, peasants, and soldiers, and
played a positive role in the revolution. The weakness was that
after the country was liberated and we entered the big cities,
many comrades failed to resist the corrosion of bourgeois
ideology in the ranks of our writers and artists, with the result
that some of them have fallen out in the course of advance.
Ours is the literature and art of the proletariat, the literature
and art of the Party. The principle of proletarian Party spirit
is the outstanding feature distinguishing us from other classes.
It must be understood that representatives of other classes
also have their principle of Party spirit, and that they are also
very stubborn. We must firmly adhere to the principle of pro-

letarian Party spirit and combat the corrosion of bourgeois ideology in creative thinking, in organizational line, and in style of work. As for bourgeois ideology, we must draw a clear line of demarcation and must on no account enter into peaceful coexistence with it. A variety of problems now exist in literary and art circles which, for most people, are problems of ideological understanding and of raising such understanding through education. We must earnestly study Chairman Mao's works, creatively study and apply them, tie up what we learn from them with our own thinking, and practice and study them with specific problems in mind. Only in this way can we really understand, grasp, and master Chairman Mao's thought. We must plunge into the thick of life for a long period of time, integrate ourselves with the workers, peasants, and soldiers to raise our class consciousness, remold our ideology, and wholeheartedly serve the people without any regard for personal fame or gain. It is necessary to teach our comrades to study Marxism-Leninism and Chairman Mao's works and to remain revolutionary all their lives, and pay special attention to the maintenance of proletarian integrity in later life, which is not at all easy.

III

By taking part in the forum, we have acquired a relatively clear understanding of all the questions mentioned above, and our opinions on them now correspond with the realities in the work in literature and art among the armed forces. As a result, the level of our political consciousness has been raised, and our determination to carry out the socialist cultural revolution and our sense of responsibility in this respect have likewise been strengthened. We will continue to study Chairman Mao's works conscientiously, make serious investigations and studies, and do well in our cultivation of "experimental plots" and the production of good models, so as to take the lead in the current struggle of the cultural revolution to foster proletarian ideology and liquidate bourgeois ideology.

17

ARMY MEDICAL WORKERS SERVE
WORKERS, PEASANTS, AND SOLDIERS*

New China News Agency

Directing their service at the rural areas and units at the grassroots level, the medical workers of the Chinese People's Liberation Army are wholeheartedly serving the workers, peasants, and soldiers. They have thus made important contributions in the struggle to carry out and defend Chairman Mao's proletarian line in medical and health work.

They have followed Chairman Mao's great teachings, "Be prepared against war, be prepared against natural disasters, and do everything for the people" and "In medical and health work, put the stress on the rural areas."

During the Great Proletarian Cultural Revolution the PLA medical workers have made a living study and application of Mao Tse-tung thought and mercilessly criticized the counter-revolutionary revisionist line in medical and health work pushed by the arch renegade Liu Shao-ch'i. In the course of the struggle between the two classes, the two roads, and the two lines, they have inherited and carried forward the PLA medical workers' glorious revolutionary tradition. Brimming with revolutionary enthusiasm and taking their medical kits with them, large numbers have gone to the countryside and units at the grassroots level to give the workers, peasants, and soldiers medical service.

---

*English-language release of the New China News Agency, Peking, January 15, 1970. Minor editorial revisions have been made.

According to rough statistics, over 6,100 PLA medical teams, made up of more than 40,000 medical workers, had gone to rural areas by the end of 1969. In addition, 22,000 medical workers had been sent to give medical service to armymen on the frontiers and islands and at work sites.

The medical teams are also Mao Tse-tung thought propaganda teams. They popularize Mao Tse-tung thought wherever they bring medical service.

Carrying their treasured books of Chairman Mao's works and climbing mountains, medical team members of the PLA General Hospital, who had made medical tours of Yenan, learned from the revolutionary spirit of the people in this old revolutionary base while taking medical service to the caves of the poor and lower-middle peasants.

Braving storms and violent waves, the roving seaborne health work team of the PLA Kwangchow units has plied among scores of islands year in and year out, bringing medical service to the commanders and fighters there who are defending the islands and to the poor and lower-middle peasants, and making Chairman Mao's concern for them felt in the southernmost part of the motherland.

A medical team of a hospital of the PLA General Logistics Department, which makes the rounds of plateaus, went to the Chinghai-Tibet plateau, some four to five thousand meters above sea level, after overcoming many difficulties and served the armymen and Tibetan peasants and herdsmen. It has brought the radiance of Mao Tse-tung thought to the icy and snowcapped mountains.

Disregarding bitter cold and sweltering summer weather, members of the medical teams in the countryside have taken their service into the fields and the homes of the poor and lower-middle peasants and have done operations right in the peasants' homes. They have been warmly praised by the members of the people's communes.

Armed with Chairman Mao's great theory of continuing the revolution under the dictatorship of the proletariat, the medical workers have constantly heightened their consciousness of class struggle and the struggle between the two lines, and their spirit is vigorous and militant. In treating the workers, peasants, and soldiers, they have shown a boundless sense of responsibility in their work and boundless warmheartedness toward all comrades and the people.

After a poor peasant woman with cancer of the breast had been examined at the outpatient department of a hospital under the PLA Nanking units, she immediately returned home. Having discussed her case later, the doctors felt that the woman should be hospitalized, only to learn that she had not given her address. The hospital medical workers went searching for her through the nearby villages. They did everything they could to find her, and finally located the woman and brought her back to the hospital, where she was operated on.

Through their practical experience, the army medical workers concluded that to realize Chairman Mao's proletarian line in medical and health work, it is imperative to "liberate" medical technique from the hands of a small number of medical workers and popularize it among the broad masses of workers, peasants, and soldiers. In addition, greater attention should be paid to the use of Chinese medicine, including local medicinal herbs. With the revolutionary spirit of fearing neither hardship nor death, they went deep among the masses and, by carrying out innumerable experiments, including trying various medicines on themselves, discovered and developed many new remedies and prescriptions, using Chinese medicine which proved to be highly effective, easy to make and use, and cheap.

The army medical teams in different parts of the country have thus far trained 274,000 peasant medical workers, or "barefoot doctors" as the poor and lower-middle peasants affectionately call them. In addition, they have helped more than 7,500 production brigades in rural people's communes set up or improve their cooperative medical services. A medical team of the Peking units of the PLA has helped the people's communes in Hsinglung hsien, Hopei Province, train a whole contingent of medical and health workers, with an average of 8 to a production brigade. This has enabled the people's communes in this mountainous county to treat locally minor and normal diseases and injuries in the production teams or brigades. A medical team of a hospital of the PLA Kwangchow units touring the rural areas has successfully conveyed basic knowledge of Chinese medicine and medical herbs, new acupuncture methods, and first-aid to every family of the commune members.

Directing their attention to the rural areas and the organizations at the grassroots level, the army medical workers have treated and cured a number of difficult diseases formerly regarded as "forbidden zones" in treatment, thus scaling one peak after another in medical technique.

Ever since the army "advanced health section serving the people wholeheartedly" successfully removed a 45-kilogram tumor from the abdomen of woman commune member Chang Chiu-chu, a miracle in medical history, many more tumor cases once considered "incurable" have been cured. More than 1,000 tumor cases have been successfully treated by medical workers of the Peking, Kwangchow, Nanking, Shenyang, and Tsinan units and of the air force units. Three of the tumors removed weighed more than 50 kilograms.

Because they are simple and effective, the new acupuncture methods created by the army medical workers are being popularized among the workers, peasants, and soldiers, and an increasing number of people are able to apply them. These new methods have helped restore paralytics' ability to move, blind people's sight, and deaf-mutes' voices, enabling them to utter joyfully the strongest sound of this era: "Long live Chairman Mao!"

The army medical workers are now earnestly engaged in summing up their experience and arming themselves further with Chairman Mao's instruction: "Be prepared against war, be prepared against natural disasters, and do everything for the people." They are determined to make ever new contributions in 1970 to the carrying out and defense of Chairman Mao's proletarian line in medical and health work.

18

THE WHOLE COUNTRY MUST
LEARN FROM THE PLA*

People's Daily

A rushing tide of study of the Liberation Army is just starting to sweep through the nation. It is now at the point of communist competition, of emulating the advanced, learning from
the advanced, overtaking the advanced, and helping the backward. "Learn from the PLA" has already become the new
fighting slogan.

The Chinese People's Liberation Army is a workers' and
peasants' army founded under the leadership of the Communist
Party and Comrade Mao Tse-tung. It is an army that has become extremely proletarian, extremely militant. For some
decades the People's Liberation Army has carried on our Party's fine tradition and excellent work style. What is more, in
this new era the PLA has shown new growth. This is the result
of instructions from the Party Central Committee and Comrade
Mao Tse-tung. It is also the result of long-term study of Mao
Tse-tung thought by the officers and fighting men of the entire
Liberation Army, and of thoroughgoing and meticulous
political-ideological work carried out by the Liberation
Army over a long period. The recent army-wide PLA Political Work Conference decided to make the PLA's political-
ideological work even better than before, and to make the whole
army become even more proletarian, even more militant. This

---

*"Ch'üan-kuo tou yao hsüeh-hsi chieh-fang-chün," Jen-min
jih-pao, February 1, 1964.

is a great, inspiring task! We are preparing to congratulate
the Liberation Army as it accumulates even richer experience
in strengthening political-ideological work. We are preparing
to celebrate the even more brilliant accomplishments of the
Liberation Army on every front. At the same time, we hope
that the whole country will learn even more deeply and widely
from the Liberation Army's invaluable experience in political-
ideological work, and that the whole country, just like the PLA,
will work to become even more proletarian, even more militant.

The primary reason why the Liberation Army is able to
grow into an extremely proletarian, extremely militant army
is that the Liberation Army raises high the great red banner
of Mao Tse-tung thought and uses Mao Tse-tung thought as its
standard in every endeavor. The Liberation Army strongly
enters upon political-ideological work, adhering firmly to the
principle of the "four firsts"; the Liberation Army adheres
firmly to our national revolutionary army's fine tradition of
the "three-eight work style"; the Liberation Army emphasizes
the creation of "four-good companies," the strengthening of
basic-level construction, etc. These are all reasons why the
Liberation Army is victorious wherever it goes. The entire
country, in learning from the Liberation Army, should study
the rich experience of these aspects of the PLA until they are
familiar enough to be put into practice. By really undertaking
the living study and living application of this precious experience, we can bring into full play the proletarian and militant
revolutionary spirit while carrying out all enterprises of the
socialist revolution and socialist construction.

Mao Tse-tung thought is a combination of the universal truth
of Marxism-Leninism and the concrete practice of the Chinese
revolution. It serves as the guideline for the Chinese people's
revolution and for socialist construction. The basic task in
PLA political work is to arm the minds of all the officers and
soldiers with Mao Tse-tung thought, and to resolutely do all
work in accordance with Mao Tse-tung thought. The great Liberation Army fighters and all levels of cadres should vigorously

study Mao Tse-tung's works and use Mao Tse-tung thought to direct their own work, direct their own actions, and transform their own thought. There has already developed a great movement of awakening among cadres and soldiers in the Liberation Army to "read Chairman Mao's books, listen to Chairman Mao's words, do things according to Chairman Mao's directions, and be Chairman Mao's good soldier." The Liberation Army emphasizes study and practice of Mao Tse-tung thought to such an extent that it is well worth having the whole nation learn from the PLA. If comrades on every battlefront in the whole country are to learn from the PLA, they should raise the red banner of Mao Tse-tung thought even higher and arm themselves with Mao Tse-tung thought. They should resolutely take Mao Tse-tung thought as their guiding principle. They should constantly examine their own thought, work and actions, and look into and sum up their own work experience. They should repeatedly study Comrade Mao Tse-tung's works and apply Comrade Mao Tse-tung's stand, viewpoint, and method to concrete analysis, examination, and handling of practical problems. If we make a living study and living application of Mao Tse-tung thought, then we will have a firm standpoint. We will be farseeing and have a long, prosperous life of conviction, complete in both wisdom and courage. All of our work will show a correct orientation, a direct approach, and will develop smoothly, full of vigor.

Following Comrade Mao Tse-tung's directions, the Liberation Army has correctly handled the problem of the "four relationships" in political-ideological work and army-building, and has also firmly grasped the principle of "four firsts." The principle of "four firsts" has universal significance for all work in the entire country, and the entire country should consider it well deserving of study.

When we deal with the relationship between man and matter in all our work, we should, like the Liberation Army in its correct handling of the relationship between man and weapons, put the human factor first, because the human factor is the decisive factor in carrying out all work. Comrade Mao Tse-tung

said: "Weapons are an important factor in war, but they are
not the decisive factor. The decisive factor is man, not matter.
In comparing power we should not only compare military and
economic power, but also bring the power of man and the power
of the human spirit into the comparison. Military power and
economic power have to be controlled by men." Can our socialist revolution and socialist construction develop smoothly?
Material conditions are an important factor, but the decisive factor is the socialist consciousness and revolutionary
spirit of the people of our nation, as well as the socialist
activism and creativity of the broad masses of cadres and
the people.

We should, like the Liberation Army, deal correctly with the
relationship between political work and all other kinds of work,
putting political work first. Politics is the commander, the
soul. Political work is to do well the work of men. Political
work is not only the lifeblood of the Liberation Army, it is also
the lifeblood of all revolutionary work and the basic guarantee
of all work. Only if political work has been well conducted
can human initiative and creativity be brought into full play.

We should, like the Liberation Army, deal correctly with
the relationship between the routine part of political work and
the ideological part, putting the ideological work first. In all
work we should embrace the proletarian ideology and conquer
nonproletarian ideology because, under certain material conditions, the state of people's ideology determines the result of
the work. Correct ideology is the necessary condition for successful work. Incorrect ideology is the root of failure in work.
The impact of the struggle to foster proletarian ideology and
liquidate bourgeois ideology on the ideological front will even
go so far as to decide the outcome of the struggle to foster proletarian ideology and liquidate bourgeois ideology on the economic and political fronts. Therefore, in order to make a success of any work we should put ideological work first, and
start by completing the ideological work.

We should, like the Liberation Army, deal correctly with the
relationship between bookish ideology and living ideology in

the course of ideological work, and put living ideology first.
We must read ideology in books, but the important thing is to
grasp living ideology, combining book-learning with practice.
We should, like the Liberation Army, earnestly grasp living
ideas. We should take problems that come up in the course of
our work and, by studying Comrade Mao Tse-tung's works,
learn to solve concrete problems with Mao Tse-tung thought.
We should learn to take the pulse of the life of the masses in
a timely way, to grasp the laws of ideological change in the
masses, in order to be able to conduct ideological work on the
basis of reality. In all work it is only by resolutely grasping
living ideas and putting living ideas first that we will be able
to encourage nascent progressiveness and to rectify bad tendencies in time.

As a result of creatively applying Mao Tse-tung thought, the
Liberation Army has grasped the principle of "four firsts" in
the course of its political work and army-building. All sections and units throughout the country should earnestly
study the way in which the Liberation Army holds resolutely
to the principle of the "four firsts," and greatly strengthen
every aspect of political-ideological work. In this way we can
give completely free play to the people's activism and creativity on all fronts, and develop even further the people's revolutionary spirit.

The Liberation Army, under the leadership of the Party and
Comrade Mao Tse-tung, and in the course of long and bitter
struggle, has cultivated an excellent work style. Comrade Mao
Tse-tung summed up this kind of work style in three phrases
and eight characters. Therefore it is known in its abbreviated
form, the "three-eight work style." The three phrases are
a firm and correct political direction, a persevering and simple work style, and flexible strategy and tactics. The eight
characters are unity [t'uan-chieh], intensity [chin-chang],
solemnity [yen-su] and liveliness [huo-p'o]. The "three-eight
work style" of the Liberation Army is the revolutionary work
style of our nation's proletariat. It is the fine traditional work
style of our nation's revolutionary forefathers developed to a

new grandeur. This work style deserves to be studied by the
entire nation.

In studying the "three-eight work style" of the Liberation
Army, we should first have a firm and correct political direction. This means that we should take Mao Tse-tung thought as
the correct political orientation in the course of all work. The
Liberation Army demands that every officer and every soldier
obey the Party and Chairman Mao and press fearlessly ahead
in the direction pointed out by the Party and Chairman Mao.
The Liberation Army cherishes the nation, cherishes the people, cherishes socialism, and is boundlessly devoted to the
proletarian cause. Every day and every night the officers and
men of the Liberation Army are on the alert, keeping watch
over the socialist motherland and defending world peace. They
enthusiastically rush to wherever the Party or the nation needs
them. Wherever they go and whatever they must endure, they
always devote themselves heart and soul to the protection of
the nation. They spill their heart's blood for national construction. They are public-spirited and unselfish. They neglect their own private interests for the sake of the public interest, and care only for others, not caring in the least for
themselves. They even go so far as to contribute their own
youth and life to socialism. In learning from the Liberation
Army, we should be true to the motherland from beginning to
end, be true to the people, and be true to the revolutionary
cause of the proletariat. Like the men of the Liberation Army,
who, unmindful of their own safety, plunge into the flaming
struggle of socialist construction, contributing their utmost
strength, we should consistently maintain a firm proletarian
stand, be able to see clearly in the midst of the storms of
class struggle, stand firm and not waver the slightest bit.
In the most difficult and dangerous situations we should
stand firm and steadfast and on no account waver. We should
embrace the ideology of uninterrupted revolution, resolutely
and thoroughly carry through the socialist revolution, and oppose stalling and coming to a standstill, degeneration and de-
moralization. We should fiercely hate the enemies of the

revolution and be brave and unyielding in the midst of struggle against the enemy, ready to die rather than surrender. We should serve the people with our whole heart and mind, unconditionally subordinating individual interests to the revolutionary interests. We should resolutely implement the Party line and all general and specific policies, and struggle irreconcilably against all tendencies toward opposing the Party's lines, principles, and policies.

While studying the "three-eight work style," we should also study the Liberation Army's work style of hard work and plain living. The Liberation Army requires every officer and soldier to carry on and develop the fine tradition of hard work and plain living. The Liberation Army, whether in revolutionary struggle or in the construction struggle, can fight resolutely under the most difficult circumstances. It should always take the initiative in shouldering the most arduous, most strenuous tasks, suffer greatly, endure the strain of great labor, and consider all this an honor and a pleasure. In studying the Liberation Army's bitter and fierce fighting style, we should resolve to diligently and frugally build up the nation, using the work style of diligence and frugality in all enterprises, the work style of sharing weal or woe with the people and the masses. We should oppose all work styles of extravagance and waste, corruption and degeneracy, and all other manifestations of the capitalist life style and ideology. In studying the Liberation Army's simple, honest work style, we should resolutely adopt the scientific attitude of seeking truth from facts in the course of work. We should investigate and explore thoroughly, starting from reality, and handle affairs according to objective laws, combining revolutionary energy and the scientific spirit. Resolutely oppose the bureaucratic practice of departing from reality and departing from the masses. Oppose magnificence without reality, and oppose pompous, exaggerated work styles. Oppose excessive timidity and all conservative work styles that follow old rules in managing affairs.

In studying the "three-eight work style," we should also study the strategy and tactics of flexible maneuver used by the

Liberation Army to conquer the enemy and achieve victory. The Liberation Army despises the enemy strategically, but takes the enemy seriously tactically. It uses these strategical and tactical principles effectively. It fights battles according to the types of enemy, weapons, and conditions it encounters. In other words, it can attack the enemy's weak point with its strong point and can greatly develop its subjective initiative in the course of the struggle. Not only should these principles be carried out in fighting actual battles but also in doing all other work. To learn from the Liberation Army is to learn to despise all difficulties strategically, while tactically taking any specific difficulties seriously. It is also to learn to be good at adopting a manner and method of flexible maneuver according to varying times, places, and conditions in order to conquer difficulties and do successful work. We should, like the Liberation Army, embrace the idea of actively crushing our enemies, embrace the idea of actively fulfilling responsibilities, of doing things bravely and with intelligence, and of using our own initiative to attack and demolish all difficulties one by one. We should oppose the attitude of being self-satisfied and setting oneself apart from others, and the empirical approach of following old, existing rules. We should also oppose the dogmatism of not inquiring into actual conditions and of mechanically applying the experience of others.

We should learn from the unity apparent in the Liberation Army's work style. There is unity between officers and soldiers, between the upper and lower ranks, between departments, between neighbors, as well as between the army and the government and between the army and the people. This sort of political unanimity, ideological unanimity, and unanimity of action constitute a work style that deserves to be studied by the whole nation. In learning from this kind of unity of effort in the Liberation Army's unified work style, we should learn to be strict with ourselves and lenient with others when handling all questions involving mutual respect, personal interrelations, and mutual aid. We should develop the communist style of "overcoming the difficulties we encounter, refusing any glory and handing it to others, learning from the advanced, and helping the backward." We should develop the communist spirit of concerted action, which asserts that "if one person has a job to be done, 10,000 people help him; if one place runs into difficulties, help will come from all directions." We should always embrace an all-round point of view, taking the whole situation into consideration and understanding the main idea, and we should oppose departmentalism and excessive decentralization. We should maintain an attitude of humility. On questions not involving matters of principle, we should be able to have a tolerant and conciliatory attitude and oppose the conceited and self-aggrandizing ideological tendency, which hinders agreement and unity. No matter how important cadres are, they should all have the status and appearance of ordinary workers, treat people equally, and look upon their subordinates and the masses alike as brothers.

We should study the intense work style of the Liberation Army. In battle, the Liberation Army is energetic, brave, not afraid of tiring in body or spirit; it always fights on, attacking like a fierce tiger, and defending as firmly as the great Mt. T'ai. Soldiers follow orders resolutely, promptly, and scrupulously. They are always fair and honest. In their work, the men of the Liberation Army carry out their mission in a sweeping manner. They do what they say they are going to do, making every effort in tackling their task and doing it thoroughly; they are easily encouraged to be bold and strong and see their work through from beginning to end. In daily life they rise in great vigor, pull themselves together, and oppose any slackening or diffusion of energy and any aimless activity. These excellent qualities of the Liberation Army are all worth studying. In studying the Liberation Army we should particularly stress its sense of time and its speed in action. We should cultivate a work style of fierce upstream struggle at a high speed. We should take harsh manual labor and combine it with skilled labor, take quantity and combine it with quality. In order to manage affairs in quantity well, fast and frugally, there must be both work and idleness, incisive action and needed rest and consolidation.

We should study the solemn work style of the Liberation Army. The Liberation Army requires every officer and soldier to stand resolutely for the principle of truth, to correct mistakes, and to struggle against all tendencies that run counter to the interests of the Party and the people. They must also resolutely conquer liberalism. In studying the Liberation Army's highly principled, solemn kind of work style, we should not only carry out practical criticism of other people's mistakes but, even more important, every comrade should have a highly developed spirit of self-criticism. We should take the responsibility of our work seriously, be honest, devote ourselves to hard work, and accept as fate the hardships of labor. We should have a highly developed sense of organization and of discipline. We should resolutely follow orders and directions from our superiors, and strictly observe all sorts of codes and conventions.

We should study the Liberation Army's lively work style. The Liberation Army requires all officers and soldiers to live a vivid life, moving with the vigor of youth, with flaming spirit, at peace with the world and themselves. They must not be dispirited and phlegmatic, with a weak and decadent spirit. They must not be mechanical, wooden people who do things spiritlessly. In studying this kind of revolutionary optimism in the Liberation Army's work style, we should bring revolutionary creativity into full play, and forever safeguard lively and vigorous political enthusiasm and a forward-looking spirit. We should not only enable young comrades to be physically and mentally lively in their work, life, and study, but we should also enable older comrades to study well and get ahead, considering their age as an advantage. We should, like the Liberation Army, energetically carry out cultural recreation and regular education in all collective units with a joyful and ardent approach.

The "three-eight work style" is a great spiritual force, and once the masses consciously act on it, it will be transformed into a mighty material force. If we study the Liberation Army's "three-eight work style," everyone's spirit will flourish and every unit's work will develop vigorously.

The Liberation Army particularly stresses using the company as the key unit in all work. The company is the primary unit for carrying out fighting, training, and all other tasks. The company is the swordpoint, and therefore should definitely be built up well. Our success in building up the company will be decided first by the strength of our political-ideological work, and also by whether or not we insist on the "four firsts" and develop the "three-eight work style." The Liberation Army has therefore devoted strenuous efforts to launching the "four-good company" movement, taking the "four goods" as the guideline for all work. The "four goods" refer to being good in political ideology, good in the "three-eight work style," good in military training, and good in management of the living conditions of the men. When creating four-good companies, the Liberation Army makes every fighting man responsible for launching the "five-good soldier" movement. "Five-good" refers to being good in political ideology, good in military techniques, good in the "three-eight work style," good in carrying out assigned tasks, and good in physical training. In this way, political-ideological work and cultivation of the "three-eight work style" will take root firmly at the basic level, going into the midst of the soldiers and building an incomparably strong foundation. All departments and other units in the entire nation should seriously study the way in which the Liberation Army emphasizes basic-level construction. Industrial and business units just now starting activity in "five-good industry" and "five-good business" movements and rural villages now starting model company and model production brigade movements particularly need to draw on the Liberation Army's experience in launching "four-good company" and "five-good soldier" movements. Comrade Lin Piao has said: "Things are always very complicated. For a few decades we have been doing various kinds of work, but the most important factors in this work are still these: do good political and ideological work, have a good work style, do good training, and manage living conditions well. These are very difficult. If we manage this sort of thing well, even though we still cannot claim that our work is complete, we will at least be able to cope with any situation that comes up. We cannot neglect basic-level units in our military construction; nor should we try to manage work in the basic-level units without these four goods." These words of Comrade Lin Piao, although directed toward the army, are in fact also entirely correct for and applicable to all our other work departments. In learning from the Liberation Army, the whole nation should make sure that all work, particularly political-ideological work, penetrates down to the grass roots level. Only then can all our work truly be established on an improved and consolidated base.

All levels of Party and government leadership organizations, all factories and mines, all other enterprises, and all people's communes should strengthen their political and ideological work. Like the Liberation Army, they should carry political-ideological work down into the basic-level units, conducting intensive and conscientious ideological work so as to lay an indestructable, reliable, firm, and steady foundation. The work of the correct handling of men should have first priority, and so should the work of the correct handling of living ideology. We should sincerely and effectively carry out ideological work among all of our 600 million people. What is more, we should set up the beginnings of a continuing, systematic political work system.

The Liberation Army, as a result of its long-term, unremitting effort in carrying out thorough and meticulous political-ideological work, has become an extremely proletarian, extremely militant army. In learning from the Liberation Army, the whole country should learn from the Liberation Army's extremely proletarian revolutionary spirit. All departments and units in the entire country should, like the Liberation Army, strive to heighten their revolutionary spirit. Comrades on all fronts throughout the country should strive to heighten their revolutionary spirit. In this way, on every front of our socialist construction, we can, like the Liberation Army, gradually forge a brave army, truly red and expert, capable of fighting great battles, capable of fighting hard battles, and capable of fighting vicious battles. Our socialist revolution and the cause of socialist construction can then develop by leaps and bounds.

Learning from the Liberation Army is the new essence of
the communist competition of emulating the advanced, learning
from the advanced, overtaking the advanced, and helping the
backward that is now going on throughout the country. All advanced experience, including that of the Liberation Army, should
be widely propagated and put to even greater use so that this
wealth of experience will belong to the whole people. Important
obstacles to the study of advanced experience are obstinacy,
conceit, pride, and self-satisfaction. Only by studying all advanced experience with an open mind and enthusiasm, learning
from other people's good points, and patching up your own bad
points can you continuously improve your own work. This session of the PLA Political Work Conference particularly pointed
out: "We hope that comrades of the Liberation Army, when
looking at their accomplishments, will at the same time look
at the shortcomings in army work." The Conference demanded
that comrades of the whole army should keep clearly in mind
the teachings of the Party and of Comrade Mao Tse-tung, and
that they should at all times adopt a Marxist dialectical method in analyzing their own work, seeing accomplishments but
also seeing shortcomings and mistakes, exploring the aspect
of accomplishments but also exploring the aspect of shortcomings and mistakes. Only in this way can obstinacy, conceit,
pride, and self-satisfaction be prevented; only in this way can
the work move forward. The Conference also appealed to the
comrades of the entire army to have an open mind and sincerely
learn from comrades working in local areas. They should
learn all good experiences in local work, good work styles, and
good methods, to the point where they can put them into practice to improve the work of the Liberation Army. We believe
that by having local areas learn from the Liberation Army and
having the Liberation Army learn from local areas we can improve the unity between the army and the people. The people
will understand and support the army, and the army will understand and help the people. This is a great thing. If the army
and the people become even more united, then our great

motherland will be even more invincible.

The experience of the Liberation Army has been accumulated over a long period; it is constantly being summed up and improved and becoming more joyful day by day. It is a comparatively complete, comparatively systematic experience, reaching a very high standard. Therefore, when studying the Liberation Army, we should learn and apply its experience with full vigor, integrating it with the actual conditions in each department and unit. We should also adopt a method of using experimental models and then extending them gradually by stages and by groups. At present, there are a few advanced units that have already achieved noteworthy success in learning from the Liberation Army. They have created some advanced experiences that are integrated with their own practical situations and that are relatively complete and relatively systematic. These experiences should be sincerely summarized and propagated.

This is the year for large-scale study and emulation. Study on a large scale Comrade Mao Tse-tung's works; study and apply with full vigor Mao Tse-tung thought. Study on a large scale the PLA and all advanced experience; study and apply with full vigor all advanced experience. Emulate the advanced. Emulate the advanced on every front and in every post. Everyone should carry out mutual comparisons and look for mutual discrepancies, starting up communist competition and cooperation. In this way the people of our country will be able to raise the great red banner of Mao Tse-tung thought even higher, go all out, aim high, and carry out all aspects of our work better and better!

19

WANG CHIEH, CHAIRMAN MAO'S
GOOD SOLDIER*

New China News Agency
and Liberation Army Daily

Wang Chieh, a twenty-three-year-old squad leader in an engineering company of the Chinese People's Liberation Army, died a glorious death on July 14, 1965, while saving the lives of eleven militiamen and a cadre during a blasting operation. He thus became a type of hero in the mold of Tung Tsun-jui (1) and Huang Chi-kuang (2), and the great communist fighter Lei Feng. (3) His name has spread far and wide throughout the country, stirring the hearts of millions. His life story and his dedication to revolution are an inspiration for all to make ever more energetic efforts under the great red banner of Mao Tsetung's thought.

Wang Chieh's life was short but brilliant. This was what he wrote in his diary on July 14, 1961: "The greatest happiness in a man's life is to serve his country."

---

*"Ke-ming ch'ing-ch'un ti tsan-ko: chi Mao chu-hsi ti hao chan-shih Wang Chieh" [A Song in Praise of Revolutionary Youth: The Story of Wang Chieh, Chairman Mao's Good Soldier], in I-hsin wei ke-ming [The Whole Heart for the Revolution] (Peking: Chung-kuo ch'ing-nien, 1965), pp. 5-16. This translation is taken, with minor editorial revisions, from The Diary of Wang Chieh (Peking: Foreign Languages Press, 1967), pp. 1-20. The subtitle of the original text is used as the title for this selection.

Young Wang Chieh steeled himself in the revolutionary army
from the time he wrote this pledge until his heroic sacrifice
four years later. Nourished by Mao Tse-tung's thought and
tested in practical struggles, this middle-school student from
an ordinary peasant family rapidly developed into a great communist fighter.

With deep emotion and profound respect we begin the story
of Wang Chieh, our closest comrade in arms and Chairman
Mao's good soldier.

Read Chairman Mao's Works, Set Out on
the Path of Revolution

Wang Chieh belonged to a new generation of Chinese youth
who have matured so quickly under the brilliance of Mao Tse-
tung's thought, which illuminates the whole of China.

Wang Chieh joined the Chinese People's Liberation Army
shortly after graduating in July 1961 from a middle school in
Chinhsiang hsien, Shantung Province. He was glowing with
enthusiasm. He was so excited, in fact, when he put on his
army uniform and cap for the first time that he asked his political instructor, "I'm a revolutionary fighter now, aren't I?"
"The first thing you must do to become a real revolutionary
fighter," the political instructor replied in a soft voice, "is to
change the way you think about things, and the only way to do
that is to study Chairman Mao's works."

When Wang Chieh joined the new recruits' company, they
were organized to study Chairman Mao's article "Analysis of
the Classes in Chinese Society" as part of a political education
campaign aimed at getting the men to recall all their sufferings in the old society.

From the stories told by the men at the "recall bitterness"
meetings, it emerged that out of ninety-odd men in the company, sixty-six had fathers or brothers who had worked as
farmhands for landlords, and fifty-six had had their homes
broken up and relatives killed by the imperialists, Kuomintang
reactionaries, or landlords. For instance, while the father of

one of the men, Tsao Chien-yüeh, was being taken away by
Japanese invaders, his grandmother was bayoneted to death.
Chu Yu-pei also had a bitter story to tell. He could still vividly
remember the time when he had to go begging as a little boy.
His parents were so poor that they didn't even have a rice bowl,
so he had to collect scraps of food with a broken tile. From
these and many other painful tales of the old society, young
Wang Chieh learned about the bitter past of his comrades in
arms. He began to see the real meaning of classes, oppression,
and exploitation, the reason for revolution. No longer able to
control his anger and hatred, he jumped on the platform and
declared: "Comrades, I haven't been through the bitterness
you've suffered, but I feel as if all your sufferings have hap-
pened to me as well. I'm determined to avenge my class brothers!"

Soon Wang Chieh was assigned to the First Engineering Company. When he first took up the job, everything was new and
fresh to him. What struck him most was the company's good
fighting record. For instance, Wang Chieh's squad — the company's sixth — had fought a more-than-thirty-hour battle during
the War to Resist U.S. Aggression and Aid Korea. With the
help of a tank unit, the squad destroyed three tanks of the U.S.
aggressive forces in this action, for which it was awarded a
second-class citation of honor. Wang Chieh felt proud to belong
to this company. He was also fascinated by stories of battles
told by Kao Shao-chung, the company's deputy commander, a
battle hero and an old soldier of the company. I wish I could
be a hero like him, thought Wang Chieh. But how?

Not long afterward, the company was ordered to build defense works. At first Wang Chieh was full of enthusiasm. But
after a few days of swinging a twelve-pound hammer his hands
became blistered and his waist and legs felt sore and leaden.
"It's all right being a tankman or a truck driver," he grumbled,
"but it's really hard work in the engineering corps!"

Political instructor Feng An-kuo knew what Wang Chieh and
some other new soldiers were thinking, so he ran a class to
study three of Chairman Mao's articles — "Serve the People,"

"The Foolish Old Man Who Removed the Mountains," and "In Memory of Norman Bethune." He also told them the stories of Chang Szu-teh and Norman Bethune. Wang Chieh was deeply inspired. He seemed to see the beacon light guiding him forward.

As soon as Wang Chieh got his first month's pay, he went to a bookshop and bought some of Chairman Mao's works. He read them during rest breaks, as soon as he got up in the morning, just before he turned in at night, and on Sundays and holidays. His love for these books grew as he read them, and he tried to live the way Chairman Mao taught. Having repeatedly studied the great leader's teachings about wholeheartedly serving the people, Wang Chieh came to understand the meaning and purpose of work. He no longer looked at building defense works as arduous and difficult. Once he had been slow and clumsy in handling the hammer. Now he became the fastest worker in his platoon. He would do the heaviest job and go wherever there was the greatest difficulty. When the work was nearly completed, Wang Chieh was commended as the company's crack hammerer. Of all the new soldiers who joined up with him, Wang Chieh was the first to be admitted into the Communist Youth League.

Wang Chieh had learned from his own experience that, as he wrote in his diary, "just as a locomotive cannot move once it is off the tracks, so a revolutionary fighter will become muddle-headed and go astray if he doesn't study Chairman Mao's works." Therefore, he studied hard and regularly. He never missed his studies for a single day, no matter how busy and tired he was. When his right hand was badly burned by smoldering pitch on April 5, 1964, for instance, he still kept on studying Chairman Mao's works, though his company commander and comrades implored him to rest. And with his right hand lying helpless across his chest, he even learned how to take notes with his left. "My body may need a rest," he remarked, "but not my mind!"

His diary of over 100,000 words was written in every spare moment he could find during his training and construction work or after late night sentry duty.

Chairman Mao made a nationwide call in March 1963, asking the Chinese people to "learn from Comrade Lei Feng." This acted as a great new stimulus to Wang Chieh, helping his progress along the revolutionary road. He set Lei Feng up as his model, measuring everything he did by his actions. But the more he compared himself with Lei Feng, the greater the distance seemed between them. By studying Chairman Mao's teachings on class analysis, he began to understand his own family background and how he was still influenced by a lot of petty-bourgeois individualistic ideas. If he wanted to come closer to his ideal — Lei Feng — he had to work really hard at getting rid of this "burden."

One day he went out to help someone without asking for leave of absence. To his surprise and dismay, the squad leader criticized him for it. That night he slept very badly. Then he thought of Lei Feng: here was a soldier who had always observed discipline, while he had violated elementary discipline by not asking for leave of absence. Didn't that show how far he was behind Lei Feng? It was this thought that made him realize how right the squad leader had been to criticize him. This was the way Wang Chieh learned from his heroes and so changed his character, layer after layer.

Wang Chieh made greater conscious efforts to do this, making stricter and stricter demands on himself. With the help of his leaders and comrades he constantly fought against his own selfish ideas. He couldn't stand the sort of person who said one thing and did another. He would not neglect the smallest thing in his battle against selfishness. And so he made a point of not picking the best seat when he went to a film show with his comrades, or the best bath in the bathhouse, and he was not particular about which work tools he used. To behave in any other way was quite incompatible, in Wang Chieh's eyes, with the noble character worthy of a revolutionary soldier. After he had studied Chairman Mao's teachings about the five requirements for revolutionary successors to the proletarian cause, he set an even higher standard for himself. In his every action he tried to live by the standard set by such heroes as

Chang Szu-teh, Norman Bethune, Tung Tsun-jui, Liu Hu-lan (4), Huang Chi-kuang, Hsiang Hsiu-li, and Lei Feng.

Wang Chieh worked all the harder at changing himself and made even stricter demands on himself the more progress and the better results he achieved. During his time in the army he was commended every year as a five-good soldier, twice won a third-class merit, and became the company's choice as a model member of the Communist Youth League. He had often thought about the question of joining the Communist Party. Having repeatedly studied Chairman Mao's teachings about ideological remolding and the requirements for a Communist Party member, he adopted a correct attitude towards this question.

"It's my earnest wish to join the Party," he said. "All my efforts are being put in that direction. But I still have a lot of individualistic ideas. I shouldn't take such shortcomings into the organization."

Wang Chieh never felt self-satisfied even though his progress and success were obvious to his comrades, and the company's Party branch was seriously grooming him for Party membership. He took careful note of his slightest failings and never expected the Party to be lenient towards them. He once told a comrade: "The Party is always ready to admit comrades who are qualified for membership. I believe some day I'll be admitted into the Party."

Wang Chieh's noble character manifested itself in his utter devotion to revolution, and his heroic deeds testify to his worthiness of being a great communist fighter.

A Servant of the People, A "Willing Ox" for Revolution

Many visitors shed tears at the exhibition of Wang Chieh's life. Why were they so deeply moved by the sacrifice of an ordinary soldier whom they had never met? Because Wang Chieh was a fine son of the people, the embodiment of the excellent qualities found in a revolutionary soldier. His dedication to the service of the people had earned the heartfelt respect of millions of working people.

In his illuminating diary he expressed again and again the desire to be a servant of the people, a "willing ox" for revolution. He frequently mentioned Lei Feng's glorious name and pledged that, like him, he would devote his limited life to the unlimited service of the people. Putting his lofty aim of serving the people into practice, Wang Chieh performed many good deeds wherever he went. Here are some instances:

On a march he once saw a soldier carelessly step on some wheat stalks. He immediately straightened them and patted earth around them.

While transporting grain he saw an old woman walking with difficulty. He offered her a ride on his cart and took her to her home several miles away.

Several times during bus trips and train journeys he paid the fares of passengers who had lost their tickets or purses.

On his way to a bookshop one Sunday morning with Chou Yu-lu, another soldier, Wang Chieh saw a long line of carts full of stones being hauled by workers across a bridge. He and Chou immediately began to help the workers, who were clearly having a hard time. Because of an urgent errand Chou left first, telling Wang Chieh to meet him at the bookshop. When Wang Chieh failed to turn up at the bookshop, Chou went back to the bridge. Wang Chieh was still there. He had taken his cotton-padded coat off and was helping to push one cart after another. Trickles of sweat ran down his face. It was only when Chou reminded him that their day's leave was up that he reluctantly agreed to leave the place. "The workers are building socialism by pushing these heavily loaded carts," said Wang Chieh. "I hate to leave them when they've still got so much to do!" Chou Yu-lu always feels deeply moved whenever he recalls this event.

Wang Chieh had a profound class feeling for his revolutionary comrades. He looked on every good deed done for his comrades as part of his service to the people. On one march he carried more than half of the whole squad's three-day ration. He brought a full canteen, but instead of using it himself he shared it with his comrades. During a snowstorm once, the soldiers got their cotton-padded coats soaked through after working a whole day repairing a bridge. In the evening they put their coats by the fire and went to sleep. Wang Chieh then went around the billet and made sure everyone was well covered by a quilt. Outside the wind howled. If the coats were not dry by the next day, thought Wang Chieh, then how could the comrades go to work? At the thought of this, he began to hold the wet coats up to the fire until the last one was dry. It was then three o'clock in the morning. When the men learned that Wang Chieh had done yet another good deed, they felt the warmth of comradeship.

Wang Chieh always made a point of doing a good turn for his comrades whenever the opportunity arose. Whatever he could do himself he would do to the best of his ability. If he could not manage a job alone, he would go all out with others to do it. When his right hand was burned by pitch, he used his left hand to help his comrades collect gravel. With his left hand he also fetched basins of water from a ditch at the bottom of the hill and then filled up the washing basins for his comrades before they went to work. While in the hospital he helped the nurses polish the floor and carried medicine and boiled water for them.

Whatever work he did — his own or that of others — he would give all he had, working with increasing vigor. He was only interested in working for the revolution and for the benefit of his comrades. When the company set up a barber shop to give the men free haircuts, he insisted on working as a barber. The men argued that he would be no good at the job. But Wang Chieh did not give up: he still thought he could be useful in some other way. So he volunteered for work the day the shop opened, bringing a towel and soap to shampoo the "customers." He also made a stand out of bits of spare wood so that his comrades could have their faces and hair washed without having to squat on the ground. He literally "squeezed" himself into the barber shop and made himself indispensable.

In his short span of life Wang Chieh served the people and his comrades with a passionate zeal. For his many good deeds he was called the living Lei Feng. Yet he always kept in mind

Chairman Mao's teachings about serving the people wholeheartedly and unreservedly. He believed that the more he contributed to the people and the less he demanded from them, the
better. He made a rule for himself: do not seek fame, privileges, or material comforts. He was the first to face hardships,
the last to enjoy comforts. While camping out he would give
others the best sleeping place. Whenever there was an errand
to run, he would always be willing to do it. When everyone was
tired after a march, he stood on sentry duty longer than necessary. He often rose very early to sweep and clean the room
and fetch washing water for the whole platoon.

In early July 1965 he was sent to train the local militia at
the Changlou People's Commune in Pihsien County, Kiangsu
Province. He was full of enthusiasm and took his new work
very seriously. He got up at four every day, even in the pour-
ing rain, making his way along the muddy road to the militia
quarters some distance away. If there were pools of water on
the ground by the time he got there, he would immediately
clear them away. Sometimes he arrived at the quarters before the militiamen were up, whereupon he would sit under the
eaves and quietly read Quotations from Chairman Mao Tse-
tung by the early light of the dawn. In his spare time he explained Chairman Mao's works to the militiamen and told them
the story of Lei Feng. He chatted with them about things of
common interest, about their homes and daily life. The men
knew him so well that they called him Teacher Wang and liked
to have heart-to-heart talks with him.

Wang Chieh was always earnest and hard-working, and he faced
complaints without a murmur. He was a "willing ox" for revolution till he breathed his last. The night before his death he
read Chairman Mao's works as usual, stood his turn on sentry
duty, and then did another spell of duty for a comrade. The
next morning he fetched washing water for his comrades, put
the toothbrushes tidily together, and left for the militia training ground, talking and laughing on the way with Chen Hsüeh-i,
assistant leader of the third squad.

In such a way did he finish the last page of his glorious life.

He had lived up to his own pledge: "I will work hard for the Party, country and people as long as I live."

A Noble Heart; Keep the Whole World in Mind

One wintry night the men of the first company were driving stakes through thin ice into a river bed. It was so bitterly cold that even their vigorous hammering could not keep them warm. They began to shiver so much, in fact, that they could not keep up their work chant. Working as enthusiastically as ever, Wang Chieh called out to them: "Comrades, think of Lo Sheng-chiao (5) and you'll soon forget the cold!"

This was the way Wang Chieh encouraged his comrades. It was typical of his attitude. When he was in a difficult situation, he thought of those who were worse off. When he felt cold, he thought of those class brothers who were in a colder place. When he faced a problem, he thought of the two-thirds of the people of the world still under oppression.

Wang Chieh's utter devotion to revolution and his broad revolutionary outlook revealed themselves in his good habits. He did not smoke or drink. He did not waste money and liked to save things. After his death his comrades found a pouch filled with used toothpaste tubes. He had intended to sell them to buy booklets of Chairman Mao's works for the company's club. He wrote in his diary on August 21, 1963:

Eating and dressing well don't bring real happiness. This will only come when all the poor people of the world lead a happy life. Being particular about food and clothes will make one eventually forget one's past suffering and become alienated from the masses. Then one will gradually lose one's revolutionary zeal.

When his service time was up in the latter part of 1964, his family asked him several times to return home to get married, but he decided to put off his marriage and stay on in the army. He said: "At the moment, U.S. imperialism is stepping up its aggression against Vietnam. How can a revolutionary soldier lay down his arms and return home?" He also wrote a poem entitled "Is There a Time Limit for Revolution?" This verse from his poem expressed his thoughts:

> Though my service time is up,
> How can I take off my uniform and retire to the farm?
> Johnson is piling up arms and preparing for war,
> How can I change my sword for a plough?

Wang Chieh always thought about how the enemy was getting ready to attack us. And with this in mind, he trained hard. When the wind was howling one bitingly cold wintry night, he went out with some of his comrades to a tank training ground to lay mines. The ground was so hard that the men's pickaxes were hardly able to penetrate it, and their hands became blistered. Someone suggested that they switch to softer ground. By torchlight Wang Chieh read "The Foolish Old Man Who Removed the Mountains" during the break and explained Vice-Chairman Lin Piao's instructions to the men about how stiffer training and higher skills were needed to kill the enemy in close range fighting up to two hundred meters. "U.S. imperialism is our most ferocious enemy," he said. "We must train in the most difficult conditions and get as much training as possible. We must be able to destroy enemy tanks on soft or hard ground." With this lesson the soldiers' enthusiasm rose; they went on with the hard training.

Wang Chieh was very careful about doing every job thoroughly. Even a relatively simple task like laying a mine, he practiced again and again during his four years in the army, and each time he would do it as if for the first time. He said: "You may only have to use it once or twice on the battlefield, but you have to practice it thousands of times!"

In the spring of 1963 the soldiers started a practice of laying a mine a day. Wang Chieh and an experienced soldier, Chi Chang-chun, worked together as a team laying and removing mines. At first Wang Chieh could not find the mines laid by

Chi, while Chi easily discovered his, however well he camou-
flaged them. A puzzled Wang Chieh asked Chi if he had a "secret" method. Chi said: "You've improved a bit recently, but
you're still not good enough. Look at the mine you've just laid.
Don't you see you've forgotten to straighten up the two small
plants you stepped on? A clever enemy will easily be able to
detect the spot." Wang Chieh learned a lot about minelaying
that day. From then on he worked even harder at the job and
improved his skill: sometime later he was able to lay a mine
that was almost impossible to discover. He also introduced
a new method of minelaying which would inflict heavier casualties on the enemy and made seven kinds of instruments for in-
structing soldiers on a crash course.

Closely following the development of world events, Wang
Chieh carefully read the daily papers, paying particular attention to the situation in Southeast Asia. After hearing a report
on current events made on May 1, 1965, by the deputy political
commissar, he was incensed with indignation against the U.S.
imperialists for their savage bombing of North Vietnam and
the increasing number of troops they had sent to South Vietnam
to slaughter the people there. He immediately wrote the
following words in his diary: "I'm determined to support the
struggle of the Vietnamese people. I wish to be a volunteer!"
He also wrote a letter to the battalion headquarters on behalf
of the comrades in his squad, expressing their firm determination to support the fraternal Vietnamese people in their battle to defeat the U.S. aggressors.

Wang Chieh loved to sing a song called "Our Generation."
It ran:

Our generation,
Hearts full of aspiration,
Standing on mountains and by rivers,
We keep the whole world in mind.

This stirring song expressed Wang Chieh's strong fighting
will and broad vision. It reflected the lofty spirit of interna-

tionalism that becomes part of the whole being of a revolutionary soldier nourished and matured by Mao Tse-tung's thought.

Dedicated to Revolution, Fearless of Death

Wang Chieh's revolutionary spirit of not fearing hardship or death is fully shown in the following passage from his diary:

I'll always be faithful to the cause of the Party. I'll be brave enough to make sacrifices for the victory of the revolution. A communist should be ready to face death fearlessly. A revolutionary soldier doesn't worry about his own safety.

Wang Chieh did every kind of commonplace work seriously and enthusiastically. He was always the first to volunteer for a difficult job. He led his comrades in carrying gravel across a ditch over a long, narrow wooden board. He worked on jobs high in the air and in narrow tunnels and drilled blast holes in danger spots. He was always the first to deal with unexploded charges. Whether in construction work or flood prevention, in training or in productive labor, comrades always found Wang Chieh doing the most arduous and dangerous job.

In his diary Wang Chieh wrote:

The path of revolution is rugged and full of danger. The old revolutionaries who trod this path have set shining examples for us. As their successors, we should not fear hardships or run away from difficulties. We young people should be like hardy grass in the storm or pines in winter: we must be able to go through all trials. . . .

One wintry night the troops went out to build a bridge over a river covered with thin ice. It was windy and drizzling. Wang Chieh was the first to volunteer as soon as it was decided that six of the strongest men should work in the water.

But the squad leader would not let him go, saying he was not strong enough. "If you want to make a good fighter out of me," pleaded Wang Chieh, "then please let me go and toughen myself up!" Without waiting for a reply he took off his cotton-padded coat and jumped into the river, sinking waist-deep in the water. Other comrades then followed him. When he had finished his work and come out of the water, his lips were blue with cold, but all he did was to wipe himself, put on his cotton-padded coat, and go off to carry planks for the bridge.

In August 1963, when the troops were sent out on flood-prevention work, Wang Chieh determinedly wrote down in his diary:

> I've become a soldier for the people, the Party, and the motherland. I'll go wherever the Party sends me without any hesitation. If necessary I will willingly sacrifice my youthful life.

In the battle against the flood he carried more earth and worked quicker than anyone else. For each straw bundle carried by his comrades, he shouldered two.

One night an urgent call came to carry timber from a lumberyard. They had to cross a flooded stretch of land on the way. The company commander called for a volunteer who could swim and lead the way through the water. "I'll go!" said Wang Chieh as he jumped into the water. Groping his way in the dark with the water up to his chest, he sank into deep muddy holes several times. As he bobbed up, he warned his comrades about the danger spots. Finally he found a safe way leading to the lumberyard.

Wang Chieh's fearless spirit of defying all difficulties was also demonstrated in his willingness to tackle dangerous jobs single-handed where there was no help available. One night about the end of July 1964, a sudden downpour lashed across the construction site in the hills where his unit was working. When two soldiers, Liu Cheng-ko and Wu Ching-chung, were awakened by the noise, they went out to see what was happening.

The flood waters were sweeping stones down the hill amidst lightning and thunder. Then they saw a shadowy figure moving around on the site. It was Wang Chieh rushing about trying to save the building material. The two men immediately joined him, and after a forty-minute desperate rescue operation, they succeeded in saving all the material which the flood had threatened to sweep away.

Wang Chieh went through several severe tests in his young life. His loyalty to the Party and revolution was expressed in these two passages from his diary:

Through studying Chairman Mao's works I've come to understand that revolution is my ideal and struggle is true happiness.

... I'll never be afraid of going through fire or water for the Party's sake.

These words present a vivid picture of his exemplary life.

* * *

Wang Chieh's life was powerful and beautiful, a song in praise of revolutionary youth.

His heroic story was on everyone's lips in the army, in the cities and countryside, in the factories and schools. A popular movement to learn from Wang Chieh vigorously spread throughout the country and the entire People's Liberation Army.

Wang Chieh is dead, but millions of Wang Chiehs are growing up. They will hold aloft the great red banner of Mao Tse-tung's thought, take up the heavy task of revolution, and march forward with big strides in the direction indicated by the Party and Chairman Mao.

Let the imperialists, reactionaries of all countries, and modern revisionists tremble before us!

Glory to the heroic new generation armed with Mao Tse-tung's thought!

Notes

1) Tung Tsun-jui (1929-48) was a member of the Chinese Communist Party and a hero of the Chinese People's Liberation Army. On May 26, 1948, during the War of Liberation, he was assigned the task of blowing up an enemy fortification on a bridge at Lunghua, Jehol Province (now Hopei Province). When he dashed under the bridge and found no place to lay his charge of dynamite, he held it up against the fortification and died a heroic death accomplishing his mission.

2) Huang Chi-kuang (1930-52) was a hero of the Chinese People's Volunteers in the War to Resist U.S. Aggression and Aid Korea. On October 20, 1952, in the famous Battle of Sangkumryung, he was assigned the task of blowing up certain enemy pillboxes. He had used up all his hand grenades by the time all but one were demolished, so he blocked its machine-gun aperture with his chest, enabling his unit to advance and capture the height.

3) Lei Feng (1939-62) was a squad leader in the People's Liberation Army and a member of the Chinese Communist Party. Besides doing his own work well, he was always ready to help others in work and study or when they were in trouble. He was therefore honored as a good fighter of Chairman Mao's. On August 15, 1962, he died in the course of duty.

4) Liu Hu-lan, a Chinese Communist Party member, born in Wenshui hsien, Shansi Province, led the people in 1946 in land reform and in supporting the War of Liberation. The Kuomintang reactionary army entered her village in January 1947 and captured her. Refusing to surrender to the enemy, she pointed her accusing finger at them and finally died a hero's death. Comrade Mao Tse-tung wrote these words in her honor: "A Great Life! A Glorious Death!"

5) Lo Sheng-chiao, first-class model soldier of the Chinese People's Volunteers and an internationalist fighter, died a heroic death in saving the life of a Korean boy. In January 1952 in Sokchon-ni, Songchon County, Korea, when the temperature was 20° C below zero, he dived into the icy water three times and saved Choi Yong, who had sunk through a crack in the ice while skating. Lo was drowned.

V
The Functions of
the Militia

20

ORGANIZE THE MILITIA IN A BIG WAY*

Fu Ch'iu-t'ao

In September, after Chairman Mao had inspected several provinces of the Yangtze River region and returned to the capital, he said, "The organization of the militia is very good and ought to be broadened." He pointed out, moreover: "The imperialists have been insulting us so much that it is necessary to deal with this seriously. We not only want to have a strong regular army; we also want to organize militia in a big way." All the people enthusiastically supported this great call of Chairman Mao's. At the same time, during the vigorous development of the people's commune movement, they launched the mass movement of "everyone a soldier" and "organize militia in a big way." In particular, after the broadening of the struggle of our people against the American imperialists' occupation of Taiwan, this movement, like ten thousand horses stampeding a thousand li in a day, has already realized [the program of] "everyone a soldier" in the majority of provinces and cities in the short period of one month. Peking, for example, has in less than a month organized 156 militia divisions and 356 militia regiments; Kiangsu Province has organized 185 militia divisions and more than 2,400 militia regiments; Kwangsi has organized 224 militia divisions and 2,400 militia regiments. At

---

*Fu Ch'iu-t'ao, "Ta-pan min-ping-shih," Jen-min jih pao [People's Daily], October 30, 1958. The author was then head of the Mobilization Department of the General Staff of the PLA.

present the organization of militia divisions and regiments in various areas is developing very quickly. After they are organized, the militia carry out the militarization of organization, the "combativization" of operations, and the collectivization of life, and adopt the method of communist cooperation. Learning the combat spirit of the People's Liberation Army, they produce iron and steel on a large scale, practice deep plowing, and carry out the cultural revolution and the technological revolution in a big way. Moreover, relying on the principle of the unity of labor and military training, they launch rich and colorful activities for spare-time military training of a mass nature. A great many militia regiments in the front line of Fukien Province produce on the one hand, and support the war front on the other. They dig battle trenches, transport ammunition, and join together with the People's Liberation Army in fighting the war and attacking the enemy. In Lien-chiang hsien, Fukien, the militia exuberantly sing this military song: "Workers, peasants, merchants, students, and soldiers intertwine into a big rope. In peacetime they carry out production; in wartime they kill the enemy. The waves are howling, and the winds are roaring. The angry fire of six hundred million people burns. The American imperialists have invaded our land. If this animosity is not revenged, our hatred will never diminish." From October 7 through October 18, the General Staff Department of the People's Liberation Army, in order to sum up and exchange advanced experience in time, called a series of on-the-spot nationwide meetings on militia work at Shih-ching-shan Electric Power Plant, Shih-ching-shan Iron and Steel Factory, Peking Industrial College, and Hsü-shui hsien, Hopei. All the comrades who were present unanimously agreed that the implementation of the program of "everyone a soldier" and "organizing the militia in a big way" is a great realization of the military thought of Chairman Mao on people's war, and an important measure in liberating 600 million Chinese people for carrying out the great socialist construction and the transition to communism.

In organizing the militia, every locality has utilized fully the experience of our Party in building the People's Liberation Army and in carrying out the method of leading mass movements. Moreover, they have already discovered many good practices:

1. Let the Party committee lead, and put politics in command. The militia are military organizations, and are also labor organizations, educational organizations, and physical education organizations. They are very closely related to the entire people's economy and to the interests of the masses. Organizing the militia is a great military task, a political task, and an organizational task of a mass nature. A great many Party secretaries have taken personal command. Comrades like Liu Hsüeh-ch'ü, Party secretary of Peking Industrial College; Ai Chih-sheng, deputy Party secretary of Tsinghua University; Li Shih-min, Party secretary of Shih-ching-shan Electric Power Plant; Ku Ai-min, deputy Party secretary of Shih-ching-shan Iron and Steel Works; Chang Kuo-chung, Party secretary of Hsü-shui hsien; Ch'en Ch'en-hua, Party secretary of Shui-ch'eng People's Commune, Hsü-shui hsien; Chan Teng-k'o, Party secretary of Shang-ch'uang People's Commune — these men have all taken personal charge of work. Under the unified leadership of the Party committee, they have firmly combined production with labor and study, adopted the democratic methods of great contending, great blooming, and great debates to mobilize the masses ardently, and carried out the organization [of the militia] on the basis of elevating the political consciousness of the masses. All militia work is carried out under the unified leadership and management of the Party committees of factories, mines, schools, administrative organs, or people's communes. All the work stresses taking into consideration the entire situation and following the mass line. The mass line is the basic line of our Party; it is also the basic line in the building up of militia. It is only by using just and egalitarian attitudes in treating the masses, consulting with the masses on all affairs, being good at the method of "from the masses, to the masses," giving play to the wisdom of the masses, and employing the positive elements

of the masses that one is enabled to carry out the Party's policies on militia work, to be effective in guarding against commandism, formalism, and the tendency to disregard the masses.

2. Thoroughly carry out the class line. Through more than twenty years of armed struggle and, since liberation, a continuation of political education under the leadership of the Party and Chairman Mao, our people have elevated their political consciousness to an unprecedented level. Now they are again firmly uniting around the Party committees and the government at every level to raise high the banner of Chairman Mao and to make progress victoriously. But within our country class enemies still exist, so we must maintain a high degree of vigilance. In the movement to organize the militia, the class enemies within and outside of our country are able to carry on destruction. Therefore, in the militia's organizational work, every locale should pay attention to investigative work and carry out the class line. No landlords, rich peasants, counterrevolutionary elements, bad elements, or rightists shall be allowed to sneak into the ranks of the militia. The purity of this armed force should be protected. As for the weapons of the militia, they should be kept in the hands of trustworthy militia. The militia should be educated to pay attention to, to take good care of, and to safeguard the weapons. With regard to militia cadres, they should be selected from among excellent Communist Party members and Communist Youth League members who are demobilized military men, workers, farmers, and students in order to ensure the absolute leadership of the Party over the militia organizations. In Hsü-shui hsien, every level of Party committee establishes a Military Affairs Department, i.e., an Armed Forces Department. The Party secretaries and Party branch secretaries serve concurrently as political commissars, political instructors, and political supervisors of militia divisions, regiments, battalions, and companies. The basic-level organizations of the militia rely on the active leadership of the Party and League members to carry out the policy and line of the Party.

3. Grasp the principle of getting the best out of each time

and place. Our country is wide, and its people are many. The
cities and the countryside are different, and the working conditions of each area are also different. Therefore, with regard
to the organizational work of the militia, it should be carried
out by differentiating geographical areas and units and grasping the principle of getting the best out of each time and place.
In the countryside, many areas take people's communes as
units, which are organized into divisions, regiments, battalions,
companies, platoons, and squads, or into large-sized brigades,
medium-sized brigades, and teams on the basis of production
organization and the size of militia. In the cities, they take
factories, mines, schools, and government organizations as
units — or else they take the urban people's communes as
units — and these are organized on the basis of the conditions
of production, work, and study. For example, the Shih-ching-
shan Electric Power Plant's militia regiments and battalions
are combined with the workshops, work sectors, and work
groups. The task of organizing militia in the areas of national
minorities may gradually be carried out in accord with their
needs and capabilities.

4. Persist in the principle of the unity of labor and military
training. After hundreds of millions of people were organized,
they all actively plunged into making iron and steel, reaping
the autumn harvest and planting, deeply plowing the land, and
other productive and construction activities. For example, Kuo
Kuang-chü, P'u Ts'un-hui (a woman), and other militia comrades of the Iron Department of Shih-ching-shan Iron and Steel
Works utilized their spare time to design and prepare materials. After 20 days of hard struggle, they built a furnace with
a daily capacity of 60 tons of iron, based on the combination
of native and foreign techniques. On September 23, it started
production, and it was estimated that by the end of the year it
could produce more than 7,000 tons of iron. The more than
12,000 members of the militia of Ta-wang-tien Commune of
Hsü-shui hsien built 4,850 crude furnaces for making iron in
one day and one night. On each production front and at each
work post the militia have demonstrated their great effective-

ness. At the same time, they carry on political education and military training according to the principle of the unity of labor and training in order to raise the level of their political consciousness and military knowledge. Naturally, in the three-year period of painstaking work, all training work has to be flexible, to be united with production, and to promote production. However much they can train, that is how much they are going to train. The training should rely on demobilized and retired army men acting as the backbone, on the mobilization of the masses, and on the adoption of the technique of guaranteeing teaching and learning. The content of military training, aside from the study of marksmanship and terrain and other geographical phenomena, should include, if possible, a systematic study of the experience of specialized military units in combination with that of the specializations of various militia units and the nature of their work, production, and study. In training, [the militia] ought to develop the fine tradition of the People's Liberation Army that the officers teach the soldiers, the soldiers teach the officers, and the officers and soldiers teach each other. The militia should combine militia training with cultural and physical education activities, and transform it into the regular cultural entertainment and physical activities of the masses.

5. Cultivate backbone cadres and develop models. The backbone of the militia is the basic militia; the backbone of the basic militia is the demobilized and transferred armymen. Of the more than six million demobilized and transferred armymen, the great majority have received a long period of Party education and have been tempered by hard combat. They have a comparatively high political consciousness, rich work experience, and strong organizational discipline. Thus, in the process of organizing and building up militia, the demobilized and transferred armymen are relied on as the backbone in each area. Their education should be strengthened. In peacetime they are needed to serve as instructors for militia training. In time of war they are needed to act as the basic-level cadres for organizing military forces. To control well the

strength of the demobilized and transferred armymen and to develop their backbone functions in production, education, study, and the struggle against the enemy will have a great effect on the implementation of the Party's policy, the creation of progressive models, the development of new standards, the spreading of the red flags, and the performance of tasks. The experience of Sui-ch'eng People's Commune in Hsü-shui hsien proves that villages with a good work record are inseparable from the backbone function of demobilized armymen. Among branch secretaries, battalion commanders, and other cadres in that commune, demobilized armymen constitute forty-eight percent [of the total number].

6. Strengthen political work and carry out education in the glorious tradition of the People's Liberation Army. The People's Liberation Army, under the direct leadership of the Party Central Committee and Chairman Mao, has wholeheartedly and thoughtfully served the people. It has developed the fine tradition and work style of the unity of officers and men, the unity of superior and inferior, the unity of the army and the people, the unity of the army and the government; military democracy, economic democracy; preserving discipline, listening to commands, sacrificing for the masses, being just and selfless, working hard and living simply, and fighting courageously. We should spread this fine tradition to the work of making "everyone a soldier." We should strengthen political work, smash individualism and departmentalism, establish the ideology of collectivism and communism, develop the communist style of "getting rid of the white flags and raising the red flags," constantly repudiate various evil thoughts and work styles, and mobilize the masses to struggle against all kinds of enemies. A variety of mass rallies, adult schools, theatrical performances, movies, poems and songs, and pictures should be utilized fully to carry out education in communism, patriotism, internationalism, and revolutionary heroism.

7. In the process of making "everyone a soldier," the army has done a tremendous task. Our nation's militia organization, with the strong help of the People's Liberation Army,

has developed and grown stronger. The powerful militia organization has become not only a useful helping hand of the People's Liberation Army but also a rich source for the continual recruitment and expansion of the People's Liberation Army. At present, in the movement to organize the militia on a large scale, the People's Liberation Army is giving significant assistance to local Party committees and local military organizations in terms of manpower and materials in order to better organize training, educate the militia, and move one step ahead in bringing about intimate relations between the army and the people. For example, the People's Liberation Army [unit] stationed in Paoting Special District, Hopei, transferred a large group of cadres to help train the militia of Hsü-shui hsien. During the training, the army cadres ate together, lived together, and worked together with the militia, exerting a very good influence on it. On Nan-jih Island in Fukien Province, the People's Liberation Army actively helped the local militia to train many excellent artillery men for joint defense against any enemy who dares to attack.

As is evident in the situations presently reflected in various locales, the organization of the militia is excellent. The militia has a profound effect and great influence on the nation's economic construction, national defense, and the changing political and ideological outlook of the people.

1. The militia can strengthen the people's courage and spirit, raise their confidence, and destroy the enemy's spirit. It can strengthen the people's determination to make progress, their daring to scorn all domestic and foreign class enemies, and their daring to demand that high mountains bow their heads, and that rivers change their course.

2. The militia can not only create hundreds of millions of reserve troops that possess a high level of political consciousness and that are qualified militarily, it can also cultivate tens of millions of talented reserve officers. This can solve the contradiction of maintaining only a small number of soldiers in peacetime, while having a large number of troops in wartime.

3. Internally, the militia can exercise effective control over

landlords, rich peasants, counterrevolutionary elements, bad elements, and rightists in order to consolidate the dictatorship of the proletariat. Externally, the militia can effectively defend against aggression. If the imperialists invade our country, the militia can make it difficult for them to move even one step. The imperialists will finally be drowned in our great sea of people who are all soldiers.

4. The militia can establish unified, well-controlled labor organizations based on democratic centralism. It can transfer manpower scientifically, raise the efficiency of the labor of the people, and promote a great leap forward in production.

5. The militia can strengthen further the organization, discipline, and combat abilities of the people.

6. The militia can cultivate the communist personality of the people through the militarization of organization, the "combativization" of operation, the collectivization of life, and livelihood based on the free supply system.

7. The militia can develop further the excellent tradition of hard work and struggle of the People's Liberation Army, and strengthen the people's strong will to fear no difficulties, dangers, or setbacks.

8. The militia can effectively open up cultural, physical, and military training activities of a mass nature, strengthen the people's bodies, and promote the technical and cultural revolutions.

9. The militia can develop jacks-of-all-trades equipped with both military and nonmilitary abilities, who can enter factories as workers, go to the fields as farmers, take up the pen as intellectuals, and carry guns as soldiers. They can become talented in being both red and expert.

10. The militia can advance further the intimate relations between the army and the people, uniting them as close as bones and flesh.

11. The militia can join together the workers, peasants, merchants, and soldiers around the Party and Chairman Mao to facilitate the implementation of the Party's policies and the building of socialism in a faster, better, and more economical way.

12. The militia can make everyone participate in both economic construction and the development of national defense. The whole national economy can be built on the principle of [making things available] for civilian use in peacetime and for military use in wartime. In peacetime the militia can participate systematically in production and construction. Once the imperialists launch an attack, the whole people can make the switch easily and systematically to wartime mobilization. The national economy can be converted in time into a war economy for supporting on all fronts a war to oppose aggression and for winning a final victory.

21

REGULATIONS CONCERNING THE POLITICAL
WORK OF THE HSIEN (OR MUNICIPAL)
PEOPLE'S MILITIA DEPARTMENT OF THE
CHINESE PEOPLE'S LIBERATION ARMY*

The CCP Central Committee

Article 1

Each hsien (or municipal) people's militia department [jen-
min wu-chuang-pu] shall establish a political commissar and
a political work section or a political cadre, in order to conduct
political work pertaining to the militia and the military service. In its political work the hsien (or municipal) people's
militia department shall accept the leadership of higher political commissars and political organs, the hsien (or municipal)
Party committee, and the Party committee of the people's
militia department itself.

The basic tasks of the hsien (or municipal) people's militia
department are — using the thought of Mao Tse-tung as the
guiding compass — to implement thoroughly the lines and pol-

---

*"Chung-kuo jen-min chieh-fang-chün hsien (shih) jen-min
wu-chuang-pu cheng-chih kung-tso t'iao-li," issued by the Central Committee of the Chinese Communist Party together with
eighteen other political work regulations on March 27, 1963.
The Chinese text for this translation is taken from Fei-chün
cheng-chih kung-tso t'iao-li [The Political Work Regulations

icies of the Party, the laws and regulations of the state, and the directives and decisions pertaining to the work of the militia and the military service; to consolidate the Party's absolute leadership among the militia; to raise the proletarian consciousness of the militiamen and strengthen their conception of national defense; to consolidate and purify the militia's organization; to mobilize the militia to participate actively in socialist construction; and to ensure the accomplishment of combat training, maintenance of social order, military conscription, war mobilization, and other tasks.

Article 2

[The political work personnel of the hsien (or municipal) people's militia department should] direct the local Party organizations at the basic level in strengthening the political work of the militia; ensure the thorough implementation by the militia of the resolutions of the Party and the orders and directives of higher authorities; resolutely obey the leadership of the Party; thoroughly implement the class line in the construction of the militia; coordinate with the pertinent authorities in directing the political scrutiny work of the militia; prevent infiltration into the militia organization by landlord, rich-peasant, capitalist-rightist, and counterrevolutionary elements; and ensure that the arms of the militia are in the hands of the upright and reliable activists among the workers, poor peasants, and lower-middle peasants.

Article 3

[The political work personnel of the hsien (or municipal)

for the Bandit Army] (Taipei: Kuo-fang-pu, Ch'ing-pao-chü, 1965), pp. 88-91. For complete English translations of all the political work regulations, see Ying-mao Kau et al., The Political Work System of the Chinese Communist Military (Providence: East Asia Language and Area Center, Brown University, 1971).

people's militia department should] conduct political education
and ideological work in the militia; constantly keep track of and
study the ideological condition of the militia; coordinate with
the pertinent authorities to conduct education among the militia
on social class, domestic and international situations, Party
lines and policies, socialism, the duties of the militia, the revolutionary tradition, and the "three-eight work style"; publicize
good persons and good deeds; promote the proletarian consciousness and patriotic thinking of the militia; and strengthen
their concept of national defense and their fighting will.

Article 4

[The political work personnel of the hsien (or municipal)
people's militia department should] constantly keep track of
the political and ideological conditions and work ability of the
full-time cadres at the basic level; coordinate with the pertinent
authorities to administer their training, evaluation, selection,
distribution, appointment, dismissal, etc.; be concerned with
their life and welfare; take charge of work pertaining to reserve cadres and foster close contact with such cadres; conduct the registration and war mobilization of the reserve cadres;
and strengthen the education and training of the "backbone"
militia cadres.

Article 5

[The political work personnel of the hsien (or municipal)
people's militia department should] conduct political work in
the militia units while they are performing fatigue duties and
ensure the accomplishment of such duties; educate the militia
to regard the taking on of fatigue duties as an honorable responsibility and to carry out various tasks enthusiastically;
educate the militia to carry out thoroughly policies and directives pertaining to domestic defense, as well as to frontier
defense struggles on land and at sea, and to observe discipline
in performing its duties; and educate the militiamen to sharpen

their vigilance, to keep secrets strictly, to hold firmly to their
standpoints, and to prevent the sabotage activities of counterrevolutionaries and other bad elements.

Article 6

[The political work personnel of the hsien (or municipal)
people's militia department should] conduct political work in
the militia in time of war; ensure the accomplishment of combat tasks and combat service duties; successfully conduct wartime political mobilization; stimulate the militia's enthusiasm
for participating in combat and rendering support to the front
and for actively accomplishing combat tasks and combat service duties; educate the militia to execute orders resolutely,
to obey commands, and to develop a combat style of coura-
geousness, staunchness, hard work, perseverance, tactfulness,
and flexibility; direct the militia in developing mass campaigns
to destroy the enemy and perform meritorious deeds; protect
the interests of the masses in the combat zone and maintain
the discipline of the army units toward the masses; and thoroughly carry out the policies of disintegrating enemy forces
and granting lenient treatment to prisoners.

Article 7

[The political work personnel of the hsien (or municipal)
people's militia department should] conduct political work in
the militia during military training; ensure the accomplishment of military training tasks; propagate the thought of Comrade Mao Tse-tung on people's war and on making all the people soldiers; publicize the significance and demands of militia
training; mobilize the militia to participate actively in military
training and national defense-oriented athletic activities; thoroughly implement the mass line furthering training; organize
the activities of mutual teaching and learning, as well as comparisons and contests; bring into play the "backbone" function
in military training of servicemen who have been relieved of

military service, transferred to civilian work, or retired; and
educate the militia to take good care of their weapons and equipment, to prevent accidents, and to ensure safety.

Article 8

[The political work personnel of the hsien (or municipal)
people's militia department should] conduct political work during the recruitment and selection of conscripts, as well as during war mobilization; propagate and thoroughly implement the
military service system of the state; educate militiamen and
young people reaching the age for military service to respond
actively to the call of the fatherland; strengthen ideological
education among prospective conscripts and their families; and
conduct effectively the work of political investigation of prospective
conscripts and political work during their assembly and transfer.

Article 9

[The political work personnel of the hsien (or municipal)
people's militia department should] be acquainted with the conditions of settlement for servicemen who have been relieved,
transferred to civilian work, retired, or disabled; be informed
about the status of preferential treatment and relief arrangements for the dependents of servicemen and martyred patriots,
and for militiamen wounded or disabled in combat; help the
pertinent authorities to fulfill their legitimate demands; educate them to uphold their honor, to develop further the revolutionary tradition, and to observe the policies of the Party and
the laws and regulations of the state; and bring into full play
the "backbone" function of servicemen who have been relieved
of military service, transferred to civilian work, or retired,
in socialist construction and militia work.

Article 10

[The political work personnel of the hsien (or municipal)

people's militia department should] coordinate pertinent authorities to educate the masses of the people in matters of national defense, sharpen their revolutionary vigilance, strengthen
their concept of national defense, and make them cherish the
people's armed forces ardently and support national defense
construction enthusiastically.

Article 11

[The political work personnel of the hsien (or municipal)
people's militia department should] be acquainted with the relationship between the army units stationed in the area and the
local Party and government organs, and between such army
units and the masses of the people; make suggestions on promoting the work of supporting the government and cherishing
the people, and of supporting the army and giving preferential
treatment to the servicemen's families; inform servicemen on
home leave about the condition of local affairs and carry on education among them; and handle letters and visits from the
masses.

Article 12

[The political work personnel of the hsien (or municipal)
people's militia department should] conduct political work
among the personnel of the people's militia department; organize the study of the writings of Comrade Mao Tse-tung and
the lines and policies of the Party; promote the proletarian
consciousness; develop a working style of hard work and thrift;
strengthen the work of the Party branch; thoroughly implement
the principle of democratic centralism; perfect and animate
Party life; strengthen Party unity; maintain Party discipline;
and ensure the accomplishment of tasks.

Article 13

In political work, the hsien (or municipal) people's militia department must accept the leadership and supervision of the hsien (or municipal) Party committee; take the initiative in co-operating closely with the pertinent organs; advance the construction of the militia through the fulfillment of production tasks and other major local tasks; regularly go into villages, factories, and schools in order to foster close ties with the masses; earnestly conduct investigation and research; summarize and publicize advanced experiences; report current conditions in good time to higher political organs and the hsien (or municipal) Party committee; and report on its work and request pertinent instructions.

VI
The Struggle
Between "Two Lines"

22

UNSWERVINGLY TAKE THE ROAD OF
PUTTING POLITICS TO THE FORE*

Liberation Army Daily

Chairman Mao is the founder, organizer, and leader of the
Chinese People's Liberation Army. Over the past decades,
our army has advanced from victory to victory under the brilliant leadership of Chairman Mao and along his proletarian
political and military lines.

However, as Chairman Mao has said: "Correct political and
military lines do not emerge and develop spontaneously and
tranquilly, but only in the course of struggle." The struggle
between two different military lines in our army has always
centered on the question of putting politics or military affairs
to the fore.

The big careerists and conspirators P'eng Te-huai and Lo
Jui-ch'ing, two agents in the army of the top Party person in
authority taking the capitalist road, all along opposed Chairman Mao and his proletarian military line. They openly advocated putting military affairs in first place and attacked Chairman Mao's concept of building up the army politically. They
attempted to usurp the command of the armed forces to serve
the aim of restoring capitalism in China.

---

*This selection is a summary of an article originally pub-
lished in Chieh-fang-chün pao [Liberation Army Daily].
The translation is taken, with minor editorial revisions, from
the English-language release of the New China News Agency,
Peking, August 30, 1967.

Under the Pretext of "Regularization and Modernization," P'eng Te-huai Promotes the Bourgeois Military Line

After the founding of new China, the Chinese People's Liberation Army was confronted with the question of whether it should continue along the road of putting politics to the fore and building a revolutionary army which is very militant and highly proletarianized, or take the road of putting military affairs to the fore and change its qualities of a people's army into those of a bourgeois army.

P'eng Te-huai, Lo Jui-ch'ing, and company, under the pretext of "Regularization and Modernization," alleged that our army's experience was "outdated" and "not systematic" and opposed Chairman Mao's concept on army-building and the putting of politics to the fore.

They asserted that in modern war it was technique, steel, and machines that counted, and that relative to these the factor of man and politics was negligible.

P'eng Te-huai once openly said: "What's the use of relying entirely on political and ideological work? It can't fly." He declared: "The results in training our units and the results in the study of military science of our cadres at all levels should constitute the fundamental criteria in the future for judging the fighting power of our army." He preached "the system of one-man leadership" in an attempt to do away with political work in the army.

Lo Jui-ch'ing also said: "Military training is the regular central task for our army in ordinary times."

They did their utmost to stress the importance of military affairs and technique, all with the aim of bringing into effect the bourgeois military line.

Chairman Mao teaches: "Weapons are an important factor in war, but not the decisive factor; it is people, not things, that are decisive."

Vice Chairman Lin Piao says: "What is the best weapon? It is not aircraft, heavy artillery, tanks, or the atom bomb.

The best weapon is the thought of Mao Tse-tung. What is the greatest fighting power? It is men who are armed with the thought of Mao Tse-tung. It is courage, being unafraid to die."

All weapons must be handled by men. Rockets can be fired thousands of miles, but in the end the issue is settled by men, by men's bravery, consciousness, spirit of self-sacrifice, that is, the spiritual atom bomb. This spiritual atom bomb is the monopoly of our army, which all imperialists and reactionaries can only envy.

P'eng Te-huai, Lo Jui-ch'ing, and company tried their utmost to put the cart before the horse by stressing the role of weapons as above that of men. What they wanted was not the ideological revolutionization of our army but a bourgeois army.

Our army takes politics as its special feature; politics is in command of military affairs. Chairman Mao teaches that politics is the supreme commander, politics is the soul of everything, and that "not to have a correct political point of view is like having no soul."

Equipment and technique vary in a hundred and one ways, but the true nature of our army can never be changed. Our military affairs are subordinate to the proletarian political line and serve proletarian politics.

The more modernized the equipment, the greater prominence should be given to proletarian politics. Otherwise, no matter how good the weapons are, the army will suffer defeats in battles. Only by persisting in putting politics in command and placing politics in command of military affairs and in command of everything can modernized equipment play its part to the fullest.

With the constant improvement in equipment and technique, does political work still retain an important position? Our answer is that it is not only important but of primary importance.

Chairman Mao teaches: "Soldiers are the foundation of an army; unless they are imbued with a progressive political spirit, and unless such a spirit is fostered through progressive political work, it will be impossible to achieve genuine unity

between officers and men, impossible to arouse their enthusiasm for the war of resistance to the full, and impossible to
provide an excellent basis for the most effective use of all our
technical equipment and tactics."

Vice Chairman Lin Piao says: "Of the various factors in the
fighting strength of our army, the factor of prime importance
is political ideological work."

Political work takes precedence over the diverse kinds of
work in the army. When political work is well done, man's
enthusiasm and creativeness can be brought into play, and all
kinds of work can be done well.

Let us illustrate this from experience in the navy. With
Vice Chairman Lin's personal attention and repeated guidance
and by the resolute struggle of the revolutionary leading cadres
in the navy, the naval units have held high the great red banner
of Mao Tse-tung's thought, defeated the bourgeois military
line, and put politics in the forefront. The mass movement for
the creative study and application of Chairman Mao's works
has become broader and deeper among the naval units.

They have persisted in the "four firsts," vigorously established the "three-eight work style," undertaken the campaign
for "four-good" companies, and effectively promoted the revolutionization of man's thinking, which has improved all kinds
of work.

In the past three years and more, the naval units have won
many victories in sea and air battles. Six outstanding units
and individuals were awarded titles of honor by the Ministry
of National Defense. These included the outstanding "Heroic
Sea Eagle Air Regiment" and combat heroes Mai Hsien-te and
Shu Chi-cheng.

Lo Jui-ch'ing Peddles Eclecticism and Opposes Putting Proletarian Politics to the Fore

The Eighth Plenary Session of the Party's Eighth Central
Committee in 1959 exposed the criminal plots of the anti-Party
clique headed by P'eng Te-huai, dismissed him from office,

and took army power out of his hands. P'eng Te-huai's bourgeois military line was criticized and repudiated in the army.

Since Vice Chairman Lin took charge of the work of the Military Commission of the Party's Central Committee, he has held high the great red banner of Mao Tse-tung's thought, led the army to study and apply Chairman Mao's works in a creative way, persisted in the "four firsts," put proletarian politics to the forefront, and intensified the work of building our army into a highly revolutionary one, so that it has advanced with big strides in the direction indicated by Chairman Mao.

But the top Party person in authority taking the capitalist road and another agent of his in the army, Lo Jui-ch'ing, did not take their defeat lying down. Lo Jui-ch'ing stubbornly opposed giving prominence to politics, made "a big show of military skills" to obstruct politics, and kept trying to promote his bourgeois military line of giving first place to military affairs and to technique.

Because Mao Tse-tung's thought has unparalleled prestige and absolute authority among the commanders and fighters of our army, Chairman Mao's principle of building the army politically and Vice Chairman Lin's instruction on the "four firsts" and putting proletarian politics to the forefront have gone deeper into the hearts of the people day by day; Lo Jui-ch'ing and company had to use more devious methods to fly "red flags" to oppose the red flag, to spread the fallacies of eclecticism, namely, opportunism, and to oppose putting proletarian politics to the fore.

Under cover of the slogan of putting politics to the fore, Lo Jui-ch'ing and company exerted efforts to spread the notions of "giving equal emphasis to military affairs and politics" and "giving prominence to military affairs and politics in turn." He also uttered such nonsense as this: "If political work is not done well, the soldiers will retreat in battle. But if soldiers have no military skill and their shooting is inaccurate, when the enemy rushes them in battle, will the soldiers not then retreat?"

Chairman Mao teaches us to look at problems from all sides,

to look at the essential or main aspects and not at the nonessential or minor ones. He says: "Of the two contradictory aspects, one must be principal and the other secondary. The principal aspect is the one playing the leading role in the contradiction. The nature of a thing is determined mainly by the principal aspect of a contradiction, the aspect which has gained the dominant position."

Of the two contradictory aspects — politics and military affairs — politics is the principal aspect of the contradiction, the one playing the leading role and determining the nature of a thing.

The proletarian revolutionary nature of our army determines that it must give prominence to proletarian politics. Otherwise the nature of our army would change.

By putting military affairs on a par with politics and alleging that politics and military affairs are equally important, Lo Jui-ch'ing and company were deliberately confusing the principal and secondary aspects of the contradiction, blurring the nature of our army, and diverting the orientation for building up our army.

Lo Jui-ch'ing did his utmost to spread the fallacy that giving prominence to politics must find concrete expression in military affairs. He uttered such nonsense as "politics must not be stressed in isolation." He said, "It cannot be described as good politics; it is empty politics, I'm afraid, if our political work is good while all other work is not good and collapses."

In the eyes of Lo Jui-ch'ing and company, if giving prominence to politics does not find concrete expression in military, professional, and technical work, then it is "empty politics."

The purpose of giving prominence to politics is definitely not confined to doing military and other work well. It has much greater significance, that is, revolutionizing people's thinking, enabling our army to retain its proletarian nature forever, and making it a genuine cornerstone of the dictatorship of the proletariat.

Vice Chairman Lin Piao says: "Innumerable as our tasks are, we must not forget our orientation or lose sight of our central task; we must never forget political power."

"Political power grows out of the barrel of a gun." The consolidation of proletarian political power depends on the gun, on a highly revolutionized army completely loyal to Chairman Mao and Mao Tse-tung's thought.

The argument that giving prominence to politics must find concrete expression in military and professional work is pernicious because it lacks the fundamental purpose of giving prominence to politics, because the argument takes military and professional work as the point of departure and the reason for giving prominence to politics, thereby leading people away from the central task.

When prominence is given to politics and Mao Tse-tung's thought takes root in people's minds, they will generate inexhaustible wisdom, drive, and energy. They will be invincible and able to create wonders.

Chairman Mao says: "It is man's social being that determines his thinking. Once the correct ideas characteristic of the advanced class are grasped by the masses, these ideas turn into a material force which changes society and changes the world."

The army's experience has proved time and again that if political work is not done well, military, technical, and other work certainly will not be done well. Even if some success is achieved for a time, it cannot last long and be consolidated. In the long run, it collapses.

When political work is done well, military, technical, and other work certainly can be done well. Even if it is not so good at a given moment, it will become good in the long run.

The allegation that "only our political work is good, while all other work is no good and collapses" is the fabrication of a nonexistent problem, a vicious distortion of the relation between political and other work. It first describes giving prominence to politics as an obstacle to success in other work and then levels unscrupulous attacks on giving prominence to politics.

Chairman Mao says that "We should be vigilant against those

people who have no faith in giving prominence to politics, who on the surface agree to giving prominence to politics and covertly oppose it, while, on the other hand, spreading eclecticism (that is, opportunism)."

Waving "red flags" to oppose the red flag, Lo Jui-ch'ing and company were deceptive as they spread utterly fallacious eclectic, opportunist notions. His fallacies won acclamation from the handful of Party persons in authority taking the capitalist road and misled a number of people whose world outlook had not been sufficiently remolded and who subscribed to the purely military viewpoint.

But fraud is fraud. Chairman Mao and Vice Chairman Lin in good time saw through and exposed this big double-dealing conspirator and careerist. So his scheme to promote the bourgeois military line by eclectic methods collapsed.

The Aim of P'eng Te-huai and Lo Jui-ch'ing in Pushing Through the Bourgeois Military Line Is to Restore Capitalism

Chairman Mao says: "All the warlords have clung to their armies for dear life, setting great store by the principle 'Whoever has an army has power.'"

This is also a vivid description of the big warlords P'eng Te-huai, Lo Jui-ch'ing, and company. In order to usurp political power with the top Party person in authority taking the capitalist road, they tried their utmost to usurp the leadership of the army.

On the one hand, they placed their accomplices and followers in the army and formed factions serving their private interests. On the other hand, they attempted to take over ideological work so as to wrest leadership of the army in this way.

To give prominence to politics or to military affairs is in fact a question of whether proletarian politics or bourgeois politics is put to the fore, a question of who will lead the political and ideological work of our army. In the final analysis, it is a question of who will hold leadership of the army.

The vicious aim of P'eng Te-huai, Lo Jui-ch'ing, and company in giving first place to military affairs and stubbornly opposing putting proletarian politics in the forefront was to lead our army onto the wrong road of striving to raise military technique alone, so that it would forget proletarian politics, lose the general orientation, and degenerate into a bourgeois army. Then, when conditions were ripe for them to seize political power, the army would follow them blindly and become a "docile tool" for their restoration of capitalism.

Vice Chairman Lin has pointed out: "To give prominence to politics is not an optional policy which you may or may not follow. It is a fundamental measure put forward in accordance with the law governing development of socialist society and required by its economic base. To go against it means to violate the law governing the development of socialist society." During the socialist stage of our country, the reason why we must give prominence to politics in our army-building lies not only in the fact that we have to defeat imperialist aggression but also in the fact that classes, class contradictions, and class struggle continue to exist in socialist society, and there exists the danger of capitalist restoration.

Our great leader Chairman Mao pointed out on the eve of the founding of new China: "Our national defense will be consolidated and no imperialist will be allowed to invade our territory again. Our people's armed forces must be maintained and developed with the brave and steeled People's Liberation Army as their foundation." "The imperialists and domestic reactionaries will certainly not take their defeat lying down, and they will struggle to the last ditch. After there is peace and order throughout the country, they will still engage in sabotage and create disturbances in various ways and will try every day and every minute to stage a comeback. This is inevitable and beyond all doubt, and under no circumstances must we relax our vigilance."

These teachings of Chairman Mao's have indicated to our army the task in the new historical period. That is, in the historical period of socialism our army must shoulder the task

not only of defeating imperialist aggression and supporting the
revolution of the people of the whole world, but also the task
of preventing a capitalist comeback within the country. If we
pay attention only to aggression by the imperialists, revisionists, and other reactionaries but ignore a possible capitalist
restoration from within, we shall commit the gravest mistake.

Chairman Mao has with genius and in a creative way developed Marxist-Leninist theory on class struggle and the dictatorship of the proletariat. He put forward the theory, line,
principles, and policies on how to make revolution under the
dictatorship of the proletariat and how to prevent the restoration of capitalism. He has taught us that the class struggle
under the dictatorship of the proletariat is still concentrated
in the struggle for political power. Our most dangerous enemy, who attempts to subvert the proletarian dictatorship, is
made up of those in authority who are taking the capitalist
road; they are the main target.

In order to prevent representatives of the bourgeoisie from
usurping the political power of the proletariat, it is necessary,
first of all, to ensure that our military power is not usurped
by them and that our army will never change its political color.

Therefore, we must adhere to Chairman Mao's principle
of building up the army politically, energetically put proletarian
politics to the fore, and arm all our commanders and fighters
with Mao Tse-tung's thought. Putting politics to the fore is
the fundamental guarantee that our army will never change its
color.

In the course of the unprecedented Great Proletarian Cultural
Revolution, acute and complicated class struggle has enabled
us to understand even more profoundly the great, far-reaching
strategic significance of Chairman Mao's principle of building
up the army politically and the "four firsts" and the putting of
politics to the fore set forth by Vice Chairman Lin. We have
also gained a better understanding of the counterrevolutionary
nature of putting military affairs first, as advocated by P'eng
Te-huai, Lo Jui-ch'ing, and company.

We are determined to hold high the great red banner of Mao

Tse-tung's thought, thoroughly criticize and repudiate the bourgeois military line, eradicate its pernicious influence, and ensure that Chairman Mao's proletarian military line is carried
out in an even more thoroughgoing way in all spheres of our
work of army-building.

23

THE FUNDAMENTAL DIFFERENCES BETWEEN
THE PROLETARIAN MILITARY LINE AND THE
BOURGEOIS MILITARY LINE*

Thoroughly Criticize and Repudiate Lo Jui-ch'ing's
Bourgeois Revisionist Military Thought

The Proletarian Revolutionaries of the
Headquarters of the General Staff of the PLA

In order to seize political power and consolidate political
power, and to win a final victory in the revolutionary struggle,
the proletariat "requires not only a correct Marxist political
line but also a correct Marxist military line." Without the
guidance of a correct political line, there can never be a correct military line. Without a correct military line, it is not
possible to carry through and realize a correct political line.
But "a correct military line and a correct political line do not
evolve and develop naturally and peacefully. They evolve and
develop in the process of struggle. On the one hand, they must
wage a struggle against 'leftist' opportunism. On the other
hand, they must wage a struggle against rightist opportunism.

---

*Chung-kuo jen-min chieh-fang-chün tsung-ts'an-mou-pu chi-
kuan wu-ch'an chieh-chi ke-ming-p'ai, "Wu-ch'an chieh-chi
chün-shih lu-hsien ho tzu-ch'an chieh-chi chün-shih lu-hsien ti
ken-pen fen-chih," Jen-min jih-pao [People's Daily], September 7, 1967; reprinted in Fei-ch'ing nien-pao [Yearbook on Chinese Communism] (Taipei, 1968), pp. 862-867.

If these harmful tendencies, detrimental to the revolution and the revolutionary war, are not struggled against and thoroughly destroyed, the establishment of the correct line and the victory of the revolutionary war would be impossible."

In the various historical stages of the last several decades of development of revolution in China, there always existed in our Party and army two diametrically opposed military lines, which involved acute and violent struggles. One was the proletarian military line represented by Chairman Mao. The other was the bourgeois military line supported by the "Leftist" and Rightist opportunists. Chairman Mao's proletarian military line evolved and developed continually in struggles against the bourgeois military line.

Our great leader Chairman Mao brilliantly created the most complete, the most scientific, and the greatest proletarian military theory. In the Decision of the Ku-t'ien Conference, personally drafted by him, and in his other military writings, Chairman Mao laid down the most correct proletarian military line. This represents the zenith of Marxist-Leninist military thought. This is the strongest and sharpest weapon with which the proletariat and the revolutionary people of the whole world defeat imperialism, modern revisionism, and all reactionary cliques.

The great triumph in the revolutionary war of the Chinese people and the world-shaking achievements of the Chinese People's Liberation Army were a great victory of the proletarian revolutionary line represented by Chairman Mao, a great victory of Chairman Mao's proletarian military line, and a great victory of Mao Tse-tung thought.

Chairman Mao's most intimate comrade-in-arms and our deputy commander, Comrade Lin Piao, has always carried out with the greatest loyalty, determination, and thoroughness Chairman Mao's proletarian revolutionary line and military thought. Over the past forty years, at every crucial historical moment, Comrade Lin Piao has always prominently and resolutely sided with Chairman Mao's correct line, and made outstanding contributions to protecting Mao Tse-tung thought, waging uncompromising struggles against the erroneous lines in the Party and the army.

The agents of China's Khrushchev in the army, P'eng Te-huai and Lo Jui-ch'ing, consistently opposed Chairman Mao's proletarian military line while frantically pushing their bourgeois military line. After P'eng Te-huai was singled out at the Lushan Conference, Lo Jui-ch'ing became the front guard in promoting the reactionary bourgeois military line. He and P'eng Chen, Lu Ting-i and Yang Shang-k'un banded into a clique against the Party. Under the protection and support of China's Khrushchev, they tried their best to usurp the military power for the bourgeois headquarters. They coordinated their efforts from both the government and the army side and waited to launch a counterrevolutionary coup to topple the proletarian dictatorship once conditions were ripe.

Throughout the socialist period, the struggle between the two military lines has been essentially a struggle between the proletariat and the bourgeoisie for the military power. This is a component of the struggle between the bourgeois restoration and the proletarian counterrestoration under the conditions of proletarian dictatorship.

Whether Or Not to Put Proletarian Politics to the Fore Is a Focal Point in the Struggle Between Chairman Mao's Military Line and the Bourgeois Military Line in the Building of Our Army

During the past forty years, the struggle between Chairman Mao's line in army-building and the bourgeois line in army-building has always centered around the basic problem of whether it should be politics first or military affairs first, whether we should put politics to the fore or put military affairs to the fore.

The core of Chairman Mao's thought and line on army-building is to put politics to the fore in the building of the people's army, to build an army first and foremost on the basis of politics.

Early in the beginning of our army-building, Chairman Mao pointed out in the historic Decision of the Ku-t'ien Conference, which he drafted: "Military affairs is only one of the tools to complete political missions." "China's Red Army is an armed league for the implementation of revolutionary political missions." He correctly explained the relationship between military affairs and politics; namely, military affairs must be subservient to politics, and politics must command military affairs.

P'eng Te-huai and Lo Jui-ch'ing, those bourgeois agents who sneaked into the Party and the army, persistently resisted Chairman Mao's thought and line on army-building, opposed putting proletarian politics to the fore, championed military affairs first and technology first.

During the War of Resistance Against Japan, two diametrically opposed lines formed around the question of how to handle correctly the cooperation between the Nationalists and the Communists and the question of the united front. The proletarian revolutionary line represented by Chairman Mao advocated "an independent stand within the united front — united but independent," and insisted on "the principle of the Party's absolute command over the Eighth Route Army." The capitulationist line represented by Wang Ming and China's Khrushchev advocated handing over the leadership of the anti-Japanese united front to the Nationalist Party. China's Khrushchev, moreover, slavishly extolled Chiang Kai-shek as the "banner of revolution," and he wanted to hand over the leadership of the army under the Communist Party to the "Nationalist Government." Lo Jui-ch'ing put forward his book on "The Political Work in the Anti-Japanese Army" to meet the needs of the capitulationist line. In this book he never talked about class struggle and the seizure of political power by the proletariat. Instead, he tried his best to publicize the reactionary Nationalist politics, shamelessly put forward the life style of Chiang Kai-shek — "intelligence, benevolence, courage," "loyalty and filial piety, kindness and love" — as the basis of political work in the army. He even wanted the political commissars to "guarantee that

the troops be absolutely obedient" to the command of Chiang
Kai-shek, and he handed over the guns of the proletariat to
Chiang Kai-shek. Lo Jui-ch'ing also publicized the horrors of
war and spread the gloom of national subjugation. He said,
"War casualties are the greatest psychological threat to man,"
in a vain attempt to riddle the morale of our army. He urged
the Chinese people to lay down their weapons and submit to the
slaughter of the Japanese aggressors. This is Lo Jui-ch'ing's
thorough capitulationist politics at the service of the capitulationist line of Wang Ming and China's Khrushchev.

During the War of Liberation, Lo Jui-ch'ing, in his report
on "How to Strengthen Political Work in the Army," ranked
politics, military affairs, and rear services equally and opposed putting political work at the fore. He said, "It is wrong
to overemphasize political work." In fact, what he meant by
not overemphasizing political work was to abolish proletarian
politics and replace it with bourgeois politics.

Our deputy commander, Comrade Lin Piao, has consistently
held high the great red banner of Mao Tse-tung thought, carried
out loyally and resolutely Chairman Mao's line on army-building, and emphasized army-building on the basis of politics. After he took charge of the work in the Military Affairs Commission, he summarized the experience of the struggle between
the two military lines since the establishment of the People's
Republic in the light of Chairman Mao's thought on army-
building and the historical experience of our army. He personally laid down the "Decision on the Strengthening of Political
and Ideological Work in the Army"; creatively advanced the
idea of the "four firsts"; put forward the policies, principles,
and measures of putting politics to the fore, making a living
study and living application of Mao Tse-tung thought; insisted
on the "four firsts"; promoted the "three-eight work style";
fostered "three democracies"; launched the "four-good"
movement; and others, thus initiating a new stage in our army-
building.

Chairman Mao pointed out that the "four firsts" are good.
They are an innovation. The ideological and political work and

the military work of the Liberation Army have been greatly developed; they have been more concrete but also more theoretical compared with the past, ever since Comrade Lin Piao put forward the "four firsts" and the "three-eight work style."

To put politics to the fore is to put Mao Tse-tung thought to the fore, is to arm the minds of the broad masses of commanders and soldiers with Mao Tse-tung thought and to establish the absolute authority of Mao Tse-tung thought. Great Mao Tse-tung thought is the soul of our army, the basis of our army-building, and the basic guarantee of the unchanging quality of our army. Owing to his personal ambition and his reactionary class instincts, Lo Jui-ch'ing deeply feared and hated Mao Tse-tung thought. He consistently opposed Comrade Lin Piao, who held high the great red banner of Mao Tse-tung thought, and opposed the mass movement to make a living study and living application of Chairman Mao's works throughout the army, the Party, and the country as advocated by Comrade Lin Piao. He tried his best to keep the broad masses of commanders and fighters from making a living study and living application of Mao Tse-tung thought. At the same time, he canonized China's Khrushchev's "Cultivation" and assigned it as compulsory reading for the whole army, emphasizing "serious and repeated study," "living study and living application," and "contrast and review." His purpose was to corrode the soul of our army with the revisionist "Cultivation" so as to lead us astray from Chairman Mao's proletarian line on army-building, to make us forget class and class struggle and forget proletarian dictatorship in a vain attempt to change the proletarian nature of our army at its very foundation.

Lo Jui-ch'ing also used the big contest [of military techniques] to bombard politics, to bombard the study of Chairman Mao's works. The big contest was to put military affairs to the fore, to put technology to the fore, to engage in formalism, to award winning and individualism. In fact, it was to put bourgeois politics to the fore. The big contest completely exposed Lo Jui-ch'ing's bourgeois thought on army-building, completely exposed his plot to usurp military power and to oppose the Party.

Vice Chairman Lin corrected the mistakes of the big contest in time and once again ordered that politics be put to the fore. Lo Jui-ch'ing still resisted and said: "Military training is politics, the highest form of politics"; "Military affairs are politics pure and simple." This equating of politics with military affairs and replacing politics with military affairs is a thoroughly bourgeois military viewpoint. Chairman Mao teaches us that politics is the commander, the soul. Political work is the lifeline of all work. By spreading his revisionist fallacies, Lo Jui-ch'ing actually wanted to subordinate politics to military affairs, to command politics with military affairs, to extract the soul from our army, and to convert the proletarian army into a bourgeois army.

In a society where class and class struggle exist, no sphere is a vacuum. If it is not subject to the guidance of proletarian thought, it is subject to the guidance of bourgeois thought. The army is a tool of class struggle. If it is not at the service of proletarian politics, it is at the service of bourgeois politics. There can never be an army divorced from politics.

All persons of the Khrushchev persuasion who want to usurp proletarian political power for the capitalist restoration must of necessity start by corroding the army ideologically so as to usurp military power and grab the gun. Therefore, whether or not to put proletarian politics to the fore, whether or not to engage in the ideological revolutionization of man concerns whether or not the proletarian army can change its nature, whether the gun is wielded in the hands of the proletariat or in the hands of the bourgeoisie. In the final analysis, it concerns whether or not the proletariat can consolidate its political power after it is won. Lo Jui-ch'ing's fierce opposition to putting proletarian politics to the fore, to Chairman Mao's thought on army-building and line on army-building, was a vain attempt to transform our army with the bourgeois world outlook, to convert our army into a bourgeois army serving as its tool for the usurption of proletarian political power and for capitalist restoration.

Whether Or Not to Implement the People's War Is a Watershed Between Chairman Mao's Military Thought and Bourgeois Military Thought

Chairman Mao's great theory on people's war creatively develops Marxism-Leninism. It is not only the sole correct way to win a nationwide victory for the Chinese people; it also points out a promising avenue for the suppressed peoples and classes of the whole world to win complete liberation.

To complete their own liberation, all suppressed peoples and classes must, first of all, arm themselves according to Chairman Mao's theory on people's war and smash the old state machinery, strike down imperialism and its lackeys, and change the whole world with guns.

Whether the people's war is carried out or not represents a watershed between Chairman Mao's military thought and bourgeois military thought, a dividing line between Marxism-Leninism and revisionism, between true revolution and false revolution.

Chairman Mao teaches us: "The revolutionary war is a mass war. Only when the masses are mobilized can the war be fought. Only when the masses are relied upon can the war be fought." "When millions of the masses are gathered around the revolutionary government to launch the revolutionary war, we can annihilate all counterrevolutions."

Chairman Mao's thought on people's war is built on the foundation of a complete trust of and reliance on the masses. It mobilizes the broad masses of people, organizes and arms them, annihilates counterrevolutions with the people's war, and seizes national political power. After the seizure of political power, it is always ready to resist aggression initiated by the imperialists and their lackeys in order to protect the proletarian political power.

Like all opportunism, Lo Jui-ch'ing's military thought was built on the basis of weapons. He basically distrusted the masses, opposed the arming of the masses, opposed the militia system, and opposed Chairman Mao's great strategic thought on people's war.

China's Khrushchev advocated technology first and the decisive role of technology. Lo Jui-ch'ing argued that with modern technical equipment "all aggressive enemies can be annihilated either at sea, in the sky, or in the bases from which their offensive started." They used the argument of weapons superiority to oppose the arming of the masses and the use of people's war to resist imperialist aggression, and they vainly hoped that the enemies could be beaten purely on the basis of technical equipment. This is typical bourgeois military thought. Are the masses of people and the people's war dispensable in wars fought under modern conditions? No, definitely not. "The contest of strength is not only between military power and economic power but also between human power and human feelings. Military power and economic power must be controlled by people." No matter how advanced the modern weapons and technical equipment and no matter how complex the conduct of modern warfare, the winning of a war must still be conditioned on the support of the masses of people, on the struggle of the masses of people and, in the final analysis, on the people's war. This is the most important and reliable guarantee for defeating the enemies.

Our great leader Chairman Mao has most fully and deeply explained the importance of arming the masses. After the nationwide victory, Chairman Mao taught us more than once: "Since the imperialists are so hostile toward us, we must handle them with extreme caution. We must not only have a strong regular army but also train militia on a large scale. Thus, when the imperialists invade our country, they will be completely bogged down." "If the imperialists dare to launch aggressive wars against us, then we will put into practice the system of every person a soldier. The militia will be coordinated with and supplement the People's Liberation Army to thoroughly defeat the aggressors."

Vice Chairman Lin points out that militia work is a fundamental question in the building of China's national defense, a component of the question of strategy, and a concrete application of the Party's mass line on war. To combine the building of a modern revolutionary army with large-scale militia-training is a concrete application of the policy of "walking on two legs" toward the building of a national defense, a significant development of Chairman Mao's thought on the people's war under modern conditions.

The militia has consistently been a component part of our armed forces, and has served as a solid foundation for people's war. Without the militia, our regular army would be like a river without sources, a tree without roots, or a general with only one arm, and thus could never fight a genuine people's war.

The militia is a tool of the proletarian dictatorship. China's Khrushchev and his agents in the army like Lo Jui-ch'ing regarded the militia organized according to Chairman Mao's thought as an obstacle to the fruition of their plot to usurp the Party and the army and to restore capitalism. On the one hand, they tried their best to destroy militia-building, to oppose the arming of the masses. On the other hand, they fermented the purely military viewpoint in militia-building and opposed putting proletarian politics to the fore in a vain attempt to transform our militia with the bourgeois world outlook and to turn the militia into a tool for the realization of their personal ambition.

Chairman Mao teaches us: "This army is powerful because it is divided into two parts: the main forces and the regional forces. The former can be deployed for war missions in any region and at any time, while the latter can concentrate on defending their own localities and attacking the enemies in cooperation with the local militia and self-defense corps." "If such a correct division is not made . . . and if attention is paid only to the role of the main forces while that of the regional forces is neglected . . . it would be impossible to defeat the enemies." After the nationwide victory, Chairman Mao more than once instructed that the building of regional armed forces should be greatly strengthened. Besides the strengthening of its own units, the regional armed forces must help the regions strengthen the

mass work in militia-training in peace, and augment its forces
with militiamen in war.

China's Khrushchev and his accomplice Lo Jui-ch'ing, simultaneous with their opposition to the militia system, vehemently
opposed the building of regional armed forces. China's Khrushchev asked if we should have "part-time regional armed forces,
partly detached from production, but returning to their homes
during the busy farming season?" This is an argument for the
abolition of regional armed forces. In accordance with his
boss's wishes, Lo Jui-ch'ing first tried his best to block
Chairman Mao's directive concerning the strengthening of the
building of regional defense, and he refused to implement it for
five years. Then he halfheartedly carried it out, but still tried
his utmost to sabotage the building of regional defense.

Vice Chairman Lin points out: "Our army has not only its
own main forces but also its regional forces. In addition, it establishes and develops militia organizations and implements
the system of armed forces through the three-in-one combination of the main forces, the regional forces, and the militia."
The implementation of the system of armed forces through the
three-in-one combination of the main forces, the regional forces, and the militia can mobilize the mass activism of hundreds
of millions of people to form a fighting entity, with the power
of the people's war developed to the full. When imperialists invade our country, the militia are not only an unlimited source
of supply for our army, they can also lead the broad masses of
people to engage in widespread guerrilla warfare. Every person is a fighter, every household a fortress, every village a
battleground — thus an inescapable trap for the enemies is set.
Regional forces are the backbone for regional combat. They
lead the broad masses of people to fight battles in consort with
the main forces. They continually enlarge, elevate, and strength-
en the main forces. With the help of the regional forces and the
broad masses of militiamen in battles, the main forces can
spare a free hand to form a powerful "fist," seeking and creating advantageous opportunities to fight concentrated battles
of annihilation.

China's Khrushchev and persons like Lo Jui-ch'ing wanted to chop off the militia and the regional forces so as to undermine our system of a three-in-one combination of the main forces, the regional forces, and the militia and sabotage the basis of implementing the people's war. They opposed the arming of the masses of people, opposed the use of the people's war against the aggressive war of the imperialists. They staked the country on technical equipment and negated the basic concept of people's war. If we were to follow what Lo Jui-ch'ing said, we would lose our hard-won victory and the whole proletarian revolutionary enterprise.

Active Defense and Passive Defense Are Two Diametrically Opposed Policies Based Respectively on the Strategic Guidance of Chairman Mao's Military Line and on the Bourgeois Military Line

Active defense is Chairman Mao's consistent strategic thought, the basic guiding thought for winning our historical revolutionary war and for resisting the imperialist aggression. It is also the only correct guiding thought for winning the revolutionary war for the people of various countries.

Chairman Mao teaches us: "Active defense is also called offensive defense and defense for a final battle. Passive defense is also called defensive defense and pure defense. Passive defense is in fact false defense. Active defense is the only true defense. It is defense for counterattack and attack." In strategic guidance, whether the strategic policy of active defense or the policy of passive defense is adopted involves every basic question in the winning of the revolutionary war.

Active defense is built on the ideological basis of complete revolution and thorough annihilation of the enemies by the proletariat. Its crux is to fight battles of annihilation. Only by fighting battles of annihilation can the energy of the enemies be drained and our strength be developed and increased so as finally to defeat the enemies. The battle of annihilation is the basic guiding thought of our warfare. Whether it is mainly guerrilla warfare or mainly mobile warfare, whether it is with respect to strategic guidance or to combat activities, this guiding thought should be implemented.

The history of the revolutionary war of the Chinese people shows that if our great commander, Chairman Mao's, active strategic policy is followed closely, victory can be assured and revolution smoothly developed. If not, losses and setbacks in revolution are inevitable.

Our deputy commander, Comrade Lin Piao, has always loyally and thoroughly guarded and carried out Chairman Mao's correct policy of active defense and opposed the erroneous policy of passive defense. Comrade Lin Piao more than once has instructed us to seriously learn Chairman Mao's great strategic thought and to resolutely guarantee the thorough implementation of Chairman Mao's strategic policy of active defense.

Lo Jui-ch'ing has always opposed Chairman Mao's strategic thought and strategic policy of active defense. He advocated passive defense, pure defense, and head-on battles. As early as in the War of Resistance Against Japan, Lo Jui-ch'ing echoed P'eng Te-huai's opposition to Chairman Mao's correct policy of freely mobilizing the masses behind the enemy lines to engage in independent guerrilla warfare, establishing anti-Japanese bases, and developing people's armed forces for the resistance against Japanese aggression. They started the "battle of one hundred regiments" on their own initiative by concentrating the main forces of the Eighth Route Army in attrition warfare with the Japanese devils. As a result, heavy losses were suffered in the anti-Japanese bases in North China and in the development of our army, thus lending support to the Nationalist Party. After Lo Jui-ch'ing usurped an important position in our army, he tried his utmost to advocate the erroneous policy of passive defense to meet the need of China's Khrushchev's class capitulationist and national capitulationist line. China's Khrushchev said: "We must stop the enemies"; "Once the enemies are in, it is difficult to handle them." Lo Jui-ch'ing echoed: "Conditions are different now"; we can only adopt "the method of damming the flood." Such fallacies of theirs were not new tricks but worn out goods that had been criticized and repudiated by Chairman Mao in the thirties as the passive defense of "defense at the door."

We consider the method of "stopping gaps" and "damming the flood" a fear of losing ground, a fear of "breaking jars and urns," and a fear of angering the American imperialists. This is proof positive of the submission to imperialism and the fear of war common among the heirs to Khrushchev's revisionism. The Chinese people are a great people armed with Mao Tse-tung thought. They dare to lure the enemies inside, dare to adopt the strategic policy of active defense. To annihilate the enemy in large numbers, they actively and systematically abandoned some ground temporarily to let the enemy in, thus forcing the enemy to spread his forces thin, to carry extra burdens, and to commit mistakes. While the enemy rejoices and relaxes, his feet sink deep into the quicksand. In this way we can concentrate our superior forces to annihilate the enemy one by one, and swallow him bite by bite. Only when the life source of the enemy is stopped can the ground be firmly held. Persons like Lo Jui-ch'ing, who were afraid of losing ground, afraid of breaking jars and urns, held on to passive defense for dear life. They put up defense everywhere and divided the forces over the points of advance to engage in attrition warfare with the enemy. If this disastrous strategic policy had been followed, our defense would have been weak all over and easily beaten by the enemies. Adventurism would have turned into capitulationism, and our proletarian land would have been lost.

They shouted, "Conditions are different now." What conditions are different? This simply means that the imperialists have atomic bombs and nuclear weapons. What's the big fuss! Marxists have always thought that whatever the change in technical equipment, the basic law governing the war of revolution will never change. "Weapons are an important factor in warfare, but not a deciding factor. The deciding factor is man, not material." The final victory or defeat in warfare still depends on the continual combat of ground forces, on the political consciousness of man, on the courage and spirit of the sacrifice of man, on rifles and grenades, on bayonet combat, close-range combat, and night combat. In resisting the aggressive wars of the imperialists, whatever their weapons, once they dare to penetrate into our country we will have the greatest power of initiative to exploit our advantages in the people's war to cut off their retreat.

They nonsensically said that "once the enemies are in, it is difficult to handle them." This was blatant propaganda for defeatism and capitulationism. Such fallacies of theirs amounted to fear of war, fear of imperialism, fear of revolution, and fear of losing their heads. Chairman Mao teaches us: "In front of wild animals, we must not display any sign of cowardice." Imperialism and the reactionary cliques of various countries are all paper tigers. They appear ferocious, but are in fact weak. If they dare to start aggressive wars against us, they are "asking for it." Then welcome! The more enemies there are, the more they will be annihilated and the greater our contribution to the world revolution. Isn't that a good thing?

China's Khrushchev and persons like Lo Jui-ch'ing frantically opposed Chairman Mao's strategic policy of active defense and tried their utmost to promote the strategic policy of passive defense for the sole purpose of meeting the political requirements of imperialism and modern revisionism. They completely betrayed the basic interests of the Chinese people, the people of the world, and the revolutionary enterprise of the proletariat.

On the eve of the Great Proletarian Cultural Revolution, personally launched and led by Chairman Mao, counterrevolutionary revisionist Lo Jui-ch'ing's plot to oppose Chairman Mao, Mao Tse-tung thought, and Chairman Mao's military line and to usurp the army and betray the Party is thoroughly bankrupt. The reactionary bourgeois military line promoted by him, as well as he himself, were unanimously rejected by the broad commanders and soldiers of the whole army. In the upsurge of great revolutionary criticism and repudiation to thoroughly smash the bourgeois headquarters with the great banner of Mao Tse-tung thought held high throughout the country, we must topple the bourgeois military line, thoroughly purge its residual poisons, and establish the absolute authority of Mao Tse-tung thought and Chairman Mao's military line. We must put proletarian politics further to the fore and advance the ideological revolutionization and organizational revolutionization of the whole army so that the guns are forever firmly in the hands of the proletariat to protect the proletarian dictatorship and to ensure that the proletarian motherland will never change its color!

24

REPORT ON THE PROBLEM OF
LO JUI-CH'ING'S MISTAKES*

The Work Group of the CCP Central Committee

To the CCP Central Committee and Chairman Mao:
On December 8, 1965, the CCP Central Committee and Chairman Mao held a meeting in Shanghai exposing and criticizing Lo Jui-ch'ing's mistakes. They struggled against him in his absence. After the meeting, the Party Central Committee and Comrade Chou En-lai patiently tried many times to educate and help him. Not only did Lo Jui-ch'ing refuse to investigate honestly his own mistakes, but he even expressed grievances and in many instances made excuses for himself. After the proceedings of the Party Central Committee meeting in Shanghai were transmitted, the army's political work conferences among high-level cadres in the Party and army further exposed Lo Jui-ch'ing's many and serious wrongdoings. In accordance with the directive of Mao Tse-tung and the decision of the Standing Committee of the Party Central Committee, a group meeting was held from March 3 to April 8 under the direct guidance of the Party Central Committee to discuss Lo Jui-ch'ing in order to thoroughly eradicate this problem. The participants followed a policy of putting the facts on the table and talking

---

* Chung-kung chung-yang kung-tso hsiao-tsu, "Kuan-yü Lo Jui-ch'ing ts'o-wu wen-t'i pao-kao," a Red Guard publication reprinted in Chung-kung nien-pao [Yearbook on Chinese Communism] (Taipei, 1970), II, Section 7, pp. 14-21.

sense, of warning him first so that afterwards he could exert himself to change his ways, of "curing the sickness and saving the patient," and they conducted face-to-face struggle with Lo Jui-ch'ing.

The group meeting was conducted in two stages, the first of
which lasted thirteen days. Participating members included
responsible comrades from each general department in the Military Affairs Commission, the Ministry of Public Security, the
Office for National Defense Industry, the Committee on National
Defense Science, the Academy of Military Science, and most
military districts and services, and Lo Jui-ch'ing himself; all
together X X* people. Beginning on March 22, the meeting entered its second stage. In accordance with the instructions of
the Party Central Committee, a total of X X people were added,
including various departments of the Party Central Committee
and related departments of the State Council concerned, and
responsible comrades of the Central Committee bureaus. A total of X X people participated in the second stage of the meeting. Because of Lo Jui-ch'ing's jump from a building (and his
injuries) on March 18, the second stage of the struggle had to
be conducted in his absence.

According to the great quantity of materials uncovered by
the meeting, Lo Jui-ch'ing's chief wrongdoings had several
aspects:

First, Lo Jui-ch'ing was hostile and opposed to Mao Tse-tung
thought. He slandered and attacked Comrade Mao Tse-tung.

Lo Jui-ch'ing was abysmally hostile to Mao Tse-tung thought.
When Comrade Lin Piao pointed out that we should "consider
Mao Tse-tung's books as the highest command in all tasks
throughout the army," Lo Jui-ch'ing spoke such nonsense as
"It doesn't fit in with our state system." When Comrade Lin
Piao put forward the statement that "Mao Tse-tung thought is
the highest, most vital Marxism-Leninism of our present era,"
Lo Jui-ch'ing spoke such nonsense as "You can't talk that way.
Do you mean to say that there are not other higher ones; that
it can't be any higher? Most vital? Do you mean to say that

---

*The Xs that appear in this article are reproduced as they
appear in the Chung-kung nien-pao version — Ying-mao Kau.

there are not more vital ones? It is not easy to understand which
is the highest and the most vital. Foreigners can't easily trans-
late it either!" Comrade Lin Piao put forward: "Read Mao Tse-
tung's books, listen to Mao Tse-tung's words, do things according to Mao Tse-tung's instructions, and be Mao Tse-tung's
good soldier."

Lo Jui-ch'ing opposed publicizing and introducing this mes-
sage to foreigners. Comrade Lin Piao pointed out that "Mao Tse-
tung thought is the culmination of Marxism-Leninism in the
present era." Lo Jui-ch'ing spoke such nonsense as "You
shouldn't phrase it like that. It won't make a good impression
on foreigners." Lo Jui-ch'ing also would not allow it to be said
that there were factors of "individual genius" included in the
formation of Mao Tse-tung thought, and he said such things as
"Now there is no one bold enough to bring up 'individual genius'
again!" When Comrade Lin Piao pointed out that the Liberation
Army Daily must regularly print the sayings of Mao Tse-tung,
Lo Jui-ch'ing felt that it was overdone. The General Political
Department followed up Lin Piao's directive in pointing out that
instructions from Chairman Mao and the Party Central Committee and documents of the Military Affairs Commission
should be turned into teaching materials and made into a required course for cadres and soldiers. Lo Jui-ch'ing refused
to approve the issuance of these teaching materials, using the
excuse that there were already too many materials issued to
the company units. Comrade Lin Piao pointed out that the militia should begin by studying Chairman Mao's works, but
Lo Jui-ch'ing answered with the nonsense that "It is un-
necessary to arrange separately for the task of studying
Mao's works in the militia." Lo Jui-ch'ing also made the criticism that in the musical play "The Sailor's Glory" the song
"Respected and Beloved Chairman Mao" was sung too often.
He said that it should be linked with praise for the Communist
Party, not sung in isolation.

Lo Jui-ch'ing distorted and opposed Chairman Mao's theory
on class struggle. Chairman Mao has taught us time and again
that there is also class struggle among the people. Lo Jui-ch'ing
said such nonsense as "The peasants have a certain spontaneous

tendency. They want to go it alone.* This is not class struggle, but rather an internal contradiction among the people"; he further uttered such nonsense as "There are no class contradictions existing in our army itself, but there do exist some problems regarding the need for a firm standpoint, raising class consciousness, resisting the intrusion of bourgeois and feudal ideologies, and also the need for a dialectical method in analyzing political questions."

When Lo Jui-ch'ing was Minister of Public Security, he denied Chairman Mao's doctrine regarding the existence of class struggle in socialist societies. Chairman Mao, in 1957, had just published his "On the Correct Handling of Contradictions Among the People," pointing out that class struggle was still protracted, devious, and sometimes even very fierce.

In 1958 Lo Jui-ch'ing started on a large scale the "ten-eliminations movement," which was limited strictly to eliminating counterrevolutionaries, eliminating thieves, eliminating vagrants and rowdies, eliminating fire damage, eliminating automobile accidents, etc. What is more, he took Soviet revisionist material and turned it around into an argument to agitate for the idea that there are no classes in the Soviet Union, and that criminal elements are all derived from external causes. This is a typical theory of the dying out of class struggle. It is a revisionist point of view from top to bottom. Although the Party Central Committee repeatedly criticized this way of doing things, Lo Jui-ch'ing still persisted in his mistakes. Not only did he spread the theory of the dying out of class struggle, but he also continued to set forth the theory of the withering away of the dictatorship of the proletariat.

In November 1958, he publicly said: "At the present time the basic level of state power is beginning to disappear, and this is also true of the tools of dictatorship." "Now that there are even fewer counterrevolutionary elements, the important thing for our basic-level state power is not to carry on class struggle but rather to build up the economy and build up culture. In

---

* I.e., they want to be individual farmers, not join cooperatives — Ying-mao Kau.

this sense the class struggle has begun to die out." The Party
Central Committee and Chairman Mao have repeatedly stressed
that the work of public security should definitely be under the
leadership of the Party and should follow the mass line. Lo
Jui-ch'ing, on the other hand, stressed vertical leadership directly under the Ministry of Public Security, and practiced
"secret-ism," "independent-ism," and other things in the tradition of the Soviet Union's "GPU."*

On the question of the struggle to oppose the subversive activities of the Soviet revisionists in X X region, Lo Jui-ch'ing
disobeyed and acted in opposition to the line and policy of the
Party Central Committee and Chairman Mao. He maligned the
"artificial alert" set up along the Sino-Soviet border and defended the Soviet revisionist criminals in the Sino-Soviet border dispute, saying such things as "It is impossible to say that
the majority of incidents were instigated by them; we must
make a concrete analysis of the situation." The violence on X
day of X month in 1962 at X X place was clearly planned and
organized by the Soviet revisionists. He too was entirely clear
on this point, but he still did his best to defend the crimes of
the Soviet revisionists, only mentioning lightly in passing that
"I see there is some small connection with their consulate."
Then he continued, again with hidden intentions, saying, "I don't
know how to interpret this piece of history." He also disobeyed
the instructions of Chairman Mao and the stipulations of the
Party Central Committee, and took it upon himself to proclaim
that the "three bad elements" in the border areas should not
move into China's interior. He criticized the X X Military Region for making a "no-man's land" in the Sino-Soviet border
area. He uttered such nonsense as "Modern revisionism attacks us for persecuting our national minorities; if we don't
deal with the relationship between the Party and the three bad
elements well, then there really will be persecution!"

Lo Jui-ch'ing opposed Chairman Mao's idea of people's war,

---

* The GPU was the predecessor of the KGB (Secret Police)
in the 1920s — Ying-mao Kau.

opposed our traditional system of armed forces. Our traditional system of armed forces links together the main military forces, regional forces, militia, and guerrilla bands. Lo Jui-ch'ing obstructed and opposed the establishment of local forces and neglected militia work.

Lo Jui-ch'ing refused to carry out Chairman Mao's instructions regarding the establishment and strengthening of the local forces. As early as 1960 Chairman Mao clearly pointed out that some divisions should be selected from the main force to serve as the backbone of regional forces in the provinces along the coast. Lo Jui-ch'ing neither transmitted nor implemented these extremely important instructions for military preparedness. He even went so far as to delay their implementation for five years. On X day of X month in 1964, at two conferences, Chairman Mao again continued to give the same instructions. Lo Jui-ch'ing said again: "Do you mean to say that regular divisions should be transferred, or that parts of regular divisions together with some newly replenished soldiers should be transferred, or that newly recruited soldiers should be combined with original local forces? We can still look into all this." The result was that he still discounted Chairman Mao's instructions.

Chairman Mao's instructions were that in carrying out the "four-cleaning campaign,"* militia work should be completed. Comrades Lin Piao and X X X also pointed out that from start to finish in the "four-cleaning campaign" we should grasp militia work, and that the army cadres participating in the "four-cleaning campaign" should do militia work. Lo Jui-ch'ing opposed this time and again, saying that in the "four-cleaning

---

* Chou En-lai, in a report to the Third National People's Congress in December 1964, said that in the socialist education movement "it is necessary to carry out cleaning and basic construction in the political, economic, ideological, and organizational aspects." From this came the "four-cleaning campaign," in which the masses and the lower-level cadres were called upon to give clean accounts of their political and ideological stand, family background, and financial situation — Ying-mao Kau.

campaign" "it is all right if we grasp militia work briefly in the stage of construction." What is more, he stipulated that army cadres going down to take part in socialist education work need not be entrusted with the further responsibility of doing militia work.

On the question of concrete implementation of the three aspects of militia work, Lo Jui-ch'ing also sang a tune opposing Chairman Mao. For the last few years Chairman Mao has repeatedly given instructions on the "three aspects" of militia work: first, the organizational aspect; second, the political aspect; third, the military aspect. The first thing is whether or not there is a militia; after that we can talk about its political orientation. Lo Jui-ch'ing mounted a frenzied opposition to this instruction of Chairman Mao's. He said repeatedly: "Among the three aspects of militia work, the primary one is the political aspect. Having built the foundation of the political aspect, then we can get to the organizational and military aspects." "If we don't do the political and ideological work well, it will even be a bit better not to carry out the aspect of organizational work at all. The more we carry out organizational work, the more the powers of leadership will be turned over to bad people, or bad cadres will learn to take control. The more thoroughly they carry out organization, the more they can do bad things." "We must make these relationships clear." In this, Lo Jui-ch'ing seems to stress politics strongly, but in fact he used a false argument to negate Chairman Mao's important instructions to organize the militia first. At the same time, Lo Jui-ch'ing completely violated Chairman Mao's instructions to "carry out work properly in the three aspects" of militia work by carrying out competition in military techniques in the militia.

Lo Jui-ch'ing opposed Chairman Mao's policies in literature and art. Chairman Mao, up to now, has instructed us that the first criterion in literature and art is the criterion of politics. The second criterion is that of artistic values. First, the question of the political orientation of literature and art must be resolved. In June 1964, Chairman Mao criticized literary and art circles, saying: "For fifteen years literary and art circles (not just a few people) have basically failed to carry out Party policy. They wanted to be officials and overlords, rather than drawing close to the workers, peasants, and soldiers and reflecting the socialist revolution and construction. In the last few years they even went so far as to reach the brink of revisionism." Lo Jui-ch'ing, in the military literary and art troupes, emphasized time and again that the problem of the orientation of literature and art had been resolved and that artistic values should be emphasized. He uttered this nonsense: "If we give priority to political and strongly militant things, then it could seem too simple and boring." "Our army has some comparatively rough literary and art works, in which the artistic process has been very careless. People who are exposed to them are bored. I don't advocate this sort of work. Otherwise, why bother with art at all; just read Mao's Selected Works and that will be enough."

Lo Jui-ch'ing openly revised Chairman Mao's theory that wherever the masses are there will be three kinds of conditions: progressive, intermediate, and backward. In November 1965, Lo Jui-ch'ing said such things as "Our troops don't need to worry about progressive and backward. They shouldn't raise such concepts as 'progressive soldier' and 'backward soldier.' These concepts can be eliminated. Our troops should only have the few titles of Party member, League member, 'five-good soldier,' model hero, and revolutionary soldier. That will be enough."

Lo Jui-ch'ing mounted a campaign of wicked slander and attack against our great leader Chairman Mao. He repeatedly spread dissatisfaction in public toward Chairman Mao. He even said to other people that Chairman Mao did not trust him and would purge him, and that he wanted to be transferred to Shanghai as mayor in order to get away from Chairman Mao as soon as possible. Afterwards, because Chairman Mao didn't ask him to be in his company on Tien-an-men, and didn't let him ride with him in the same plane on the flight to a meeting at X X X, he again said that Chairman Mao did not trust him and would purge him. This proves that his hatred towards Chairman Mao was deep-seated.

In this way, Lo Jui-ch'ing, in eyeing with hostility and opposing Mao Tse-tung thought, and in slandering and attacking Comrade Mao Tse-tung, was in fact opposing, eyeing with hostility, and attacking proletarian politics and trying hard to replace proletarian politics with bourgeois politics.

Second, he promoted the bourgeois military line and opposed Chairman Mao's military line, and he acted on his own authority to decide to carry out competition in military techniques throughout the army and opposed putting politics to the fore.

Lo Jui-ch'ing's bourgeois military ideas were completely unmasked when he acted on his own authority to decide to carry out competition in military techniques throughout the army and opposed putting politics to the fore. His plot to strive to pull our army out of the orbit of proletarian politics was completely unmasked, and so was his strong attempt to replace the proletarian military line represented by Comrade Mao Tse-tung with the bourgeois military line.

In January 1964, without going through the Conference of the Staff Offices of the Military Affairs Commission or through the Training and Research Committee of the Military Affairs Commission, and without asking Comrades Lin Piao, X X, and Nieh Jung-chen for instructions, Lo Jui-ch'ing decided on his own authority to carry out competition in military techniques throughout the army. He also decided on his own authority to carry out competition in military techniques in every province and city.

Competition in military techniques was competition in military affairs and technology. It advocated giving first priority to military affairs and technology. As soon as he carried out competition in military techniques, he denied the "four firsts" and denied the 1964 guideline for all army work. Competition in military techniques conflicted with politics, conflicted with the study of Chairman Mao's works, and weakened the troops' military and ideological work. Competition in military techniques has brought about serious evil consequences. In order to compete for first place in military techniques, an elite was created, and false appearances became a very common phenomenon. The purely military viewpoint and the tendency to care only for winning trophies developed in a big way, seriously harming the troops' work style, seriously alienating them from the masses, and seriously affecting the unity within the army. Because of competition in military techniques, the ill wind and malevolent influence of bourgeois ideology were on the rise, inundating the army. The number of "four-good companies" was greatly diminished. In order to carry out competition in military techniques, quite a few units emphasized technology and slighted politics in their choice of cadres and in developing Party and League members. Some units squeezed out cadres of worker and peasant origin. They put a high value on politics and ideology, but cadres who were slightly lacking in technical skills were often transferred. They completely denied Chairman Mao's instructions regarding the five criteria for successors to the revolutionary enterprise of the proletariat. Competition in military techniques conflicted with regular military training. It was training for show rather than training for fighting, and it made for a great deal of formalism and empty display, completely out of keeping with the demands of real fighting. The amount of waste and extravagance in competition in military techniques was astonishing; training accidents increased greatly. In the militia, competition in military techniques conflicted with "carrying out work properly in three aspects," influenced production, made the militia lose touch with the masses, added greatly to the burdens borne by the people and the masses, and gave rise to a great number of accidents.

At the end of 1964, Comrade Lin Piao, in accordance with the line of Chairman Mao's military thought, with the historical experience of our army's development, and with the great quantity of information reflected in military units at that time, gave instructions to put politics to the fore and severely criticized the mistake of competition in military techniques. Lo Jui-ch'ing not only failed to carry out these instructions but also resorted to all sorts of tricks to oppose them, alter them, and distort

them. Within ten days he repeatedly altered the substance of
Comrade Lin Piao's instructions more than eight times, did
his utmost to ruin their revolutionary spirit, and introduced
many extraneous elements. At the beginning of 1965, at the
Eighth Enlarged Conference of the Staff Offices of the Military
Affairs Commission and at an all-army conference to study the
experience in the revolutionization of the army, and later during
the many times he spoke at military academies, Lo did his utmost to oppose Comrade Lin Piao's instructions to put politics
to the fore, and moreover he incited others with his evil intentions. For example, in 1965, on X day of X month, in his
concluding speech to the reading class for high-level cadres
at the advanced military academies, Lo Jui-ch'ing openly incited everyone, saying, regarding Comrade Lin Piao's instructions to put politics to the fore, "Whether you agree or not is
a matter open to discussion. You will be leaving today, so
those comrades who don't agree can write letters back after
they have gone." He had ulterior motives in saying everywhere
that there should be a "correct," "complete," "dialectical" understanding of Comrade Lin Piao's instructions. He also said
that the work of military training in 1964 was the best of any
year since the founding of the country, and that the most important accomplishments were those in competition in military
techniques, which kept up the morale of the troops and prevented
their spirits from being dampened. Everywhere he spread the
fallacy of eclecticism (i.e., opportunism) and intensely opposed
Chairman Mao's basic viewpoint on putting politics in command
of military affairs. He also stressed the purely military point
of view, saying such things as that military affairs were the
same as politics, and military affairs and politics should receive equal emphasis, and that he opposed so-called "armchair
politicians." He said things such as "There is a theory that if
we don't handle politics well we can't handle anything well, and
that if politics is good, everything else will be good. I'm afraid
that finally this sort of good politics cannot be considered really
good. It is 'armchair' politics. What good is this kind of politics?" "We must definitely have a correct understanding of

Commander Lin's instructions. If we don't handle politics well, then our soldiers will run in retreat when they begin to fight; but, on the other hand, if we don't handle military affairs well, since our training is for the purpose of fighting, then, if the fighting goes badly, and as soon as we strike everyone is beaten, wouldn't our soldiers be even more likely to run in retreat?" "If we do military training badly, it will not only lead to waste, but even more important, as a result of the fighting, the Party will be exterminated and we will face national disaster," and on and on.

In November 1965, after Comrade Lin Piao brought up the five principles of putting politics to the fore, he quickly ran up against Lo Jui-ch'ing's opposition and contradiction. Lo Jui-ch'ing opposed using Chairman Mao's books as the highest guidance in all our army work. He also said that the principle of "well-tempered and tested techniques and the techniques of close combat and night fighting" were the most important of the five principles, and he put the living study and living application of Chairman Mao's works, grasping living thought, and other important principles in a subordinate position. In 1966 the Military Affairs Commission had already established the five principles as the guideline for work throughout the army, but Lo, on the contrary, deliberately stressed that the important thing was to resolve questions of method. He said such things as "If the question of method is not solved, then even the best possible guideline will not enable us to carry out work well!" He hinted that the five principles put forward by Comrade Lin Piao were just muddled talk.

Third, Lo Jui-ch'ing ignored organization and discipline and wanted to create an independent kingdom and destroy the Party's system of democratic centralism.

What was said above about Lo Jui-ch'ing deciding on his own authority to carry out competition in military techniques, opposing the instructions put forward by Comrade Lin Piao on putting politics to the fore, carrying out the "ten-eliminations movement" in the Ministry of Public Security, etc. — all of these were not only serious mistakes politically, but they were also serious in regard to the aspects of organization and discipline.

Concerning the question of struggle against the enemy in X X [Fukien] along the coast, Chairman Mao, the Party Central Committee, and the Military Affairs Commission all repeatedly and clearly pointed out that the struggle in the Taiwan Straits was not only a struggle against bandit X [Chiang Kai-shek], but more importantly a struggle against U.S. imperialism; not only a military problem, but more importantly a political problem. Therefore all military actions against bandit X [Chiang Kai-shek] should be considered in terms of politics, military strategy, and all other aspects and then decided by the Party Central Committee according to its understanding of the requirements of the overall situation. No person should take his own stand or act lightly without due consideration or without getting authorization from the Party Central Committee. Lo Jui-ch'ing, without asking Chairman Mao, the Party Central Committee, or the Military Affairs Commission for instructions, all by himself brashly instructed X X Military Region that from X day X month on they should fight on the sea. He said to the military region that they could, "on their own initiative, attack the enemy; in order not to waste any opportunity, strike first and report later."

Lo Jui-ch'ing, in many important military actions and military combat plans, repeatedly neglected to report to and ask instructions of the Standing Committee of the Military Affairs Commission. Sometimes when the Standing Committee of the Military Affairs Commission held a meeting and made decisions that did not agree with his ideas, Lo Jui-ch'ing got angry and rejected the decisions. For instance, in the X X combined operation plan drafted in X X, there were two defensive actions on the X X border in September and October 1956, and in both cases Lo Jui-ch'ing neither sought instructions from the Standing Committee of the Military Affairs Commission nor reported to it. Another example of this occurred in X month 1962, when the Standing Committee of the Military Affairs Commission held a meeting to discuss the two problems of the X X border conflict and the army's industrial production. Everyone decided, according to the situation at that time, that it would be best to move a unit to X section of the X border and at the same time to increase the production of regular weapons so as to build up stockpiles. At the meeting, some comrades of the Standing Committee asked some comrades in the Operations Department to convey the above opinions to Lo Jui-ch'ing, asking him to think them over and decide. After he heard this he burst into anger in front of a crowd of people and kept on saying, "We shouldn't be led astray in military strategy." "Tell me, where has there been any influence on military production?"

The Party Central Committee, Chairman Mao, and the Military Affairs Commission decided on a series of guidelines and policies concerning the question of establishing national defense industry, national defense science, and technology work. However, Lo Jui-ch'ing not only refused to put these into practice and to implement them, but he even changed and canceled them at will. At the end of 196X, at the meeting of the National Defense Industries Staff Office, he suddenly made a frantic proclamation, saying that "after the setting up of the new Military Affairs Commission, the Party Central Committee, the Military Affairs Commission, and Commander Lin put forward a series of guidelines for national defense industry. X X summed these up in his 'seventeen points of experience and good lessons' at a conference of three levels of cadres. If these guidelines are correct, then we must definitely support them. Where they are partly or mostly correct we should improve them, and where they are incorrect we should cancel them." He denied the important achievements of the National Defense Science Commission, under the direct leadership of Comrade Nieh Jung-chen. Even after the appearance of our atomic bomb he still frantically attacked our national defense scientific research work as going from data to data, from design to design, without ever completing anything.

Comrades Lin Piao and Nieh Jung-chen disagreed with Lo Jui-ch'ing's assertion that the system of military representatives should be quickly abolished in national defense industry.

Lin and Nieh repeatedly pointed out that "changing the system of military representatives should be thought over carefully, and until the situation has been clarified we should not make any changes for the time being." Lo Jui-ch'ing said: "There are people who say that doing away with the military representative system is the idea of P'eng Teh-huai and Huang K'o-ch'eng, but I'll take that risk."

During the period of his work with the Ministry of Public Security, Lo Jui-ch'ing frequently erred in ignoring organization and discipline. In November 1949, for example, he decided on his own authority, without asking instructions from Chairman Mao, the Party Central Committee, or the Military Affairs Commission, to transform X X Division and X Regiment of regular units guarding Peking into a central public security column directly under the command and organization table of the Ministry of Public Security. This matter was criticized by Chairman Mao and the Military Affairs Commission. Later, Lo Jui-ch'ing did his utmost to extend his own power, actively enlarging the public security forces and even trying to set up a system of direct leadership over public security work and public security forces.

Although Lo Jui-ch'ing held the positions of secretary of the secretariat of the Party Central Committee, secretary general of the Military Affairs Commission, and chief of the General Staff, he very seldom sincerely and systematically transmitted either the spirit of Central Committee meetings or the instructions of Chairman Mao and the Party Central Committee down to the cadres. Sometimes he would transmit instructions in part, but even then very seldom in their original form. Often he added his own interpretation in the transmission so that the cadres were not clear as to which parts consisted of directives from the Party Central Committee and Chairman Mao and which parts were Lo Jui-ch'ing's own addenda. Lo Jui-ch'ing sealed himself off from the Party Central Committee, the Military Affairs Commission, and especially from Comrade Lin Piao. From 1961 on, Comrade Lin Piao repeatedly tried to criticize and educate Lo, hoping to be in constant contact with him.

In April 1965, Comrade Lin once again clearly pointed out that from that time on all appointments and dismissals of cadres above X level in the army and of all heads of departments in the PLA general headquarters should be made only after reporting for instructions from all the comrades on the Standing Committee of the Military Affairs Commission, and then reporting to the Party Central Committee for it to pass judgement. Lo Jui-ch'ing acted as though he had never heard about this instruction. In May 1965, in determining grades for X number of leaders with the rank of general in the army, he did not report to Comrade Lin Piao or the Standing Committee of the Military Affairs Commission for instructions; instead, on his own initiative, he decided to use the name of the Military Affairs Commission in reporting to the Secretariat of the Party Central Committee. Lo Jui-ch'ing also often issued orders in the name of Comrade Lin Piao and of all the comrades on the Standing Committee of the Military Affairs Commission, and he would not allow others to go to ask for instructions.

Lo Jui-ch'ing is a typical example of someone self-centered and abysmally undemocratic. He seriously damaged the Party's system of democratic centralism. On many important questions he didn't go through the Standing Committee of the Military Affairs Commission, through the Military Affairs Commission's Staff Offices Conference, through the Headquarters of the General Staff, or through the General Political Department, and he often used his own personal judgement to decide questions. He overthrew and changed at will decisions of the Standing Committee of the Military Affairs Commission, and of the Staff Offices Conference of the Military Affairs Commission especially. Often he alone would speak at the Staff Offices Conference of the Military Affairs Commission. When others started to speak, he would often interrupt them. He wouldn't let others finish what they were saying. He even went so far as to sarcastically ridicule others, wounding them with his slanderous words. When the Standing Committee of the Military Affairs Commission held a meeting, he talked the most. When the vice chairmen of the Military Affairs Commission talked, he often interrupted them. He didn't have even the slightest spirit of self-criticism, and didn't listen to opinions that differed even slightly from his own. He acted like a tiger which could not be tampered with. If anyone tried to tell him his opinion, he nursed a long-standing resentment in his heart and seized any opportunity to attack in revenge.

Fourth, Lo Jui-ch'ing was a bad character, speculating and profiteering, supporting the standpoint of the exploiting class, and he had a bourgeois individualist desire to reach the top.

Lo Jui-ch'ing likes to stand out from the crowd. He is high-flying and arrogant, boasting and lording over others. He tries in every way to get fame and position and will use any means to make political capital for himself. He devoted himself especially to publishing his essays and speeches. He tried to get more space in the papers for his writings, sought front-page coverage, and wanted to make his name known and to be in the camera's eye. He often made speeches to express his opinion on important national and international political questions, pretending to be the plenipotentiary spokesman for the Party and the nation.

Lo Jui-ch'ing is the biggest speculator and profiteer. In 1964, for example, X X X himself adopted the teaching method of Kuo Hsing-fu and opened an on-the-spot conference to discuss this method. He also suggested to the Military Affairs Commission that it should further popularize the method. Chairman Mao and Comrade Lin Piao agreed with this suggestion and even praised it. As soon as Lo Jui-ch'ing saw that there was considerable profit in this, he pushed Comrade X X X out of the way, and, urging others to follow him, he himself opened an even larger-scale on-the-spot conference. He and his followers gave themselves all the credit and also seized this opportunity to start carrying out competition in military techniques throughout the army and to push forward their bourgeois military line. And Lo Jui-ch'ing made himself seem a hero by opposing P'eng Te-huai and Huang K'o-ch'eng, saying everywhere that he was their victim and that during the period of the Yenan rectification campaign he had criticized P'eng Te-huai and that as a result P'eng hated him fiercely. In fact, in the period of the War of Resistance Against Japan, when Lo Jui-ch'ing worked in the political department of a field army, he was an intimate follower of P'eng Te-huai's. When he saw P'eng Te-huai being criticized during the Yenan rectification campaign, he did a turnabout and began to criticize P'eng Te-huai. Later, during the attack on Taiyuan [city in Shansi] in the period of the War of Liberation, he saw that P'eng Te-huai was assuming important responsibilities again and had come to the fore in Taiyuan, and once again he began to lean on him. At that time, when P'eng Te-huai expressed dissatisfaction with the Yenan rectification campaign, Lo added quickly: "I too think that you have been criticized too strongly." In 1953, at the time of the P'eng, Kao [Kang], Jao [Shu-shih] anti-Party alliance, he again fell in with them. All of this demonstrates that Lo Jui-ch'ing is the very prototype of an opportunist.

When he worked on the Military Affairs Commission, Lo Jui-ch'ing was always climbing upward, divorcing himself from the masses and from reality. He never went to the basic level to investigate and do research and was not willing to listen to other people's briefings. He completely failed to take responsibility in his work and seriously neglected his duties, but tried to give the appearance of being very busy and advertised everywhere how terribly busy he was. In fact he was only busy reaping political gains and carrying out scheming activities, busy eating, drinking, and making merry. It went so far that in the very tense periods of fighting or preparing for battle he still went out as usual to see plays, go dancing, go fishing, and go sightseeing. He was lavish and a spendthrift in his way of life, rotten to the core.

Although Lo Jui-ch'ing entered the Party several decades ago, he still has not changed his standpoint from that of the exploiting class. Lo Jui-ch'ing had not the slightest bit of revolutionary class feeling toward Chairman Mao and Comrade Lin Piao, who had tried to cultivate and educate him over these few decades, nor did he have any feelings of revolutionary class empathy with revolutionary comrades or comrades-in-arms. He was coldhearted and treated them unsympathetically as enemies.

Lo Jui-ch'ing's attitude in dealing with his service personnel, with Comrade Tuan Kuang-fu, and with his own landlord relatives completely reveals his exploiting class standpoint. Comrade Tuan Kuang-fu had suffered greatly in the past and was full of deep class hatred. He was born a poor peasant, the son of a revolutionary martyr. He worked in Lo's residence for ten years, always extremely diligently and earnestly, enduring both hard work and insult, working more than ten hours a day. He cared for Lo's livelihood and ruined his own life, but Lo still treated him badly, in all respects like a slave. Lo had lots of sympathy for his landlord family, however. He even went so far as to shelter and offer support to his wife's father, who had carried out counterrevolutionary activities, thus becoming an air-raid shelter for a counterrevolutionary landlord.

Fifth, he tried to make use of the Party and to compel Comrade Lin Piao to "give way to the wise man" and "yield authority." He plotted to usurp the leadership of the army and opposed the Party.

In his activities to usurp leadership of the army and to oppose the Party, Lo Jui-ch'ing first pointed his spearhead at Comrade Lin Piao. He treated Comrade Lin Piao as an enemy and often spread rumors and false accusations about him. He attacked Comrade Lin Piao and used all kinds of plots and tricks to compel Comrade Lin Piao to "give way to the wise man" and "yield authority."

In the middle of September 1964, Comrade Liu Ya-lou explained that Lo Jui-ch'ing told him that Commander Lin said that his health was not good and that from now on he, Lo, should independently supervise the work of the Military Affairs Commission and all matters concerning the army. Lo should be concerned with solving problems on a large scale. It was not necessary to regularly ask for instructions from Commander Lin or to go all over the place asking for instructions. He also said that Comrade Lin Piao wanted Lo Jui-ch'ing to spend more time going out to look over the terrain and battlefields throughout the country so that when war broke out one day he could depend on Lo Jui-ch'ing to take command. When this matter was checked out it was found to be entirely a fabric of false reports spread by Lo, and thus clearly exposed his ambition to usurp leadership of the army and to oppose the Party.

After National Day in 1964 and before the preparations to open the Third Session of the National People's Congress, Lo Jui-ch'ing was impatient for Comrade Lin Piao to hand over his position and "give way to the wise man." At that time he ran over to Comrade Lin Piao's place and, under the cover of a discussion about cadre problems, he criticized Comrade Lin Piao, blaming him by indirect metaphors, saying: "A sick room is only for recuperating in. You can't handle business there. Give way to the wise man and don't interfere!" He walked out of the door and into the corridor, then shouted: "Don't stand in the way!"

In January 1965, at the first meeting of the Third Session of the National People's Congress, Comrade Lin Piao was chosen as the first vice premier and concurrently as defense minister. On January 17 and 18, Lo Jui-ch'ing went to Shanghai, where he said privately to Comrade Liu Ya-lou: "I had no idea that man would rise up again." In order to betray Comrade Lin Piao's trust, Lo Jui-ch'ing said to Comrade Liu Ya-lou: "This time I am really determined to follow Comrade Lin Piao. I will be like a small bird following the flock, never separated, not even by bullets or thunder. Even if I, Lo Jui-ch'ing, should die and be cremated, I will still remain loyal and faithful to Comrade Lin Piao." What is more, he wanted Comrade Liu Ya-lou to report these words to Comrade Lin Piao. On February 22, Lo Jui-ch'ing went to Shanghai again. First he talked a long time with Comrade Liu Ya-lou, and then on the morning of the second day he went to see Comrade Lin Piao and said to him: "From now on I will have even more faith in Comrade Lin Piao's leadership and support it even more strongly. From now on I will steadfastly follow you." Comrade Lin Piao told him he should follow the Party Central Committee and Chairman Mao. He also wanted him to rectify his past way of thinking and to improve his work. Comrade Lin Piao criticized

Lo Jui-ch'ing for having said a lot of things to Comrade Liu Ya-lou that he should not have said. Just after having said in the morning that he had faith in and supported Comrade Lin Piao even more strongly and "steadfastly followed" Comrade Lin Piao, an hour later, in the afternoon, in Canton Lo Jui-ch'ing started wild rumors concerning Comrade Lin Piao.

On February 14 and 15, 1965, Comrade Liu Ya-lou, following directions given him by Lo Jui-ch'ing, told Comrade Yeh Ch'ün about "four suggestions," hoping that she would persuade Comrade Lin Piao to accept them. These "four suggestions" were, first, any person, sooner or later, should leave the political arena. This general principle cannot be altered by the wishes of the individual. Even if a person does not want to leave the political arena he still has to leave. In the future Commander Lin too should leave the political arena. Second, Lin Piao's health should be carefully protected. In this we depend on you. Third, from now on Commander Lin should not pay so much attention to the army's affairs, because it can take care of itself. The army has everything it needs. The important question is that of carrying things out properly, and there is no need for Commander Lin to handle it any longer. Fourth, once he hands things over to Lo, he should show more respect to Lo and should let go and let him take over. Comrade Liu Ya-lou also said to Comrade Yeh Ch'ün: "Chief Lo said that if you only handle this matter well, Chief Lo will never treat you badly." After Liu Ya-lou made these suggestions, Comrade Yeh Ch'ün said: "It is not suitable for you to talk about such big questions with me. If you have something to say, please talk directly with Comrade Lin Piao."

On February 19, Liu Ya-lou went to Comrade Lin Piao's place and reported to Comrade Lin Piao the general content of the above "four suggestions," saying that he should respect Lo, have more faith in Lo, let go of army affairs, and let Lo take care of them. At that time Comrade Lin Piao severely criticized Comrade Liu Ya-lou. He pointed out Lo Jui-ch'ing's ideological situation since 196X and his bad tendencies. He also told Liu his own experience in recent years in conducting criticism of Lo. Comrade Liu Ya-lou told Comrade Lin Piao that he had been fooled and swindled by Lo Jui-ch'ing. Comrade Liu Ya-lou's wife, Comrade Ch'ü Yün-yin, heard about this matter, and both Comrades Yang Ch'eng-wu and Wu Fa-hsien also heard of it shortly before Comrade Liu Ya-lou's death.

In the afternoon of X month X day 1965, Lo Jui-ch'ing used the opportunity provided by a reception given by the Standing Committee of the Party Central Committee for members of the X X Conference of the Military Affairs Commission, and brought up a difficult topic to embarrass the Standing Committee of the Party Central Committee, and especially to embarrass Comrade Lin Piao. Lo Jui-ch'ing, without prior instruction from the Standing Committee of the Military Affairs Commission, arranged to have the representatives chosen from small groups act in consort with him in bringing their ideas before the Standing Committee of the Party Central Committee. He adopted the method of "surprise attack," and led them in putting forward the opinion that there was a need to greatly expand the number of military units and to merge military regions. After he spoke, he wanted comrades from each military region to speak. He vainly attempted to put strong pressure on the Standing Committee of the Party Central Committee to express its attitudes immediately. Comrade Lin Piao and other comrades of the Standing Committee of the Party Central Committee immediately criticized Lo Jui-ch'ing's evil way of doing things. Comrade Lin Piao had consistently, over a period of many years, condemned merging military regions and expanding the number of military units, as advocated by Lo Jui-ch'ing. What is more, when Lin Piao had reported to Chairman Mao for instructions, Chairman Mao entirely agreed with Comrade Lin Piao's opinion. Lo Jui-ch'ing was entirely clear on this matter. In this, Lo Jui-ch'ing was playing with a scheme. He calculated that, in the light of his desires, if the Standing Committee of the Party Central Committee agreed with his opinion, then he would have made his meritorious achievement known in front of the comrades of all the military regions, and he also would have achieved his purpose of attacking Comrade Lin

Piao. If the Standing Committee of the Party Central Committee did not agree with his opinion, then he could arouse the dissatisfaction of all the military regions toward the Party Central Committee and toward Comrade Lin Piao.

Lo Jui-ch'ing said in front of a lot of people: "Comrade Wang X X [Tung-hsing] said that the chairman made the criticism that the sentence about the human factor being first among the 'four firsts' lacked class analysis. There are good men and bad men; there are men of this class and men of that class." Comrade Wang X X [Tung-hsing] proved that Chairman Mao had never said these words at all. Nor had Comrade Wang X X [Tung-hsing] ever said these words to Lo Jui-ch'ing. The sentence about the human factor being first was put forward by Comrade Lin Piao in his "four firsts," and it referred to the relationship between men and weapons. This is exactly the consistent line of Chairman Mao's military thought. Chairman Mao, for several years, had repeatedly praised the "four firsts" put forward by Comrade Lin Piao. Lo Jui-ch'ing also spread the rumor that, when Comrade Lo Jung-huan was sick and dying and wanted to see Comrade Lin Piao for a moment, Comrade Lin Piao feigned illness and would not see him, and that he waited until after Comrade Lo Jung-huan had passed away before he finally went to the dead man and paid his respects and then went to follow the funeral procession, doing all this to make amends and for others to see. Lo Jung-huan's wife, Comrade Lin Yüeh-ch'in, and Comrade Lin Piao's secretary both testified that there was never such an occurrence and that it was entirely a fabrication and slander.

On X X day, in May 196X, just at the time of the X X Conference, after Comrade Lin Piao had continually criticized Lo Jui-ch'ing, Lo Jui-ch'ing and Liang X X had a secret talk, trying to sow discord in the relations between Comrade Lin Piao and Lo Jung-huan, and to slander and attack Comrade Lin Piao.

Over a long period of time, Lo Jui-ch'ing set up a barrier against Comrade Lin Piao. Although outwardly he engaged in some spurious self-examination after being criticized by Comrade Lin Piao, in reality he not only failed to rectify his mistakes but also harbored feelings of hatred, and going from bad to worse, made up poisonous rumors about Comrade Lin Piao, slandering and attacking him. Not only did he himself fail to make reports and to harmonize, he did not allow others to report or to harmonize, either. If anyone did try to harmonize, he attacked them and excluded them. Occasionally he would try to harmonize a little, and then again he would falsely twist Comrade Lin Piao's instructions, stir up contention, and carry out a campaign of vilification.

Lo Jui-ch'ing not only plotted to usurp the highest authority in the army but also tried to make use of people everywhere, from the Party Central Committee down to the local areas. He was originally in charge of military work, but he abused his authority and position, often giving directions in his own name on great quantities of papers already considered by the members of the Party Central Committee Secretariat, vice premiers of the State Council, and Party secretaries of Central Committee bureaus, provinces, cities, and autonomous regions. There were many matters that he did not submit to investigation and research, but merely added his criticisms, castigations, and commands in a blind way. There are many examples like this.

In order to realize his plot to usurp leadership of the army and to oppose the Party, Lo Jui-ch'ing also turned his back on the Party and formed a secret alliance with people of a like kind, boasting, flattering, and touting. Lo Jui-ch'ing's relations with Yang X X, Yang X X, Liu X X, Hsiao X X, and Liang X X were very improper.

The comrades who went to the conference realized all along that Lo Jui-ch'ing's mistakes were not just common mistakes, that, on the contrary, he was using the bourgeois line in military affairs to oppose the proletarian line and using revisionism to oppose Marxism-Leninism and Mao Tse-tung thought. He opposed Comrade Lin Piao, the Party Central Committee, and Chairman Mao, and he tried vainly to seize armed power in order to achieve his wicked purpose of usurping leadership of the army and opposing the Party. He is an extreme bourgeois individualist, an ambitious schemer, and a false gentleman; waving the red flag to oppose the red flag, he is like a time bomb placed within our Party and army.

This group meeting followed the principle of presenting the facts and explaining the reasons, punishing the ringleader as an example to others, and curing the sickness to save the patient in carrying out patient education and severe criticism of Lo Jui-ch'ing. Those attending did their utmost to try to change him and save him, but he not only utterly refused to recognize his crimes and mistakes, but he repeatedly refused to be educated, and he deceived and threatened the Party. In his self-examination made on March 12, although he admitted that he had committed some mistakes, and although he put several different labels on himself, when it got down to basic questions he still tried in a thousand and one ways to equivocate and deny his guilt. What is more, he set up lots of "traps," carried out a counterattack, and prepared to reverse the verdict afterwards. His self-examination made the comrades who were at the meeting extremely indignant, and they made many rebuttals on the spot. Afterwards, using the excuse that he did not have enough time for his self-examination, he asked for understanding and said that everyone should go back to work and wait until he was well prepared before opening the meeting again. When this plan failed he even "committed suicide" by jumping from a building in order to demand things from the Party under threat. He removed himself from the Party and from the people, following the line of a deserter from the Party. In his "last will and testament," written before he jumped from a building, he retracted even his admission to a few small mistakes, which he had made in the last few days.

The meeting recognized that it was no coincidence that Lo Jui-ch'ing's mistakes had developed to such a serious stage. It was a reflection of the class struggle within and outside of the country, and it had profound class, historical, and ideological roots. Lo Jui-ch'ing was born into a landlord family, and although he entered the Party some thirty years ago he had by no means changed his standpoint from that of the oppressor class. During the period of the National Revolution and the Democratic Revolution, he became more and more alienated from the Party until eventually the traits of a power-holder within the Party taking the capitalist road appeared in him, and he carried out activities to usurp leadership in the army and to oppose the Party. He became a yes-man of imperialism, modern revisionism, and reactionary elements of all nations, and he played the role of an agent of landlords, rich peasants, counterrevolutionaries, bad elements, and rightists. During every revolutionary period, Lo Jui-ch'ing committed numerous mistakes. In the period of the Second Revolutionary Civil War, for instance, he ran along behind the Wang Ming line. In relations with the Third Regiment of the X X Army, and in questions involving the treatment of . . . cadres [characters in original document unclear], he created factionalism and destroyed all unity. During the War of Resistance Against Japan, he was an active supporter of P'eng Teh-huai in the battle of the 100th Regiment, and he poured cold water on the masses. In 1941, after the Incident of South Anhwei, when P'eng Teh-huai turned his back on the policies of the Party Central Committee and on his own authority issued an order "confiscating the land belonging to big landlords and distributing it to landless peasants and peasants owning a small amount of land," the order was drafted by Lo Jui-ch'ing. After the establishment of the nation, in the incident of the anti-Party clique involving P'eng Te-huai, Kao Kang, and Yao Shu-shih, Lo also fell in with them. The Party Central Committee, Chairman Mao, the Military Affairs Commission, and Comrade Lin Piao tried repeatedly to criticize and educate him. Since 1961, Comrade Lin Piao repeatedly, with the greatest patience, tried to criticize him and educate him regarding his mistakes, and he gave him stern warnings. However, Lo still was outwardly compliant but inwardly unsubmissive, and he failed to rectify his mistakes, until finally in the last one or two years his evil character broke through and he was exposed. Lo Jui-ch'ing's world outlook is that of the capitalist class and of extreme individualism. He would use any means and do all sorts of bad things, even take advantage of the Party, in order to look after his own fame, profit, and position. As a result, he lifted his own disguise and revealed his essential nature.

The comrades at the meeting considered that the Party Central Committee, Chairman Mao, the Military Affairs Commission, and Comrade Lin Piao had shown exceptional brilliance in their timely discovery and resolute handling of the problem of Lo Jui-ch'ing's anti-Party plot. After the meeting of the Party Central Committee in Shanghai, this group meeting was held to thoroughly expose and criticize Lo Jui-ch'ing's mistakes and to crush his plot to usurp leadership of the army and to oppose the Party. This was a great victory for Mao Tse-tung thought and a great victory for the correct line of the Party. This proves once again that our Party is a great, glorious, and correct Party. It proves that our army is the incomparably loyal and reliable armed force of the Party. For the last few years, under the leadership of the Party Central Committee, Chairman Mao, the Military Affairs Commission, and Comrade Lin Piao, the army has accomplished great things in its work. It has shown great resistence to Lo Jui-ch'ing's mistakes. When the anti-Party element, Lo Jui-ch'ing, made his appearance, it did not harm the glory of our People's Liberation Army, founded by Chairman Mao himself, in the slightest. The comrades at the meeting always profoundly believed that after crushing the plot of Lo Jui-ch'ing to usurp leadership of the army and to oppose the Party, bad things would turn into good, and that our Party's undertakings and our army-building and the building of our national defense would all develop even more vigorously and achieve one glorious victory after another.

The meeting made the following recommendations to the Party Central Committee, in accordance with the facts of Lo Jui-ch'ing's serious mistakes and of his alienation from the Party:

First, Lo Jui-ch'ing should be dismissed from all his duties in the military affairs system.

Second, Lo Jui-ch'ing should be dismissed from his duties as vice minister of the State Council.

Third, Lo Jui-ch'ing should be dismissed from his duties as

member of the Secretariat of the Standing Committee of the Party Central Committee.

Fourth, a political and organizational summing up should be made regarding Lo Jui-ch'ing's mistakes.

Fifth, the report of the work group of the Party Central Committee and several important pronouncements of the group meeting should be transmitted to the proper levels in order to thoroughly eradicate his evil influence in all aspects.

In the course of this meeting, on a whole series of important questions, P'eng Chen maintained an attitude of trying to minimize, cover up, apologize for, and support Lo Jui-ch'ing's mistakes. He even tried to make various preparations to wait for an opportunity to reverse the verdict on Lo Jui-ch'ing. In fact, P'eng Chen had the same standpoint as Lo Jui-ch'ing, opposing Chairman Mao, opposing the Party Central Committee, and opposing Comrade Lin Piao. Another report regarding other facts on his mistakes will be prepared by Comrades [Yeh Chien-ying, Hsiao Hua, Liu Chih-chien],* and Yang Ch'eng-wu for submission to Chairman Mao and the Party Central Committee. This report is hereby submitted for approval.

The Work Group of the CCP Central Committee
April 30, 1966

---

*According to CCP Documents of the Great Proletarian Cultural Revolution, 1966-1967 (Hong Kong: Union Research Institute, 1968), p. 32 — Ying-mao Kau.

VII
The Military and the Cultural Revolution

25

DECISION CONCERNING THE PLA'S RESOLUTE
SUPPORT OF THE REVOLUTIONARY MASSES
OF THE LEFT (JANUARY 23, 1967)*

The CCP Central Committee,
The State Council,
The Military Affairs Commission of the
Central Committee,
The Cultural Revolution Group of the
Central Committee

To all regional bureaus of the Central Committee, all military regions, provincial, municipal and autonomous region Party committees and people's councils, and, through them, to Party committees and people's councils at lower levels, military districts, and military subdistricts:

Under Chairman Mao's leadership, a new stage in the Great Proletarian Cultural Revolution has begun. The principal characteristic of this new stage is the great alliance of proletarian revolutionaries to seize power from the grasp of a handful of power-holders within the Party taking the capitalist road and the diehards clinging to the bourgeois reactionary line. This

---

* Chung-kung chung-yang, kuo-wu-yüan, chung-yang chün-wei, chung-yang wen-ke hsiao-tsu, "Kuan-yü jen-min chieh-fang-chün chien-chüeh chih-ch'ih ke-ming tso-p'ai ch'ün-chung ti chüeh-ting," issued on January 23, 1967; reprinted in Fei-ch'ing nien-pao [Yearbook on Chinese Communism] (Taipei, 1968), pp. 578-579.

struggle to seize power is a general counteroffensive by the proletariat against the frantic attacks by the bourgeoisie and its representatives within the Party over the last seventeen years. This is a class struggle carried on in every corner of the entire nation. It is a great revolution in which one class overthrows another.

The People's Liberation Army is a revolutionary army of the proletariat fashioned by Chairman Mao's own hands, and it is the principal instrument of the dictatorship of the proletariat. In this great struggle of the proletariat to seize power from the bourgeoisie, the PLA must stand resolutely on the side of the proletarian revolutionaries and support and aid resolutely the proletarian revolutionary left.

Recently, Chairman Mao directed that the PLA should support the broad masses of the left. Henceforth, wherever there are genuine revolutionaries who seek the army's support and aid, their demands should be satisfied. So-called "noninvolvement" is not true, for the army has been involved for some time. The question is not whether to become involved or not, but which side to stand on. The question is whether to support the revolutionaries or support the conservatives or even the rightists. The PLA ought to support actively the revolutionary left.

All of our army's commanders and fighters must resolutely carry out Chairman Mao's directive.

1. The previous directives concerning the army's noninvolvement in the Cultural Revolution on the local level and other directives that violate the spirit of the above are all nullified.

2. Actively support the broad revolutionary masses' struggle to seize power. Whenever the genuine proletarian leftists ask the army to come to their aid, the army should dispatch a unit to actively support them.

3. Resolutely suppress counterrevolutionary elements and counterrevolutionary organizations that oppose the proletarian revolutionary left. If the counterrevolutionaries take up arms, the army should resolutely counterattack.

4. Reiterate the directive that the army cannot act as an

air-raid shelter for the handful of power-holders within the Party taking the capitalist road and the diehards clinging to the bourgeois reactionary line.

5. Conduct intensive education throughout the army on the struggle of the proletarian line, represented by Chairman Mao, against the bourgeois reactionary line, represented by Liu Shao-ch'i and Teng Hsiao-p'ing.

This directive must be conveyed in full to every fighter in the Liberation Army.

The CCP Central Committee,
the State Council, the Military Affairs
Commission of the Central Committee,
The Cultural Revolution Group of
the Central Committee

January 23, 1967

26

BULLETIN OF THE PLA MILITARY CONTROL
COMMISSION OF THE PEKING MUNICIPAL PUBLIC
SECURITY BUREAU (FEBRUARY 25, 1967)*

Investigation has revealed that organizations known as the
National Red Laborers Rebel General Corps, the National Destroy Capitalism Army Rebel Corps General Headquarters,
and the National State Farms Red Rebel Army are reactionary
organizations. They indiscriminately carried out a series of
evil acts, including spreading rumors and slanders, provoking
armed struggle, carrying out economism, attacking the leading
state organs, looting and destroying state property, seizing
buildings by force, and raping women. In accordance with the
unanimous demands of the broad revolutionary masses, it has
been decided to ban these organizations and arrest their leading elements and some particularly bad individual elements.
As for their general members who were hoodwinked, they will
only be required to recognize their mistakes, expose the evil
deeds of their reactionary chiefs, and immediately return to
their original areas and units. Their cases generally will not
be investigated any further.

Further investigation has revealed that organizations known
as the National Defend-the-Truth Revolutionary Rebel Corps
of Intellectual Youth Sent to the Mountains and the Countryside,

---

* "Chung-kuo jen-min chieh-fang-chün Pei-ching-shih kung-
an-chü chün-shih kuan-chih wei-yüan-hui pu-kao," issued on
February 25, 1967; reprinted in Fei-ch'ing nien-pao [Yearbook
on Chinese Communism] (Taipei, 1968), p. 591.

the National Red Revolutionary Rebel Corps of Intellectual Youth Sent to the Mountains and the Countryside, the National Red First Line Struggle Detachment of Intellectual Youth Sent to the Mountains and the Countryside, the National Army Reclamation Fighters Revolutionary Rebel Corps, the China Detachment of the International Red Guard Army, and the National Deaf-Mute Revolutionary Rebel United General Headquarters are unlawful organizations, and it has been decided that they will be banned. All other so-called nationwide mass organizations in Peking are also unlawful. In accordance with the announcement of the Party Central Committee and the State Council, they should immediately disband, and their members must immediately return to their original areas and units.

The PLA Military Control Commission of
the Peking Municipal Public Security Bureau

February 25, 1967

27

SOME DIRECTIVES CONCERNING THE DISPATCHING
OF THE "CENTRAL SUPPORT-THE-LEFT UNITS" IN
ALL MILITARY REGIONS AND PROVINCIAL
MILITARY DISTRICTS (JUNE 10, 1968)*

The CCP Central Committee,
The State Council,
The Military Affairs Commission of the
Central Committee,
The Cultural Revolution Group of the
Central Committee

To all provincial, municipal, and autonomous region revolutionary committees (and preparatory committees), military control committees, all military regions and provincial military districts:

The Great Proletarian Cultural Revolution, personally initiated and led by our great teacher, great leader, great commander, and great helmsman, Chairman Mao, has already gained a decisive victory. Our revolutionary situation is not just quite good; it is very good.

The great Chinese People's Liberation Army, following

---

* Chung-kung chung-yang, kuo-wu-yüan, chung-yang chün-wei, chung-yang wen-ke hsiao-tsu, "Kuan-yü 'chung-yang chih-tso pu-tui' chin-chu ko-ta chün-ch'ü sheng-chün-ch'ü ti jo-kan chih-shih," issued on June 10, 1968; reprinted in Chung-kung nien-pao [Yearbook on Chinese Communism] (Taipei, 1969), Section VII, pp. 39-41.

closely Chairman Mao's great strategy in the Great Proletarian Cultural Revolution, has bravely defended the proletarian revolutionary line represented by Chairman Mao, thoroughly smashed the frantic assaults of the bourgeois reactionary line represented by China's Khrushchev, brilliantly undertaken the formidable task of "three-support" and "two-military" work, and performed the greatest meritorious services for the Chinese people and the people of the world.

Now the bulk of the nation's provinces, municipalities, and autonomous regions have already, one after the other, formed revolutionary great alliances and established revolutionary committees with the proletariat in authority. This is a telling blow to the imperialists, the modern revisionists, and the reactionaries in every country, as well as to the handful of power-holders within the Party led by China's Khrushchev who are taking the capitalist road and are foolishly trying to overthrow our nation's dictatorship of the proletariat. Yet these enemies will not be reconciled to their defeat. As Chairman Mao teaches us: "They are a group of counterrevolutionaries who are against the Party and the people. Their struggle with us is a struggle to the death." "They still want to get in the last blow."

The fact that Fukien, Yunnan, Kwangsi, Tibet, and Sinkiang have not yet formed revolutionary committees is a sharp reflection of the class struggle within the Party. The handful of capitalist-roaders within the Party who stubbornly refuse to change, along with their lackeys — the landlords, rich peasants, reactionaries, bad elements and rightists, and all the monsters and freaks in society from the Central Committee on down to the local areas — are placing serious obstacles in the way of the great alliance of proletarian revolutionaries. They are insanely attempting to destroy the foundation of the revolutionary committees. From the right and from the extreme left, and from both sides at once, they are creating disturbances on our front and are fomenting factionalism in the revolutionary ranks, destroying solidarity, promoting a right-deviationist adverse current, and madly and audaciously trying to pressure Chairman Mao and the Party Central Committee.

Contrary to the hopes of the enemy, the more they try to obstruct and undermine the establishment of the revolutionary committees, the quicker they bring about their own extinction. The Chinese People's Liberation Army Support-the-Left Units, armed with invincible Mao Tse-tung thought and closely integrated with the broad revolutionary masses, have formed a flood tide which cannot be diverted and which no reactionary force can withstand.

In order to meet the needs of the current revolutionary situation, and in order to consolidate those revolutionary committees already established and expedite the establishment of revolutionary committees in areas where a great alliance has not yet formed, the Chinese People's Liberation Army Support-the-Left Units (called the Central Support-the-Left Units for short), in accordance with the spirit of Chairman Mao's latest directive, are directly authorized by the Military Affairs Commission of the Central Committee to take up posts in every military region and provincial military district to carry out the task of supporting the left.

The powers and duties of the "Central Support-the-Left Units" are as follows:

I. Helping the Local Military Units with Problems in Carrying Out Support-the-Left Duties

1. The "Central Support-the-Left Units" are support units under the direct leadership and direction of the Military Affairs Commission of the Central Committee. They are fully authorized agents for the Military Affairs Commission's work of supporting the left.

2. Local army units, with the help of the "Central Support-the-Left Units," should more ably and faithfully carry out Chairman Mao's order that "The PLA should support the broad masses of the left." Armed with Mao Tse-tung thought, they should effectively take up the glorious task of "three-support" and "two-military" work.

3. Wherever support-the-left units are not yet stationed,

"Central Support-the-Left Units" must quickly take up their posts. The garrisons ought to be especially strengthened in provinces and autonomous regions where revolutionary committees have not yet been established or in areas where, although a revolutionary committee has already been established, the revolution is still in turmoil. This is so that, along with the local troops, they can help the revolutionary masses and deal a solid blow to the whole reactionary adverse current trying to destroy the revolutionary great alliance and trying to split the revolutionary committee.

4. The "Central Support-the-Left Units" have the power to supervise the local army units' support-the-left work and to correct their mistakes in leadership in support-the-left work. Strictly forbid "mountaintop-ism" and "secessionism" from the respective governmental authority.

5. If responsible persons of any military services or any branches of the local forces of the Chinese People's Liberation Army make mistakes of a fundamental nature in support-the-left work and yet reject the corrections and aid of the "Central Support-the-Left Unit," they can be forcibly detained and their cases examined and dealt with accordingly. Those leading the resistance will be relieved of their military positions and weapons, and a report will be submitted to higher authorities for disposition.

II. Handling the Problems of the Revolutionary Mass Organizations That Urgently Require Solution

1. Wherever firearms and ammunition have been distributed and used in the campaign, the "Central Support-the-Left Unit" must see to it that all weapons are collected. Bad leaders and their stubborn followers who resist the turning over of weapons can be arrested, and even coercion can be used to force them to surrender their arms. Armed resistance will invariably be brought under control by military action.

2. Those leading evil elements who continue to foment armed struggle, produce incidents of bloodshed, and disrupt the course

of the Great Proletarian Cultural Revolution must be severely punished.

3. In the case of elements led by a small handful of diehards who continue to foment trouble and incite the masses to encircle and attack the Liberation Army, the "Central Support-the-Left Unit" has the power to counterattack in self-defense and to provide the necessary punishment.

4. In areas where a revolutionary great alliance cannot be realized because of factional struggles, the "Central Support-the-Left Unit" ought to help the two sides immediately negotiate and reach an agreement on the spot. When negotiations at the hsien level cannot resolve the differences, representatives may be dispatched to the provincial level to reach an agreement. When agreement cannot be reached at the provincial level, representatives can be summoned to the Central Committee to reach agreement. No side can decline on any pretext to participate in the negotiations and to overthrow resolutely bourgeois and petty bourgeois factionalism and to foster a proletarian-type party.

5. The "Central Support-the-Left Units" must devote all their efforts to propagandizing and educating the broad revolutionary mass organizations. No matter where they are, those leaders who are either openly or behind the scenes continuing to foment armed struggle or stir up resistance to participation in agreements or great alliances and trying to destroy the foundation of the revolutionary committees or promote factionalism must forthrightly confess their crimes to the people and to Chairman Mao. Those who are stubborn right to the end will be arrested. Those who were hoodwinked will then turn against their former leaders.

III. On the Question of "Rehabilitation" and "Grasp Revolution, Promote Production"

1. The "Central Support-the-Left Units" should devote all their efforts to supporting the revolutionary masses in continuing to deeply and thoroughly criticize the handful of power-

holders within the Party led by China's Khrushchev, taking
the capitalist road, and resolutely attack the rightist reverse
current. But toward those revolutionary masses who committed
mistakes and who were even labeled as "monsters and freaks,"
the Party Central Committee Cultural Revolution Group's
"Eight Directives Concerning the Question of Rehabilitation,"
promulgated on May 13, 1967, ought to be resolutely carried
out and progress on them rechecked.

2. After revolutionary alliances have been carried out, revolutionary mass organizations that have committed mistakes
of viewpoint or direction in the past must not be labeled or
discriminated against.

3. After the "Central Support-the-Left Units" have taken
their posts, they should issue to all in their area an urgent order to resume production. They should put the revolution in
order and move forward in carrying out the policy of "grasp
revolution, promote production." As for violaters, their respective dispersal of wages and leaving jobs on their own initiative should be ended across the board and their cases discussed and handled accordingly.

IV. The Question of Intensifying the Dictatorship
Over the Class Enemy

1. Intensify the dictatorship of the proletariat, deal a fierce
blow to the destructive activities of all class enemies, and protect the new proletarian revolutionary order.

2. Deal a resolute blow to all kinds of espionage by U.S.-
Chiang Kai-shek spies, Soviet revisionist spies, and Japanese
spies who have sneaked into revolutionary organizations and
carried out subversive and destructive activities. Those active
counterrevolutionaries who have stolen state information and
leaked state secrets to foreign countries must be resolutely
suppressed.

3. Intensify the supervision and control of landlords, rich
peasants, counterrevolutionaries, bad elements, and rightists.
Only allow them to behave themselves; don't allow them to

speak or act in an unruly way. In order to carry out and consolidate the red political power of the proletariat in a workable manner that will guarantee the great alliance, the four elements ought to be kept under centralized surveillance, and they ought to reform themselves through labor in accordance with the needs of each local situation.

4. Resolutely strip the four elements of any political right to reverse verdicts and stir up "rebellion." Any who are discovered to be carrying out class revenge or undermining the Great Proletarian Cultural Revolution in any way will be suppressed resolutely. No policy of benevolence will be carried out.

The CCP Central Committee,
the State Council, the Military Affairs
Commission of the Central Committee,
The Cultural Revolution Group of
the Central Committee

June 10, 1968

ATTENTION

1. Reproduction of this document is prohibited with the exception that every provincial military district may uniformly make and distribute copies to the revolutionary committee, military control commission, and local army leadership organ of every administrative region in order to provide for internal compliance.

2. This document must not be circulated or spread either to administrative units other than those mentioned above or to revolutionary mass organizations.

28

ON THE REVOLUTIONARY
"THREE-WAY ALLIANCE"*

Red Flag

Chairman Mao has stated that in every place and unit where power must be seized, the policy of a revolutionary "three-way alliance" must be carried out to establish a provisional organ of power which is revolutionary and representative and has proletarian authority. This organ of power should preferably be called a revolutionary committee.

This is a political and organizational guarantee for the victory of the proletarian revolutionaries in their struggle to seize power. The proletarian revolutionaries should understand this policy correctly and carry it out correctly

The provisional organ of power based on the revolutionary "three-way alliance" should be established by leaders of revolutionary mass organizations that really represent the broad masses, representatives of the local units of the Chinese People's Liberation Army, and revolutionary leading cadres. None of these three components may be omitted. To overlook or underestimate the role of any one component is wrong.

The vigorous mass movement of the Great Proletarian Cultural Revolution during the past half year and more has fully mobilized the masses and turned out large numbers of newly emergent representatives of the revolutionary masses. The

---

*"Lun ke-ming ti 'san-chieh-ho,' " Hung-ch'i editorial, No. 5 (March 30, 1967), 5-9.

broad revolutionary masses are the base on which the proletarian revolutionaries seize power from the handful of Party
people in authority taking the capitalist road. They are the
foundation of the provisional organ of power based on the revolutionary "three-way alliance."

True proletarian revolutionaries and newly emergent representatives of the revolutionary masses have performed im-
mortal feats in the Great Proletarian Cultural Revolution. They
are the new forces nurtured by the thought of Mao Tse-tung,
and they embody the general direction of the revolution.

This struggle to seize power from the handful of Party persons in authority taking the capitalist road is a mass movement
from the bottom to the top under the leadership of the Central
Committee of the Party headed by Chairman Mao. Within the
provisional organ of power based on the revolutionary "three-
way alliance," it is imperative to give full play to the role of
leaders of the revolutionary mass organizations, to respect
their opinions, and never to regard them simply as the supporting cast. The reason is that they are the representatives of the
revolutionary masses. If their role is not recognized or if it is
downgraded, it will amount to the negation of the revolutionary
masses and the Great Proletarian Cultural Revolution. If they
are rejected or regarded as the supporting cast, a provisional
organ of power that is revolutionary, representative, and has
proletarian authority cannot be established; and the organ cannot be a revolutionary "three-way alliance."

In all great revolutionary mass movements, the occurrence
of some shortcomings and errors is inevitable. It is imperative
to see clearly the essence, the mainstream, and the general
direction of the revolution. During this Great Proletarian Cultural Revolution, the shortcomings and errors of the leaders
of revolutionary mass organizations who truly represent the
masses are a question of one finger among the ten and a problem that arises in the course of advancement. As proletarian
revolutionaries they should recognize that their general orientation is correct, they have many strong points, and we should
learn from them modestly. As for their shortcomings and er-

rors, we should warmheartedly, patiently, and painstakingly help them to overcome them. We should also note that many revolutionary mass organizations have pointed out wrong trends within their own organizations and have proposed ways of correcting them as a result of their creative study and application of Chairman Mao's works. This is a valuable revolutionary consciousness and creativity. It is precisely the revolutionary masses themselves who have raised the task of attacking "self-interest" in their own thinking, while seizing power from the handful of Party persons in authority taking the capitalist road.

In the final analysis, the question of one's attitude toward leaders of revolutionary mass organizations that really represent the masses taking part in the provisional organ of power based on the "three-way alliance" is a question of one's attitude toward the masses, toward the mass movement itself. It is also an important indication of whether or not one can carry out the proletarian revolutionary line represented by Chairman Mao. We must at all times remember Chairman Mao's teaching: "The masses are the real heroes"; "the masses have boundless creative power"; and "the people, and the people alone, are the motive force in the making of world history." Any organization or individual, if isolated from the revolutionary masses, will definitely be unable to carry out the proletarian revolutionary line represented by Chairman Mao.

The vigorous mass movement of the Great Proletarian Cultural Revolution in the past half-year and more has put the ranks of our cadres to a severe test. The handful of Party persons in authority taking the capitalist road have been exposed. At the same time, it has proved that the majority of our cadres are good or relatively good. The idea of rejecting and overthrowing all cadres is absolutely wrong. It is necessary to point out that the masses are not to be blamed for [such a mentality]. To reject and overthrow all cadres indiscriminately is the stand taken by those few people who laid down the bourgeois reactionary line, and it was precisely what they did. This kind of poisonous influence has not been eradicated from the minds of certain comrades; and therefore they have, to a certain extent, committed such mistakes unconsciously.

In every place, department, and unit of an enterprise or business, there are great numbers of revolutionary cadres. This is also true for some places or departments where those in authority taking the capitalist road have been entrenched, except that revolutionary cadres there were, over a long period, suppressed. We must be aware of this.

The role of the revolutionary cadres in taking part in the provisional organ of power based on the "three-way alliance" must be fully weighed. They should and can play the role of nucleus and backbone of the organ. Of course, they can play such a role only by integrating themselves with the masses and by following the mass line in work.

As long as they examine their own mistakes and correct them, draw a clear-cut line of demarcation between themselves and the handful of Party persons in authority taking the capitalist road and between themselves and the bourgeois reactionary line, and really stand on the side of the proletarian revolutionary line represented by Chairman Mao Tse-tung, cadres who have made mistakes should be united with, in accordance with the principle that "early or late, all who make revolution merit equal treatment." Proper jobs should be arranged for them. Many of them may be permitted to join the provisional organ of power.

But those who persist in their mistakes and do not draw a clear-cut demarcation line between themselves and the people in authority taking the capitalist road and between themselves and the bourgeois reactionary line must not be imposed on the masses by force and arbitrarily pushed into the "three-way alliance" power organ. Otherwise, the organ would not be a revolutionary "three-way alliance," to say nothing of the seizure of power from the handful of Party persons in authority taking the capitalist road. A new reversal would occur, and the people in authority taking the capitalist road who had been defeated might even regain power.

We must be vigilant against those who distort the principle of a revolutionary "three-way alliance" and, on the pretext of "three-way alliance," carry out eclecticism, conciliationism, or "the combination of two into one," or even try a thousand ways to pull in the Party persons in authority taking the capitalist road. They aim at fishing in troubled waters, usurping the fruit of the Great Proletarian Cultural Revolution, and carrying out counterrevolutionary restoration. All revolutionary masses and all revolutionary cadres must resolutely resist, oppose, and smash this kind of conspiracy of the class enemy.

The great People's Liberation Army is the mainstay of the dictatorship of the proletariat. Chairman Mao's call to the People's Liberation Army to support actively the broad masses of the revolutionary Left is a matter of great strategic significance.

Experience proves that participation by representatives of the local People's Liberation Army units in the provisional organ of power based on the revolutionary "three-way alliance" plays a very important role in the successful completion of the task of the struggle to seize power.

With the participation of cadres of the People's Liberation Army in the "three-way alliance" provisional organ of power and with the support of the People's Liberation Army, the strength of the local proletarian revolutionaries becomes still greater. The class enemy fears most the People's Liberation Army and the revolutionary "three-way alliance" in which People's Liberation Army cadres take part. The class enemy takes pains to create rumors and fabricate stories in a vain attempt to provoke dissension between the revolutionary masses and the People's Liberation Army and to incite some people who do not know the truth to direct the spearhead of their struggle against the People's Liberation Army. Such intrigues of the class enemy must be fully exposed and resolutely smashed.

The Chinese People's Liberation Army is a thoroughly revolutionized army of the proletariat, unmatched in the world. Chairman Mao Tse-tung has said: "The sole purpose of this army is to stand firmly with the Chinese people and to serve them wholeheartedly." It is precisely because of this that all revolutionary mass organizations and revolutionary masses

have faith in the People's Liberation Army and warmly support
the participation by representatives of the local army units in
the provisional organ of power based on the revolutionary
"three-way alliance." From the top to the bottom, in all units
where power must be seized, representatives of the army or
the militia should take part in forming the "three-way alliance."
This should be done in factories and the rural areas, in the
financial and trading organization, the cultural and educational
units (universities, middle schools, and primary schools), in
Party and government organizations, and in mass organizations.
Representatives of the armed forces should be sent to the hsien
level or higher, and representatives of the militia should be
sent to the commune level or lower. This is excellent. If representatives of the armed forces are lacking, [the places for
them] may be left vacant for the time being and should be
filled in the future.

The attitude toward the People's Liberation Army means
the attitude toward the dictatorship of the proletariat, and it
is an important criterion for distinguishing whether or not a
person is a genuine revolutionary Leftist.

In a number of places, some comrades in the local army
units may commit temporary mistakes in their support work,
owing to the intricate and complex conditions of the class struggle. When such problems occur, the genuine proletarian Leftists should explain, with good intentions and in the proper way,
the conditions and put forward their opinions to responsible
comrades of the army units. They should absolutely never
adopt an attitude of public resistance and should not in the least
direct the spearhead of their struggle against the People's
Liberation Army. Otherwise, they will commit gross mistakes
and do things which will sadden friends and gladden the enemy,
and they will be used by the class enemy.

The People's Liberation Army has already made important
contributions in supporting the proletarian revolutionaries in
their struggle to seize power. All commanders and fighters
must follow Chairman Mao's teachings, closely rely on the
revolutionary masses, modestly learn from them, be their

students first before acting as their teachers, be good at discussing matters with them, and conduct in-depth and careful investigation and research. In so doing, they will be able to give the proletarian revolutionaries very powerful support in their struggle to seize power and work for still closer ties between the army and the people. And the army units, for their part, will get new tempering and improvement in the course of the struggle.

The provisional organ of power based on the "three-way alliance" must be revolutionary and representative and have proletarian authority. This organ of power must resolutely carry out the proletarian revolutionary line represented by Chairman Mao and firmly oppose the bourgeois reactionary line. It must not be "combining two into one" or eclectic. Only in this way can [the organ of power] be representative and speak for the revolutionary masses and revolutionary cadres. Only in this way can it have proletarian authority, exercise powerful centralized leadership on the basis of the most extensive democracy, impose effective dictatorship on the class enemy, and smash every kind of scheme for counterrevolutionary restoration plotted by the small handful of Party people in authority taking the capitalist road and the monsters and demons in society.

A big question now confronting the people of the whole country is whether to carry the Great Proletarian Cultural Revolution through to the end or to abandon it halfway. All revolutionary comrades must keep a cool head and never get confused. "With power to spare we must pursue the tottering foe and not ape Hsiang Yü, the conqueror seeking idle fame." At present, we should especially remember this instruction from Chairman Mao.

29

PLA THREE-SUPPORT AND TWO-MILITARY
PERSONNEL MAKE NEW CONTRIBUTIONS
TO THE CONSOLIDATION OF THE
DICTATORSHIP OF THE PROLETARIAT*

Bright Daily

During the past year or so, under the favorable conditions of
the victorious advance of the Great Proletarian Cultural Revolution throughout the country, the broad masses of commanders and fighters of the People's Liberation Army fighting on
the first line of three-support and two-military work followed
the great teaching of great commander Chairman Mao that "We
must transform the Party and the world according to the spirit
of the proletarian pioneers." Taking PLA Unit 8341, which
achieved outstanding merits in three-support and two-military work, as a model, they warmly helped revolutionary
committees at various levels and the broad masses of revolutionaries to follow Chairman Mao's great strategic plans
closely by combining the great mass movement of studying and
applying Mao Tse-tung's thought in a living manner with the
tasks of struggle-criticism-transformation. They firmly
grasped the struggle between the two classes, the two roads,
and the two lines, and thoroughly "developed the ideological
struggle of the proletariat against the nonproletariat." In this

_____
*"Chieh-fang-chün san-chih liang-chün jen-yüan wei kung-
ku wu-ch'an chieh-chi chuan-cheng tso-ch'u hsin kung-hsien,"
Kuang-ming jih-pao, July 28, 1970.

way they conscientiously transformed their world outlook, effectively pushed forward the in-depth development of the struggle-criticism-transformation movement, and made new contributions toward the further consolidation of the dictatorship of the proletariat and further victory in the Great Proletarian Cultural Revolution.

Vigorously Grasp the Fundamentals and Enthusiastically Help the Leadership Squads at Various Levels to Strengthen Revolutionary Construction

During the past year or so, under the illumination of the Party's Ninth Congress and in accordance with Chairman Mao's great teaching that "the fundamental question in revolution is the question of political power" and Vice Chairman Lin's instruction that "leadership squads are political power," all three-support and two-military personnel of each unit used their greatest revolutionary enthusiasm to help leadership squads at various levels to strengthen their revolutionization. They brought to revolutionary committees at various levels their advanced political work experience in giving prominence to proletarian politics, in persevering in the "four firsts," and in promoting the "three-eight work style" in order to build up the leadership squads as fighting bodies boundlessly loyal to Chairman Mao, boundlessly loyal to Mao Tse-tung's thought, and boundlessly loyal to Chairman Mao's revolutionary line. They turned all support-the-Left units into true great schools of Mao Tse-tung's thought and spared no efforts to consolidate the dictatorship of the proletariat from its foundation.

In the course of supporting the Left, the broad masses of commanders and fighters of the support-the-Left personnel of Unit 8341, which was boundlessly loyal to Chairman Mao, unfailingly helped the leadership squads at various levels and the broad revolutionary masses to study and apply Mao Tse-tung's thought in a living manner, so as to make them consciously and thoroughly execute Chairman Mao's proletarian revolutionary line and carry out various proletarian policies when implementing the fighting tasks put forward by the Ninth Party Congress. They made them dare to struggle against the class enemy, "Leftist" and Rightist erroneous tendencies, and nonproletarian ideas in their own heads. They were able to achieve this no matter how great and how complicated the work was, since the world never changes direction in the living study and living application of Mao Tse-tung's thought; and no matter how busy they were, they would never forget giving prominence to proletarian politics. In accordance with Vice Chairman Lin's instruction, "We must study Chairman Mao's works with problems in mind, study and apply in a living manner, combine study with application, study urgent parts first, make it work immediately, and pay special attention to 'application,'" the Mao Tse-tung thought propaganda team of a unit stationed in Peking General Knitting Works energetically helped the factory create the "read, think, ask, discuss, apply, write, and investigate" method of living study and living application of Mao Tse-tung's thought. The masses called this the "seven-character scripture," which effectively pushed forward the further development of the mass movement of living study and living application of Mao Tse-tung's thought in the whole factory.

The support-the-Left personnel of a unit under the Nanking Command stationed at the Shanghai Electrochemical Works concentrated their efforts on dealing with the poor combination of study with application in the leadership squad of the factory and actively helped them cultivate the good study style of combining theory with practice, so that they would be able to combine closely the living study and living application of Mao Tse-tung's thought with the implementation of the policies and guidelines of the Party, with diverse work in struggle-criticism-transformation, with the current situation and tasks, and with the transformation of their own world outlook. This greatly speeded up the revolutionization of the leadership squad, and moved the Electrochemical Works from among the backward units to the ranks of the advanced.

In the course of helping leadership squads to study and apply

Mao Tse-tung's thought in a living manner and strengthening
their revolutionization, the broad masses of three-support and
two-military personnel of units stationed in Peking, Shanghai,
Tientsin, Wuhan, Shenyang, Canton, Lanchow, and Kunming
regularly looked for problems in the struggle over line, together
with the members of the leadership squads at various levels,
and looked for causes of troubles from the ideology of the leadership, so as to enable the leadership squads to advance ceaselessly and vigorously along Chairman Mao's revolutionary line.
With a view to the confused idea harbored by some of the
cadres in Wuhan Heavy Machine Tool Works that "politics is
a soft target whereas production is a hard target, therefore it
is not important whether we grasp politics or not," the support-
the-Left personnel stationed in this factory actively cooperated
with the revolutionary committee to hold Mao Tse-tung thought
study classes on a large scale. They used the Resolution of the
Ku-t'ien Conference and the Resolution of the 1960 Enlarged
Conference of the Military Affairs Commission as weapons to
unfold a great debate concerning the question of how to handle
correctly the relation between politics and production. This
greatly heightened the consciousness of all the cadres and
workers in the entire factory in the struggle between the two
lines. Many cadres said with a deep understanding that when
they studied the "Resolutions" enthusiastically and gave prominence to politics with a definite orientation, they could never
go astray from the course of revolution. In order to help implement the task of consolidating the dictatorship of the proletariat down to the basic level, support-the-Left personnel of
the navy and the air force regularly worked with factory and
rural revolutionary committees at various levels to conduct
line analyses in combination with the practice of the struggle-
criticism-transformation movement and personal thinking, to
uncover contradictions hidden in "principles" and "guidelines,"
to trigger revolution deep in the soul, and to promote effectively
the revolutionization of the leadership squads at various levels.

Actively Lead the Broad Masses of Revolutionaries
in the Struggle-Criticism-Transformation Movement
and Extensively Develop the
Struggle Between the Proletarian and
the Nonproletarian Ideology

As the struggle-criticism-transformation movement developed in depth, the broad masses of three-support and two-military personnel, following Chairman Mao's great teaching — "unite for one purpose, that is, the consolidation of the dictatorship of the proletariat; it must be realized in every factory, village, office and school" — actively led the broad masses of revolutionaries and leadership squads at various levels to "develop the ideological struggle of the proletariat against the nonproletariat" under the guidance of the invincible thought of Mao Tse-tung. This has made the broad masses of Communist Party members and revolutionary masses undergo a profound ideological change and become more self-conscious in carrying out and defending Chairman Mao's revolutionary line. In the struggle-criticism-transformation movement, the support-the-Left personnel stationed in Kiangnan Shipyard actively led the broad masses of revolutionaries to study repeatedly Chairman Mao's great teaching: "The Chinese people have ambition and ability. They will catch and surpass advanced world standards in the near future." They energetically condemned the towering crime of renegade, hidden traitor, and scab Liu Shao-ch'i in advancing the "theory of crawling at a snail's pace" and the "philosophy of servility to foreign things"; and they established in the revolutionary masses the ambitious aspiration to follow the road of developing our own shipbuilding industry. This resulted in the simultaneous launching of two 10,000-ton ships within a very short period of time. In accordance with Chairman Mao's great teaching, "If socialism does not occupy the rural positions, capitalism is bound to occupy them," the Mao Tse-tung thought propaganda team of a unit stationed in Chengtu penetrated into many production teams, used Mao Tse-tung's thought to propagandize, organize, and arm the masses of commune members, and persistently eliminated the ideological influences of spontaneous capitalism and the exploiting classes. This enabled the continuous consolidation of the socialist positions in rural areas. A Mao Tse-tung thought propaganda team of a unit under the Tsinan Command, which was dispatched to Chao-chia-an Production Brigade, Ju-shan hsien, enthusiastically helped the peasants in mountainous areas to set up Mao Tse-tung thought study classes in every household. This brought about unprecedented changes in this remote mountain area. Among the thirty-two households in the village, fifteen were appraised as five-good families, and many individuals were appraised as activists in the living study and living application of Mao Tse-tung's thought. This village also became an advanced collective in Shantung Province in the living study and living application of Mao Tse-tung's thought.

Controlling the realm of the superstructure, the three-support and two-military personnel paid great attention, in support of the Left, to helping the broad masses of revolutionary cadres and revolutionary intellectuals in the living study and living application of Mao Tse-tung's thought. They carried out struggle to destroy bourgeois ideology and establish proletarian ideology and conscientiously moved the standpoint over to the side of the proletariat. Together with the poor and lower-middle peasants, the support-the-Left commanders and fighters of a unit under the Foochow Command stationed in Ching-kang-shan Area enthusiastically helped cadres who were sent there to settle, to transform their world outlook conscientiously, and to make up their minds to spend the rest of their lives following the revolutionary road laid down by Chairman Mao. The Mao Tse-tung thought propaganda team of a unit under the Canton Command stationed in the Chung-shan Medical College always considered the leading of the revolutionary teachers and students to study and apply Mao Tse-tung's thought in a living manner and the combining of themselves with the workers, peasants, and soldiers as the fundamental road in helping revolutionary intellectuals to transform their world outlook. Together with the revolutionary teachers and students, they used

Chairman Mao's "Talks at the Yenan Forum on Literature and Art" as a weapon to repudiate profoundly various bourgeois ideas, such as the "idea of fame and profit," "going to school to become bureaucrats," "belittling labor," etc., and thoroughly to eliminate the remnant poison of Liu Shao-ch'i's counterrevolutionary revisionist line, so as to heighten greatly the consciousness of the broad masses of revolutionary teachers and students in the struggle between the two lines. Revolutionary teachers and students of this medical college consciously went to the countryside to settle, and humbly received reeducation from the poor and lower-middle peasants. During a period of two years or so they treated 940,000 patients and trained more than 2,000 rural barefooted doctors, who were welcomed by the poor and lower-middle peasants.

Study and Apply Mao Tse-tung's Thought in a Living Manner Through Struggle and Ceaselessly Heighten One's Own Political Consciousness

Chairman Mao taught us: "The working class should also ceaselessly heighten its own political consciousness through struggle." In order to do a better job in three-support and two-military work, Party committees and political organs in various military units regularly held study classes, convened symposiums on three-support and two-military political and ideological work, and called meetings for discussing and applying the living study and living application of Mao Tse-tung's thought in combination with the tasks of the struggle-criticism-transformation movement and with the living ideas of the three-support and two-military personnel. The three-support and two-military personnel were sent periodically in groups for training in order to raise the consciousness of their own self-revolution. In practicing struggle, the broad masses of three-support and two-military personnel considered themselves a revolutionary force but, at the same time, also the target of revolution. Being self-conscious of the task of transforming

their own world outlook, they studied and applied in a living
manner Chairman Mao's great theory of continuous revolution
under the dictatorship of the proletariat and the new Party
Constitution, so as to raise their consciousness in the continuation of revolution and to become leaders in ideological revolutionization.

Since assuming the chairmanship of the Tung-t'ai hsien
Revolutionary Committee in Kiangsu Province, Shih K'e-li, an
activist in the living study and living application of Mao Tse-
tung's thought and deputy staff officer of a unit under the Nanking Command, humbly learned from the masses, treated himself according to the principle of "dividing one into two," ab-
sorbed rich political nourishment from the masses, and un-
ceasingly promoted his own ideological revolutionization. Upon
noticing that the masses did not criticize him much at a meeting of democratic life attended by all members of the hsien
revolutionary committee, he actively went deep into the masses,
laid his thought open, struggled against self-interest, repudiated
revisionism, and invited the masses to criticize him. He said:
"Only when you criticize me so much that my face turns red
and my heart begins to pound, can you touch my soul deeply
and make my transformation effective." On one occasion, Li
Fa-chih, a military representative from the Lanchow Command
to the revolutionary committee of a factory, heard the workers
say that in the revolutionary committee, representatives from
the cadres and masses did not act as frankly as military representatives. This incident made him think deeply. He linked
it with his ideology and immediately examined his own short-
coming of not sufficiently developing the role of other members of the revolutionary committee in his work. From then
on he always paid attention to developing the role of other members of the revolutionary committee, consciously abided by the
resolutions of the revolutionary committee, and persevered in
discussing things with the masses. As a result, he was praised
by the masses. Li Sheng-k'ai, leader of a platoon of a unit
stationed in Sinkiang, during the period when he was supporting
agriculture in the Second Commune of Chao-su hsien, con-

sciously transformed his world outlook, tempered his revolutionary spirit of fearing neither hardship nor death, and strove
to perform difficult and dangerous work before others. On
one occasion when he learned that the lives of people and animals of a livestock brigade were seriously threatened by an
avalanche, he immediately rushed to the spot on horseback to
lead the masses in the rescue operation, regardless of his own
personal safety.

Now, the three-support and two-military personnel of various
units are taking advantage of the favorable revolutionary situation to sum up their experience conscientiously for future
struggles. They are determined to do a better job in the living
study and living application of Mao Tse-tung's thought and to
treat the three-support and two-military work as the best form
of army-building and war preparation. Cherishing the great
goal of communism in their heart and maintaining always their
vigorous revolutionary fighting spirit, they will emulate the
support-the-Left personnel of Unit 8341 as the model and
closely follow Chairman Mao's great strategic plans to make
still greater contributions to carry the Great Proletarian Cultural Revolution through to the end.

VIII

The Reassertion
of the Maoist Model

30

SUM UP EXPERIENCE IN
STRENGTHENING PARTY LEADERSHIP*

People's Daily, Red Flag,
Liberation Army Daily

In line with the great leader Chairman Mao's instructions
"Read and study seriously and have a good grasp of Marxism"
and "Carry out education in ideology and political line," the
whole Party has unfolded a movement for criticizing revisionism and rectifying the style of work and has deepened it step by
step since the Second Plenary Session of the Ninth Central
Committee of the Party. The movement has attained marked
results and achieved great victories. By seriously reading works
by Marx, Lenin, and Chairman Mao, the masses of Party members, and particularly senior Party cadres, have heightened
their consciousness of class struggle and the struggle between
the two lines and of continuing the revolution under the dictatorship of the proletariat, and have gone a step further in exposing
and criticizing such swindlers as Liu Shao-ch'i. New Party
committees at various levels have generally been established
and the struggle-criticism-transformation in the Great Pro-

---

*"Tsung-chieh chia-ch'iang tang ti ling-tao ti ching-yen,"
joint editorial by Jen-min jih-pao, Hung-ch'i, and Chieh-fang-
chün pao. The Chinese text may be found in Hung-ch'i, No. 13
(December 4, 1971), 4-6. This translation is taken, with minor
editorial revisions, from Peking Review, No. 50 (December 10,
1971), 4-5.

letarian Cultural Revolution is developing in depth. Rallying all the more closely around the Party Central Committee headed by Chairman Mao, and advancing along the line of unity for victory of the Ninth National Congress of the Party, the whole Party, the whole army, and the people of the whole country have continued to win new successes in the socialist revolution and socialist construction.

The Communiqué of the Second Plenary Session of the Party's Ninth Central Committee called for strengthening Party-building and "giving further play to the leading role of the vanguard of the proletariat." In the past year and more, the whole Party has done a great deal of work in accordance with Chairman Mao's line for Party-building. The present domestic and international situation is very fine. In order to fulfill our Party's glorious tasks still better, the Party committees at all levels must sum up their experience in earnest so as to continue to strengthen Party leadership over all kinds of work.

What are the main questions to be stressed in strengthening Party leadership?

It is imperative to strengthen the Party concept. Chairman Mao teaches us: "The Chinese Communist Party is the core of leadership of the whole Chinese people. Without this core, the cause of socialism cannot be victorious." Our Party is the vanguard of the proletariat; it is the highest form of class organization of the proletariat. Of the seven — industry, agriculture, commerce, culture and education, the army, the government, and the Party — the Party gives leadership to the first six. Party committees at all levels should exercise centralized leadership in all fields of work in accordance with the Party's line and policies and, for the purpose of consolidating the dictatorship of the proletariat, strive to unite the revolutionary masses and unite all the forces that can be united so as to give fuller play to the role of the vanguard of the proletariat as the core. Chairman Mao regards Party-building as one of the three principal magic weapons for the Chinese revolution and helping to strengthen, and not discard or weaken, the leadership of the Communist Party as one of the most important political criteria for distinguishing fragrant flowers from poisonous weeds. In the complicated class struggle and the struggle between the two lines, every Party member and every revolutionary must firmly bear in mind Chairman Mao's teaching: "We must have faith in the masses and we must have faith in the Party. These are two cardinal principles. If we doubt these principles, we shall accomplish nothing." It is especially necessary for members of Party committees at all levels to strengthen the Party concept and place themselves within the Party committee and not outside it, still less above it.

It is imperative to carry on education in ideology and political line in a deep-going way. Chairman Mao has pointed out on many occasions: The correctness or incorrectness of the ideological and political line decides everything. Policies are the concrete embodiment of a political line. Fundamentally, strengthening Party leadership means the firm implementation of Chairman Mao's proletarian revolutionary line and policies. The history of inner-Party struggle between the two lines shows that the represeatatives of the bourgeoisie always change their tactics in an attempt to substitute their opportunist line and policies for the Party's Marxist-Leninist line and policies and substitute their bourgeois program for the Party's proletarian program, and thus to bring about a change in the character of the Party, turning it from a proletarian into a bourgeois Party, and achieve their criminal aim of liquidating Party leadership and undermining the Chinese revolution. This is an inevitable reflection of the class struggle in society. Under the guidance of Chairman Mao's correct line and proletarian policies, our Party is growing more consolidated and stronger in the storms of class struggle. Neither imperialism, nor social imperialism, nor revisionism within our Party has been able to defeat us. On the contrary, every triumph of the correct line over the incorrect line has dealt heavy blows to the enemies at home and abroad, brought about still greater victories in the revolutionary cause, and enabled our Party to become stronger, more united, and thriving. This is the conclusion drawn by history.

It is imperative to strengthen the unity of the Party. Chairman Mao has always stressed the importance of being able to unite with the great majority and has regarded the unity of the Party as the most essential factor in winning victory in the revolution and construction. Had it not been for the correct principle of unity of the Seventh Party Congress, the new democratic revolution could not have achieved victory. And had it not been for the line of unity for victory of the Ninth Party Congress, the fruits of the Great Proletarian Cultural Revolution could not have been consolidated and developed. Opportunism in politics is, organizationally, inevitably accompanied by the mountain-stronghold mentality, sectarianism, and fractionalism. History does not lack such lessons. Ch'en Tu-hsiu's patriarchism, Ch'ü Ch'iu-pai's punitiveness, Li Li-san's "my word is law," Wang Ming's "ruthless struggle and merciless blows," Chang Kuo-t'ao's fractionalism and war-lordism, and the "striking at many in order to protect a handful" practiced by Liu Shao-ch'i and other swindlers like him have all caused tremendous harm to the unity and unification of the Party. In his struggle against opportunist lines, Chairman Mao set forth the principles of "unity, criticism, unity" and "learn from past mistakes to avoid future ones and cure the sickness to save the patient." Only by implementing these principles is it possible to educate the cadres and strengthen the unity of the Party on the basis of the principles of Marxism-Leninism-Mao Tse-tung thought. Hidden anti-Party and antisocialist counterrevolutionaries are very few in number. The overwhelming majority of good people who committed mistakes in political line are able to return to the correct line through criticism and self-criticism.

Be open and aboveboard. Chairman Mao pointed out long ago: "We Communists have always disdained concealing our views." All Party comrades, and it goes without saying for senior Party cadres, must be frank and forthright politically. At all times one ought to state one's political views openly and, on every important political issue, express one's position, either for or against, adhering to what is right and correcting what is wrong. This is a question of the Party's style of work and of Party spirit. As chieftains of opportunist lines are en-

gaged in splitting activities, they are bound to resort to conspiracies and intrigues. In his famous talk in 1964 on bringing
up successors, Chairman Mao pointed out: "Beware of those
who engage in intrigue and conspiracy. For instance, men like
Kao Kang, Jao Shu-shih, P'eng Te-huai and Huang K'e-ch'eng
were to be found in the Central Committee. Everything divides
into two. Some persons are dead set on conspiring. They want
to do this, so that's that — even now there are such persons
at it! That there are persons conspiring is an objective fact
and not a question of whether we like it or not." In our Party's
history, those bourgeois careerists, conspirators, and persons
having illicit relations with foreign countries, who clung to opportunist lines and engaged in conspiracies, could not but bring
ruin, disgrace, and destruction upon themselves in the end.

It is imperative to strengthen the sense of discipline. Discipline is the guarantee for the implementation of the line. In
summing up our Party's struggle against Chang Kuo-t'ao's opportunist line, Chairman Mao pointed out: "Some people violate
Party discipline through not knowing what it is, while others,
like Chang Kuo-t'ao, violate it knowingly and take advantage of
many Party members' ignorance to achieve their treacherous
purposes. Hence it is necessary to educate members in Party
discipline so that the rank and file will not only observe discipline themselves, but will exercise supervision over the leaders so that they, too, observe it, thus preventing the recurrence
of cases like Chang Kuo-t'ao's." We must bear firmly in mind
this historical experience, resolutely carry out the Party's
unified discipline stipulated in the Party Constitution, and resolutely carry out "The Three Main Rules of Discipline and the
Eight Points for Attention" formulated by Chairman Mao. It is
necessary to learn and sing well "The Internationale" and the
song "The Three Main Rules of Discipline and the Eight Points
for Attention" and "educate the cadres, the masses, the Party
members, and the people in 'The Three Main Rules of Discipline
and the Eight Points for Attention.'"

It is imperative to practice Marxism-Leninism, and not revisionism. To practice Marxism or to practice revisionism?

The struggles between the two lines within our Party, in the final analysis, boil down to this question. Why is it that some people are fooled and taken in during the struggle between the two lines? The fundamental reason is that they do not read and study seriously and cannot distinguish materialism from idealism and the Marxist line from the opportunist line. This is an extremely profound lesson. Comrades throughout the Party, senior Party cadres in particular, must follow Chairman Mao's teachings, continuously persist in reading and studying seriously, have a good grasp of Marxism, consciously remold their world outlook, combine study with revolutionary mass criticism, constantly raise their ability to distinguish between genuine and sham Marxism, and carry out Chairman Mao's revolutionary line ever more consciously.

The Chinese Communist Party with Comrade Mao Tse-tung as its leader is a great, glorious, and correct Party. Through positive and negative examples, the previous struggles between the two lines have enabled us to understand ever more deeply that Chairman Mao's leadership means the greatest happiness for the whole Party, the whole army, and the people of the whole country, and that Chairman Mao's proletarian revolutionary line is the lifeblood of the whole Party, the whole army, and the people of the whole country. Under the leadership of the Party Central Committee headed by Chairman Mao, and along Chairman Mao's proletarian revolutionary line, let us unite to win still greater victories!

31

FURTHER STRENGTHEN THE
PARTY'S UNIFIED LEADERSHIP*

Ch'i Yung-hung

Study seriously Chairman Mao's theory of Party-building and
strengthen further the Party's unified leadership — this is an
important guarantee for implementing the line set by the Ninth
Party Congress and for consolidating the proletarian dictatorship.

What is the most important question in carrying out the Party's unified leadership? The question of line is the most important. "The line is the key link; once it is grasped, everything falls into place." To strengthen Party leadership, this
key link should be grasped. Chairman Mao has consistently
taught us: "To lead the revolution to victory, a political party
must depend on the correctness of its own political line and the
solidarity of its own organization." "The correctness or incorrectness of the ideological and political line decides everything." By unified leadership, we mean to guarantee the victorious implementation of Chairman Mao's proletarian revolutionary line and policies on every front. At the Ninth Party
Congress and the First Plenary Session of the Ninth Party
Central Committee, Chairman Mao called on us "to unite and
win still greater victories." Chairman Mao said: "Unite for
one purpose, that is, the consolidation of the dictatorship of the

---

*Ch'i Yung-hung, "Chin i-pu chia-ch'iang tang ti i-yüan-hua
ling-tao," Hung-ch'i [Red Flag], No. 1 (January 1, 1972), 38-43.

proletariat. It must be carried out in every factory, village, office, and school." "In speaking of victory, we must be sure of uniting with the broad masses of the people of the whole country to win victory under the dictatorship of the proletariat." To conscientiously carry out the line of the Ninth Party Congress and the various policies of the Party as put forth by Chairman Mao is a basic goal of strengthening the Party's unified leadership. To violate the line of the Ninth Congress and various proletarian policies will invariably result in dualism and pluralism and will undermine the Party's unified leadership.

Historical and practical experience tell us that implementation of the Party's unified leadership is definitely not easy. Some comrades think: "With a great victory won in the Great Proletarian Cultural Revolution, the struggle between the two lines will disappear." Others hold: "With new men, new horses, and a new squad, everything will be fine from now on." Theoretically these views are against materialist dialectics and are at variance with reality. Chairman Mao points out: "Opposition and struggle between ideas of different kinds constantly occur within the Party; this is a reflection within the Party of contradictions between classes and between the new and the old in society. If there were no contradictions in the Party and no ideological struggles to resolve them, the Party's life would come to an end" ("On Contradiction" [1937]). We should remember well this truth that Chairman Mao pointed out.

The philosophy of the Communist Party is the philosophy of struggle. In the past half century, our Party has gone through many major struggles between the two lines. Guided by Chairman Mao's correct line and various proletarian policies, our Party has defeated successive wrong lines and smashed the sinister conspiracies of the chieftains of the opportunist line to split the Party, change the character of the Party, and eliminate the Party's leadership. Each time it uncovered and defeated a wrong line, our Party advanced, won more victories, and demonstrated a greater vitality. The hard struggles in the past half century have enabled our Party to develop into a great, glorious, and correct Marxist-Leninist Party capable of

leading 700 million people. Since the Second Plenary Session
of the Ninth Party Congress, under the guidance of the Party
Central Committee headed by Chairman Mao, the whole Party
has step-by-step carried out penetratingly the campaign to repudiate revisionism and rectify the style of work, and it has
achieved remarkable results and won new and great victories.
[The fact that] these victories were won quickly shows clearly
the continued progress in socialist revolution and the unprecedented consolidation of the dictatorship of the proletariat in
our country. This also indicates that our Party is purer, more
united, and more prosperous than it has ever been at any time
in the past. Faced with this victorious situation, we must go on
fighting vigorously, seriously sum up our experience in strengthening Party leadership, further criticize and uncover Liu Shao-
ch'i and swindlers like him, and firmly carry out the line of the
Ninth Party Congress and various proletarian policies of the
Party.

The line of the Ninth Party Congress is a line of unity and
a line of victory. The Party's unity is the Party's life and is
an organizational guarantee for the Party's unified leadership.
Chairman Mao calls upon us to "unite the Party and army virtually as one man and forge close ties between them and the
masses of the people, and to carry out effectively all the policies and tactics formulated by the Central Committee of our
Party" ("Speech at a Conference of Cadres in the Shansi-
Suiyuan Liberated Area" [1948]). Only when it is solidly united
can the Party lead the hundreds of millions of the masses to
fight and build. The clarion call of "The Internationale" is:
"Unite and by tomorrow the Internationale shall be the human
race." The first verse in the song "The Three Main Rules of
Discipline and the Eight Points for Attention" says: "Obey
orders in all your actions and march in step to win victory."
Our Party's cause is the common cause of the proletariat and
the broad masses of the people. Therefore, to unite to ensure
the realization of the Party's unified leadership is a matter of
utmost importance to Party leadership at various levels and to
all the Party members; it is also a matter of primary impor-

tance to the proletariat and the broad revolutionary masses. Under the guidance of Chairman Mao's revolutionary line, we must achieve unified thinking, unified policy, unified planning, unified command, and unified action, and march in step and fight in unison. This is the basic condition for winning victories in socialist revolution and socialist construction.

Revolutionary unity can be built only on the basis of the principle of Marxism-Leninism-Mao Tse-tung thought. Liu Shao-ch'i and political swindlers like him went all out to denounce the inner-Party ideological struggle. In his black book Self-Cultivation [English edition published in 1951, 1952, 1964], Liu Shao-ch'i said that "inner-Party peace and inner-Party unity without differences over principle are very fine and necessary." They also advocated that "a 'common desire' means unity," "'harmony among men' means unity," and so on. All these are anti-Marxist fallacies. Unity has a class content. Any talk about "inner-Party peace" and "harmony among men" in isolation from the struggle between the two classes and two roads and from the Marxist principle is deceptive nonsense. One wants to exterminate capitalism; the other wants to restore it. How can the two get along "harmoniously"? Similarly, the so-called common desire in isolation from this principle is no "common" desire. One "desires" socialism; the other "desires" capitalism. How can the two share a "common" desire? Such a fallacy is itself "different in principle" from Marxism-Leninism and will cause the destruction of the "inner-Party unity." Liu Shao-ch'i and political swindlers like him had advocated this kind of fallacy as a smoke screen to deceive the good people, to cover up their counterrevolutionary desire, and to recruit deserters and traitors in a vain attempt to subvert the dictatorship of the proletariat and restore capitalism.

Chairman Mao has used the formula "unity-criticism-unity" to explain succinctly the dialectical relationship between unity and criticism. During the prolonged struggle the fine style of criticism and self-criticism has been formed in our Party, and it has become the main weapon with which to uphold truth, rectify mistakes, resolve inner-Party contradictions, and achieve unity of the whole Party. Communists must dare to fight against all erroneous tendencies opposed to Marxism-Leninism-Mao Tse-tung thought. If the Party does not constantly uncover and solve the contradictions within itself, if the Party does not carry out a struggle between the two ideologies and the two lines, and if the Party evades contradictions and bows to dangers, erroneous tendencies will grow, the Party's unity will be undermined, and the Party's fighting power will be weakened.

To carry out inner-Party struggle, it is definitely necessary to distinguish between two different types of contradictions and carry out Chairman Mao's teaching: "Expand the scope of education and narrow the target of attack." Bad elements hiding in our Party are always a very small minority. As for good people who make mistakes or even mistakes in line, we must proceed from the principle and position of Marxism and follow the policy of "learning from past mistakes to avoid future ones and curing the sickness to save the patient." While struggling against them, we must also unite with them. Struggling is for upholding principle and Chairman Mao's revolutionary line; unity is for "giving the comrades who have committed errors ample opportunity to wake up" ("On Contradiction" [1937]). [We must] actively help those comrades who have committed errors to see and correct their errors; and for those who have improved slightly and begun to wake up, [we must] proceed from the desire for unity and continue to give them help. This is an important policy which Chairman Mao has long taught us and which has been proved to be effective in practice. Why do we say "learn from past mistakes to avoid future ones"? Because we want people to accept the historical experience of class struggle so that they can do their work better, avoid making similar mistakes in the future, and raise their resistance against wrong ideas and deeds. So long as we adhere to the Party's principle and rely on the Party's policies, we shall achieve "the twofold objective of clarity in ideology and unity among comrades." We must unite with all forces that can be united, arouse all positive factors, and wage a common fight for winning still greater victories in socialist revolution and construction and for consolidating the dictatorship of the proletariat.

Chairman Mao teaches us: "One is the unity of the Party, and the other is the unity of the Party and the people. They are invaluable treasures for overcoming a difficult environment. Comrades of the whole Party must cherish these two invaluable treasures." In order to further strengthen unity inside and outside the Party and further strengthen unified leadership under the guidance of the line of the Ninth Party Congress, it is necessary to handle seriously and well the following two relationships:

One concerns proper handling of the relationship between the Party and various revolutionary organizations. "The Party is the vanguard of the proletariat and the highest form of the proletarian organization." That is to say, the Party should and must exercise leadership over all organizations of the proletariat. Otherwise, the proletariat cannot possibly carry on its victorious fight. This is a truth the proletariat the world over has learned during its prolonged revolutionary practice, and it is a basic principle for handling the relationship between the Party and the revolutionary organizations of various kinds. On the basis of this fundamental Marxist-Leninist principle, our Party Constitution provides: "The state organ of power under the dictatorship of the proletariat, the People's Liberation Army, the Communist Youth league, the workers, the poor and lower-middle peasants, the Red Guards, and other revolutionary mass organizations must accept the leadership of the Party." For only in this way can the proletarian organizations of various kinds advance in step and lead the broad revolutionary masses to defeat their common enemy. Under the unified leadership of the Party Central Committee, Party committees at all levels must concretely strengthen their political, ideological, and organizational leadership on various fronts in accordance with the line of the Ninth Party Congress and the various guidelines and policies of the Party, and in the practice of the Three Great Revolutionary Movements, they must "raise the leadership work of the Party committee to a higher level." In the process of strengthening the Party's centralized leadership, Party committees must carry out the principle put forth by Chairman Mao: "Power must be centralized in deciding major problems and decentralized in deciding minor problems. The Party committee makes a decision, and the localities carry it out. In so doing, the localities may make decisions without parting from the principle. The Party committee is responsible for examining the work done." The aim in doing this is to strengthen the leadership of the vanguard of the proletariat over the various revolutionary organizations of the proletariat, and to strengthen the leadership of the proletariat over the masses of the people of all walks of life. If the Party committee monopolizes everything, big or small, it will invariably fail to lead what it should lead, and revolutionary organizations will not be able to bring their revolutionary enthusiasm into full play. As a result, Party leadership will be weakened, not strengthened.

The second pertains to the internal relationship of the Party committee. Those who are elected to the Party committee, whether they are old or new cadres, army cadres or local cadres, and whether they are assigned to this or that front, are part of the Party committee, and all should make strenuous efforts to build the Party committee into a staunch fighting collective. Chairman Mao points out: "The Party committee system is an important Party institution for ensuring collective leadership and preventing any individual from monopolizing the conduct of affairs" ("On Strengthening the Party Committee System" [1948]). Only by firmly carrying out Chairman Mao's correct line and relying on collective experience and wisdom can the Party committee build itself into a vigorous fighting command post of the proletariat in accordance with Marxist theory and style.

Chairman Mao instructed us that it is necessary to "practice democratic centralism to stimulate the initiative of the whole Party" ("Win the Masses in Their Millions for the Anti-Japanese National United Front"). Without correct centralization, the

Party cannot fight. Without full democracy, it is impossible to develop correct centralization. Within the Party committee, it is necessary to uphold "rule by the opinions of the masses" and oppose "rule by the opinion of one man." In handling any major problem, the Party committee must practice democracy and allow its members present at its meeting to discuss the problem in full. When everyone airs his opinions, it is necessary to sum them up correctly, work out decisions or resolutions, and instruct the committee members or departments concerned to implement them. It is also essential to make sure that neither collective leadership nor personal responsibility is overemphasized to the neglect of the other. It is necessary to oppose the tendency for "the secretary to take everything into his hands, while the committee members act as his dependents" and "the situation in which everyone seems to be responsible and yet no one is actually responsible." Every committee member must have a strong sense of revolutionary responsibility and be brave in airing opinions in collective leadership, in assuming responsibility, and in doing well the job assigned to him.

Chairman Mao teaches us: "The Chinese Communist Party is the core of leadership of the whole Chinese people. Without this core, the cause of socialism cannot be victorious." The history of the Chinese revolution in the past fifty years shows that this precept of Chairman Mao's is correct. To bring the role of the Party as the vanguard of the proletariat into full play, Party committees at all levels must free themselves from certain concrete routine affairs and concentrate their energies on grasping crucial problems affecting the situation as a whole. First, they should grasp the education in ideology and political line, grasp the implementation of the Party's line, guidelines, and policies, and grasp class struggle and the work of consolidating the dictatorship of the proletariat. They should grasp the tendencies of a general nature and tendencies which are growing during a certain period of time, and so on. As the vanguard of the proletariat, the Party must, through its ideological, political and organization work, unite the working class, the poor and lower-middle peasants, and the broad masses of the people. It must be good at summing up the masses' creations and experiences and lead them to move forward. The Party organization will not be able to play its vanguard role effectively if it pays no attention to the line, does not rely on and unite with the masses, and fails to make a constant study of the conditions of the mass movement and class struggle or to rectify promptly wrong tendencies which run against the Party's line and the fundamental interests of the people. At no time should the comrades of the Party committee forget the role of the Party. The proletariat represents the interests of the broad masses of the people, and as the vanguard of the proletariat, the Party must uphold the proletarian Party spirit. Organizationally, the Party committee must "institute a sound system of Party committee meetings" and overcome the practice of calling meetings for "everything." Such a practice can easily cause us to confuse the relation between the Party committee and other organizations, between the leader and the led, and thereby weaken Party leadership.

As early as the period of the democratic revolution, Chairman Mao had said: "The unification and centralization of the leadership in a base area should find expression in the establishment of a Party committee which is unified and leads everything in each base area." By adhering to this principle, our Party has been leading the people of the whole country to win victories in the democratic revolution and socialist revolution. Under the unified leadership of the Party committee, a higher work department must and should exercise "line leadership" [tui-k'ou ling-tao] over a corresponding lower department. But if it bypasses the Party committee and makes its leadership absolute, the result will be "vertical leadership" [ch'ui-chih ling-tao] or "dictatorship along functional systems" [t'iao-t'iao chuan-cheng]. "There is only one needle below, but there are a thousand threads above" — this will not only cause confusion for the basic-level Party committees and make higher work departments exercise leadership to no purpose, but it will also impede the centralization and unity of our Party.

Chairman Mao teaches us: "In relaying to subordinate units any task (whether it concerns the revolutionary war, production, or education; the rectification movement, checkup on work, or the examination of cadres' histories; propaganda work, organizational work, or anti-espionage; or other work), a higher organization and its departments should in all cases go through the leader of the lower organization concerned so that he can assume responsibility. In this way both division of labor and unified, centralized leadership are achieved" ("Some Questions Concerning Methods of Leadership" [1943]). To oppose those practices which affect or weaken the unified leadership of the Party committee and to insist that the Party committee enforce "division of labor and centralized leadership" under unified leadership are basic ways of guaranteeing the implementation of Chairman Mao's revolutionary line, avoiding mutual isolations, and preventing the emergence of barriers in the middle. They are also important issues of organizational principle.

In view of the historical experiences of the struggle between the two lines, Chairman Mao has particularly reminded the comrades of the whole Party that: "In the struggle against deviations, we must give serious attention to opposing double-faced behavior. As Chang Kuo-t'ao's career shows, the greatest danger of such behavior is that it may develop into factional activity" ("The Role of the Chinese Communist Party in the National War" [1938]). The behavior of the double-faced elements is manifested in this way: They say one thing in public but do another in private; shake hands with people on the stage but kick them off the stage; approve decisions at a meeting but overthrow them afterward. Under socialist conditions, the handful of class enemies, daunted by the enormous power of the dictatorship of the proletariat, often resorts more to double-faced tactics and organizes counterrevolutionary conspiratorial cliques in a frenzied attempt to split the Party and restore capitalism. We can see through these counterrevolutionary double-faced elements if we "read and study seriously and have a good grasp of Marxism" and raise our consciousness of class struggle and the line struggle. We must vigorously raise our proletarian Party spirit, persist in the Party's principle, speak the truth and not tell lies, take the correct road and not the wrong one, put problems on the table, be open and aboveboard, and confirm words with deeds.

To strengthen the Party's unified leadership is an important task. Only when we overcome various wrong tendencies which weaken the Party's leadership function can we strengthen the Party's unity, increase the Party's fighting strength, and guarantee the implementation of Chairman Mao's revolutionary line. At present, the situation is excellent at home and abroad. We must unite to win still greater victories under the guidance of the line of the Ninth Party Congress and under the leadership of the Party's Central Committee headed by Chairman Mao!

32

GRASP MILITARY TRAINING ACCORDING TO
CHAIRMAN MAO'S LINE OF ARMY-BUILDING*

The Party Committee of a Certain PLA
Regiment Stationed in Peking

The great leader Chairman Mao instructs us: "The whole
Party must pay attention to war and study military affairs" and
"Improve the military art." A series of instructions by Chairman Mao on strengthening military training are an important
component of Chairman Mao's line of army-building and a fundamental guideline for improvement of military training and
for overall improvement of the fighting strength of the armed
forces. Only by carrying out strict training and setting strict
demands on the basis of Chairman Mao's army-building line
can we improve the political and military qualities of our army.

Chairman Mao has always emphasized the importance of
strengthening our army's ideological and political work, while
at the same time he has placed great stress on firmly grasping
military training under the command of politics. As early as
the time when our army was first founded, despite very difficult
circumstances and frequent battles, Chairman Mao still pointed
out that it was necessary to "try to avoid some battles in order
to find time for training." During the War of Resistance Against

*Chung-kuo jen-min chieh-fang-chün Pei-ching pu-tui mou
t'uan tang wei-hui, "An-chao Mao-chu-hsi chien-chün lu-hsien
chua-chin chün-shih hsün-lien," Hung-ch'i [Red Flag], No. 5
(May 1, 1972), 32-34.

Japan, Chairman Mao called on the whole Party to "pay attention to the study of military problems" and to "seek improvement in politics, organization, armament, technique, tactics,
and discipline." He stated: "Military consolidation and training
and political consolidation and training should be given equal
emphasis, and the two should be integrated." During the War
of Liberation, Chairman Mao again stressed: "Emphasis should
be put on military training during breaks in the fighting." After
the founding [of the Chinese People's Republic], Chairman
Mao again pointed out many times that only by undergoing strict
training and setting strict demands could the army fight. In
the past several decades, our armed forces have, in accordance
with Chairman Mao's teachings, strengthened political education, raised the consciousness of the line, firmly grasped military training, and improved the military art. [Because of this,
we have] succeeded in strengthening the overall fighting strength
of the armed forces, defeated vicious enemies of all kinds, and
fulfilled various fighting tasks entrusted to us by the Party and
the people.

Our army is armed with Marxism-Leninism-Mao Tse-
tung thought, and is a people's army led by Chairman Mao
and the Communist Party. It has a high level of consciousness
of class struggle, of the line struggle, and of continuing the
revolution under the proletarian dictatorship. It has the brave,
self-sacrificial spirit of fearing neither hardship nor death.
This is the decisive factor for the strong fighting power of our
army. Meanwhile, a fine military art is also one of the important factors for our army's fighting power. We must understand and master Chairman Mao's principles of strategy and
tactics, handle skillfully the weapons in our hands, flexibly apply various techniques, and be good both in offense and in defense, in marching and in fighting. [Only by doing so] can we
score a big victory at a small cost in battle. Strenuously opposing Chairman Mao's army-building line, Liu Shao-ch'i and
swindlers like him said such absurd things as: It was not so
serious to have a lower standard of military training; military
techniques should not be studied exclusively, for they could be

picked up quickly when they are needed; and so on. This is
naked resistance and betrayal of Chairman Mao's instruction
on strengthening military training. They attempted in vain to
negate the importance of military training, abolish military
training, and weaken our army's fighting strength. If these
fallacies are not criticized, they would interfere with the overall implementation of preparation against war. After our Party
committee has conscientiously studied Chairman Mao's series
of directives on strengthening political and military work,
it will understand that politics must be in command of and lead
military affairs, but it cannot replace military affairs. Preparation against war and training must absolutely not be based
on the standpoint of a "lower standard," but should be based on
that of "early preparation" and "incessant quest for perfection."
Improvement of military techniques is absolutely not given by
heaven; it can only be developed and cultivated from the practice of political and military training guided by the thought of
Mao Tse-tung. Therefore, military training cannot be relaxed,
but should be grasped and intensified persistently. With Chairman Mao's teachings as the weapon, we have criticized the
various fallacies spread by Liu Shao-ch'i and swindlers like
him. Under the guidance of Chairman Mao's proletarian line
of army-building, we have not only seriously conducted political
education but also seriously carried out military training.

In order to raise awareness of proper military training on
the part of the broad masses of cadres and fighters, we continue to conduct education in Chairman Mao's proletarian line
of army-building to deal with some comrades' muddled ideas.
In the course of training, we pay attention to drawing the following lines of distinction. One is the line between revolutionary heroism and championism. In military training, to work hard
to acquire the techniques for annihilating the enemy, to improve
the military quality of the armed forces, and to achieve good
records — all this should be encouraged and promoted. But
cultivating "superskills" for personal fame and material gain
should be opposed. If the idea of revolutionary heroism is also
opposed, the masses' activism for drilling will be undermined.

The second line is that between the preservation of necessary systems and formats and the promotion of "frills" and other formalistic things. All systems and formats that are compatible with actual war needs are summed up from practice and serve the content of training; they are indispensable. Those systems and formats which have been tested and found useful must not only be upheld but must also be firmly implemented repeatedly, while formalistic things incompatible with actual war needs must be criticized and eliminated. The third line is between the proper handling of advanced models and the haphazard presentation of "pacesetters." In the course of training, to grope for laws and to sum up and exchange experiences as a guide to overall training, we identify some advanced models, engage in needed evaluation and comparison, and make on-the-spot visits. This is a correct method of leadership. By emphasizing proper models, we can "light a lamp to illuminate a wide stretch" and provide cadres and fighters with an orientation for study and with an objective to achieve. This is fundamentally different from the practice of faking things, haphazardly summoning "pacesetters," and seeking "sensational surprises." The clarification of these demarcation lines will help cadres and fighters see clearly in training what is compatible with Chairman Mao's army-building line, and they should be upheld firmly. What runs counter to Chairman Mao's army-building line should be opposed in order to raise continuously their consciousness of good military training under the command of politics.

Chairman Mao has set up a series of guidelines, principles, and methods for our army's military training. They represent the scientific summing up of our army's combat and training experience over the past several decades. To train the army according to these guidelines, principles, and methods will enable us to improve the political and military quality of the armed forces. Liu Shao-ch'i and swindlers like him opposed Chairman Mao's guidelines, principles, and methods, undermined the glorious traditions of our military training, and interfered with and thwarted the firm implementation of Chairman

Mao's army-building line. In the course of intensifying military training, we have criticized black trash pushed by Liu Shao-ch'i and swindlers like him and trained the army strictly according to the guidelines, principles, and methods specified by Chairman Mao. We determine the content of a training program on the basis of actual war needs and teach cadres and fighters to "give first priority to improvement of the level of such techniques as shooting, bayonet charge, and hand-grenade throwing, and secondary priority to raising the level of tactics." Emphasis is placed on training in close combat and night fighting, swimming, and camping exercises; and the necessary time is set aside for systematic instruction ranging from single-soldier training to whole-battalion training. Concerning the methods of drilling, we follow Chairman Mao's teachings and widely promote military democracy by "unfolding a mass training movement where officers teach men, men teach officers, and men teach men." In every lesson of training, it is essential to arouse the masses to hold discussions in order to make everyone understand what and how to train and stick to the practice of "from the masses and to the masses" as a means of pooling the wisdom of the masses and improving the quality of training. We also pay attention to permeating the whole process of military training with Chairman Mao's military thinking, applying Chairman Mao's strategic and tactical principles to every military subject, combining learning with drilling, and deepening the understanding of Chairman Mao's military thinking through practice. For instance, when organizing companies to stage tactical exercises, we took them to Hsin-pao-an, the battlefield where the Thirty-Fifth Army of the Kuomintang was annihilated during the War of Liberation. There we conscientiously studied Chairman Mao's thesis: "Concentrate a superior force and annihilate the enemies one by one"; "select a relatively weak point (not two points) of the various battle positions of enemy troops and launch a fierce attack to conquer it without fail"; and so on. Leading comrades who had participated in that war were invited to recount the battle history, how our army applied Chairman Mao's strategic and

tactical principles to wiping out the enemy, and how their own
units, in accordance with Chairman Mao's teachings, chose the
attack spots and concentrated superior forces to launch a violent attack on the enemy and win the victory. Later, we organized the unit to stage tactical exercises in light of the combat
conditions in those years. Through the study of battles and
on-the-spot exercises, everyone acquired a deeper understanding of Chairman Mao's strategic and tactical principles
about concentration of superior forces in fighting battles of
annihilation, and both cadres and fighters have raised their
strategic and tactical levels.

In doing military training well in accordance with Chairman
Mao's army-building line, we must carry out strict training
and strict demands. Military affairs are a science. "There is
no flat and broad path in science." We must be prepared to
overcome great difficulties and work arduously. If we do not
experience strict training and strict demands and just try to
avoid work and find an easy way out, no real skills can be acquired. In time of war, fighting between the enemy and ourselves is very severe and complicated, and it becomes an overall test for the political and military quality of our army. If
we are a bit lax in peacetime training, then in fighting we cannot cope well with various complicated situations and will mud-
dle important things and will suffer a great deal. Only by imposing on ourselves strict training and strict demands without
any compromise can we really master military science and
improve our skills for defeating all enemies. In order to train
our army rigorously, we persist in training it in accordance
with how battles should be fought. Every crucial lesson of
combat techniques required by actual war needs must be practiced repeatedly. Conditions likely to appear in war should be
perceived in a more complicated way, so that more training
and exercises can be carried out for each situation and every
kind of terrain. For instance, once during a winter field-
camping exercise, the weather suddenly changed. Snow fell
heavily and the air temperature dropped to over thirty degrees
below zero. We took this as a very good opportunity for rigor-

ous training of our army, and we decided to organize the unit to make a long-distance "raid." We also arranged a training program in line with actual war needs. Fully equipped, the cadres and fighters of the whole regiment braved wind and snow, and marched 160 li nonstop for a day and night on a pla-teau 1,000-odd meters above sea level. During the march, var-ious tactical and technical maneuvers were attempted. Thus, the unit not only trained in the revolutionary spirit of fearing neither hardship nor death but also raised the level of its mil-itary techniques. The comrades said: "Though this kind of training is a bit tiring, we have received a rigorous tempering."

To grasp well military training in compliance with Chairman Mao's army-building line is an important task of the Party com-mittee. "The Party should give military work positive at-tention and discussions." If a perfunctory attitude is taken toward military training, the Party actually abandons its lead-ership over military work. We demand that every Party com-mittee member concern himself with military work, share his labor but not his household belongings, grasp military and po-litical affairs simultaneously, and strengthen energetically ideological and political work in the course of military training. To guarantee implementation of military training, our Party committee should make overall plans and unified arrangements for all items of work and make military training an important part of the Party committee's work plan, so as to ensure ef-fective leadership of the Party over military work. By doing so, we have [specific] arrangements for each plan, safeguards for its timetable, and personnel in charge of organization. [Work is] constantly studied and examined to make sure mil-itary training is effectively carried out. In the final analysis, whether or not military training is well grasped is a question of consciousness of the line. Only by raising consciousness of implementing Chairman Mao's proletarian line of army-building can we distinguish between right and wrong, eliminate interference from the "Left" or the Right, and consciously grasp military training for the consolidation of the proletarian dictatorship. We must firmly grasp the line as the key link and, through "reading and studying conscientiously and mastering Marxism-Leninism," we must strengthen education in ideology and the political line, incessantly raise the consciousness of the line struggle, do well in military training, and fight for the overall improvement of the fighting power of the armed forces.

Bibliography

Abbreviations

CB   Current Background
ECMM   Extracts from China Mainland Magazines
JPRS   Joint Publications Research Service
NCNA   New China News Agency
SCMM   Selections from China Mainland Magazines
SCMP   Survey of China Mainland Press

I.   Chinese Sources

Chang Kuo-chiang. Chung-kung chün-shih [Military Affairs
    of Communist China]. Taipei: Chung-yang kai-tsao wei-
    yüan-hui, n.d.

Chang Tso-hua. K'ang-Jih chün-tui chung ti cheng-chih kung-
    tso [Political Work in the Resistance Army]. Hankow:
    Shang-hai tsa-chih, 1938.

Chang Yü-sheng. Kung-fei kung-nung hung-chün chien-shih
    [A Concise History of the Red Army of Workers and
    Peasants of the Communist Bandits]. Taipei, 1962.

Chang Yün-t'ien. "Tui Chung-kung-chün chan-k'ai 'Hsiang-
    jen-min hsüeh-hsi' yün-tung ti fen-hsi" [An Analysis of
    the "Learn from the People" Movement of the Chinese
    Communist Army]. Chung-kung yen-chiu [Studies on
    Chinese Communism], VI: II (November 1972), 83-90.

Ch'en Ch'eng, comp. Ch'ih-fei fan-tung wen-chien hui-pien
    [A Collection of the Reactionary Documents of the Red
    Bandits]. Taipei: Chung-yang wen-wu, 1962.

Ch'en I. Pa jen-min chieh-fang-chün ti wen-i kung-tso t'i-kao i-pu [Raise Higher the Cultural and Artistic Work of the People's Liberation Army]. Peking: Jen-min wen-hsüeh, 1953.

Ch'en Wan-li. Pa-lu-chün ti chan-tou li [The Combat Strength of the Eighth Route Army]. Shanghai: Hsin Chung-kuo, 1938.

"Cheng-chih t'ung-shuai chün-shih, cheng-chih t'ung-shuai i-ch'ieh" [Politics Commands the Army, Politics Commands Everything]. Chieh-fang-chün pao [Liberation Army Daily], editorial, February 18, 1967.

Cheng-feng wen-hsien [Documents on Party Rectification]. Hong Kong: Hsin min-chu, 1949.

Chi P'eng. "Tui Lin Piao chi-t'uan cheng-pien kang-ling ti yen-hsi" [A Study of the Coup d'Etat Guidelines of the Lin Piao Group]. Chung-kung yen-chiu [Studies on Chinese Communism], VI: 6 (June 1972), 5-8.

————. "Chang-wo she-hui chu-i shih-ch'i chieh-chi tou-cheng ti kuei-lü" [Grasp the Law of Class Struggle in the Socialist Period]. Hung-ch'i [Red Flag], No. 8 (August 1972), 6-10.

Chiang Ch'ing. "Wei jen-min li hsin-kung" [Give New Meritorious Service to the People]. Chung-kung yen-chiu [Studies on Chinese Communism], IV: 6 (June 1970), 114-130.

Chiang I-shan. Chung-kung chün-shih wen-chien hui-pien [Source Book on Military Affairs in Communist China]. Hong Kong: Yu-lien, 1965.

————. "Chung-kung chün-tui ti cheng-chih kung-tso" [Political Work in the Chinese Communist Army]. Tsu-kuo [China Monthly], No. 18 (September 1965), 2-15.

————. "Chung-kung chün-tui hsüeh-hsi ch'üan-kuo jen-min ti huo-tung" [Activities of "Learn from the

People of the Whole Country" Among the PLA Units].
Tsu-kuo [China Monthly], No. 100 (July 1972), 19-23.

―――. "Chung-kung chün-tui ti cheng-pien yü fu-yüan" [The
Reorganization and Demobilization of the Chinese Communist Army]. Tsu-kuo [China Monthly], XIX: 11 (September 16, 1957), 16-18.

―――. "I-nien-lai Chung-kung chün-tui ti hsün-lien"
[The Training of the Chinese Military in the Past Year].
Tsu-kuo [China Monthly], No. 105 (December 1972), 9-12.

―――. "Kung-chün tang-wei-chih ti chin-hsi" [The Present
and Past of the Party Committee System in the Communist
Army]. Tsu-kuo [China Monthly], XXIV: 11 (December
15, 1958), 14-17.

―――. "Lin Piao tao-t'ai ch'ien-hou ti jen-min chieh-
fang-chün" [The PLA Before and After the Downfall of
Lin Piao]. Tsu-kuo [China Monthly], No. 101 (August
1972), 13-16.

―――. "Ts'ung ch'ih wei-tui tao ch'üan-min chieh-ping"
[From Red Guards to Everyone a Soldier]. Tsu-kuo
[China Monthly], XXIV: 13 (December 29, 1958), 13-15, 32.

"Chieh-fang-chün chin-i-pu fa-yang chi-chung ling-tao-hsia
ti san-ta min-chu" [Develop a Step Further the Three
Great Democracies Under Centralized Leadership in the
PLA]. Ta-kung pao, June 8, 1965.

"Chien-chüeh kuan-ch'e chih-hsing cheng-chih kung-tso t'iao-
li" [Resolutely and Thoroughly Carry Out the Political
Work Regulations]. Jen-min jih-pao [People's Daily],
May 10, 1963.

Chin-Ch'a-Chi chün-ch'ü cheng-chih-pu. Pa-lu-chün ho lao-
pai-hsing [The Eighth Route Army and the Common Peo-
ple]. N.p., 1946.

Chin-Chi-Lu-Yü chün-ch'ü cheng-chih-pu. Pu-tui tang-wei
kung-tso [Party Committee Work in the Army]. N.p., 1947.

Ching Ch'in. Chan-shih cheng-chih kung-tso [Wartime Political Work]. Shanghai: Shih-tai shih-liao pao-ts'un-she, 1938.

Chou Ching-wen. Mao Tse-tung ti chün-tui [The Army of Mao Tse-tung]. Hong Kong: Shih-tai, 1964.

Chu Teh. Lun chieh-fang-ch'ü chan-ch'ang [On the Battlefronts of the Liberated Areas]. N.p.: Chung-kuo ch'u-pan-she, 1946.

————. Lun yu-chi-chan [On Guerrilla Warfare]. Shanghai: Chien-she, 1938.

"Ch'üan-kuo min-ping cheng-chih kung-tso hui-i" [The Nationwide Conference on the Political Work of the Militia]. Jen-min jih-pao [People's Daily], November 17, 1964.

Chün-shih wei-yüan-hui wei-yüan-chang Nan-ch'ang hsing-yin ti-ssu-t'ing, comp. Ch'ih-fei wen-chien hui-pien [A Collection of the Documents of the Red Bandits]. 11 vols. N.p., 1933-1934.

Chung Hua-min. "Lin Piao shih-chien p'o-hsi" [An Analysis of the Lin Piao Case]. Tsu-kuo [China Monthly], No. 102 (September 1, 1972), 2-8.

"Chung-kung chung-yang chün-wei pa-t'iao ming-ling" [The Eight-Article Order of the Military Affairs Commission of the Central Committee]. Fei-ch'ing nien-pao [Yearbook on Chinese Communism], 1968, p. 588.

"Chung-kung chung-yang chün-wei shih-t'iao ming-ling" [The Ten-Article Order of the Military Affairs Commission of the Central Committee]. Fei-ch'ing nien-pao [Yearbook on Chinese Communism], 1968, pp. 591-592.

"Chung-kung chung-yang pan-pu 'Chung-kuo jen-min chieh-fang-chün cheng-chih kung-tso t'iao-li'" [The Central Committee of the Party Issues the Political Work Regulations of the Chinese People's Liberation Army]. Jen-min jih-pao [People's Daily], April 29, 1963.

Chung-kung nien-pao [Yearbook on Chinese Communism],
    1966-1970.

"Chung-kuo jen-min chieh-fang-chün ch'üan-chün cheng-chih
    kung-tso hui-i" [The All-Army Political Work Conference
    of the Chinese People's Liberation Army]. Jen-min jih-
    pao [People's Daily], March 6, 1963.

"Chung-kuo jen-min chieh-fang-chün ch'üan-chün cheng-chih
    kung-tso hui-i" [The All-Army Political Work Conference
    of the Chinese People's Liberation Army], Jen-min jih-
    pao [People's Daily], January 18, 1964.

"Chung-kuo kung-ch'an chu-i ch'ing-lien-t'uan lien-tui chih-
    pu kung-tso t'iao-li" [Regulations Concerning the Work
    of the Company Branch of the Chinese Communist Youth
    League]. Chung-kuo ch'ing-nien pao [China Youth News],
    November 24, 1961.

Chung-kuo kung-ch'an-tang k'ang-chan wen-hsien [Papers of
    the Chinese Communist Party on the War of Resistance].
    Hong Kong: Hung-mien, n.d.

Chung-kuo kung-nung hung-chün cheng-chih kung-tso chan-
    hsing t'iao-li (Ts'ao-an) [Draft Provisional Political Work
    Regulations for the Chinese Red Army of Workers and
    Peasants]. N.p., 1932.

Chung-kuo kuo-min-tang chung-yang ti-liu-tsu, comp. Fei-
    chün cheng-chih kung-tso chih-tu ti yen-chiu [A Study of
    the Political Work System of the Bandit Army].
    Taipei, 1957.

————. Kung-fei chung-yao tzu-liao hui-pien [A Collection
    of Important Materials on the Communist Bandits]. 16
    vols. Taipei: Chung-yang wen-wu, 1952.

Fei-chün cheng-chih kung-tso t'iao-li [The Political Work
    Regulations for the Bandit Army]. Taipei: Kuo-fang-pu
    ch'ing-pao-chü, 1965.

Hai Feng. "I-chiu-ch'i-i nien ti Chung-kung tang-wu" [Communist China's Party Affairs in 1971]. Tsu-kuo [China Monthly], No. 100 (July 1972), 2-11.

Ho Lung. "Chung-kuo jen-min chieh-fang-chün ti min-chu ch'uan-t'ung" [The Democratic Tradition of the Chinese People's Liberation Army]. Hung-ch'i [Red Flag], No. 8 (1965), 1-15.

Hou Mi. Chung-kung tsen-yang tui-tai fu-lu [How the Chinese Communists Treat Prisoners of War]. Hong Kong: Yu-lien, 1953.

Hsiao Hua. "Hsiang-cho hsien-tai-hua mai-chin ti Chung-kuo jen-min chieh-fang-chün" [The PLA Marches Toward Modernization]. Hsin-Hua yüeh-pao [New China Monthly], (August 1952), 6-9.

————. "I Mao Tse-tung ssu-hsiang wei chih-chen cho huo-ti ssu-hsiang chiao-yü [Use Mao Tse-tung's Thought as the Guiding Compass to Carry Out Living Ideological Education]. Jen-min jih-pao [People's Daily], November 15, 1961.

————. "Liang-nien-lai chün-tui ch'uang-tsao ssu-hao lien-tui ti chi-pen ching-yen" [Basic Experience in Creating Four-Good Companies in the Army in the Past Two Years]. Jen-min jih-pao [People's Daily], April 1, 1963.

————. "Mu-ch'ien pu-tui cheng-chih kung-tso chien-she ti chi-ko wen-t'i" [Some Problems in the Army's Political Work and Construction at the Present Time]. Chung-kuo ch'ing-nien pao [China Youth News], January 23, 1964.

————. "P'ei-yang san-pa tso-feng shih wo-chün chien-she ti chung-yao jen-wu" [To Cultivate the Three-Eight Work Style Is an Important Task of Our Army-Building]. Jen-min jih-pao [People's Daily], May 24, 1960.

————. "Wo-chün chih-chan-yüan tsen-yang hsüeh-hsi Mao Tse-tung chu-tso [How Commanders in Our Army Should

Study the Writings of Mao Tse-tung]. Hung-ch'i [Red Flag], No. 10 (May 1964), 27-34.

Hsin Chung-k'o. Kung-fei wu-chuang chien-she chih yen-chiu [A Study of the Army-Building of the Communist Bandits]. Taipei: Yang-ming-shan chuang, 1957.

Hsüan Mo. "Lin Piao Ch'en Po-ta lien-ho fan Mao fen-hsi" [An Analysis of the Joint Anti-Mao Activities Led by Lin Piao and Ch'en Po-ta]. Chung-kung yen-chiu [Studies on Chinese Communism] VI:7 (July 1972), 4-14.

"Hsüeh-hsi ho chih-ch'ih jen-min kung-she" [Study and Support the People's Communes]. Chieh-fang-chün pao [Liberation Army Daily], August 22, 1958.

"Hsüeh-hsi ho fa-yang jen-min chieh-fang-chün ti min-chu ch'uan-t'ung" [Learn and Develop the Democratic Tradition of the People's Liberation Army]. Jen-min jih-pao [People's Daily], editorial, June 8, 1965.

Hung-ch'i p'iao-p'iao pien-chi pu, comp. Chieh-fang chan-cheng hui-i-lu [Reminiscences of the War of Liberation]. Peking: Chung-kuo ch'ing-nien, 1961.

Jen-min chieh-fang-chün tsung-pu. Chung-kuo jen-min chieh-fang chan-cheng chün-shih wen-chi [A Collection of Military Documents on the Liberation War of the Chinese People]. 6 vols. N.p., 1951.

"K'ai-chan ch'un-chieh yung-cheng ai-min huo-tung yao-ch'iu ch'üan-chün ta-li chih-yüan nung-yeh" [Spread the "Support-the Government and Love-the-People" Movement During the Spring Festival, and Call Upon the Whole Army to Support Agriculture in a Big Way]. Jen-min jih-pao [People's Daily], February 2, 1961.

"Kan-tang jen-min ch'ün-chung ti hsiao-hsüeh-sheng" [Be Willing to Be Pupils of the Masses]. Hung-ch'i [Red Flag], No. 2 (February 1, 1972), 87-89.

"Kao chü Mao Tse-tung ssu-hsiang ti wei-ta hung-ch'i chien-chüeh kuan-ts'e chih-hsing cheng-chih kung-tso t'iao li"

[Raise High the Banner of Mao Tse-tung's Thought and Carry Out Thoroughly the Political Work Regulations]. Chieh-fang-chün pao [Liberation Army Daily], editorial, May 8, 1963.

"Kuan-yü chün-tui ch'an-chia ho chih-yüan nung-yeh ho-tso-hua yün-tung chi nung-yeh sheng-ch'an ti shih-shih fang-an" [The Plan for Implementing the Army's Participation in and Support of Agricultural Cooperativization Movement and Agricultural Production]. Jen-min jih-pao [People's Daily], February 9, 1956.

"Kuan-yü 'chung-yang chih-tso pu-tui' chin-chu ko-ta-chün-ch'ü sheng-chün-ch'ü ti jo-kan chih-shih" [Some Instructions Concerning the Dispatching of the "Central Support-the-Left Forces" to Various Military Regions and Provincial Military Districts]. Chung-kung nien-pao [Yearbook on Chinese Communism], 1969, Section VII, pp. 39-41.

"Kuan-yü Nan-ching-lu shang hao-pa-lien cheng-chih ssu-hsiang kung-tso ching-yen ti chieh-shao" [Introduce the Experience in Political and Ideological Work of the Good Eighth Company on Nanking Road]. Chung-kuo ch'ing-nien pao [China Youth News], May 14, 1963.

Kung-fei "Min-ping she-hui chu-i chiao-yü chiao-ts'ai" ["Socialist Education Teaching Materials for the Militia" of the Communist Bandits]. Taipei, 1964.

Kung-fei wen-hua ta-ko-ming chung-yao wen-chien [Important Documents on the Great Cultural Revolution of the Communist Bandits]. 2 vols. Taipei: Kuo-fang-pu ch'ing-pao-chü, 1969.

Kung-tso t'ung-hsün [Bulletin of Activities], January-August 1961.

Kuo-fang-pu ch'ing-pao-chü. Fei min-ping cheng-chih chiao-ts'ai "Tsen-yang tang-ko hao min-ping" [Political Teaching Materials for the Bandit Militia: "How to Be a Good Militia"]. Taipei, 1966.

Kuo-min cheng-fu chu-hsi Wu-han hsing-yüan ti-erh-ch'u. Chien-fei chung-yao wen-chien hui-pien [A Collection of Important Documents of the Traitors and Bandits]. N.p., 1947.

Kuo-min cheng-fu chün-shih wei-yüan-hui wei-yüan-chang Nan-ch'ang hsing-ying ti-ssu-ting. Ch'ih-fei wen-chien hui-pien [A Collection of Red Bandit Documents]. 11 vols. N.p., 1934.

Kuo-min ko-ming-chün ti-shih-pa chi-t'uan-chün cheng-chih-pu, comp. Chung-kuo kuo-min ko-ming-chün ti-shih-pa chi-t'uan-chün (ti-pa-lu-chün) cheng-chih kung-tso t'iao-li (Ts'ao-an) [Draft: Political Work Regulations for the Eighteenth Group Army (Eighth Route Army) of the Chinese National Revolutionary Army]. N.p.: Chiao-tung Hsin-Hua, 1940.

Li Kuang. Hung-chün shih tsen-yang tuan-lien ti [How the Red Army Is Trained]. Canton: K'ang-Jih hsün-k'an, 1938.

"Liang-i san-ch'a chiao-yü yün-tung tsung-chieh pao-kao" [The Summing-Up Report on the "Two-Remembrances and Three-Investigations" Education Movement]. Kung-tso t'ung-hsün [Bulletin of Activities], 15 (April 5, 1961).

Lien-tui cheng-chih kung-tso ching-yen [Political Work Experience in Company-Level Units]. Shanghai: Shang-hai jen-min, 1965.

Lien-tui kuan-li chiao-yü kung-tso [Management and Educational Work in the Company]. Shanghai: Shang-hai jen-min, 1965.

Lin Piao. Lin fu-chu-hsi chün-shih chu-tso hsüan-tu [Selected Military Writings of Vice Chairman Lin]. N.p., n.d.

———. "Shen-ju lien-tui chia-ch'iang ssu-hsiang kung-tso" [Go Deep into the Company-Level Units to Strengthen Ideological Work]. Jen-min jih-pao [People's Daily], October 8, 1960.

————. "Tsai Chung-kuo kung-ch'an-tang ti-chiu-tz'u ch'üan-kuo tai-piao ta-hui-shang ti pao-kao" [Report at the Ninth Congress of the CCP]. Hung-ch'i [Red Flag], No. 5 (May 1, 1969), 7-48.

Lin Piao chuan-chi [Special Collection on Lin Piao]. Hong Kong: Chung-kuo wen-t'i yen-chiu chung-hsin, 1970.

Lin Piao shih-chien yen-hsi [Analysis of the Lin Piao Affair]. Taipei: Kuo-min-tang ti-liu-tsu, 1972.

"Lin Piao t'ung-chih tui pu-tui kuan-li chiao-yü kung-tso ti ssu-t'iao chih-shih" [Comrade Lin Piao's Four-Point Directive on the Management and Education Work of the Armed Forces]. Kung-tso t'ung-hsün [Bulletin of Activities], March 29, 1961.

Liu Chih-chien. "Chia-ch'iang pu-tui ch'ing-nien ti ssu-hsiang cheng-chih chiao-yü p'ei-yang yu-hung yu-chuan ti chieh-pan-jen" [Strengthen the Ideological and Political Work of the Youth in the Army and Cultivate Revolutionary Successors of Red and Expert]. Chung-kuo ch'ing-nien pao [China Youth News], May 3, 1961.

Lo Jui-ch'ing. K'ang-Jih chün-tui chung ti cheng-chih kung-tso [Political Work in the Anti-Japanese Military Forces]. N.p.: Chung-kuo wen-hua she, 1939.

Lo Jung-huan. "Chi-hsü fa-yang wo-chün ti kuang-jung ch'uan-t'ung" [Continue to Develop the Glorious Tradition of Our Army]. Jen-min jih-pao [People's Daily], August 1, 1955.

"Lu-hai-k'ung san-chün ta-li chih-yüan kang-t'ieh sheng-ch'an" [The Three Armed Forces of Army, Navy, and Air Force Support Steel Production in a Big Way]. Jen-min jih-pao [People's Daily], September 21, 1958.

Mao Tse-tung. Chung-kuo kung-ch'an-tang hung-chün ti-ssu-chün ti-chiu-tz'u tai-piao ta-hui chüeh-i-an [Resolution of the Ninth Party Congress of the Fourth Army]. Hong Kong: Hsin-min-chu, 1949.

————. [Collection of Statements by Mao Tse-tung, 1956-67; a Red Guard publication]. N.p., 1967; partly translated in JPRS, No. 52029 (1970).

————. Mao chu-hsi wen-hsüan [Selected Writings of Chairman Mao, 1959-1967]. N.p., n.d., a Red Guard publication; translated in JPRS, Nos. 49826 and 50792 (1970).

————. Mao chu-hsi yü-lu [Quotations from Chairman Mao]. Peking: Jen-min, 1966; published in English as Quotations from Chairman Mao Tse-tung. Peking: Foreign Languages Press, 1966.

————. Mao Tse-tung chi [Collected Writings of Mao Tse-tung]. 10 vols. Tokyo: Hokubō sha, 1971-72.

————. Mao Tse-tung ssu-hsiang wan-sui [Long Live Mao Tse-tung Thought]. N.p., 1967.

Min-ping chi-pen chih-shih [Basic Knowledge for the Militia]. Peking: K'o-hsüeh p'u-chi, 1958.

Min-ping chün-shih hsün-lien shou-ts'e [Manual of the Military Training of the Militia]. Peking: Chung-kuo ch'ing-nien, 1959.

Pa-lu-chün cheng-chih-pu. Chung-kuo ti-hou k'ang-Jih min-chu keng-chü-ti kai-k'uang [The Condition of the Anti-Japanese Democratic Bases Behind Enemy Lines in China]. N.p.: Hsin-Hua, 1944.

Pa-lu-chün lien-fang cheng-chih-pu. Pu-tui lao-tung ying-hsiung ti tai-piao [The Representatives of the Army's Labor Heroes]. N.p., 1944.

————. Sheng-ch'an, yung-ai ho hsüeh-hsi [Production, Support, Love and Study]. N.p., 1944.

————. Fa-chan sheng-ch'an yung-cheng ai-min wen-hsien chi [A Collection of Documents on Advancing Production and on Supporting the Government and Loving the People]. N.p., 1944.

Pa-lu-chün liu-shou ping-t'uan. Sheng-ch'an ching-yen t'an [Discussions on Production Experiences]. N.p., 1944.

Pa-lu-chün liu-shou ping-t'uan cheng-chih-pu. I-nien lai ti yung-cheng ai-min kung-tso [The Support-the-Government and Love-the-People Work of the Past Year]. N.p., 1944.

————. Wei feng-i chu-shih erh tou-cheng [Struggle for Sufficient Clothing and Food]. N.p., 1943.

"Pa wo-chün pan-ch'eng Mao Tse-tung ssu-hsiang ti ta-hsüeh-hsiao" [Turn Our Army into a Great School of Mao Tse-tung's Thought]. Chieh-fang-chün pao [Liberation Army Daily], editorial, August 1, 1966.

Pei-yüeh-ch'ü jen-min wu-chuang-pu. Min-ping cheng-chih chiao-ts'ai [Political Teaching Materials for the Militia]. N.p., 1944.

"Pu-tui kan-pu tang-ping ti ko-ming i-i" [The Revolutionary Significance of Having Army Cadres Work as Privates]. Jen-min jih-pao [People's Daily], November 8, 1958.

San-pa tso-feng [Three-Eight Work Style]. Shanghai: Shanghai jen-min, 1965.

"Shang-yeh pu-men yeh-yao hsüeh-hsi chieh-fang-chün" [Commerce Departments Should Also Learn from the Liberation Army]. Jen-min jih-pao [People's Daily], editorial, February 20, 1964.

Shih Ch'eng-chih. Lun Chung-kung ti chün-shih fa-chan [On the Development of the Chinese Communist Military]. Hong Kong: Yu-lien, 1952.

"Shu-wan chün-tui kan-pu chiang ch'an-chia cheng-she" [Tens of Thousands of Military Cadres Are to Participate in the Adjustment of Communes]. Jen-min jih-pao [People's Daily], December 24, 1958.

Ta-chung jih-pao-she. Min-ping kung-tso shou-ts'e [Handbook on Militia Work]. N.p., 1942.

Tai Fu. Jen-min ho chün-tui [The People and the Army].
Shanghai: Shang-hai tsa-chih, 1950.

T'an Cheng. "Chien-she hsin-chieh-tuan chung cheng-chih
kung-tso ti jo-kan wen-t'i" [Some Problems of Political
Work During the New Stage of Construction]. Jen-min
shou-ts'e [People's Handbook], 1957, pp. 102-106.

T'ao Chu. "Kuan-yü pu-tui cheng-chih wen-hua cheng-hsün
wen-t'i" [Concerning the Question of Political and Cultural
Training in Military Units]. Ch'ang-chiang jih-pao
[Yangtze Daily], April 4, 1950.

Ti-shih-pa chi-t'uan-chün tsung-cheng-chih-pu hsüan-ch'uan-
pu. Chung-kuo chieh-fang-ch'ü chan-ch'ang shang ti min-
ping [The People's Militia in the Combat Zones of China's
Liberated Areas]. Peking: Chieh-fang jih-pao she, 1945.

Ti-shih-pa chi-t'uan-chün tsung-cheng-chih-pu hsüan-ch'uan-
pu, comp. Chün-min kuan-hsi [Army-People Relations].
Shanghai: Shang-hai tsa-chih, 1949.

————. K'ang-chan pa-nien lai ti pa-lu-chün yü hsin-ssu-
chün [The Eighth Route Army and the New Fourth Army
During the Eight Years of the War of Resistance].
N.p., 1945.

————. Kuan-ping kuan-hsi [Officer-Men Relations]. Shanghai: Shang-hai tsa-chih, 1949.

————. Ling-tao tso-feng [Style of Leadership]. Shanghai:
Shang-hai tsa-chih, 1949.

————. Ti-hou chan-ch'ang shang ti min-ping [The Militia
Behind Enemy Lines and in the Battlefield]. N.p., 1945.

Ting Li. "Lun Chung-kung ti ping-i-fa ts'ao-an yü chün-kuan
fu-i t'iao-li" [On the Draft Conscription Law and the Regulations on the Service of Officers of Communist China].
Tsu-kuo [China Monthly], IX: 12 (March 21, 1955), 13-14.

"Tsai lien-tui chin-hsing nung-yeh fa-chan kang-yao chiao-yü"

[To Carry Out the Education of the Outline of Agricultural Development at the Company Level]. Chieh-fang-chün pao [Liberation Army Daily], June 12, 1958.

"Tsai she-hui chu-i chiao-yü yün-tung chung chia-ch'iang min-ping chien-she" [Strengthen the Militia Construction Through the Socialist Education Movement]. Jen-min jih-pao [People's Daily], editorial, November 17, 1964.

Ts'ao Ch'ih-ch'in. "Kuan-yü Lin Piao fan-Mao cheng-pien yen-hsi" [An Analysis of Lin Piao's Coup Against Mao]. Fei-ch'ing yüeh-pao [Chinese Communist Affairs Monthly], XV: 3 (May 1972), 12-17.

"Tsen-yang t'u-ch'u cheng-chih" [How to Give Politics Prominence]. Chieh-fang-chün pao [Liberation Army Daily], editorial, February 22, 1965.

Tsung-cheng-chih-pu hsüan-ch'uan-pu, comp. Ling-tao tso-feng [Style of Leadership]. Shanghai: Shang-hai tsa-chih, 1951.

"Tsung-cheng-chih-pu pan-pu lien-tui cheng-chih kung-tso ssu-ko t'iao-li" [The General Political Department Issued Four Sets of Political Work Regulations for the Company-Level Units]. Jen-min jih-pao [People's Daily], November 22, 1962.

"Tsung-cheng fa-ch'u chün-tui ch'an-chia chien-she kung-tso kang-yao" [The General Political Department Issued the Outline for the Army's Participation in Construction Work]. Jen-min jih-pao [People's Daily], February 26, 1959.

"Tsung-cheng kung-pu hsin-ti wu-hao chan-shih t'iao-chien" [The General Political Department Issued the New Criteria of the Five-Good Fighter]. Chung-kuo ch'ing-nien pao [China Youth News], November 30, 1961.

Wang Chia-hsiang et al. Cheng-chih kung-tso lun-ts'ung [Discussions on Political Work]. N.p.: Pa-lu-chün-cheng tsa-chih-she, 1941.

Wang Chien-min. Chung-kuo kung-ch'an-tang shih-kao [History of the Chinese Communist Party]. 3 vols. Taipei: Hsien-ping yin-shua-ch'ang, 1965.

Wang Hsiang-li. Jen-min ti chün-tui [The People's Army]. N.p.: Kuang-hua shu-tien, 1948.

"Wu-ch'an chieh-chi pi-hsü lao-lao chang-wo ch'iang-kan-tzu" [The Proletarian Class Must Firmly Control the Gun]. Hung-ch'i [Red Flag], No. 12 (August 1, 1967), 43-47.

Wu Yün-kuang. "Chung-kung-chün cheng-chih kung-tso ti san-ko shih-ch'i" [The Three Periods of the Chinese Communist Army's Political Work]. Fei-ch'ing yen-chiu [Studies on Chinese Communism], I:4 (April 30, 1967), 29-71.

———. "I-chiu-ch'i-erh-nien ti Chung-kung chün-shih" [The Chinese Communist Military Affairs in 1972]. Chung-kung yen-chiu [Studies on Chinese Communism], VII:1 (January 1973), 32-46.

Yin Ch'ing-yao. "Jen-min chün-tui" [People's Army]. Fei-ch'ing yüeh-pao [Chinese Communist Affairs Monthly], XV: 12 (February 1973), 66-71.

"Yung-cheng ai-min chih-yüan sheng-ch'an ta-yao-chin" [Support the Government, Love the People, and Support the Great Leap Forward in Production]. Jen-min jih-pao [People's Daily], editorial, February 19, 1958.

"Yung-yüan t'u-ch'u cheng-chih" [Always Give Politics Prominence]. Chieh-fang-chün pao [Liberation Army Daily], editorial, February 3, 1967.

II. Japanese Sources

"Bōchō suru Chūkyō jimmin busōtai" [The Expanding Chinese Communist People's Militia]. Tairiku, I:3 (March 1952), 25-31.

Chūgoku Kenkyū geppō [Monthly Research Report on China,

Tokyo], Nos. 261-262 (November-December 1969). Special issues on writings of Lin Piao, part I-II. Translated in Translations on Communist China, No. 102, JPRS, 50477 (May 7, 1970).

Fukada Yūzō. Shina kyōsangun no gensei [The Present Condition of the Chinese Communist Army]. Tokyo: Kaizōsha, 1939.

Hatano Ken'ichi. Sekishoku Shina no kyūmei [An Investigation of Red China]. Tokyo: Daitō shuppansha, 1941.

————, comp. Chūgoku kyōsantō shi [History of the Chinese Communist Party]. 7 vols. Tokyo: Jiji tsūshin sha, 1961.

Izaki Kiyota. "Chūkyōgun ni okeru seijibu seido ni tsuite" [On the Political System in the Chinese Communist Army]. Tairiku mondai, II: 9 (September 1953), 42-51; and II: 10 (October 1953), 37-47.

Kawai Kazuo. "Sekigun junen shi" [Ten-Year History of the Red Army]. Hankyō sōsho, 13 (March 1940), 48-67; 14 (April 1940), 64-89; and 15 (May 1940).

Kōain Kahoku renrakubu. Kaisan made no shinshigun [The New Fourth Army to the Time of Its Dispersal]. Shanghai, 1941.

Kōain Seimukyoku. "Kyōsangun nai ni okeru seiji kunren" [Political Training Within the Communist Army]. Jōhō, 10 (January 15, 1940), 65-87.

————. "Shinshigun no seiji kōsaku soshiki kōyō sōan" [The New Fourth Army's Draft Outline of the Organization of Political Work]. Jōhō, 43 (June 1, 1941), 19-45.

"Mimpeisei no kenkyū" [Study of the Militia System]. Tairiku mondai, IX: 8 (August 1960), 4-15.

Minami Manshū tetsudō kabushiki kaisha chōsabu. Daihachirogun oyobi shimpen daiyongun ni kansuru shiryō [Materials on the Eighth Route Army and the Newly Organized Fourth Army]. Dairen, 1939.

Mō Takutō bunken shiryō kenkyūkai, comp. Mō Takutō shū [Collected Writings of Mao Tse-tung]. 10 vols. Tokyo: Hokubō sha, 1971-1972.

Nakajima Mineo. "Mō Takutō mikōkai jūyō shiryō" [Important Unpublished Materials by Mao Tse-tung]. Chū kōron, 7 (July 1969), 351-400; 8 (August 1969), 209-235.

Nihon gaiji kyōkai, comp. Shina ni okeru kyōsan undō [The Communist Movement in China]. Tokyo: Nihon gaiji kyokai, n.d.

Ōtsuka Reizō. Shina sekishoku seiryoku no gendankai [The Present Strength of China's Red Forces]. Dairen: Mantetsu, 1936.

Suzue Gen'ichi. "Shina sekigun no gensei to kongo no hatten" [The Present Situation and the Future Development of the Chinese Red Army]. Kaizō, XII: 9 (September 1930), 49-57.

Tōa keizai chosakyoku. "Kyōsantō Shin-Satsu-Ki henku seifu to guntai oyobi minshu dantai to no kankei" [The Communist Party's Chin-Ch'a-Chi Border Region Government and Army and Their Relation to the Mass Organization]. Tōa, XII: 1 (January 1939), 35-56.

————. Shina sovieto undō no kenkyū [A Study of the Chinese Soviet Movement]. Tokyo: n.d.

III. Sources and Works in English

"Against One-Sided Emphasis on Modernization." Chieh-fang-chün pao [Liberation Army Daily], editorial, August 17, 1958; translated in JPRS, No. 6471 (1959).

"Army Cadres and Local Cadres Learn from Each Other and Advance Together Under the Guidance of the Line of Unity and Victory of the Ninth Party Congress." Jen-min jih-pao [People's Daily], January 18, 1972; translated in SCMP, No. 5065 (1972).

"Army Cadres Should Humbly Learn from the Local Cadres and the People." Jen-min jih-pao [People's Daily], January 2, 1972; translated in SCMP, No. 5054 (1972).

"Armymen, Workers and Cadres in North China Region Learn from Each Other." NCNA-English, Shih-chia-chuang, January 20, 1972; in SCMP, No. 5066 (1972).

Asia Research Center, comp. The Great Cultural Revolution in China. Tokyo: Tuttle, 1968.

Barnett, A. Doak. China After Mao. Princeton: Princeton University Press, 1967.

————, ed., Chinese Communist Politics in Action. Seattle and London: University of Washington Press, 1969.

Bobrow, Davis B. "The Civic Role of the Military: Some Critical Hypotheses." Western Political Quarterly, XIX (March 1966), 101-111.

————. "The Good Officer: Definition and Training." The China Quarterly, 18 (April-June 1964), 141-152.

————. "Peking's Military Calculus." World Politics, XVI:2 (January 1964), 287-301.

————. "The Political and Economic Role of the Military in the Chinese Communist Movement, 1927-1959" (Ph.D. thesis, Massachusetts Institute of Technology, 1962).

"Break with One-Sided Military View and Promote Political Work." Chieh-fang-chün pao [Liberation Army Daily], June 16, 1958; translated in JPRS, No. 10343 (1959).

Bridgham, Philip. "Mao's Cultural Revolution." The China Quarterly, 29 (January-March 1967), 1-35.

Brohm, John F. Lessons for Civic Action: The Experience of the People's Liberation Army. Washington, D.C.: Bureau for the Far East, Agency for International Development, 1962.

"Campaign for Enrollment in Military Cadre Institutions Concluded." NCNA, February 1, 1951; translated in SCMP, No. 62 (1951).

CCP Documents of the Great Proletarian Cultural Revolution, 1966-1967. Hong Kong: Union Research Institute, 1968.

Chang, Parris H. "The Changing Patterns of Military Participation in Chinese Politics." ORBIS, XVI: 3 (Fall 1972), 780-802.

————. "Mao's Great Purge." Problems of Communism, 18 (March-April 1969), 1-10.

Charles, David A. "The Dismissal of Marshal P'eng Teh-huai." The China Quarterly, 8 (October-December 1961), 63-76.

Chen, Kuang-shen. Lei Feng, Chairman Mao's Good Fighter. Peking: Foreign Languages Press, 1968.

Ch'en, Po-ta. Notes on Ten Years of Civil War: 1927-1936. Peking: Foreign Languages Press, 1954.

Ch'en, Tsai-tao. "Army Officers, Upholding their Fine Tradition, Go to the Companies to Serve as Privates," Jen-min jih-pao [People's Daily], April 27, 1959; translated in CB, No. 579 (1959).

Cheng, J. Chester, ed. The Politics of the Chinese Red Army. Stanford: Hoover Institution, 1965.

————. "Problems of Chinese Communist Leadership as Seen in the Secret Military Papers." Asian Survey, IV:6 (June 1964), 861-872.

"Chieh-fang-chün pao Editorial on Class Struggle on Literature and Art Front." NCNA-English, Peking, May 23, 1967; in SCMP, No. 3946 (1967).

"Chinese Army Daily Acclaims Summary of the Forum on Literature and Art." NCNA-English, Peking, May 29, 1967; in SCMP, No. 3951 (1967).

"Chinese Army Unit Combines Political Education with Military Training." NCNA-English, Tsinan, April 2, 1972; in SCMP, No. 5113 (1972).

"Chinese Armymen Help in Construction Work." NCNA, February 4, 1962; translated in SCMP, No. 2682 (1962).

"Chinese Armymen on Revolutionary Literature and Art." NCNA-English, Peking, February 6, 1968; in SCMP, No. 4114 (1968).

Chinese Law and Government, V: 3-4 (Fall-Winter 1972-73). Special Issue on "The Case Against Lin Piao."

"Chinese PLA Makes New Progress in Farming." NCNA-English, Peking, February 2, 1972; in SCMP, No. 5075 (1972).

"Chinese PLA Makes Remarkable Achievements in Agricultural and Sideline Production." NCNA-English, Peking, January 13, 1967; in SCMP, No. 3862 (1967).

Chiu, Sin-ming. "Chinese Communist Military Leadership." Military Review, XXXIX:12 (March 1960), 59-66.

————. "A History of the Chinese Communist Army" (Ph.D. thesis, University of Southern California, 1958).

————. "Political Control in the Chinese Communist Army." Military Review, XLI: 8 (August 1961), 25-35.

Chu, Teh. The Battle Front of the Liberated Areas. Peking: Foreign Languages Press, 1955.

"Commanding Cadres of PLA Live and Work in Combat Units." NCNA, July 28, 1960; translated in SCMP, No. 2317 (1960).

Communist China: Ruthless Enemy or Paper Tiger? A Bibliographic Survey. Washington, D.C.: Headquarters, Department of the Army, March 6, 1962.

Compton, Boyd, ed. Mao's China: Party Reform Documents, 1942-1944. Seattle: University of Washington Press, 1952.

"Conscientiously Apply Democratic Centralism, Strengthen Collective Leadership by Party Committee." Kuang-ming jih-pao [Bright Daily], February 7, 1972; translated in SCMP, No. 5080 (1972).

"Country-Wide Upsurge in Supporting and Learning from the PLA." NCNA-English, Peking, February 6, 1970; in SCMP, No. 4597 (1970).

"Discuss Line Education Every Day and Pass on Revolutionary Traditions from Generation to Generation." Jen-min jih-pao [People's Daily], December 24, 1971; translated in SCMP, No. 5050 (1972).

"Do Good Propaganda Work Outside the Army." Chieh-fang-chün pao [Liberation Army Daily], May 18, 1958; translated in JPRS, No. 10239 (1959).

Domes, Jurgen. "The Role of the Military in the Formation of Revolutionary Committees, 1967-1968." The China Quarterly, 44 (October-December 1970), 112-145.

Fan, Ke. "The Orientation of Political Work for the Army." Jen-min jih-pao [People's Daily], July 28, 1961; translated in SCMP, No. 2556 (1961).

Fang, Chün-kuei. "Military Dictatorship Under Mao's Regime. Issues & Studies, VIII: 1 (October 1971), 23-37.

"Fine Models of Revolutionary Literature and Art." NCNA-English, Peking, May 31, 1967; in SCMP, No. 3952 (1967).

"Forge Bravely Ahead Along Chairman Mao's Army-Building Road." Jen-min jih-pao [People's Daily], January 11, 1972; translated in SCMP, No. 5062 (January 26, 1972), 87-93.

"Four Sets of Regulations on Political Work in Company-Level Units of the PLA Promulgated for Enforcement." NCNA, November 21, 1961; translated in SCMP, No. 2630 (1961).

"From the Defeat of Peng Teh-huai to the Bankruptcy of

China's Khruschov." Peking Review, No. 34 (August 18, 1967), 18-21.

Fu, Chung. "Achievements Made by the Armed Forces in Support of Socialist Construction." Jen-min jih-pao [People's Daily], April 6, 1960; translated in CB, No. 624 (1960).

Garvey, James E. Marxist-Leninist China: Military and Social Doctrine. New York: Exposition Press, 1960.

"General Political Department Notifies Units to Study the Five Documents in Earnest." Chieh-fang-chün pao [Liberation Army Daily], July 19, 1956; translated in Union Research Service, VI: 6 (January 18, 1957).

"General Training Supervisory Department Vigorously Studies the Five Documents." Chieh-fang-chün pao [Liberation Army Daily], August 28, 1956; translated in Union Research Service, VI: 6 (January 18, 1957).

George, Alexander. The Chinese Communist Army in Action. New York: Columbia University Press, 1967.

Gittings, John. "China's Militia." The China Quarterly, 18 (April-June 1964), 100-117.

———. "The 'Learn from the Army' Campaign." The China Quarterly, 18 (April-June 1964), 153-159.

———. "Military Control and Leadership." The China Quarterly, 26 (April-June 1966), 82-101.

———. "Political Control of the Chinese Army." World Today, XIX: 8 (August 1963), 327-336.

———. The Role of the Chinese Army. London: Oxford University Press, 1967.

"Give All-out Help to Factories, Mines and Other Industrial Enterprises in Grasping Revolution and Stimulating Production." Chieh-fang-chün pao [Liberation Army Daily], March 22, 1967; translated in SCMP, No. 3906 (1967).

"The Great Chinese PLA — Reliable Pillar of Our Proletarian Dictatorship and Great Proletarian Cultural Revolution." Peking Review, No. 36 (September 1, 1967), 5-6.

"Greater Successes by PLA in 1968 Farming and Sideline Occupations." NCNA-English, Peking, February 11, 1969; in SCMP, No. 4361 (1969).

Griffith, Samuel B. The Chinese People's Liberation Army. New York: McGraw-Hill, 1967.

————. "The Glorious Military Thought of Comrade Mao Tse-tung." Foreign Affairs, XLII: 4 (July 1964), 669-674.

"Hail Victory of Mao Tse-tung Line on Literature and Art." NCNA-English, Peking, May 27, 1967; in SCMP, No. 3950 (1967).

Hanrahan, Gene Z. Chinese Communist Guerrilla Tactics. Washington, D.C.: U.S. Army, July 1952.

Hinton, Harold C. "Political Aspects of Military Power and Policy in Communist China," in Harry L. Coles, ed., Total War and Cold War. Columbus: Ohio State University Press, 1962.

"Hold Aloft the Banner of the Party Committee System." Chieh-fang-chün pao [Liberation Army Daily], editorial, July 1, 1958; translated in SCMP, No. 1881 (1958).

Ho, Lung. "Democratic Tradition of the Chinese PLA." Peking Review, 32 (August 6, 1965), 6-17.

"Hold Aloft the Great Red Banner of Mao Tse-tung's Thought and Thoroughly Criticize and Repudiate the Bourgeois Military Line." Chieh-fang-chün pao [Liberation Army Daily], editorial; NCNA, Peking, July 31, 1967; translated in SCMP, No. 3994 (1967).

Hsiao, Hua. "Participation in National Construction Is a Glorious Task of the People's Liberation Army." Hung-ch'i [Red Flag], No. 15 (August 1959); translated in ECMM, No. 182 (1959).

Hsiao, Tso-liang. Power Relations within the Chinese Communist Movement, 1930-1934: A Study of Documents. Seattle: University of Washington Press, 1961.

Hsieh, Alice L. "China's Secret Military Papers: Military Doctrine and Strategy." The China Quarterly, 18 (April-June 1964), 79-99.

———. Communist China's Military Doctrine and Strategy. Santa Monica: Rand Corporation, 1963.

Hsüeh, Chün-tu. The Chinese Communist Movement, 1921-1937: An Annotated Bibliography of Selected Materials in the Chinese Collection of the Hoover Institution on War, Revolution, and Peace. Stanford: Hoover Institution, 1960.

———. The Chinese Communist Movement, 1937-1949: An Annotated Bibliography of Selected Materials in the Chinese Collection of the Hoover Institution on War, Revolution, and Peace. Stanford: Hoover Institution, 1962.

———, and Robert C. North, trans. "The Founding of the Chinese Red Army," in E. Stuart Kirby, ed., Contemporary China. Hong Kong: University of Hong Kong Press, 1964, VI, pp. 59-83.

Huang, Yi-mei. "The People's Liberation Army Is Marching toward Modernization." Kung-jen jih-pao [Worker's Daily], July 31, 1955; translated in SCMP, No. 1163 (1955).

"Humbly Learn from Local Cadres and Masses." Jen-min jih-pao [People's Daily], December 14, 1971; translated in SCMP, No. 5044 (1971).

"Humility in Learning from the Masses Stimulates Army-Building." Kuang-ming jih-pao [Bright Daily], January 7, 1972; translated in SCMP, No. 5060 (1972).

Hung, Yi-ping. "A People's Army Is Invincible Before the Enemy." Peking Review, No. 7 (February 13, 1970), 17-18.

"Important Measures in the Modernization and Regularization of China's Armed Forces." Jen-min jih-pao [People's Daily], editorial, September 28, 1955; translated in SCMP, No. 1147 (1955).

Joffe, Ellis. "The Chinese Army in the Cultural Revolution: The Politics of Intervention." Current Scene, VIII: 18 (December 7, 1970).

————. "The Communist Party and the Army," in E. Stuart Kirby, ed., Contemporary China. Hong Kong: Hong Kong University Press, 1961, IV, pp. 55-69.

————. "The Conflict Between Old and New in the Chinese Army." The China Quarterly, 18 (April-June 1964), 118-140.

————. Party and Army: Professionalism and Political Control in the Chinese Officer Corps, 1949-1964. Cambridge: Harvard University Press, 1965.

Johnson, Chalmers. Ideology and Politics in Contemporary China. Seattle: University of Washington Press, 1973.

————. "Lin Piao's Army and Its Role in Chinese Society." Current Scene, IV: 13-14 (July 1966).

Kashin, A. "Chinese Military Doctrine." Bulletin for the Study of the USSR, VII: 11 (November 1960), 36-46.

Kau, Ying-mao. "The Case Against Lin Piao." Chinese Law and Government, V: 3-4 (Fall-Winter 1972-73), 3-30.

————. "The Organizational Line in Dispute." Chinese Law and Government, V: 1 (Spring 1972), 3-23.

————. "Patterns of Recruitment and Mobility of Urban Cadres," in John W. Lewis, ed., The City in Communist China. Stanford: Stanford University Press, 1971, pp. 91-121.

————, et al. The Political Work System of the Chinese

Communist Military. Providence: East Asia Language
and Area Center, Brown University, 1971.

Kim, Ilpyong J. "Mass Mobilization Policies and Techniques
Developed in the Period of the Chinese Soviet Republic,"
in A. Doak Barnett, ed., Chinese Communist Politics in
Action. Seattle: University of Washington Press, 1969,
pp. 78-98.

"Learn Humbly from the Masses." Hung-ch'i [Red Flag],
No. 4 (April 1, 1971); translated in SCMM, No. 704 (1971).

"Let the People of the Whole Country Learn from the PLA and
Vice Versa." Jen-min jih-pao [People's Daily], January
4, 1972; translated in SCMP, No. 5056 (1972).

Lewis, John W. "China's Secret Military Papers." The China
Quarterly, 18 (April-June 1964), 68-78.

————. Leadership in Communist China. Ithaca: Cornell
University Press, 1963.

————. Major Doctrines of Communist China. New York:
Norton, 1964.

————, and Morton H. Halperin. "New Tensions in Army-
Party Relations." The China Quarterly, 26 (April-June
1966), 58-67.

"Liberation Army Units to Make Work of Support of the Government and Love of People a Regular Task." NCNA,
February 17, 1957; translated in SCMP, No. 1477 (1957).

Li, Hsü-ku. "The People's Liberation Army on the Industrial
Front." Shih-shih shou-ts'e [Current Events Handbook],
3 (February 6, 1959); translated in ECMM, No. 167 (1959).

Li, T'ien-min. "Conflicts Between the CCP and the PLA and
Between Mao and Lin." Issues & Studies, VIII: 6 (March
1972), 48-56.

Lindsay, Michael. "The North China Front: A Study of

Chinese Guerrillas in Action." Amerasia, VIII: 7 (March 31, 1944), 100-110; VIII: 8 (April 14, 1944), 117-125.

Lin, Piao. Long Live the Victory of People's War. Peking: Foreign Languages Press, 1965.

————. March Ahead under the Red Flag of the Party's General Line and Mao Tse-tung's Military Thinking. Peking: Foreign Languages Press, 1959.

————. "The Victory of the Chinese People's Revolutionary War Is the Victory of the Thought of Mao Tse-tung." Hung-ch'i [Red Flag], No. 19 (October 1, 1960); translated in SCMM, No. 231 (1960).

"Lin Piao and the Cultural Revolution." Current Scene, VIII: 14 (August 1, 1970).

Liu, F. F. A Military History of Modern China, 1924-1949. Princeton: Princeton University Press, 1956.

Liu, Ya-lou. "Seriously Study Mao Tse-tung's Military Thinking." Chieh-fang-chün pao [Liberation Army Daily], May 23, 1958; translated in SCMP, No. 1900 (1958).

Mao, Tse-tung. "Long Live Mao Tse-tung Thought: A Collection of Statements by Mao Tse-tung." CB, No. 891-2 (1969).

————. Quotations from Chairman Mao Tse-tung. Peking: Foreign Languages Press, 1966.

————. Selected Military Writings of Mao Tse-tung. Peking: Foreign Languages Press, 1963.

————. Selected Readings of Mao Tse-tung. Peking: Foreign Languages Press, 1967.

————. Selected Works of Mao Tse-tung. Peking: Foreign Languages Press, 1961-1965, 4 vols.

————. "Selections from Chairman Mao." Parts I-II. Translated in JPRS, Nos. 49826 and 50792 (1970).

————. "Talks and Writings of Chairman Mao." Translated in JPRS, No. 52029 (1970).

"Marshal Lin Piao on Political Work in the Chinese People's Liberation Army." NCNA, October 8, 1960; translated in SCMP, No. 2358 (1960).

"Military Service Law of the People's Republic of China." NCNA, July 30, 1955; translated in CB, No. 344 (1955).

"Ministry of Defense Promulgates Regulations for PLA Management and Education at Company Level." NCNA, July 5, 1961; translated in SCMP, No. 2540 (1961).

"More Officers Serve as Company-Level Soldiers." NCNA, October 7, 1958; translated in SCMP, No. 1877 (1958).

Mozingo, David P., and T. W. Robinson. Lin Piao on "People's War": China Takes a Second Look at Vietnam. Santa Monica: Rand Corporation, 1965.

"Nationwide Activities to Support the Army and Cherish the People." Peking Review, No. 8 (February 20, 1970), 11-14.

"Northwest China Veteran Communists Active in Industry." NCNA-English, Sian, February 20, 1971; in SCMP, No. 4848 (1971).

O'Ballance, Edgar. "The Officer Cadre of the Chinese Red Army." Army Quarterly, 91 (October 1965) 50-57.

————. The Red Army of China. London: Faber and Faber, 1962.

"Old Red Armyman Keeps Advancing on Road of Continuing Revolution." NCNA, August 6, 1970; translated in SCMP, No. 4719 (1970).

Oksenberg, Michel. "China: Forcing the Revolution to a New Stage." Asian Survey, VII: 1 (January 1967), 1-15.

P'eng, Te-huai. "Build Our Army into an Excellent Modernized Revolutionary Force." Chieh-fang-chün pao [Liberation

Army Daily], March 30, 1958; translated in JPRS, No. 10239 (1959).

—————. "The Chinese People's Liberation Army." CB, No. 422 (1956).

"PLA Academies Start to Study Chairman Mao's Works in Earnest." NCNA, June 19, 1958; translated in SCMP, No. 1802 (1958).

"PLA Active in Production and Political Life in Countryside." NCNA-English, Peking, October 27, 1967; in SCMP, No. 4051 (1967).

"PLA Assigns Commanders to Basic Units." NCNA, July 27, 1960; translated in SCMP, No. 2316 (1960).

"PLA Engages in 'Support the Government and Cherish the People' Activities." NCNA, February 6, 1970; translated in SCMP, No. 4597 (1970).

"PLA Farm Leads People's Communes in Learning from Tachai." NCNA-English, Tsinan, July 28, 1971; in SCMP, No. 4592 (1971).

"PLA Firmly and Victoriously Advances Along Chairman Mao's Proletarian Line on Army-Building." NCNA, October 21, 1970; translated in SCMP, No. 4768 (1970).

"PLA Gets Stronger Every Day Through Modernization and Regularization." NCNA, February 28, 1954; translated in SCMP, No. 760 (1954).

"PLA Helps in China's Industrial Production." NCNA-English, Peking, March 22, 1967; in SCMP, No. 3906 (1967).

"PLA Issues Notification on Showing Support to Government and Love to the People." NCNA, January 8, 1960; translated in SCMP, No. 2179 (1960).

"PLA Medical Workers Go to Countryside to Temper Themselves." NCNA-English, Peking, August 2, 1969; in SCMP, No. 4472 (1969).

"PLA Medical Workers Serve People Wholeheartedly." NCNA, September 7, 1970; translated in SCMP, No. 4740 (1970).

"PLA Men Develop Revolutionary Tradition in Learning from the Masses." NCNA-English, Peking, January 29, 1972; in SCMP, No. 5072 (1972).

"PLA Men Help Militia Study Chairman Mao's Ideas on People's War." NCNA-English, Peking, September 3, 1966; in SCMP, No. 3776 (1966).

"PLA Men on Revolutionary Mass Repudiation in Literature and Art." NCNA-English, Peking, June 3, 1968; in SCMP, No. 4194 (1968).

"PLA Officers Serve in the Ranks." NCNA, January 20, 1960; translated in SCMP, No. 2184 (1960).

"PLA Propaganda Team Helps Mine Cadres to Come Out and Make Revolution." Jen-min jih-pao [People's Daily], July 16, 1967; translated in SCMP, No. 3992 (1967).

"PLA Practices 'Three-Eight' Work Style." NCNA, July 20, 1960; translated in SCMP, No. 2309 (1960).

"PLA Scores New Gains in Farm and Sideline Production Last Year." Jen-min jih-pao [People's Daily], January 29, 1972; translated in SCMP, No. 5071 (1972).

"PLA Three-Support Two-Military Personnel Make New Contributions to the Consolidation of the Dictatorship of the Proletariat." Kuang-ming jih-pao [Bright Daily], July 28, 1970; translated in SCMP, No. 4713 (1970).

"PLA Unit Builds Dyke to Turn Lake into Farmland in South China Province." NCNA-English, Canton, March 26, 1970; in SCMP, No. 4628 (1970).

"PLA Unit Turns East China Lake into Farmland." NCNA, May 5, 1970; translated in SCMP, No. 4656 (1970).

"Perfect the Party Committee System and Guarantee the

Party's Collective Leadership." Jen-min jih-pao [People's Daily], December 25, 1971; translated in SCMP, No. 5051 (1972).

"Persevere in Learning from the Masses, Stimulate Army-Building." Jen-min jih-pao [People's Daily], January 10, 1972; translated in SCMP, No. 5061 (1972).

"Political Work Will Always Be the Lifeline of Our Army." Chieh-fang-chün pao [Liberation Army Daily], September 4, 1958; translated in JPRS, No. 10240 (1959).

"Politics Must Lead Technology." Chieh-fang-chün pao [Liberation Army Daily], August 20, 1958; translated in JPRS, No. 10240 (1959).

Powell, Ralph L. "Commissars in the Economy: 'Learn from the PLA' Movement in China." Asian Survey, V: 3 (March 1965), 125-138.

———. "Communist China's Mass Militia." Current Scene, III: 7-8 (November 15 and December 1, 1964).

———. "Everyone a Soldier: The Communist Chinese Militia." Foreign Affairs, XXXIX: 1 (October 1960), 100-111.

———. "The Increasing Power of Lin Piao and the Party Soldiers, 1956-1966." The China Quarterly, 34 (April-June 1968), 38-65.

———. "The Military Affairs Committee and Party Control of the Military in China." Asian Survey, III: 7 (July 1963), 347-356.

———. "Military Affairs of Communist China." Current History, 51 (September 1966), 140-146.

———. "The Party, the Government and the Gun." Asian Survey, X: 6 (June 1970), 441-471.

———. "Politico-Military Relationships in Communist China." Washington, D.C.: Policy Research Study, External

Research Staff, Bureau of Intelligence and Research, U.S. Department of State, 1963.

————. The Rise of Chinese Military Power. Princeton: Princeton University Press, 1955.

"Raise Aloft the Great Red Banner of the Thought of Mao Tse-tung, Resolutely Implement Regulations Governing PLA Political Work." Chieh-fang-chün pao [Liberation Army Daily], editorial, May 8, 1963; translated in SCMP, No. 2984 (1963).

"Regulations Governing Work of YCL Branch in Company-Level Units of the PLA." Chung-kuo ch'ing-nien pao [China Youth News], November 24, 1961; translated in SCMP, No. 2632 (1961).

"Regulations on the Service of Officers of the Chinese People's Liberation Army." CB, No. 312 (1955).

Report on Mainland China, Nos. 26-27 (June 26 and October 18, 1972).

"The Revolutionary Committee and the Party in the Aftermath of the Cultural Revolution." Current Scene, VIII: 8 (April 15, 1970).

Rhoads, Edward J. M., et al. The Chinese Red Army, 1927-1963; An Annotated Bibliography. Cambridge: Harvard University Press, 1964.

Robinson, Thomas W., ed. The Cultural Revolution in China. Berkeley: University of California Press, 1971.

————. A Politico-Military Biography of Lin Piao, Part I, 1907-1949. Santa Monica, California: Rand, 1971.

————. "The Wuhan Incident: Local Strife and Provincial Rebellion During the Cultural Revolution." The China Quarterly, 47 (July-September 1971), 413-438.

Scalapino, Robert A. Elites in the People's Republic of China. Seattle: University of Washington Press, 1972.

Schram, Stuart R. "The Military Deviation of Mao Tse-tung."
     Problems of Communism, XIII: I (January-February 1964),
     49-56.

————. The Political Thought of Mao Tse-tung. New York:
     Praeger, 1963.

Schwartz, Benjamin I. Chinese Communism and the Rise of
     Mao. Cambridge: Harvard University Press, 1951.

Schwartz, Henry. "The Chinese Communist Army in Sinkiang."
     Military Review, XLV (March 1965), 69-79.

"Seriously Practice Democratic Centralism and Give Play to
     the Role of Collective Leadership." Jen-min jih-pao
     [People's Daily], January 22, 1972; translated in SCMP,
     No. 5069 (1972).

"'Serve in the Ranks' System Widely Carried Out Among PLA
     Units Throughout China." NCNA, October 20, 1958; trans-
     lated in SCMP, No. 1882 (1958).

Snow, Edgar. Red Star Over China. New York: Random House,
     1938.

Snow, Helen. Red Dust. Stanford: Stanford University Press,
     1952.

Solomon, Richard H. Mao's Revolution and the Chinese Polit-
     ical Culture. Berkeley: University of California Press,
     1971.

————. "On Activism and Activists." The China Quarterly,
     39 (July-September 1969), 76-114.

"Strengthen Party-Mindedness, Abide by Party Discipline."
     Jen-min jih-pao [People's Daily], December 6, 1971;
     translated in SCMP, No. 5037 (1971).

"Strengthen Party-Mindedness and Centralized Party Leadership."
     Jen-min jih-pao [People's Daily], December 20, 1971;
     translated in SCMP, No. 5048 (1972).

"Strengthen Party-Mindedness, Voluntarily Uphold Collective Party Leadership." Kuang-ming jih-pao [Bright Daily], January 8, 1972; translated in SCMP, No. 5057 (1972).

"Strengthen Regard for the Party and Uphold Party's Centralized Leadership." Kuang-ming jih-pao [Bright Daily], December 4, 1971; translated in SCMP, No. 5035 (1971).

Strong, Anna. "Political Work of a Chinese Army." Amerasia, II: 6 (August 1938), 304-308.

"Study Chairman Mao's Ten Military Principles." Chieh-fang-chün pao [Liberation Army Daily], June 20, 1958; translated in JPRS, No. 10239 (1959).

"Troops Stationed in Fukien Active in Strengthening Link Between Military and Administration." NCNA, February 13, 1957; translated in SCMP, No. 1477 (1957).

Tsou, Tang. "The Cultural Revolution and the Chinese Political System." The China Quarterly, 38 (April-June 1969), 63-91.

————, and Ping-ti Ho, eds. China in Crisis. Chicago: University of Chicago Press, 1968.

"Use Chairman Mao's Writings as a Weapon to Review Instructions." Chieh-fang-chün pao [Liberation Army Daily], June 20, 1958; translated in JPRS, No. 10239 (1959).

"Veteran Red Armyman Who Never Stops on Road of Revolution." NCNA, November 18, 1970; translated in SCMP, No. 4787 (1970).

Vogel, Ezra F. "From Revolutionary to Semi-Bureaucrat: The 'Regularization' of Cadres." The China Quarterly, 29 (January-March 1967), 36-60.

Wang, Chieh. The Diary of Wang Chieh. Peking: Foreign Languages Press, 1967.

Whitson, William. The Chinese High Command, 1927-71. New York: Praeger, 1973.

Yang, Mei-sheng. "The Army Must Be Forever the Handy
    Tool of the Party and the People." Hsin Hu-nan pao [New
    Hunan News], November 22, 1959; translated in SCMP,
    No. 2155 (1959).